Leslie Alexander

The Arctic Voyages of Adolf Erik Nordenskiöld from 1858 to 1879

Leslie Alexander

The Arctic Voyages of Adolf Erik Nordenskiöld from 1858 to 1879

ISBN/EAN: 9783337310639

Printed in Europe, USA, Canada, Australia, Japan

Cover: Foto ©Andreas Hilbeck / pixelio.de

More available books at **www.hansebooks.com**

THE ARCTIC VOYAGES

OF

ADOLF ERIK NORDENSKIÖLD.

CIRCUMPOLAR MAP

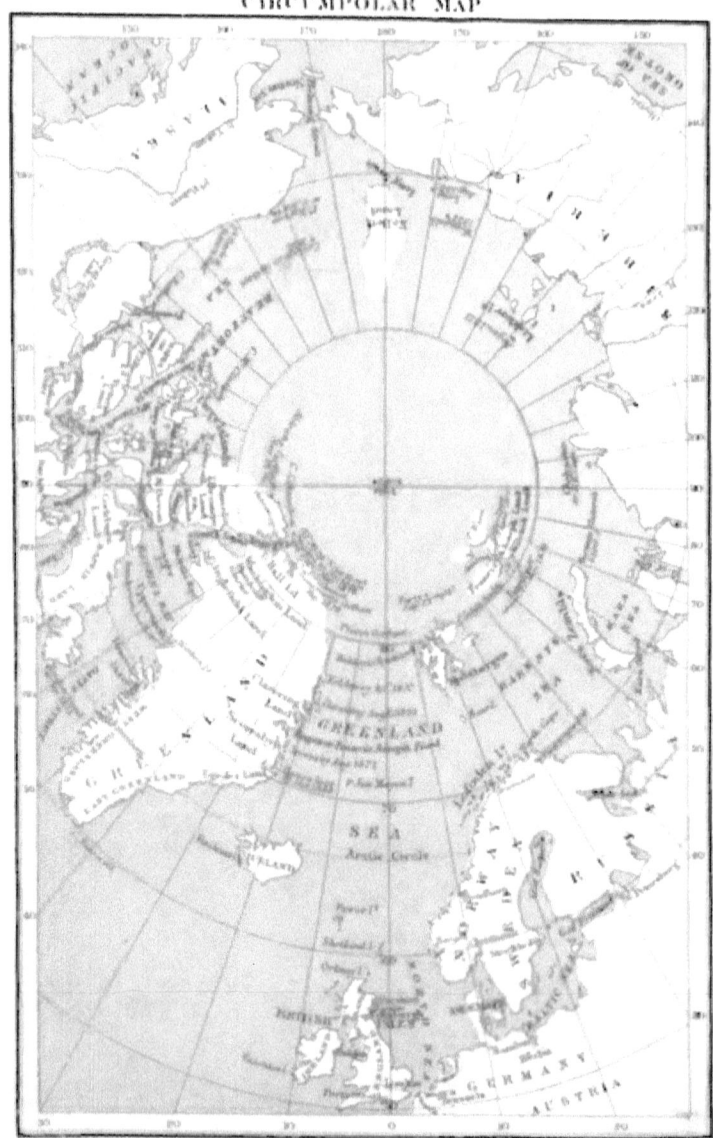

London: Macmillan & Co.

THE ARCTIC VOYAGES

OF

ADOLF ERIK NORDENSKIÖLD.

1858—1879.

WITH ILLUSTRATIONS AND MAPS.

London:
MACMILLAN AND CO.
1879.

LONDON:
R. CLAY, SONS, AND TAYLOR,
BREAD STREET HILL.

TO

OSCAR DICKSON

OF

GOTHENBURG,

THE MUNIFICENT PATRON OF

ARCTIC EXPLORATION AND RESEARCH,

THIS VOLUME

IS

(BY PERMISSION)

Respectfully Dedicated.

PREFACE.

THE brilliant success which has attended the North-East Passage Expedition under the leadership of Professor Nordenskiöld will naturally awaken a desire on the part of the English-speaking peoples for some account of his previous achievements in the field of Arctic exploration and research in which he has won for himself an imperishable name. Professor Nordenskiöld's Arctic experience extends over a period of twenty-one years, and more than half that time has elapsed since he carried the flag of his country to the highest latitude that has been reached by a vessel in the old hemisphere. In opening up communication by sea with the great Siberian rivers he has rendered a service of incalculable value to commerce, but he would doubtless prefer that his fame should rest on the contributions which have been made to our knowledge of the past history and present condition of our globe by his own scientific labours and those of his colleagues.

An accomplished and skilful mineralogist and geologist, Professor Nordenskiöld has examined, on Spitzbergen alone, more than a thousand English miles of rock sections, and in all his expeditions he has been accompanied by a staff of naturalists and physicists who have made thorough and comprehensive scientific surveys of the regions they have visited, and by their collections have made the Swedish museums the richest in the world in objects of natural history from the North Polar Basin.

With Professor Nordenskiöld's kind permission I had undertaken to prepare from the abundant materials that were available, a popular account of his Arctic voyages before the North-East Passage Expedition was planned; and not to leave my work incomplete, I have added a sketch of the history, so far as yet known, of this memorable voyage, by which, when it is finished, the *Vega* will have, for the first time, circumnavigated the twin continents of Europe and Asia. The slight outline here given will, I trust, increase the reader's appetite for the fuller details of the narrative which the illustrious explorer will write on his return home.

I have thought the valuable and interesting report of Dr. Envall on the hygiene of the Polar Expedition of 1872-73 deserving of a place in this volume, and the scientific reader will find in the List of Books and Memoirs in the Appendix, a sort of index to the large mass of printed matter, consisting of more than 6,000 pages of type and 150 plates, to which the Swedish Arctic Expeditions have given rise.

It is my pleasant duty to acknowledge the valuable assistance that has been kindly rendered to me in many ways in the preparation of this volume by my friend HERR GUSTAF LINDSTRÖM, Assistant in the Mineralogical Department of the Riks Museum, Stockholm. I am also indebted to the eminent firm of NORSTEDT and SÖNER for the use of some of the original woodcuts, to the proprietors of the *Geological Magazine* for others, and to the proprietors of the *Nya Illustrerad Tidning* for the one given at page 360, representing the *Vega* saluting Cape Chelyuskin.

ALEX. LESLIE.

ABERDEEN, 30th September, 1879.

CONTENTS.

CHAPTER I.
THE NORDENSKÖLD FAMILY: AUTOBIOGRAPHICAL SKETCH ... 1—39

CHAPTER II.
THE SWEDISH ARCTIC EXPEDITIONS OF 1858 AND 1861 ... 40—103

CHAPTER III.
THE SWEDISH ARCTIC EXPEDITION OF 1864 ... 104—127

CHAPTER IV.
THE SWEDISH POLAR EXPEDITION OF 1868 ... 128—152

CHAPTER V.
EXPEDITION TO GREENLAND ... 153—175

CHAPTER VI.
THE SWEDISH POLAR EXPEDITION OF 1872—3 ... 176—277

CHAPTER VII.

VOYAGE TO THE YENISSEJ IN 1875 AND ASCENT OF THE RIVER . 278—319

CHAPTER VIII.

SECOND VOYAGE TO THE YENISSEJ IN 1876 . . . . 320—342

CHAPTER IX.

THE NORTH-EAST PASSAGE EXPEDITION, 1878—79 . . . . . . 343—387

APPENDICES.

APPENDIX I.—OFFICIAL REPORT TO THE (SWEDISH) ROYAL BOARD OF HEALTH ON THE HYGIENE AND CARE OF THE SICK DURING THE SWEDISH POLAR EXPEDITION, 1872—73, BY DR. ENVALL, MEDICAL OFFICER . . . . 391—417

APPENDIX II.—LIST OF BOOKS AND MEMOIRS RELATING TO THE SWEDISH ARCTIC EXPEDITIONS . . . . 418—440

LIST OF ILLUSTRATIONS.

	PAGE
PROCELLARIA GLACIALIS	50
LARUS EBURNEUS	57
GRAVE ON SPITZBERGEN	59
"MAGDALENA" IN ICE HARBOUR (MIDSUMMER DAY)	61
"ÆOLUS" IN TREURENBERG BAY	62
GROUP OF POLAR BEARS IN MURCHISON BAY	67
BEAN OF ENTADA GIGALODIUM. (NATURAL SIZE)	73
SAXIFRAGA FLAGELLARIS	76
CHARLES XII.'S ISLAND AND DRABANTEN	83
REINDEER HUNTING	87
HEAD OF WALRUS	89
MAINLAND AT SMEERENBERG—GRANITE	91
DANES' ISLAND	92
IN THE INTERIOR OF KING'S BAY	97
FOX AND DEAD REINDEER	103
PHOCA BARBATA	126
DRAGGING BOAT OVER ICE	127
THE "SOFIA"	131
SHARK FISHING	132
MUSHROOMS AT ADVENT BAY	138
KING'S BAY—WESTERN SIDE	140
BEDTIME DURING A BOAT VOYAGE	141
MORMON ARCTICUS	148
THE "SOFIA" CROSSING THE ARCTIC CIRCLE, 14TH JULY, 1868	152
INLAND ICE ABUTTING ON LAND	171

LIST OF ILLUSTRATIONS.

	PAGE
INLAND ICE EXTENDING INTO THE SEA	172
INLAND ICE ABUTTING ON THE BOTTOM OF AN ICE-FJORD	172
INLAND ICE ABUTTING ON A MUD-BANK	173
THE "POLHEM"	183
VIEW OF GOTHENBURG ROADS	184
THE "GLADAN"	190
GLACIER IN FAIR HAVEN	192
LAPP WITH REINDEER	198
POLHEM—WINTER STATION	199
BURIAL IN 80° N.L. DURING THE POLAR NIGHT	212
ASTRONOMICAL OBSERVATORY	216
DREDGING UNDER THE ICE IN WINTER	217
MUSSEL BAY	220
CLEFT IN THE INLAND ICE (CANAL)	259
MATTILAS' WINTER QUARTERS AT GREY HOOK	273
NORTH POINT OF PRINCE CHARLES' FORELAND	276
WINTER DRESS AND HUNTING WEAPONS	277
THE "VEGA" SALUTING CAPE CHELYUSKIN, THE NORTHERNMOST POINT OF THE OLD WORLD	360

MAPS.

To be placed at the end of the Volume.

1. MAP OF SPITZBERGEN.
2. MAP ILLUSTRATING NORDENSKIÖLD'S VOYAGES TO THE YENISSEJ IN 1875 AND 1876.
3. MAP SHOWING THE COURSE OF THE "VEGA" FROM THE MOUTH OF THE YENISSEJ TO THAT OF THE LENA.

THE ARCTIC VOYAGES

OF

ADOLF ERIK NORDENSKIÖLD.

NORDENSKIÖLD'S ARCTIC VOYAGES:

1858—1879.

CHAPTER I.

THE NORDENSKIÖLD FAMILY: AUTOBIOGRAPHICAL SKETCH.

ADOLF ERIK NORDENSKIÖLD was born at Helsingfors, the capital of Finland, on the 18th November, 1832, the third in order of seven children, four brothers and three sisters, all of whom, with the exception of a sister who died young, still survive. His parents were Nils Gustaf Nordenskiöld, a well-known naturalist, chief of the mining department of Finland, and Margareta Sofia von Haartman. The race from which Nordenskiöld sprang had been known for centuries for the possession of remarkable qualities, among which an ardent love of nature and of scientific research was predominant. Its founder is said to have been a Lieutenant Nordberg, who was settled in Upland about the beginning of the seventeenth century. His son Johan Erik, born 1660, changed the name to Nordenberg. He was chief inspector of the saltpetre manufactories of Nyland, in Finland, and was considered by the enlightened a master in agriculture and by the common people a proficient in the black art. His only art, however, consisted in a persevering study of Nature, in closely following her footsteps. In the year 1710, when he heard that the plague had broken out all over Finland, he protected himself against the epidemic in a very peculiar way. He loaded a vessel which belonged to him with provisions and other necessaries, went on board with all his family, and cruised about in the open sea for several months, taking good care to have no communication with the land. If his voyage had a certain resemblance to Noah's in the ark, it had the same successful issue. About the beginning of 1711, when the plague had ceased, all on board landed safe on Åland.

Johan Erik Nordenberg died in 1740, leaving two sons, Anders Johan and Carl Frederik, both of whom, though the latter was only lieutenant, were elected members of the Swedish Academy of Sciences when it was founded in 1739. Both were ennobled in 1751. Carl Frederik is the common ancestor of the families bearing the name of Nordenskiöld now living in Sweden and Finland. One of his many remarkable sons, the third in order, Colonel Adolf Gustaf Nordenskiöld, became owner of Frugord in Finland. This property, situated in a forest-crowned valley in the department of Nyland, is still in the possession of the Nordenskiölds. Here Colonel Adolf Gustaf Nordenskiöld built a peculiar residence, the middle of which is taken up with a hall two stories high, round the upper part of which runs a broad gallery in which collections in natural history are arranged. Life in this home has always borne a certain old Norse stamp. In the surrounding park a sepulchral mound has been thrown up, which forms the last consecrated resting-place of a portion of the Finnish members of the Nordenskiöld family. In these arrangements, as in much else at Frugord, there was something uncommon, indicating a peculiar idiosyncrasy in the owner, and undoubtedly not without an influence on the youth that grew up there. Many of the Nordenskiöld family were devoted to literature and scientific research. Otto Magnus Nordenskiöld, a brother of Adolf Gustaf, after undertaking extensive tours in Holland, France, Germany, &c., for the purpose of studying the commerce of those countries, was the first to introduce " many-bladed " saw-mills into Finland, on an island on the coast of which he planned the foundation of a manufacturing town, for which he wished to secure neutrality in the wars between Sweden and Russia. His scheme, however, was frustrated by the outbreak of the war of 1742, when the Russians burned down the only manufacturing establishment that had been erected on Fagerö, a wind-driven saw-mill. Soon after, the unlucky Otto Magnus drew on himself persecution and threats of capital punishment both in Sweden, for being concerned in the surrender of Tavastehus in the war of 1742, and in Russia, for a very well-meant proposal made to the Czarina Elizabeth concerning perpetual peace between all Christian nations. He died excommunicated by the clergy of Finland.

Colonel Adolf Gustaf Nordenskiöld had many children, one of whom, August, was a zealous alchemist, and laboured with Bernhard Wadström for the abolition of negro slavery. He died at Sierra Leone from injuries received from the blacks during an attempt at colonisation, undertaken with a view to form a free negro state. August's youngest brother, Nils Gustaf, was born in 1792. After passing his examination in mining at the University of Upsala he was for several years a pupil of Berzelius, with whom he formed the warmest friendship, which was only broken off by death. Nils Gustaf, early known as a distinguished mineralogist, was appointed a government inspector of mines in his native country, and by means of liberal grants of public money was enabled to undertake extensive foreign tours, which brought him into communication with most of the eminent mineralogists and chemists of the day in England, France, and Germany. After three years of foreign travel he returned to Finland, and was promoted in 1824 to be chief of the mining department, and devoted thirty years of restless activity to the improvement of that important branch of the industry of his native land. He travelled through Finland in all directions in the prosecution of his untiring mineralogical and geological researches. His travels extended as far as the Ural. He published his views, discoveries, and experiments, in many scientific periodicals and in several independent works, and a large number of minerals discovered by him afford evidence of his keen research. He was made Councillor of State, and obtained many distinctions for his scientific services from the sovereign and from learned bodies. On the 21st of February, 1866, he ended his active life at Frugord, and was laid to rest in his father's grave. "His simple frank manner," said A. E. Arppe in his *éloge* on this veteran of science, "his wit and his extensive experience, made his society equally agreeable and instructive.

The young, who were interested in his researches, could especially reckon on his friendship; they enjoyed his company, and were strongly attached to him. He had the uncommon happiness of seeing one of his sons not only devote himself to the same kind of studies, but maintain with distinguished success by his scientific travels and labours the ancient honour of the family name."

Frugord, with its old books and natural history collections accumulated from generations of nature-loving ancestors, was a fitting home for the future naturalist and explorer, Adolf Erik, who was to make the name of Nordenskiöld world-famous. While yet a boy he was an industrious collector of minerals and of insects, and was permitted to accompany his father on his tours, acquiring thus early the keen eye of the mineralogist. After studying for some time with a private tutor he was sent to the gymnasium at Borgo, where, as at similar institutions elsewhere, there then prevailed, as he tells us in the autobiographical sketch which he wrote for Bejer's "Swedish Biographical Lexicon," an almost unlimited freedom, the teachers taking no oversight whatever of the pupils' attention to their studies. "Even in this respect," he says in the sketch already quoted, "the gymnasium was a connecting link between the school and the university—in my opinion a fortunate circumstance, which is now changed. It must, however, be admitted," he continues, "that the liberty was used badly enough by many. This was the case with myself, for instance, during my first year at the gymnasium, for during the first term I distinguished myself, as the rector expressed it, 'only by absolute idleness.' At the close of the spring term I was not only not advanced, but I was marked in my certificate 'unsatisfactory' in nearly the whole of the subjects. My parents were judicious enough not to attach any importance to this well-deserved mishap. Instead of breaking out in reproaches and increasing the control which my mother's presence at Borgo, and a private tutor installed for the purpose during the first year of our attendance at the gymnasium were intended to exert, the watch kept upon us was now completely removed. We[1] were boarded in very modest quarters for five silver roubles a month for board and lodging, and got full liberty to manage our studies in our own way. Self-respect was thus awakened. I became exceedingly industrious, and was soon one of those then attending the gymnasium who obtained the best reports."

Among the teachers of the gymnasium at Borgo at this time was Johan Ludvig Runeberg, the distinguished poet. He held the Greek lectureship, and was greatly esteemed both by his colleagues and his pupils, which, however, did not prevent him having much unpleasantness during the year of his rectorship, 1848. For taking part in an unseemly brawl two of the pupils were condemned to rustication, and two others, according to the school laws, which were then new, to corporal punishment. The two former obtained a mitigation of their sentence by an appeal to the ordinary courts, but the latter had to submit to their punishment, which was inflicted with due severity by the then rector Runeberg. This was indeed quite legal, but by no means in accordance with the old traditional freedom of the gymnasium, and it took place in the eventful

[1] Adolf Erik and his elder brother.

year 1848. Not even Runeberg's rectorship could prevent a revolution, which in the end led near the half of the pupils to leave the institution. Among those who did so were Adolf Erik and his younger brother Otto Nordenskiöld.

Nordenskiöld entered the University of Helsingfors in 1849, devoting himself chiefly to the study of chemistry, natural history, mathematics, physics, and above all, of mineralogy and geology. "Already before I became a student," he writes, "I had been allowed to accompany my father in mineralogical excursions, and had acquired from him skill in recognising and collecting minerals and in the use of the blowpipe, which he, being a pupil of Gahn and Berzelius, handled with a masterly skill unknown to most of the chemists of the present day. I now undertook the charge of the rich mineral collection at Frugord, and besides, during the vacations made excursions to Pitkeranta, Tammela, Pargas, and others of Finland's interesting mineral localities. By practice I thus acquired a keen and certain eye for recognising minerals, which has been of great service to me in the path of life I afterwards followed."

After passing his candidate examination in 1853 Nordenskiöld accompanied his father on a mineralogical tour to Ural, devoting most of his attention to Demidoff's iron and copper mines at Tagilsk. Here he planned an extensive journey through Siberia, but the breaking out of the Crimean war put a stop to it.

"After my return," says Nordenskiöld, "I continued to prosecute my chemical and mineralogical studies with zeal, and wrote as my dissertation for the degree of Licentiate a paper 'On the Crystalline Forms of Graphite and Chondrodite,' which was discussed under the presidency of Professor Arppe on the 28th February, 1855. The following summer I was employed on a work of somewhat greater extent—" A Description of the Minerals found in Finland," which was published the same autumn. Various short papers in mineralogy and molecular chemistry were printed in *Acta Societatis scientiarum Fenniæ*: I also published along with Dr. E. Nylander 'The Mollusca of Finland' (Helsingfors, 1856) as an answer to a prize question proposed by one of the faculty. In the interval I had been appointed Curator of the Mathematico-Physical faculty, and had obtained a post at the Mining Office as mining engineer extraordinary, with inconsiderable pay, and an express understanding that no service would be required from me in return. A salary was also attached to my curatorship."

"I did not, however, long enjoy these, which were my first paid appointments. Before I received my second quarter's salary I was removed from my offices in consequence of some political speeches made at the tavern at Thölö on the occasion of a dinner arranged by us on Friday, the 30th November, 1855. The gay circle of youth to which I belonged, instead of celebrating our namedays and birthdays each by himself according to the usual practice, determined to combine all the separate fêtes which occurred during the autumn term of 1855 in one giant entertainment with military music, floral decorations, &c. It went off pleasantly, and as a fact the discussion of politics, which was common enough among us, was that day almost wholly forgotten. But we had appearances helplessly against us, and justice requires the acknowledgment that we had before dabbled in politics and sinned so much that our truthful account of the occurrences of that day was everywhere received with distrust."

"The way in which the thing happened was this: Some time before Palmerston had made his famous speech about the taking of the Baltic fortresses. Our entertainment was opened by what we considered a well-executed parody of this speech by K. Vetterhoff, on which followed in the course of the dinner toasts to the French wines, Crimean fruits, sardines, &c., all in heedless fun and frolic. We had all been concerned a hundred times before in affairs similar or worse, but on this occasion things were on a grander scale—and that was our misfortune. We had a band of music belonging to the Finnish navy, which played tunes to our toasts. The leader of the music thought himself obliged to make a report of the speeches to his chief, with the distinct declaration that the whole appeared merely to be a frolic. The first who were informed of the unfortunate report by the naval officer, an intimate acquaintance of most of us, were those who had taken part in the entertainment. He swore at us for not having chosen a Russian band, which would not have understood any of our nonsense, and said that he was obliged to let the report go further. But he would delay it as long as possible, in order to give us an opportunity of arranging the affair in the meantime. This seemed at first to be very easy of accomplishment until Governor-general Count von Berg got a list of the delinquents, when, struck with surprise, he probably exclaimed, 'Ah! these are all old acquaintances!'"

"Indeed most of us were previously known by name to the Count for a reason that was very unpleasant to him. On accepting the post of Governor-general of Finland during the war with the western powers, Count von Berg—unfamiliar as he was with the position of affairs in a country where all gave free and unreserved expression to their sentiments, but where, on the other hand, there had never been any trace of actual conspiracy, secret societies, or anything of the sort—became much alarmed by the probably untrue and exaggerated reports which he received of the state of feeling in the country. He endeavoured to procure spies who should give him information of expressions of dissatisfaction, and the like. In this he was completely unsuccessful, and he appears himself to have even come to the conclusion that the odious measure was unnecessary. He had succeeded, however, at first in getting a young student to act as his tool, who was sent to Stockholm to find out about the authors of many correspondence-articles which were sent from Finland to the Swedish newspapers, and which at that time attracted the attention of the public to a degree of which we can now scarcely form any idea. After his return he was to act as a spy among the students. An official of high position, since dead, who had a post in von Berg's office, became acquainted with the fact, and considering the odious and pernicious consequences which would follow espionage in private life, determined to bring about an unexpected disarrangement in von Berg's plans. He told some students about it, on whose silence he could rely, and suggested that they should make short work with the rascal. He did not require to say it twice. Some leading persons among the students met in a private house. The delinquent was sent for without being informed of the reason. Supposing that it related to some literary society he made his appearance, flattered by the attention shown him. Scarcely had he entered when the door was fastened, and he was addressed by one of those present with the words: 'We have proof that you are a spy.' Pale as a corpse, he stammered out, after some moments, 'I must acknowledge that an offer has been made to me, but I have not accepted it.' The beginning was made, and a full confession soon followed. He was now ordered to leave the university and the town. The Governor-general, who was nearly out of his wits, especially because we had obtained such accurate information about the greatest secrets of his office, attempted at first to take the discovered spy under his own protection, but was soon obliged to desist. To protect a spy who has been found out is impossible, even for a nearly all-powerful Governor-general. The misguided youth, who was said to be very talented, was removed to some office in Russia, and disappeared from Helsingfors. Von Berg kept the list of the members of the tribunal, and promised to keep them well in mind."

"The Thölö affair offered an excellent opportunity for this, as the names of those who took part in the entertainment were mostly well-known to von Berg from the former list, and possibly also from others of which we had no knowledge. The first sacrifice was the singers invited to the feast, young students who were known as æsthetic, respectable youths, little given to politics. But, fired by the speeches and wine, they had, while going home through the streets of the town, sung the Marseillaise, with offensive words added by Topelius. They were all rusticated for a term, some for a longer period. I got a double dismissal without further ceremony."

"We all bore our misfortune very calmly. I betook myself to two respectable persons, obtained their security, borrowed money, and went abroad by St. Petersburg to Berlin. While driving during my stay in St. Petersburg in an 'isvoschik' in the Nevski Prospect, I quite unexpectedly encountered my father, who had returned sooner than he intended from a new journey to the Ural. He was exceedingly surprised to meet his son, but, after an explanation, quite approved of my journey, and provided me with letters of introduction to the friends of his youth, the brothers Rose, Mitscherlich, &c."

"I stayed at Berlin during the spring and early summer of 1856, working in Rose's laboratory at researches in mineral analysis. I besides made use of the opportunity to make the acquaintance of several of the world-renowned men of science of the city, by whom, thanks to my father's well-known name, I was particularly well received."

"During the summer of the same year I returned through Sweden to Finland. I was now asked by Professor Arppe, the dean of the mathematico-physical faculty, whether I wished to apply immediately for the newly-established professorship in mineralogy and geology, or whether I preferred by getting some of the large travelling stipends of the university to provide myself with funds for extensive foreign travel. I chose the latter, but on my first application for 'the literary travelling grant' I was passed over by my friend, the distinguished philologist Ahlquist, under the express promise, however, that I should have as an equivalent the Alexander stipend, which would be vacant some months after. The plan of travel which I gave in to the Consistorium was for a geological excursion to Siberia, and above all to Kamschatka. The plan was abandoned for the time, but I hope now, twenty years after, to bring about a scientific expedition to the same regions, though on another and far grander scale than would then have been possible for me." [1]

"Immediately thereafter I obtained the Alexander stipend for a tour of study through Europe. Before my departure, however, I wished to be present at the Promotion festival of 1857, when I was at the same time to be promoted to the degree of master (magister) and doctor, with the first place of honour among the masters and the second among the doctors. This 'promotion' became an unexpected turning-point in my life."

"At the invitation of the young men who were to become laureates, there was present at the 'promotion' a deputation from the universities of Upsala and Lund, consisting of a professor and five eminent younger academicians. They were received by us, and everywhere as they travelled in Finland, in the most cordial manner. Innumerable speeches were spoken in their honour, and even the older men did not weigh with any special care the words with which the guests from the dear old mother-country were welcomed, all to the great provocation of Count von Berg, who was childish enough to consider as treason such a reception, called forth by

[1] This was written in 1877.

grand and illustrious common memories of many centuries' old, and a debt of gratitude for culture, freedom, national existence, which can never be forgotten. In von Berg's favour it may be mentioned that he had not yet been able to comprehend the peculiar Dualism which then prevailed in Finland between Russian despotism and the habit of freedom centuries old."

"At the parting festival I, who otherwise seldom appeared as a speaker, was asked to propose a toast—a request which from my position among the 'promoti,' I could scarcely decline. My speech was not long, and was naturally in the tone that prevailed during the course of the entertainments, perhaps somewhat more pointed than the others, which had the fortune to fall unnoticed into the sea of forgetfulness. I concluded with a verse by K. Vetterhoff in which he calls for a toast 'to our memories all, and to the time that has been and the time that shall come, if only it does not bring Finland's fall, a toast to the days of memory that have fled and the hope that still remains.'"

"The preceding part of my speech was a repetition of the same clearly very prudent, sensible, and resigned sentiment which the verse contained, naturally embellished according to use and wont to some inconsiderable extent with such flourishes as intelligent practical folk describe as 'rhetorical tropes.' It is well known that such figures of speech are as indispensable to a speaker, especially to a speaker at such an entertainment, as salt is to meat."

"Either it was the case that I now 'salted' too much, or that the temper of the guests from the long continued feasting had become more than usually receptive of the impressions of the moment. At all events my words were received with a storm of applause from one quarter, mixed with a prudent dissent from another. The affair, however, would certainly have passed unobserved, like so many other similar effusions on such occasions, if a highly-esteemed, warm-hearted, and patriotic academic teacher, Professor Cygnæus, had not been seized with the insane and impolitic idea of seeking, while the temper of the meeting was so heated, to counteract the unfavourable impression the behaviour of the youth might make in higher quarters by a speech directed against some verses read a short time before at a student festival at Hasselbacken, in which J. G. Carlén said of Finland: 'Soon a gilded nest of thraldom.' *An historian of literature now made Carlén a representative of opinion in Sweden, and our guests were reproached on account of his poetical effusions.* A general and well-grounded displeasure, this time I believe quite independent of all politics, broke loose: and urged by many, I went up to the speaker's chair, where Cygnæus still stood, and cried: 'He does not speak for us.'"

"This occurrence attracted much attention and gave rise to much talk, and came the following day to von Berg's ears. He had been lying in wait the whole time for an opportunity to get hold of some suitable scapegoat, and I became the scapegoat. The rector was sent for and got instructions to inquire into the circumstance. He applied to me. I gave him a correct account of the whole affair. 'Now why in Heaven's name did you talk so?' cried he. On this I drew from my pocket the draft of my speech, and handed it to 'uncle' Rein—as all the former members of the Viborg division, of which he had been the much-liked inspector, called him."

"After reading it the rector's countenance cleared. He declared that my words did not contain anything offensive, and was confident that to communicate them to the Governor-general would certainly mollify him, if he were permitted to give him a copy — a request which I considered myself bound to answer in the affirmative, although I doubted the prudence of the step he intended to take."

"The written word, as is well known, has many meanings, at least when it is interpreted according to the prepossessions of the readers. Governor-general von Berg immediately declared to the good rector that what lay before him almost amounted to high treason, and took steps to have the crime punished. I treated the whole affair with contempt, and betook myself to Frugord, where a couple of days after I received a communication from a Finn, one of von Berg's most intimate friends, advising me either to go abroad immediately, or to remain and boldly declare that the whole affair arose from mistake, misunderstanding, &c. I chose the former alternative, and crossed over to Sweden with a passport which I had taken out some months before. Soon after there came a Government missive from St. Petersburg, in which I was said to have been declared to have forfeited, not the stipend which I had, but one which I had never possessed, and to be deprived of the right of ever holding office in the university. I never obtained a complete copy of this document, although I made repeated application for it, quite certainly

because the whole judgment was rash and perhaps not
quite legal. Late in the autumn of 1858 I returned to
Finland, after having taken part in Torell's first expedition to Spitzbergen, and having received an offer of an
appointment as successor to Mosander in the mineralogical department of the Riks-Museum. On receiving
a telegram that I was nominated to this post I applied
for a passport in order to return to Sweden. Difficulties
were raised. I got a message to call on the Governor-
General. He received me at first in a friendly way,
and found fault with me for having travelled on the
former occasion without a passport. To this I replied
that that was not quite the fact, as I had travelled with
a passport which I had already taken out during the
winter. 'But that passport was over three months
old,' said von Berg. To this I answered that the passport regulations were completely unknown to me, and
that it was the duty of his officials to see that they
were complied with. Von Berg—'You must at least
admit that those acted wrongly who allowed you to
travel with an old passport.' Nordenskiöld—'With the
greatest pleasure, your Excellency.'"

"This reply was evidently gratifying to von Berg.
He now began to speak in a very judicious way, on
the whole, about the promotion catastrophe, declaring
that everything could easily be made right again, and our
relations be put on a better footing than before. To this
I answered evasively that even if I had sinned through
my speech at the festival, I had now suffered so much
loss of money and annoyance on account of the affair
that I thought the whole might be forgotten. Turning
to a Finnish official who was present at our meeting

von Berg said : 'It is not enough for a man to recognise his errors, he should be sorry he made them.' On my replying to this, 'That I shall never be!' von Berg answered somewhat impetuously, 'You shall have your pass, but you may say good-bye to Finland, I shall see to that.' Thus was the conversation concluded. The following day I obtained a passport, and in fourteen days had crossed the frontier."

"I have been informed that von Berg afterwards formally urged in the senate my being exiled from the country, not however with reference to the occurrence at the promotion, but because I had entered foreign service without asking permission of the Government. The proposition, however, was negatived, and it was declared that I had in the circumstances only availed myself of the rights belonging to the ennobled class. Instead, he obtained an order to the Russian minister at Stockholm, forbidding him to *visé* my passport to Finland. A *visé* accordingly was repeatedly refused to me till the summer of 1862, when von Berg was no longer Governor-General. Since then I have been allowed to go to Finland whenever I pleased."

" After having married a Finnish lady, I applied in the year 1867 for the professorship of mineralogy and geology in the University of Helsingfors, and obtained the unanimous recommendation of the consistory for the post. Daschkoff, who was then Russian minister at Stockholm—with whose family I became acquainted through my wife, being received by them with much friendliness—asked me at an accidental meeting, somewhat doubtingly, if I *really* wished to have the post. When I answered that this of course was the case, as

I had applied for it, he said he could answer for the result if only I would promise him privately not to mix myself up with politics in Finland. This promise I could not give, but I told him that of course I had the intention after my return of submitting with 'loyauté' to the legally existing state of affairs. With this, however, he was not satisfied. He afterwards, with good intentions towards me, endeavoured to reach his object through the ladies, and applied to my wife, asking her to put the matter right. He got the answer, 'But my husband is a very decided person,' and thus the negotiation was closed. I was not appointed."

"After my departure from Finland in 1857, I passed the summer principally in visiting Swedish mineral localities for mineralogical purposes. The following winter I settled in Stockholm, where my old father also happened to be staying at the time. I employed myself in working out a couple of papers published in the Transactions of the Academy of Sciences, to one of which the Lindbom prize was awarded by the Academy. At the same time I was engaged in chemical researches at the laboratory of the Caroline Institute and in practical studies in the mineralogy of Scandinavia at the mineral cabinet of the Academy of Sciences, rich in Swedish and Norwegian minerals. Here I was received with special good-will by my illustrious predecessor Mosander, a zealous mineralogist, and, though his sight was much impaired by incipient cataract, still very skilful at recognising the minerals of Scandinavia. Mosander was a fully developed Conservative and did not spare now and then furious attacks on the Liberal views of his younger colleague, which, however, did not in the least disturb the good understanding between us."

"In the spring of 1858 I received an offer through Professor Sven Lovén to take part as geologist in Torell's first expedition to Spitzbergen, during which the fjords on its west coast were visited and rich zoological, botanical, and geological collections made. With reference to the geological collection, it may be stated that I was successful in finding at Bell Sound a number of fossil plants belonging to the tertiary period, which were afterwards described by Professor Oswald Heer, of Zurich, and form the commencement of the comprehensive collections in this field which have been brought home by the Swedish Arctic expeditions, and which in the experienced hands of Heer have yielded such important new contributions to our knowledge of the former geological history of our globe. There were obtained, besides a large number of fossils from the carboniferous and Jurassic formations, fine minerals from the limestone veins on the Norways, Cloven Cliff, &c."

"Immediately after my return from my first Arctic voyage Mosander died, and I was asked privately if I was willing to take his place at the Riks-Museum, in case the Academy should appoint me to it. When, after no little hesitation, I had declared myself willing to do so, I was appointed on the 8th December the same year Professor and Intendent of the mineralogical department of the Riks-Museum. I was then, as has been said, in Finland, and had the conversation narrated above with the Governor-General, in connection with which it deserves to be mentioned that von Berg then was clearly ignorant that I had been appointed to an honourable scientific post in the neighbouring country."

"I started from Helsingfors in the last days of December, 1858, in order to return to Sweden by the Sea of Åland. I passed New Year's Eve with relatives at Björkboda, in Kimitto parish, and had the good fortune to make once more a remarkable mineral discovery in Finland; for during an excursion from the works I found, at some quartz quarries the working of which had been lately resumed for the puddling furnaces situated at a place called Rosendal, a very considerable quantity of the exceedingly rare mimeral Tantalite, previously found only at two places in Finland, two in Sweden, and one in France, important as the only mineral occurring in any considerable quantity into which the simple substance Tantalum enters as a main constituent. The passage of the Sea of Åland was exceedingly difficult. I skated over Skiftet, and, from my impatience to get across, over such weak ice that three times on the same day I got a cold bath up to the throat."

"Immediately after my return to Stockholm I entered on my new employment and began to work partly at the arrangement of the museum, partly at scientific researches which formed the subjects of several of my papers published either in the Transactions of the Academy of Sciences or of the Geological Society. At Professor Mosander's death, when the rebuilding of the Academy's house had just begun, the mineralogical collection was stuffed into three small rooms, where there was so little space that the exhibition of the collection could not be thought of. The new spacious apartments intended for the Riks-Museum were finished in the summer of 1865, and already by the following autumn the arrangement and removal of the collections were so far advanced that the Museum could be opened to the public. It has since been my constant endeavour to enlarge the collection not only by purchases from dealers in minerals, but mainly by visits to the most important mineral localities in Scandinavia, undertaken on account of the Museum, partly by the Intendent himself, partly by Assistant Lindström, or by students of mineralogy from the Universities. In consequence of the extraordinary richness of the Scandinavian peninsula in rare and remarkable minerals, the Mineralogical Museum at Stockholm, with the help of the collections, valuable in certain directions, which have existed from Mosander's time, has in this way become one of the most considerable in Europe. In the summer of 1859 I made a tour for mineralogical purposes to Jemtland and Dalecarlia, during which for a time I lay very ill of gastric fever at a peasant's house at Storsjön. The following winter I had the pleasure of receiving as *collaborateur* at the laboratory the friend of my youth and promotion-comrade, J. J. Chydenius, afterwards professor of chemistry at Helsingfors, and in the summer of 1860 we made together a pleasant and agreeable journey rich in mineral discoveries to Arendal, Brevig, Kragerö, Kongsberg, and other places in southern Norway well known to the mineralogist. In the following year, 1861, I took part in Torell's carefully equipped polar expedition, on which occasion I had an opportunity of surveying the northern part of Spitzbergen and of clearing up the main points of the geognosy of the country. It was fully described by one of those who took part in it, K. Chydenius, who unfortunately died prematurely, so that it is not necessary for me to say anything more concerning an expedition, through which the first foundation was laid of a true knowledge of the natural history of the polar countries."

"After von Berg quitted the post of Governor-General there were, as I have said, no longer any obstacles placed in the way of my visiting Finland by the authorities. I took advantage of the fact, and passed part of the summer of 1862 in my old country, where I had the pleasure of finding my father in good health, and of undertaking a tour with him to several of the most interesting mineral localities of Finland. During the time when I had not been allowed to visit Finland my mother had died at Frugord, on the 26th January, 1860, without my being permitted to come across to bid her a last farewell. As my father spent a great part of his time in travelling, both at home and abroad, it was my mother who conducted and arranged our first education. Her good judgment, and her liking for employment of all kinds, and for generous, impartial, and frank behaviour, exercised a powerful influence on all within her family circle, and created a home at Frugord where singular unanimity and mutual affection prevailed."

"In the month of December, 1862, I again travelled by the difficult and, during winter, even dangerous way of Grisslehamn and Åland to Finland, in order, at Professor Edlund's request, to make some investigations concerning the formation of ice in the sea. After having in Finland betrothed myself to Anna Mannerheim, daughter of Ex-President Count Carl Mannerheim and Eva von Schantz, I returned on 1st January, 1863, to Stockholm. On the 1st July in the same year our marriage was celebrated at Willnäs, near Åbo."

"I had now of course abandoned all thoughts of further Arctic journeys. Circumstances, however, so arranged themselves that just from this time they were resumed by me, and on a greater scale than before. The occasion was the following :—

"Torell's polar journey of 1861 had for its object, among other things, to carry into effect a proposal, made several years before by the President of the Royal Society of London, to examine how far it is possible in these high latitudes to obtain the measurement of an arc of meridian of sufficient extent. The north part of the triangulation for this measurement had been staked out during the expedition of 1861 by Dr. K. Chydenius, who took part in the expedition as physicist on board the schooner *Æolus*. But the plan for examining the southern part of the proposed triangulation could not be carried out, it having been impossible during the course of the summer for the other vessel of the expedition, the sloop *Magdalena*, which was a bad sailor, and was long shut up by ice on the north coast of Spitzbergen, to reach Stor Fjord, the part of Spitzbergen along which the southern part of the triangulation should lie. On this account the Royal Academy of Sciences applied for and obtained from the estates a grant of 10,000 crowns (about 550*l.*) to defray the expenses of an expedition on a small scale, having for its object the completion of the survey commenced in 1861."

"Originally K. Chydenius, a skilful, very energetic, and warm-hearted man, was appointed to the leadership of the expedition. But he fell so seriously ill during the winter of 1863-4 that he was unable to take charge of the necessary preparations. I was asked by the Academy to step into my sick friend's place under circumstances which scarcely left me any choice. The intention was that Chydenius, if he got better, should take part in the expedition. He died in the course of the winter."

"In his place I asked Docent N. Dunér, of Lund, and Dr. Malmgren, of Helsingfors, to join me. The expedition was very pleasant, and, taking into account the limited means at my disposal, rich in results. The preliminary survey for the proposed measurement of an arc of meridian was completed, the southern part of Spitzbergen mapped, and important new data collected towards ascertaining the flora and fauna of that group of islands. That year the sea was very free of ice, and when, after finishing our other work in autumn, we made an attempt in our little schooner-rigged gunboat to sail far up towards the north, we might probably have been able to reach a very high latitude, if the proposed excursion had not been interrupted by a meeting with seven boats, laden with walrus hunters from three vessels which had been wrecked upon the east side of North East Land. They had to be rescued, and such a demand was made both on the room in the vessel and on our stock of provisions that I was compelled immediately to return to Norway. During the voyage we had pretty good sport, and our sales covered part of the expenses of the expedition."

"In 1865 I was with my family over in Finland, in order once more to visit my old father. He had already been attacked by the illness, through which, on the 21st February, 1866, his active life was brought to a close. He therefore could not accompany me on the excursions which I undertook in the course of the summer to Laurinkari, Ersby, Skogböle, Kulla, and others of the most remarkable localities of Finland. The following summer I travelled in Vestmanland, Vermland, and Dalecarlia, making mineralogical researches, and took part as juryman for the department of porcelain and stone ware in the Scandinavian Exhibition, opened at Stockholm that summer. In 1867 I visited Paris, having been commissioned, along with Professor A. J. Ångström, to compare a normal metre and a normal kilogram, which had been made for the Swedish Government, with the prototypes preserved in the Conservatoire des Arts et Métiers. In consequence of the regulations in force at that institution the commission could not be executed in a way that was completely satisfactory from a scientific point of view, a circumstance which had been often complained of both before and since, and these complaints finally led to the recent changes in the way of preserving the prototypes and comparing them with copies. This journey also gave me an opportunity of visiting for a considerable time the great Paris Exhibition of 1867, and of making the acquaintance of several eminent scientific men there, by whom I was received in a very kind and friendly way."

"It almost appeared as if no resumption of the

Swedish Arctic Expeditions was to be looked for in the near future. The Diet, in voting the grant for that of 1864, declared that no further funds for the purpose in question were to be reckoned on, and most of the leading men in Stockholm repeatedly and distinctly expressed the opinion that we had now done enough in that field. I myself, however, anxiously wished to be able to renew the attempt to reach a high northerly latitude, which was made in the autumn of 1864 after the completion of the survey for the measurement of an arc of meridian, and which was interrupted on that occasion by the rescue of the walrus hunters already referred to. After several unsuccessful attempts in other directions, I approached Count Ehrensvärd, Governor of Gothenburg, a zealous friend of science, art, and literature, with a memorial setting forth the main points of my plan of a new expedition, and a request that he would endeavour to obtain in Gothenburg the considerable sum of money which was required to carry it out. My proposal was received with great interest by Count Ehrensvärd, and in a short time the amount that was considered necessary to secure the undertaking on its economic side was collected through munificent contributions from the commercial magnates Dickson, Ekman, Carnegie, &c. The new Arctic Expedition was also received with special interest by State-Counsellor Count Platen, Chief of the Marine Department, and above all by the then powerful chief of the Kommando Office of the Navy, Commander Adlersparre. Starting with the idea, doubtless correct, that some small part of the money voted to the Royal Navy for exercising might, with advantage both to it and the general interest, be employed in voyages with scientific or commercial objects, Count Platen fitted out and manned from these funds a vessel belonging to the Post Office, the iron steamer *Sofia*, which the Government placed at my disposal. The expedition was thus brought about by a harmonious co-operation of the Government, private persons of wealth, and several young men of science who took a lively interest in the matter, and it may serve as a pattern for such undertakings not only within our own land, but also in foreign countries. It was proposed to reach with the vessel as high a latitude as possible during the autumn, and to complete the researches of the foregoing expeditions in the natural history of Spitzbergen and the surrounding sea."

"Rich, and, in a scientific point of view, important collections were brought home, and we reached, on the 19th September, 1868, the highest northern latitude which any vessel can be proved to have attained in the old hemisphere. In this respect we have hitherto been only surpassed by Hall's American and Nares' English expeditions in Smith's Sound. At the third attempt to penetrate to the northward, which was made during this voyage in the beginning of October from Amsterdam Island in the neighbourhood of the 80th degree of latitude, we should probably have been able to go much farther if the vessel had not, during a storm on the 4th October, in 81° N. L., been dashed against a block of ice and thereby sprung so bad a leak that we could only with difficulty get back to our former anchorage. We owe a debt of gratitude to the skill and coolness of the captain of the vessel, Baron von Otter, afterwards Counsellor of State, for our escape that day with our lives. The vessel *Sofia*, built by Carlsund for other purposes, was much too weak to encounter an October storm in 81° N. L., in darkness, with blocks of ice driving about. The attempt to reach a high northerly latitude by sea deserves, however, to be resumed with a more suitable vessel, strong, protected against icing down and provided with abundant stock of coal and provisions. During a not too unfavourable ice-year it would certainly be possible, during autumn or early winter, to reach, from the north-western extremity of Spitzbergen, which is free of ice for the greater part of the year, a far higher latitude than Sir George Nares' vessel attained during the last English Polar Expedition."

" Mr. Oscar Dickson was among those who made the most liberal contributions to the Expedition of 1868. We are told that it is characteristic of this magnanimous, generous, but prudent Mæcenas seldom to abandon an undertaking which he has once entered on; and scarcely a year had elapsed after the return of the Expedition of 1868, when he offered, of his own accord, to contribute liberally to the equipment of a new expedition to the same regions. I joyfully accepted the offer, and it was determined that the new expedition should have for its object to winter on the north coast of Spitzbergen, in order thence to push northwards in sledges on the ice."

" It is necessary in such sledge journeys in regions where no game can be reckoned on, in order to be able to traverse a sufficiently great distance, to employ draught animals which, during the course of the journey, may be killed in proportion as the stock of provisions becomes lighter. Two different kinds of draught animals are used for such purposes in the most northerly inhabited regions of the globe, viz., reindeer and dogs. The first point to determine was which of these was to be preferred? For this purpose numerous statements were collected, by the care of Mr. Oscar Dickson, from the northern parts of the kingdom, concerning the suitableness of reindeer for such journeys, their power of draught, the possibility of feeding them with collected moss, &c.; and it was at the same time determined that I should go to Greenland to collect similar statements regarding dogs, and to purchase a large number of them in case I should determine on their employment during the ice journey towards the pole."

" This was the occasion of my journey to Greenland in 1870, which, with Mr. Dickson's consent, was extended to a small scientific expedition, in which three young Swedish scientific men took part. The journey to Greenland yielded unexpectedly rich scientific results, among which may be mentioned the following:—

The collection of new contributions to the flora of the Polar countries during several preceding geological periods of special importance for a knowledge of the history of the development of our globe.

The discovery in the miocene basaltic strata of Greenland at Ovifak, on the island Diskö, of the largest known blocks of meteoric iron, regarding the origin of which an extensive scientific controversy has arisen, and which perhaps will at some future time form the starting point for quite a new theory of the method of formation of the heavenly body we inhabit. The large blocks were brought home the following year by two vessels of war which were sent out to Greenland for that purpose by the Swedish Government under command of Baron von Otter."

"An excursion of some length was made into the wilderness of ice, everywhere full of bottomless clefts, which occupies the interior of Greenland, and which, if I except unimportant wanderings along the edge and an inconsiderable attempt in the same direction in the year 1728, by the Dane Dalager, was now, for the first time, trodden by human foot. I had here an opportunity of clearing up the nature of a formation which, during one of the latest geological ages, covered a great part of the civilised countries of Europe, and which, though it has given occasion to an exceedingly comprehensive literature in all cultivated languages, *had never before been examined by any geologist.* The equipment for the journey was exceedingly defective, because everybody with whom I conversed who had any knowledge of the circumstances, declared to me that such a journey was impracticable, and that in consequence my preparations were thrown away. It was on this account that I was compelled to return earlier than would otherwise have been the case."

"According to the original distribution of work it was Dr. Theodore Nordström who should have accompanied me in this ice journey, but after our arrival in Greenland he was still much too weak from an illness which attacked him during the voyage to be exposed to the dangers and difficulties which must be encountered during a journey on the ice. Instead I persuaded Dr. Sv. Berggren, who took part in the Greenland Expedition of 1870, to accompany me. He began not without some jocular protests about the absurdity of a botanist making a dangerous excursion in the only region of the known land of the globe where he could not expect to meet with the least trace of vegetation. Berggren was, however, mistaken, for on the inland ice itself he had the opportunity of making a very remarkable and unexpected botanical discovery. His keen accustomed eye soon observed that the inland ice was everywhere bestrewn with a scanty vegetation of microscopic algæ, which, exceedingly minute as it is, by its dark colour certainly conduced in a high degree to limit the extension of the glaciers, and to change the ice deserts of the Ice Age into the green valleys and plains of the present period. At the same time that Dr. Berggren investigated, in a very careful way, the bryology of north-western Greenland, Docent P. Öberg made rich collections of marine animals, and I succeeded in collecting about 1,000 more or less perfect stone implements from the Stone Age of Greenland, &c."

"With respect to the proper object of the Expedition, I arrived at the conclusion *that dogs could not be employed with advantage in long sledge journeys in the regions where no game was to be had.*"

"The same year that I went to Greenland two young Swedes, Docent H. Nathorst and Hj. Wilander visited Spitzbergen, at the expense of some men of business in Stockholm, in order to examine for technical purposes some phosphatic deposits, and see whether they could not be worked with advantage. The result was favourable, and a company of commercial men was formed in

Stockholm and Gothenburg to work the deposits. We determined to endeavour to found a colony in Spitzbergen for this purpose, and as the country belonged to no State in particular we petitioned the Swedish Government to take steps to obtain international protection for our undertaking. This petition gave occasion to an attempt by Count Wachtmeister, then Foreign Minister of Sweden, to take possession of the whole of Spitzbergen for Sweden and Norway. For this purpose the necessary inquiries were made of the Powers of Europe who could have any claim in this respect. Favourable answers were received from all the States, with the exception of Russia, where the question caused a brisk newspaper controversy, from which the Russian Government took occasion to give a friendly answer in the negative."

"An attempt at any rate was made by the company to found a colony at Cape Thordsen in Ice Fjord. In the summer of 1872 two vessels were sent thither with some miners, a house was built, and a small railway constructed from the intended workings to the shore. The same summer, however, the enterprise was abandoned, partly because the manager of the company considered the phosphatic deposits not rich enough for profitable working in so remote regions, partly because the share capital was too limited. The company was dissolved, after having repaid to the shareholders what remained (about 25 per cent.) of the paid-up capital."

"As son of a native Swedish nobleman, I was able, soon after becoming a Swedish subject, to sit and vote in the House of Nobles. I was also present as a member of the House of Nobles at the two last meetings of the

Estates, but without at any time speaking or following the business with any special interest. Naturally, however, I was a zealous supporter of the views of the Liberal party, and I took an active part in the agitation for a change in the representation. After the introduction of the new system of representation, I repeatedly came forward as a Liberal candidate for Stockholm for a seat in the Diet. In this way, and through my taking part in the so-much-denounced 'new Liberal society,' to which I was introduced by August Blanche, I brought upon myself for several years much unpleasantness from the Conservative circles of the city. It was perhaps on this account that I was put up in 1869 as a candidate by the Liberal party, and after a contest, vehement in our circumstances, was elected. I thus became a representative for the capital from 1869 to 1871. With regard to the part I took as a member of the Diet, I will here only mention that, together with Hedin, Gumælius, and others, I took part in an attempt which was made in 1869 to form a Liberal Opposition Party to the Country Party in the Second Chamber, which, however, was completely unsuccessful, as all the peasant representatives, who at first joined us, returned to the Country Party, when we refused to follow them in what we thought their mistaken views on the question of the national defence. Two motions were brought forward by me. In the first I proposed that the Geological Office should be placed under the Academy of Sciences, and not, as is still the case, under the Civil Department, where there is scarcely to be found that knowledge of the subject which is required for the superintendence of an office, whose work, in order that it may be truly fruitful in a practical point of view, must, like all preliminary work in the present day with a technical end in view, be founded on a purely scientific basis. The motion was rejected. My second motion met a better fate. I proposed that the Diet should take the necessary steps for the appointment of a committee with a view to reconstruct the Technological Institute, so as to form a technical high school (or rather a technical and military scientific faculty of a future university in the capital) by uniting with it several teaching institutions already existing in Stockholm, as the Pharmaceutical Institute, the Institute of Forestry, the Military High School, &c. The motion was agreed to. The committee I asked for was appointed, and drew up a complete plan for the reconstruction of the Technological Institute as a Technical High School. Part of the alterations which it recommended have already been made. Unfortunately, however, a number of considerations have prevented the carrying out of the reform to the extent and in the direction which I proposed."

"The long prepared new Polar expedition finally started for the north in 1872. The state of the ice on the north coast of Spitzbergen was more unfavourable in 1872 than it had been at any time since the coast was frequented by the Norwegians. Three days after our reindeer were landed they made their escape. Some hours before the time when two vessels acting as tenders to the expedition, which were not provided with a sufficient stock of provisions for the winter, were to start on their return to Norway, they were shut up by ice in Mussel Bay. The stock of provisions which the expedition had at its disposal then became insufficient. Some days after, in addition to this, we were like to have been compelled to receive and maintain a large number of shipwrecked walrus-hunters. In the end of January all our vessels were in danger of being wrecked during an exceedingly violent storm, which broke up the covering of ice which had previously been on the surrounding sea, &c. This expedition, notwithstanding, yielded important scientific results, among which I may mention the discovery on the Polar-ice itself of a dust of cosmic origin, containing metallic nickel-iron; researches by Dr. Kjellman on the development of algæ during the winter night, which at Mussel Bay is four months long; researches on the Aurora and its spectrum by Dr. Wijkander and Lieutenant Parent, of the Italian Marine; researches by Dr. Wijkander on horizontal refraction in severe cold; a complete series of meteorological and magnetic observations in the most northerly latitude where such observations had up to this time been carried on; the discovery of numerous new contributions to a knowledge of the flora of the Polar countries during former geological epochs; a sledge excursion undertaken under very difficult circumstances by Palander and myself, whereby the north part of North East Land was surveyed, and a journey, very instructive in a scientific point of view, made over the inland ice of North East Land, &c., &c."

"The shutting up of the transport vessels in Mussel Bay was attended with very great expense, which had not been reckoned upon when the expedition was planned, and which was defrayed exclusively by Mr. Oscar Dickson. When the news spread at home that three times the number of men that had been intended were compelled to winter on Spitzbergen, Dickson placed 100,000 (Swedish) crowns (about 5,500*l.*) at the disposal of Baron Fr. von Otter, in case he considered it possible *immediately* (in late autumn) to relieve us. Von Otter rightly declined the proposal as impracticable."

"The comparatively unsuccessful issue and the heavy expenses of the expedition of 1872-73, by no means diminished Mr. Dickson's interest in such undertakings. On the contrary these were perhaps the reasons why he shortly after my return home declared himself willing to 'go on.' A new Arctic voyage was projected to the Kara Sea and the mouths of the Obi and Yenissej, and we started from Tromsö at midsummer 1875 in a small sailing vessel. I was on this occasion successful in almost completing the programme which had been arranged before our departure, a circumstance of rare occurrence in the history of northern voyages of discovery. We came here to a new, previously untouched field of inquiry, and succeeded in bringing home exceedingly numerous contributions to a knowledge of the flora and fauna of the region we visited. I made my way without difficulty in my little sailing vessel to the mouth of the Yenissej, and thus inaugurated, as I hope, a new and important route for the commerce of the world. From the mouth of the Yenissej the vessel was sent back under charge of Docent Kjellman to Norway, while, in company with Docent Lindström, Dr. Stuxberg, and three sailors, I ascended the river in a Nordland boat, which we had taken with us for the purpose to Dudino, where we fell in with a steamer. From this point we continued our journey by steamer to Yenisseisk, and thence overland by Ekaterineburg, Moscow, Petersburg, Helsingfors, and Åbo to Sweden. During this journey the Swedish *savants* were received in the large cities with fête after fête in consequence of the enthusiasm with which the foremost geographical and commercial circles in Russia hailed the prospect of a sea route between Siberia and Europe."

"There were, however, many doubters who affirmed that the success of the *Pröven* in 1875 depended only on the uncommonly favourable state of the ice, which prevailed that year in the Siberian Polar Sea. This gave occasion to the expeditions of the following year (1876), which had for their object partly to continue the interesting scientific researches of the year 1875 in the Kara Sea, and along the river valley of the Yenissej, and partly to show that the success of the preceding year did not depend on a fortunate accident. Their expenses were defrayed by Messrs. Oscar Dickson and Alexander Sibiriakoff, and they were completely successful, notwithstanding that 1876 was a bad ice year. Before I started on this occasion for the Polar Sea, I took part as juryman in the department of porcelain and stoneware in the Philadelphia Exhibition. I returned from America on the 1st July, and at Trondhjem stepped on board the vessel that had been chartered for the voyage. On the 15th August I was at the Yenissej, although I had halted at several places on the way. It had been arranged that I should meet a party at the Yenissej which was to make its way by land under Docent Théel to an appointed rendezvous near the mouth of the great river. I waited there seventeen days for these comrades in vain, and then returned successfully to Europe.

"For the present (July 1877) I am engaged in making arrangements on account of Mr. Sibiriakoff to send this summer to the Yenissej the steamer *Fraser*, which has been purchased specially for the purpose, with a cargo of commercial goods, and with the equipment of a new expedition, having for its object to extend farther westwards, if possible to Behrings Straits, the scientific explorations in the Siberian Polar Sea commenced in 1875 and 1876. His Majesty King Oscar takes a lively personal interest in this enterprise, and has made a liberal contribution to it from his privy purse. The balance of the expenses is to be defrayed by Messrs. Oscar Dickson and Alexander Sibiriakoff, and I hope to obtain for this undertaking support from the Royal Navy like that which was extended to the Expeditions of 1868 and 1872-73."

CHAPTER II.

THE SWEDISH ARCTIC EXPEDITIONS OF 1858 AND 1861.

WE shall now proceed to fill in with the more important details the rapid outline which Nordenskiöld has sketched of those Arctic Expeditions which have revived the ancient glories of Sweden, and shown that the thirst for adventure, the love of the sea, and the cool, daring, and unflinching intrepidity which characterised the old Norsemen, still run in the veins of their descendants, and that the love of nature and of science still animates the countrymen of Linnæus and Berzelius. It was with a scientific object in view that the first Swedish Arctic Expedition was projected, and the series has always retained a strongly scientific character, though practical results of the greatest importance are already visible.

The credit of originating the series of expeditions by which that part of the Polar Basin, which lies to the north of Europe, has been explored, and its natural history investigated during the last twenty years with such energy, skill, perseverance, and success by Swedish men of science, must be ascribed to Otto Torell, now Chief of the Geological Survey of Sweden. The discovery of the Ice Age, the geological period during which a great portion of the northern hemisphere was in the condition in which Greenland still is—covered with an immense sheet of ice—had conferred on the natural conditions of the high north a special significance for Scandinavia. To the study of glacial phenomena, the importance of which had been first perceived by Professor Playfair of Edinburgh, by the Norwegian Esmarck, and the Swiss Venetz, and Charpentier, Otto Torell, while Adjunct in the University of Lund, determined to devote himself, and with that end in view to make himself acquainted with the nature of the high north by travelling. His first voyage was to Iceland. In 1857, accompanied by Olsson Gadde, he travelled for three months in various directions across the island, making observations on its glacial phenomena, and rich collections of its marine fauna along the coast. The following year he visited Spitzbergen.

Spitzbergen, a group of islands, of which three are large and the others small, having a total area estimated at about 30,000 English square miles, lies 300 miles north of Scandinavia, and 325 east of Greenland. It was discovered on the 19th June, 1596, by the famous Dutch explorer William Barentz, in the course of his third voyage to discover the North East Passage. Barentz is said to have circumnavigated Spitzbergen, but considerable doubt rests on this statement, and if it is correct the feat was not repeated until the year 1863, when it was performed by Captain Carlsen, a Norwegian walrus-hunter.

The sea to the west of Spitzbergen was once a favourite whale-fishing ground, to which most of the seafaring nations of Europe sent fleets of whalers;

but the "right whale" is now extinct on its coasts, and the whale-fishing in that sea has long since terminated.

Spitzbergen was next visited by Russians, who built huts in all directions along the coast, and carried on fishing and hunting, their principal game being walruses, foxes, bears, and seals. The visits of the Russians became less and less frequent, and about 1830 it was only some private persons and the rich monastery, Solovetskoj, on the White Sea, that sent any vessels. The last Russian expedition to Spitzbergen for fishing and hunting appears to have been before 1850, though the date is not exactly known.

It is only the Norwegians that in our days visit Spitzbergen in order to hunt the walrus, with the exception of a stray Englishman like Mr. Lamont. According to Keilhau it was a Hammerfest merchant who, in company with a Russian, carried out the first Norwegian hunting and fishing enterprise in Spitzbergen in 1795. Part of the crew consisted of fishing Lapps and Russians, and they passed the winter in Spitzbergen. But the now existing Norwegian fishing and hunting dates properly from the year 1819, when an English mercantile firm at Bodoe sent a galeasse, with a crew of eleven men, to Bear Island and Spitzbergen, for the purpose of ascertaining whether fish and other animals existed in sufficient numbers to make fishing and hunting profitable. They returned from Spitzbergen—they had missed Bear Island—with accounts of the abundance of walrus, reindeer, and down, on Spitzbergen. A vessel with eight men was accordingly sent out from Hammerfest. But when they reached Bear Island, and the greater part of the crew had landed for the purpose of hunting, a fog and a high wind made the skipper lose sight of land, and finding it impossible to regain it, he left his men behind and returned to Hammerfest. The abandoned men provisioned their boat with walrus beef, and returned in it to Norway. Another expedition, similar in all points to the preceding, with the same skipper, the same crew, and precisely the same result, was undertaken in 1821. In 1822 a party of Norwegians wintered on Spitzbergen at Cross Bay, and their success induced others to imitate their example, not always with the same fortunate result. The fishing and hunting is still carried on in these waters by vessels from Tromsoö and Hammerfest; and these voyages, while on the whole a source of considerable profit to the owners of the vessels, have also been a school for the masters and crews in which the best qualities of a good seaman have been developed, especially those required for navigation among ice.

For more than a century Spitzbergen has formed the base from which a number of expeditions have endeavoured to reach the North Pole. For this it is well adapted. A branch of the Gulf Stream gives its west coast a much higher temperature than is due to its geographical position. The existence of land to the north of it is exceedingly probable; and, if it does exist, it would form a very convenient stepping stone to the Pole. We shall briefly enumerate the expeditions that have endeavoured to make Spitzbergen a point of departure.

In 1765 Admiral Tschitschagoff was sent by the Czarina Catharine of Russia with three vessels to

Spitzbergen to sail towards the North Pole. He reached the latitude of 80° 21′, but found it impossible to advance farther. The following year he reached the latitude of 80° 28′.

In 1773 Constantine John Phipps, afterwards Lord Mulgrave, sailed with the *Racehorse* and *Carcass*, with a view of reaching the North Pole. He got as far as 80° 37′ N. L., visited some of the Seven Islands, and mapped the north of Spitzbergen. In the beginning of August he was beset, but sawed his way through the ice, which at many places was twelve feet thick, and made his way back to England.

In 1818 Captain Buchan, in the *Dorothea*, and Lieutenant (afterwards Sir John) Franklin in the *Trent*, attained the latitude of 80° 34′ north of Spitzbergen.

In 1823 Clavering and Sabine, in the ship *Griper*, visited Spitzbergen, and while Sabine carried on magnetic observations on the inner Norway Island, Clavering went to sea and steered northwards, but did not get farther than 80° 20′ N. L.

In 1827 Parry, who had a short time before returned from his third Arctic voyage, which had for its object the discovery of the North-West Passage, undertook his well-known expedition in the *Hecla*, and made Treurenberg Bay the starting-point of the sledge journey, in which he reached the latitude of 82° 45′ N., then and for long after the highest attained by man.

The same year the Norwegian geologist, Professor Keilhau, paid a visit to Spitzbergen, of which he has given an interesting account in his attractive work, *Reise i Ost og West Finmarken*.

Ten years after Professor Lovén, of Stockholm, visited

Spitzbergen, dredging along its coast, and collecting organic remains from its fossiliferous strata. This visit is remarkable as the first made from Sweden to Spitzbergen with a scientific purpose.

In the following year, 1838, the French Government sent to Spitzbergen in the corvette *La Recherche* a scientific expedition under the leadership of P. Gaimard, and invited Scandinavian men of science to accompany it, an invitation which was accepted by several Swedish, Danish, and Norwegian naturalists. *La Recherche* visited Bell Sound in 1838, and Magdalena Bay in 1839. The great work in which an account of this expedition is given is unfortunately incomplete. It contains, besides, excellent views of the regions visited; among other valuable matter, important meteorological and physical observations, and a great number of drawings of objects of natural history, made for the most part under the direction of the Danish and Norwegian members.

It was in the year 1858 that Otto Torell undertook, at the suggestion of Professor Lovén, a voyage to Spitzbergen. He fitted out in Hammerfest, at his own expense, the sloop *Frithiof*, of about sixty-four tons burden, and sailed on the 3rd June accompanied, as has been already stated, by A. E. Nordenskiöld and A. Quennerstedt. The wind was favourable until some leagues south of Bear Island, where it turned against them, and they encountered drift-ice, which made the island inaccessible. They now cruised for a week in the ice until they were about 30 miles west of Bell Sound, when they succeeded in making their way through a belt of ice which lay several miles from land. On the 18th June they neared Horn Sound, where islands and hills were still clothed in their white winter dress, which, however, was daily disappearing, as the melting of the snow went on with incredible speed. Excursions were made in all directions, the geognosy of the region was described, glaciers were ascended, moraines examined, and specimens of markings collected, and dredging was carried on at the same time with great success at different depths up to a hundred fathoms. On the 28th they sailed to Bell Sound, where, the following day, they anchored at Middle Hook. There dredging was again undertaken with abundant success, birds and mammalia were shot and prepared, a tertiary formation containing fossil plants discovered, and botanical collections made, particularly of mosses and lichens.

On 6th July they left this anchorage to sail northwards, but calms and head winds compelled them to seek the north harbour in the same fjord. There Nordenskiöld discovered thick vertical strata of limestone and siliceous slates rich in fossils of the genera Productus and Spirifer, and which therefore appeared to belong to the Carboniferous Formation, and found these strata overlain by other nearly horizontal beds belonging to the same tertiary formations with impressions of leaves as he had observed at Middle Hook. On the 24th July they again went to sea, and on the 28th anchored in Green Harbour in Ice Fjord, which they examined till the 2nd August, when they again steered northwards. On the 4th they were at Amsterdam Island, on the 7th in another harbour between the Norways and Cloven Cliff, on the 10th in Magdalena Bay, on the 13th in English Bay, and on the 16th in Advent Bay in Ice Fjord. There they remained till the 22nd, when they sailed with the view of visiting the Thousand Islands, but an easterly storm obliged them instead to shape their course for Hammerfest, where they landed on the 28th August with an abundant harvest of observations and collections from all the different places they had visited.

In 1859 Torell visited Greenland, going as far as Upernavik, the most northerly settlement. He ascended the inland ice, which covers the whole land like a single enormous glacier, and dredged along the coast to a depth of 280 fathoms. He thus accumulated rich collections and increased his experience of travelling in these remote regions.

He had no sooner returned from his visit to Greenland than he began to form plans for another expedition to the Polar Sea. The Swedish Estates voted him a sum of 8,000 rix-dollars, which was supplemented by a further grant of 12,000, the total grant, 20,000 rix-dollars, being equal to about a thousand guineas. The Crown Prince, now King of Sweden, gave a contribution of 4,000 rix-dollars. It was arranged that each of the scientific men who were to take part in the expedition should pay his own expenses. During the summer of 1860 Torell visited Copenhagen and London. Carl Petersen, the experienced Danish polar traveller, who accompanied so many Arctic expeditions from Penny's to the latest one, in which he met his death, consented to take part in this, and to assist with the preparations. In London Torell's plan was received with lively interest by Sir Leopold McClintock, Captain Sherard Osborne, and by Sir Roderick Murchison, then President of the Geographical Society. In the latter part of the summer Torell visited Norway, making observations on its glaciers, until the return to Tromsö and Hammerfest of the Spitzbergen walrus-hunters, from whom he obtained information and assistance in making preparations for his projected expedition.

During the winter Torell submitted his plan to the Swedish Academy of Sciences. It embraced two objects—a comprehensive survey of the geology and natural history of Spitzbergen and its coasts, and a geographical excursion still farther to the north and north-east. The latter was to be carried out by himself, Nordenskiöld, Petersen, and a number of picked men with boat-sledges and dogs, with a view to settle the question whether in the neighbourhood of the Pole there is really an open sea or not. During the absence of the party the attention of the other members of the expedition was to be taken up with geological, zoological, meteorological, and magnetic work. Observations on the tides, on marine currents and on optical phenomena were included in the plan. Preliminary surveys were also to be undertaken to determine as to the possibility of measuring an arc of meridian on Spitzbergen, an undertaking that had been proposed by Captain (now Sir Edward) Sabine, more than thirty years before. The Academy expressed its warmest approval and made a representation to the Government, the result of which was the increased grant to which we have already referred.

Torell was in treaty for chartering the steamer *Fox*, in which McClintock had made his famous Arctic voyage, but did not succeed, so that he was obliged to be content with the *Æolus* and *Magdalena*, two small vessels, the former of about ninety-two, and the latter of about eighty-two tons, the ordinary size of the craft that sail from the north of Norway to Spitzbergen, and also the handiest, because they can the more easily push through openings in the ice into the fjords, or between the many small islands by which Spitzbergen is surrounded. On board the *Æolus*, which was under the command of Lieutenant Lillichöök, were Torell, the chief of the expedition; Nordenskiöld, who shared the command with him, carried out the geological surveys and took solar observations; Malmgren, zoologist and botanist; Chydenius, physicist; and Petersen, guide. On the sloop *Magdalena*, under the command of Captain Kuylenstjerna, were Blomstrand, geologist and leader of the scientific work; Dunér, astronomer and physicist; Goës and Smitt, zoologist and botanist, the former also physician to the expedition; and von Ylen, hunter and artist. An old seaman, Anders Jakobsson, who had accompanied Torell in his visits to Iceland, Greenland, and Spitzbergen, was also attached to the expedition as assistant to the zoologists. Though seventy years of age, he was still very active and much interested in it.

The expedition was ready to start from Tromsoe on the 15th April, 1861, but its departure was delayed by northerly winds, accompanied by fogs and falls of snow, until the 7th May, when the two vessels were towed through Tromsoe Sound by the Norwegian mail steamer *Aegir*. After a short involuntary delay off Carlsoe the *Æolus* and the *Magdalena* put to sea.

On the morning of the 10th May the voyagers lost sight of land, and by the evening of the same day they had fallen in with the first fulmar petrel (*Procellaria glacialis*), which they looked upon as a herald from the polar regions. This bird has its home in the high north, on the Färö Islands, the rocky islands of Iceland, Greenland, Arctic America, Kamschatka, and Novaya Zemlya. It breeds among the highest fells in colonies of many thousand pairs, and every pair has but one egg, which is very large, and is laid in the beginning of May,

PROCELLARIA GLACIALIS.

exceptionally in June. The fostering of the young is not finished before the middle of September. Together with the burgomaster (*Larus glaucus*) and the "tjufjo" (*Lestris parasitica*), it is the most dangerous enemy of the other birds, plundering their nests of eggs and young. The bird and the place which it inhabits have a suffocating carrionlike smell, and when taken living, it squirts from its bill a trainlike liquid of evil odour on any one that incautiously attempts to lay hands on it.

> "Obscenæ pelagi volucres, fœdissima ventris
> Proluvies, uncæque manus, et pallida semper
> Ora fame."

On the 12th May Bear Island was sighted for the first time, and the vessels began to be surrounded continually by a great number of auks. Bear Island lies to the east of the Gulf Stream, and beyond its influence. Its climate is, in consequence, much more severe than might be supposed from its position. It is often concealed by fogs and swept by storms, and landing on it is always difficult and dangerous. Two attempts were made on this occasion, but both of them were frustrated by the drift-ice that lay close packed along the shore. Leaving Bear Island on the 13th the vessels fell in with whales ("finners") for the first time, and on the 16th they were visited by snow-buntings (*Emberiza nivalis*) on their way to the north; they settled on the rigging and decks of the vessels; among them were young a year old. They appeared to be very tired, and were not in the least shy. After a short rest they resumed their laborious flight. On the 17th and 18th May, the wind being light and the sea calm, deep dredgings were carried on. On the first day a "Bulldog" machine took bottom at a depth of 1,000 fathoms, but did not work properly. A Brooke's apparatus, however, brought up some clay with *Polythalamia* from a depth of 1,320 fathoms. On the second day the "Bulldog" machine was successfully used. It brought up from a depth of 1,050 fathoms five different layers of clay containing animals, among others Annelids, and *Holothuria*, of which classes no species had been found at so great a depth. The delight of the naturalists at this *find* was naturally great. On the 18th the vessels were in 75° 45′ N. lat., and 12° 31′ E. long. Since the 15th "finners" had been often visible, the sea had a beautiful azure blue colour, and its temperature varied between 2·5° and 3·8° C. Now the "finners" disappeared, the temperature fell to between 0° and 1·3° C., and the sea assumed a dirty green colour, arising in great part from a number of microscopical, slimy, ill-smelling algæ belonging to the families *Diatomaceæ* and *Desmidieæ*. The boundary of the Gulf Stream, with its well-known blue colour, had been passed. "Finners" were not seen again until the return of the expedition in September in 78° N. lat. The temperature of the water was then about 3·8° C. It is probable that "finners" never live in colder water than this, and that the northern limit of their distribution coincides with sea of this temperature. It has to be kept in view, however, that this boundary line lies several degrees farther to the north in summer than in winter.

After falling in among snow-covered drift-ice with a great number of rotges (*Mergulus alle*) and black guillemots (*Uria grylle*) and shooting a few of them, the expedition came in sight of Spitzbergen on the 21st. Early in the morning the mountain-tops round Bell Sound and Ice Fjord were recognised from the sloop, and at 9 o'clock Prince Charles's Foreland was visible from both vessels. The land strongly resembled Norway as it had been left in its winter dress, only the precipitous sea-faces of the glaciers with their beautiful greenish-blue colour, indicated a much colder climate. On the 21st the vessels sailed along the Foreland and passed King's Bay and Cross Bay, and the glacier fifteen miles wide, which being here and there divided by elevated rocky ridges, is called "The Seven Icebergs." On the 22nd they passed Magdalena Hook, Danes'

Island, and Amsterdam Island, but falling in with pack-ice, which lay between the mainland, the Norways, and Cloven Cliff, and extended north and north-west as far as the eye could see, they returned and anchored off Amsterdam Island. A boat party was immediately sent off to ascertain the state of the ice. Finding it impossible to make way in a north-easterly direction, they turned to the north-west and rowed to a vessel that had been driving before a gentle breath of wind. Its skipper, the experienced Quane Mattilas, whom we shall often encounter in the course of this narrative, informed the Swedes that a belt of ice to the northward, visible from his "crows' nest," completely blocked the way. They accordingly returned to the vessels.

During the whole voyage no birds had been seen but auks and black guillemots, on their way northwards in immense flocks to revisit their old breeding-places. The same night, however (23rd May), great numbers of barnacle geese (*Anser bernicla*) were seen flying towards the north-east, perhaps to some land more northerly than Spitzbergen. The existence of such a land is considered quite certain by the walrus-hunters, who state that at the most northerly point hitherto reached such flocks of birds are seen steering their course in rapid flight yet farther towards the north.

"We were occupied as best we might with the examination of this hypothesis, the clearing up of which is reserved for futurity," says Chydenius, "when we were interrupted by an adventure which ought not to be left untold, as it had for us the charm of novelty. Two of the crew were harpooners, and among the best walrus-hunters existing. The guns lay ready for use loaded with pointed bullets, the polished lances and the carefully coiled lines were in their places, and the harpoons hung in the fore where the harpooners sat, and, like the no less skilful steersman, eagerly looked for game."

"Hitherto none had been visible, but now the steersman said that he saw walruses in a direction which he pointed out with his hand. In this direction two small black specks were visible, which an unaccustomed eye would never have discovered at such an immense distance, and it certainly could not have traced in them the least resemblance to animals. The hunters, however, stated that they were two walruses sleeping on a piece of ice; and we rowed for a little with a view to ascertain how far in among the drift-ice the animals lay. A short consultation was held about the quickest and easiest way of getting at them; we resolved on going by an open channel in the ice, which extended to a point which was about 200 feet from being within range of shot. At first the animals had the appearance of two yellowish-brown shapeless lumps. Suddenly two walruses, quite close to the boat, raised their heads above the water, with a pair of long white tusks projecting from each of their mouths. They lifted a part of their round bodies out of the water, looked at the boat and ducked hastily under, head foremost. After some moments they again came up, but it was thought best not to follow them for fear of frightening the others that were the first objects of pursuit. In the meantime we had come so near the latter that the harpooner stopped rowing, fixed the line to the harpoon and stuck it on its shaft. He now stood in the fore and made a sign with his hand which way the boat should be steered. Few words, only the most necessary, were spoken, quite silently the eight muffled oars passed through the water, and silently but speedily the boat glided over its surface. The animals did not move. Finally the boat got behind an immense block of ice, against which the sea broke furiously, and thus prevented the noise of the motion of the boat among the ice from being heard. The breakers, however, had to be avoided, and the boat came again in sight of the walruses. It was not long before they began to move, and one of them raised its head. That instant the boat stood still, all bent down as well as they could, and soon it was whispered 'They are lying quiet.' The harpooner placed himself with his weapon ready for a throw and a gun close beside him. A few fathoms more and they were within reach, when the animals lifted up their heads, regarding us with unconcern, and raising the anterior part of the body, the thick hide on the neck lying in great folds. 'They will dive! Shoot! I this—you that—close behind the ear." The boat stood still, the harpoon whistled through the air, and two shots were heard. Both walruses sank down on the ice, one motionless—the steersman's bullet had hit home—the other showing signs of life. Dunér handed his gun to the steersman. Again a report, and a stream of blood from the neck where the shot had taken effect. The animal raised itself up half its length. 'Shoot; I cannot reach the gun,' cried Uusimaa, a skilful Quane harpooner. I fired, the beast sank down, and a new stream of blood from the breast gave hope that it had got enough, but already part of its body was beyond the edge of the ice, and it sank and disappeared."

"The boat was now pushed forward to the edge of the

low piece of ice, on which we all sprang up. The remaining walrus, a beast of ten feet in length, was stripped of its skin and a three-inch thick layer of blubber and deprived of its head with the ivory-like teeth eighteen inches long. This time the gun and not the harpoon had done the work. The ball had hit the right place behind the ear, the only place where it causes immediate death, for if it strikes any other part of the head it is flattened against the incredibly solid bone or passes through a part of the brain, the penetration of which is not at once fatal. If it enters any other part of the body it remains harmlessly in the thick layer of blubber —walruses are often found with balls in the blubber— or it does not cause death until the animal has reached the water, as was now the case. If a swimming walrus receives a mortal wound it sinks immediately, and therefore the gun ought only to be employed to confuse it till it can be reached by the harpoon, for it and the lance are always the main weapons in this kind of hunting. We had scarce cast loose our boat when an immense number of gulls, that had gathered in the neighbourhood immediately after the death of the walrus, alighted in order to feast on the remains. Now, as always, the glaucous gull (*Larus glaucus*), which of old Martens, for its stately bearing, obtained the name of 'Burgomaster,' was the most active and least shy among these guests; after it the pretty snow-white ivory gull (*Larus eburneus*), Marten's 'Councillor'; a kittiwake (*Larus tridactylus*) and a fulmar petrel or two bore them company."

"When a man approaches a walrus he must, especially if it is lying upon ice, make as little noise as possible not to frighten it; but this is not necessary with the seal, except it be close to its hole, for then it is very easily frightened. If it be in open water or among drift ice it may be enticed to come nearer the boat by whistling or other noise, as we observed several times during the voyage. It held its head far above water, evidently listening to the sound, went under

LARUS EBURNEUS.

water and came up in another direction. A shot frightened it only for a short time."

The naturalists of the expedition employed themselves in dredging, familiarising themselves with the extraordinary richness of the Arctic waters in marine life, in botanising and geologising on Amsterdam Island, which consists of fine-grained grey granite, passing into gneiss-granite and mica-schist. The ground was still covered with snow to a depth of eight to ten feet, but on the precipitous mountain sides where no snow could lie there were found growing *Cetraria nivalis, cucullata, islandica,* and the black *Umbilicaria arctica,* the high-northern "need-bread," on which many polar travellers have maintained life, and other lichens. On the ledges and in fissures brownish-green carpets were formed of *Salix polaris* and mosses, among which the most common were *Ptilidium ciliare, Dicranum scoparium, Rhacomitrium lanuginosum, Gymnomitrium concinnatum, Hypnum cupressiforme, Polytricha,* &c. Here and there stuck up *Cerastium alpinum* and *Cochlearia,* the scurvy grass from the former year, nearly as green as in summer.

After anchoring in Kobbe Bay and remaining there some days, Torell, seeing large masses of ice go drifting past before a northerly wind, determined to attempt to force a passage north of Spitzbergen. The vessels accordingly sailed on the 30th of May, but on reaching the latitude of Cloven Cliff pack-ice was found stretching to the north and north-east as far as the eye could reach. On the 31st the thermometer stood at $-6·5°$ C. After several days' hard work among the ice and an unsuccessful attempt to reach Brandywine Bay, the *Æolus* and *Magdalena* came to anchor in Treurenberg Bay on the 7th June. The Swedes considered themselves fortunate in having reached, at so early a period of the year, a harbour so far north, from which they could at the first opportunity reach the coast of Northeast Land, which was still blocked up with pack and bay ice. It was from this point that Parry started on his famous polar expedition. During his absence from the 21st of June to the 22nd of August, 1827, his officers carried on extensive researches in the neighbourhood, which thus became one of the best known on Spitzbergen. Near the bay there was a burying-place with about thirty stone mounds, probably dating from the time when the Dutch and other nations were drawn in thousands to Spitzbergen by the attractions of the whale

GRAVE ON SPITZBERGEN.

fishery. A Dutch inscription, dated 1730, was found by the Swedes, and Parry found another dated 1690.

The Swedes paid a visit to Hecla Cove, Parry's harbour, protected from the north by Cape Crozier with its hill of quartzite. It was on this point that Parry and his lieutenant, Crozier, carried on their magnetic and astronomical observations, and on this height they erected a flagstaff with a copper plate bearing an inscription to preserve the memory of their visit. Here was found a flagstaff, which, however, was only the highest portion of Parry's flagstaff, and the copper plate was cut away so that only a few small pieces remained under the heads of the nails with which it had been fastened. Hecla Mount, about 1,720 feet high, was ascended, and from its top an extensive view was obtained of North-east Land, which is very flat along the coast with rounded hills of inconsiderable height. In the interior it is covered with a continuous snow-plain of about the same or somewhat greater height above the sea than the top of Hecla Mount, and to the south of Niew Vriesland, the interior of which is also occupied by a similar unbroken snow-plateau. In the neighbourhood large masses of hyperite were found; and to the iron which this eruptive rock contains the Swedes attributed certain irregularities which appeared in the magnetic observations. Interesting as was the discovery of this rock on the other side of the bay to the geologists, it was not so to the physicists, who found that all their magnetic observations were affected by its presence. Scarcely had the Swedes anchored in Treurenberg Bay than they found themselves shut in along with four other vessels that had accompanied them, and were engaged in walrus hunting. An attempt to force the ice on the 12th of June was frustrated by a calm, and on the following day the bay was filled with pack ice.

Midsummer eve found the expedition still imprisoned in Treurenberg Bay, but the great Scandinavian festival was duly celebrated. The sun shone in a beautiful blue sky, but he had not been able to bring forth from the reluctant earth leaves and flowers for a garland, much less for the indispensable midsummer pole. What the land could not furnish the sea supplied. There grew luxuriant forests of seaweed, brown *Laminaria*, with leaves four feet in length, and stalks nearly as long. With these a high pole was decked, which was raised on Æolus' Mount, and ornamented with all the flags and standards that were available. Alongside of the pole was kindled an immense drift-wood fire, and round them were assembled the members of the expedition and the crews of the imprisoned vessels, among

"MAGDALENA" IN ICE HARBOUR. (MIDSUMMER DAY.)

whom were representatives of the four northern peoples —Swedes, Norwegians, Danes, and Finns: the Lapp even not being wanting. The burning pile, the midsummer pole, the cross of Æolus, the variegated assemblage lighted up by the flame, the mount with the graves, the pack ice stretching as far as the eye could reach, over which the midnight sun in the cloudless firmament right to the north beamed mild and hopeful —all formed a picture which, says Chydenius, "by its contrasts made an indelible impression on us all. The gayest sport and the most serious earnest contended for the mastery; the former won, for seldom have glasses clinked more cheerfully than by the graves in Sorge Bay."

During the weeks that elapsed from the imprisonment of the vessels till their release the zoologists carried on

"ÆOLUS" IN TREURENBERG BAY.

dredgings, the other members of the expedition being employed in copying charts, with a view to future excursions, and in calculating observations. On board the *Æolus* meteorological observations were taken hourly: and measurements were made of the tides.

At length the ice broke up, and on the 2nd of July the ships got out to sea accompanied by the *Jaen Mayen*, a fishing vessel that had been imprisoned along with them.

June is the spring month of Spitzbergen. The sun rose higher and higher above the horizon, and his rays were by no means powerless. The snow first became soft and water-drenched, and disappeared in spots from the ground. On the 11th June *Cochlearia fenestrata*, and the polar willow began to open their buds; on the 22nd June the first expanded flowers of *Saxifraga oppositifolia* were gathered, a sign that the midsummer sun had at length won a victory over the northern winter, and on the 26th there were in flower *Draba alpina*, *Cochlearia*, *Cardamine bellidifolia*, and *Saxifraga cernua*, and here and there *Oxyria*, and the willow, and in the beginning of July *Cerastium alpinum*. Small *Podura* hopped about in a lively way among the snow. By the 7th June there were seen on Hecla Mount, more than 1,500 feet above the sea, a number of gnats, and on the 21st there were captured near Æolus' cross *Diptera*, which, however, were unable to raise their wings to a higher flight than a foot or two from the ground. Small spiders and a kind of worm, like our dew-worm, living in the already thawed ground, were found here and there.

During nearly the whole stay of the expedition in Treurenberg Bay the thermometer was above the freezing point, and after the 22nd June it did not sink below it, while it once rose as high as 15° C. (66° F.) in the sun. The mean temperature of the month of June, including the cold days in the beginning, when the vessels were cruising off Red Bay, was, according to 305 observations made on the *Æolus*, 1·7° C. (35° F.). The temperature of the water, filled as it was with colossal ice masses, also underwent a remarkable rise. During the first week it had kept under the freezing point, and even fallen to −1·5° C., but afterwards it rose as far as to + 2·6° C., while the ice floating in it visibly melted, and thus took up heat from the water. This rise, which, of course, cannot be ascribed to the immediate action of the sun, was specially perceptible at those times of the day when the tide set in from the sea. By the end of the month the border of the fast ice was a little south of the position which it occupied on Parry's arrival, as stated by him.

Snow, and on one occasion rain, fell in abundance during the first part of June, but none during the remainder. Towards the end of the month the fogs, that before had been rather troublesome, also disappeared.

With the beginning of July summer set in with a surprising rapidity of which the inhabitants of more southerly regions can form no idea. The temperature now occasionally rose to 11° C. (52° F.) in the shade ; the strong light was troublesome to the eyes, and the heat oppressive, when any hard work had to be done in the sun. The ice-foot, undermined by the waves, broke asunder and tumbled down, the bare patches on the fell sides, and on the level low land hourly extended themselves, and where skating had been going on shortly before rapid torrents cut deeply into the loose gravel of the terraces and slopes.

"The promontory where we lay," says Chydenius,

"raises itself terrace-wise in gentle slopes towards Hecla Mount, and the ground, deprived of its winter covering, resembled with its loose surface of gravel and fragments of mica, hyperite, and limestone, a fallow-field sparsely overgrown with Saxifrages, *Draba*, *Cardamine bellidifolia* and *Cerastium alpinum*, the plebeians of the Arctic flora, now in their best flower. The freshwater pools were visited by small flocks of *Tringa maritima* in search of larvæ, and here and there the beautiful *Phalaropus* was seen to pluck the alga *Nostoc commune*, which is plentiful in these waters, but not yet developed. An eider or two had built here their artless nest, and had newly laid their eggs. Along the beach, and mostly near the mouths of the streams, large flocks of *Larus tridactylus*, which in company with fulmar petrels and terns, restless and noisy, luxuriated on *Limacinæ*, crustacea which are found in immense numbers at this season on the coast of Spitzbergen, and in the interior of the fjords where they in spring have their favourite habitat at the mouths of the glacier streams near the surface of the water. The terns swarmed around in the air, and darted in swift flight down on their prey, while the fulmar petrels swam about and caught their food with little exertion."

Torell proposed to repeat Parry's attempt to reach the North Pole by a sledge journey over the ice. He pointed out that though Parry concluded his account of his expedition in 1827 with the declaration that such a plan could not be carried out, yet in 1845, after many years of ripe consideration and new experience, he stated it as his belief that if a sledge expedition could start from Spitzbergen as early as the month of April it might be able to reach the pole and avoid the three main difficulties he had to contend with, namely the uneven nature of the ice, the softness of the snow, and the current which carried the ice towards the south. The ice would then, Parry thought, show a hard and unbroken surface. It would probably lie motionless and reindeer might be employed. The forming of depôts and the sending out of returning parties were also proposed. Thus the only man who had made the attempt, but failed and declared it hopeless, came in the end after many years' consideration to hold the view that such a journey was possible. Admiral Wrangel was of the same opinion. He twice travelled with dog-sledges far to the north of Siberia.

Torell had hoped to reach north Spitzbergen by the beginning or middle of May, as he had been informed that the walrus-hunters were sometimes at North East Land by the end of April. His plan was that Nordenskiöld, Petersen, and he, with two men and three teams of the best dogs should start for the north, accompanied at first by two reserve parties, one to return after four or five days and the other after nine or ten days. He reckoned that without the help of depôts or reserve parties five men could be out between forty and fifty days and with the help of reserve parties nine or ten days longer. He had devoted himself for a long time to the working out of the plan and to the perfecting of all the details. It had now to be abandoned because in the first place the continuance of northerly winds delayed too long the departure from Tromsoe, and in the second place during the long imprisonment in Treurenberg Bay the ice was found to be quite unsuitable for a sledge journey, and finally when the vessels could leave the bay the season was so far advanced and the ice to a yet greater extent so broken up that such a journey could not be thought of. Even if smoother ice might possibly have been reached after a week's work no very high latitude could have been attained. There was therefore no alternative but most reluctantly to abandon the plan of the sledge journey northwards. It was then resolved, as indeed had been agreed upon beforehand in

GROUP OF POLAR BEARS IN MURCHISON BAY.

case the first plan could not be carried out, that Torell, Nordenskiöld, and Petersen should undertake a boat voyage through Hinloopen Strait, while Chydenius went northwards to carry out the preliminary survey for the measurement of an arc of meridian.

The boat party started on the 10th July, passing the mouth of Murchison Bay, landing first on a little island where Russian sailors had raised a fine cross with numerous inscriptions, and then on what on old maps was called North East Island but which turned out to be a projecting part of North East Land. The rock here was found to be an unfossiliferous limestone, the strata of which were very much twisted, having been exposed to the action of the eruptive hyperite which traversed them at several places.

They then proceeded down the Strait, Petersen's rifle keeping the cook well supplied with fresh reindeer beef, at least after Cape Fanshawe was passed, walrus-hunting also being prosecuted occasionally. On the 13th July they ascended one of Foster's Islands. Here high mountains with steep sides bound both sides of Hinloopen Strait. At several places there are immense glaciers, one about seven miles broad and standing out into the sea with its perpendicular wall. Enormous flocks of auks sought their food among the ice. Numbers of walruses were to be seen in the sound. The splendid illumination of the sun, which at this season does not set, and the abundance of animal life, gave the whole landscape a stamp of strangeness and grandeur which made a deep impression on the spectator. South of Wahlenberg's Bay a bed containing Permian fossils in great abundance was met with. These were the first fossils found on North Spitzbergen. As the party proceeded towards South Waygat's Islands a fog came on and they found it difficult enough to make their way with the aid of the compass among the pieces of drift-ice. Innumerable walruses tumbled about in the water, or lay crowded together on the low pieces of ice that were everywhere floating about. A piece of ice was often packed so full of them that not only the ice itself but part of the bodies of the walruses were sunk under water, while others swam round and, when there was no vacant place, endeavoured by strokes of their great teeth to drive away their comrades already in possession. Once when the boat in the fog came quite close to such a low piece of ice, on which thirty or forty walruses lay close together without troubling themselves about its approach, one of the men gave a sudden cry. The walruses threw themselves immediately into the sea in great disorder and with much noise, but came immediately up again behind a neighbouring piece of ice, appeared very curious, and tramped the water, so that a third part of the body was raised out of the sea. With their great bodies and long teeth they were a very peculiar spectacle.

After visiting Wahlenberg's Island where some young of the Arctic fox, *Canis lagopus*, were seen, the Swedes rowed amid innumerable walruses to a mountain on the south-west side of North East Land, to which as it was rich in fossils they gave the name of Angelin's Mount. During the row they harpooned a walrus, and as they were towed along by it, they were surrounded by over fifty of its companions which gathered from all quarters and swam in a half circle after the boat within shot. Even Petersen, though so familiar with the animal world of the north, was at first somewhat taken aback at this, and gave orders that all guns should be loaded. The animals, however, were moved by curiosity not revenge. They followed peaceably for a considerable distance, often raising their clumsy heads as far as possible out of the water the better to view the proceedings. Even when the dead walrus was drawn up on a piece of ice to be flensed, its comrades looked on, plashing among the ice that was floating about, till the blood, mixing with the water, drove them away.

After collecting a large quantity of fossils at Angelin's Mount the party rowed along the shore to another mountain, 2,000 feet high, which strongly resembled it. This they named Lovén's Mount. Its upper part consists of hyperite and with its flat, steep, and black sides strongly resembles a roof. Underlying the hyperite are horizontal lime- and sand-stone strata with nearly perpendicular faces towards the sound, giving the whole mountain the appearance of a regular colossal building. Another rich collection of fossils was made here. The party then proceeded down the Strait, but after two hours' rowing they were met by fast ice and obliged to turn. They then rowed along the west side of the sound, taking an hour to pass a broad glacier. After it they came to another which lay like a stratum of rock on a perpendicular cliff of hyperite, and accordingly tumbled with its ice over the rocks into the sea. The hyperite was found to be beautifully polished and marked, and here, as at several other places, were found many signs that the ice in former times had occupied a larger area on Spitzbergen. On reaching Dym Point, a number of eider-nests were found containing some fresh eggs, which afforded a welcome means of varying the auk soup which for some time had formed the standing dish. Between Dym Point and Cape Fanshawe the Swedes passed the greatest auk-fell they had hitherto seen. "Black cliffs, 800 to 1,000 feet high here, for a

stretch of about a mile and a half, rise perpendicularly
out of the sea, inhabited by millions of auks which sit
close packed together in all the clefts and crevices, and
we were witnesses of the literal truth of the well-known
statement that the air is darkened by the number of
fowl flying out of such a fell when a gun is fired, without
it being possible to distinguish any diminution
in consequence in the number of those which sit still
so quietly that some, which had made their nests,
could be reached from the boat and taken with the
hand. Where we rowed forward there were besides
great flocks upon and between the ice seeking their
food." Here also was found, rising from the sea to a
height of 1,000 feet, a perpendicular wall of hyperite,
everywhere split vertically into basalt-like, upright, four-
or eight-sided columns, standing free or only connected
with the main rock by a small corner, and sometimes
crowned capital-wise by a stratum of greyish-white
limestone.

After passing Cape Fanshawe the party next entered
Lomme Bay, on the west side of which they found
the largest glacier they had yet seen on Spitzbergen.
It is about ten miles wide, and projects into the
sound with a curved front. The stratification of the
ice is horizontal. After rowing nearly seven miles
into the bay, a small sandy beach was met with, on
which they drew up their boat. Near this, a little
farther up the bay, were found some grassy terrace-like
slopes. Here Petersen landed and in a short time killed
three reindeer, which the Swedes could hardly believe
to be the same species of animals as those they had shot
at Treurenberg Bay scarcely four weeks before. Then

they were so lean, as if they had consisted entirely of skin, bone and sinew; these, on the contrary, might have competed as fat stock at an English cattle show, for the largest rein had a layer of fat four to five inches thick on the loin. After visiting an island in the sound where a walrus-skin had been left, the party sailed with a favourable wind to Depôt Island in Murchison Bay. The *Æolus* had sailed, but Lilliehöök had left according to agreement a writing in a cairn, which they found. Lightening the boat of a sackful of fossils and other superfluous articles, they proceeded without resting to Shoal Point. The beach here is everywhere covered with an enormous mass of driftwood among which are found pieces of pumice-stone, birch-bark, cork, poles and floats from the Lofodden fisheries, with other things which had been carried hither by currents from the south. The driftwood formed a broad line along the beach. Farther up was another line, where the water now scarcely comes even during spring tides, probably elevated by a raising of the land. In this line the driftwood was far older and undergoing decomposition. While Torell was examining all this, he found among other things a well-preserved bean of the West Indian plant *Entada gigalobium*. This bean, which is upwards of an inch and a half across, floats with the Gulf Stream through the Atlantic, is found not unfrequently on the coast of Norway, and being also found on North Spitzbergen, affords the most convincing evidence that the Gulf Stream reaches this high latitude.[1] Following

---

[1] De Candolle states that one of these beans was found under the roots of the oldest chestnut tree in Paris, and that on being planted it germinated and grew. There is another bean of the same kind

the *Æolus*, the boat party arrived on the 21st July at
the north side of Low Island and there fell in with
Mattilas and his sloop. He informed them that Lilliehöök had sailed the night before for the Strait, and that

BEAN OF ENTADA GIGALOBIUM. (NATURAL SIZE.)

from the top of the mast of his sloop he could see with
his glass Chydenius' boat at the border of the fast ice
that yet covered Brandywine Bay. After a rest the

in the Riks-Museum in Stockholm, which was found at Tjoern, in
Bohus Laen, in a peat moss thirty feet above the sea level.

party determined to join Chydenius, and hearing from him that Lillichöök intended to return soon they waited his return between Bird and Brandywine Bay. Ascending a high mountain, they came, at a height of about 1,500 feet, to a plateau almost free of snow and bounded on the north by Bird Bay, towards which the rocks rise perpendicularly. From this plateau the mountain top raised itself, covered with snow, or rather loose fine-grained ice. From its highest point there was a splendid and uncommonly extensive view in all directions which the glorious weather with which they were favoured enabled the Swedes thoroughly to enjoy. In the north the horizon was bounded by an endless ice-field, in which from this height no opening could be distinguished, and whose uniformity was broken only at some few places by the groups of islands lying north of North East Land, the Seven Islands, Walden Island, Great and Little Table Island, and the land marked on Parry's map "Distant High Land." Towards the east the view was bounded by the high desolate snow plain which occupies the whole of the interior of North East Land. In the west, notwithstanding the great distance, it was possible clearly to distinguish the contours of the mountain tops around the Norways and Cloven Cliff. In the south-west Grey Hook and Hecla Mount were visible, and to the south of the latter two isolated, very high, pointed, snow-covered summits, which were believed to be situated on the north shore of Stor Fjord. On the 23rd July the boat party rejoined their vessel which had again anchored off Low Island and found all well.

Chydenius in the meantime had been at work in the neighbourhood of Low Island, and with the help of

Parry's map had come to a clear understanding as to how the triangulation should be arranged as far south as the mouth of Hinloopen Strait, and the *Æolus* had revisited Treurenberg Bay and there fallen in with Mattilas, who, under a heap of driftwood, had just discovered one of Parry's depôts, containing a gun, now useless, an ammunition chest of wood, lined with lead, cartridges and loose powder, all in good preservation, and eleven hermetically sealed tins. In one of the latter, on its being opened, was found roast meat, imbedded in jelly and fat, that tasted as well as if it had been placed there the day before. On the well-made ammunition chest the word *Hecla* could be clearly distinguished, and the wood, like all wood on Spitzbergen, was scarcely in the smallest degree affected by the air.

Torell and Nordenskiöld, on the 26th July, started again with their old crew from Low Island to examine the hitherto unexplored coast of North East Land. The *Æolus* was to visit Depôt Island, and then lie at suitable anchorages between Foster's and South Waygat's Islands till the 24th August, afterwards in Lomme Bay, then in order at the Russian Islands, mouth of Wijde Bay, Red Bay, the Norways, and Kobbe Bay, and if the boat party did not turn up it was not to run the risk of an involuntary wintering, but to go by degrees to the more southerly harbours of Spitzbergen, and thence to Norway. Torell and Nordenskiöld were accompanied as far as Brandywine Bay by Lillichöök, Malmgren and Chydenius, the whole party numbering sixteen men in four boats. At Brandywine Bay, one of the boats, made of galvanised iron, was drawn up on the beach, and a depôt formed.

On a steep ridge which starts from the neighbourhood

of this point Malmgren made a rich collection of plants. On the lower slopes there is a moist and soft carpet of the liveliest green, for the most part composed of mosses, *Aulacomnium turgidum* and *Hypnum uncinatum*, spread as a thick covering over a black layer of peat a foot thick. On this damp soil there flourished in large

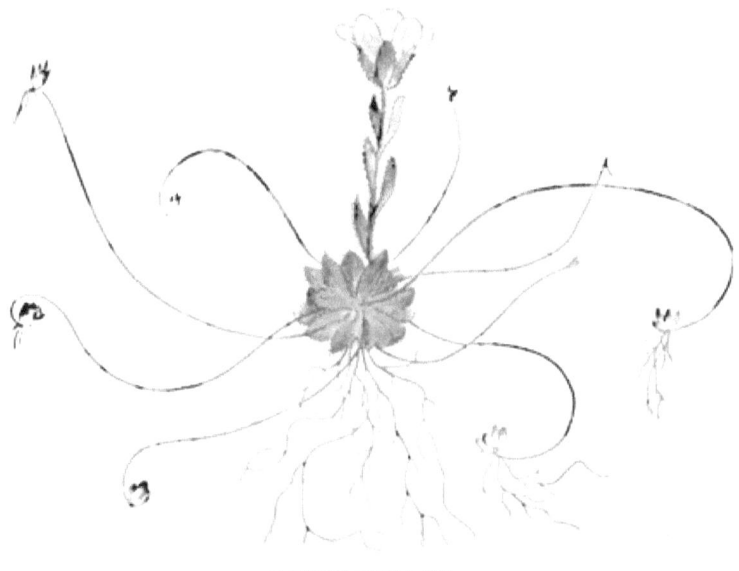

SAXIFRAGA FLAGELLARIS.

numbers several species of grass: *Alopecurus alpinus*, *Dupontia Fisheri*, *Poa cenisia*; and among other plants the little *Ranunculus hyperboreus* distinguished itself; *Oxyria reniformis*, a foot high, and large-leaved scurvy grass. *Cochlearia fenestrata* shot up in astonishing luxuriance at the less marshy places, mixed with the stately *Ranunculus sulphureus*, whose golden-yellow flowers came up to the wanderer's knees. Not to name other favourites of the Arctic soil, Saxifrages, *Cerastium alpinum*, *Potentilla emarginata* here had the fowl-fell as their home and formed a strong contrast to the stunted specimens found on the gravel wastes. Nor were the driest places without occupants; yellow *Drabæ* and poppies, with Saxifrages, *Cardamine bellidifolia*, the dwarf willow and *Dryas*, alternating with reddish patches of the hitherto unknown grass *Catabrosa vilfoidea*, were strewn like bouquets over the greyish brown ground. Among mosses the American *Pottia hyperborea* distinguished itself, and among lichens the *Usnea melaxantha*, which occurs in North and South America, in the latter along the Cordilleras, and which like many other plants is peculiar to East Spitzbergen, being absent on the west coast; so different are the natural productions of the two coasts separated only by a comparatively small extent of high land. Nor were the steep fell slopes without some, though scanty, vegetation. Torell brought down from a height of 1,500 feet several specimens of *Luzula hyperborea*, *Stellaria Edwardsi*, and *Papaver nudicaule*. The locality, however, was favourable, the slope was to the south, and sea-fowl in millions breed there.

Starting from Brandywine Bay Torell and Nordenskiöld rested first at North Cape, the northernmost point of North East Land, resuming their journey on the afternoon of the 28th July, but not proceeding farther than a small island, one of two lying to the south-east of North Cape, which they named Castréns Islands. From the top of the larger island, about 1,000 feet high, an excellent view was obtained of the sea between the Seven Islands and the mainland. The ice, which was thought to have been dispersed, was found to have collected anew, so that there appeared to be little hope of being able to force a passage through it. This, however, turned out to be practicable, and the party landed on the southern point of Parry's Island. Parry's Island is almost entirely occupied by two mountains, about 1,500 feet high, separated by a low valley. The rock is gneiss, traversed by veins of granite, in which there are to be found here and there crystals of tourmaline. Although the geological formation is thus the same as on North West Spitzbergen, and the difference in north latitude does not amount to a degree, the difference both in animal and vegetable life is very striking. It is probable that a cold ocean-current from the east is the cause of this state of things. In the valley the vegetation is extremely poor; even on the fell sides manured with birds' dung it is very scanty, consisting only of some few phanerogamous plants, among which are the yellow poppy of Spitzbergen, and stunted lichens. Here and there however there was a little green, and at one place there pastured three large and fat reins which were shot. Traces of foxes were visible in the sand.

Up to this time the weather had been fine with few exceptions. It now changed and became rainy and foggy. Bad weather compelled the Swedes to remain on Parry's Island during the 31st of July. The following day it was only with difficulty they could make their way through the mist and the closely packed ice to Marten's Island, the most easterly of the Seven Islands. They ascended the highest summit on Marten's Island, but could see nothing for the thick showers of snow that were falling. The stones at the top were covered with a loosely-sitting shining cake of ice, clearly newly formed by the condensation of watery vapour. This cake, which was several lines in thickness, loosened at the least motion and fell down, splitting asunder with great noise into a thousand pieces. No snow-field could be discovered at a height of 800 to 1,000 feet. On this island a reindeer was shot by Petersen. While hunting it he discovered the nest of a beautiful little wader, *Charadrius hiaticula*, which was here seen for the first time by the Swedes on Spitzbergen.

On August 5th they visited Phipps Island, which consists of several isolated mountains about 1,800 feet high, connected by a low land covered with driftwood and fragments of ships. Among the driftwood, there were as at Shoal Point many pieces of birch-bark, pumice-stone, and fishing-floats, often marked with Roman characters, &c. Remains of whale skeletons were found lying high above the present level of the sea, both on the low promontory on Marten's Island, and on the beach of the bay on the east side of Parry Island. All this indicates a considerable elevation of the land since the time when the Dutch whale-fishers first visited the neighbourhood. No more reins being visible it was determined to return to North East Land, and on the 8th August the party reached Castréns Islands with considerable difficulty and danger through the drift-ice, which was in continual motion, and on one occasion nipped the boat so that its form was altered and water streamed in through many joints. But the soft American elm withstood the proof, and after the water was baled out, the boat, with the exception of a trifling fracture, was as good as ever. Without much hope of being able to advance very far, the Swedes next day continued their row eastwards. The ice, however, soon became so packed that it was impossible to proceed, and they returned to the point which is incorrectly given in old maps as the most northerly point, and thus obtained the now inappropriate name of Extreme Hook. From the heights in this neighbourhood but little open water could be seen. On the 9th August an unsuccessful attempt was made to force a passage eastwards. A landing was effected on the western shore of the bay between Extreme Hook and North Cape, where a view was obtained from a neighbouring height of the state of the ice and the surrounding country and islands. Up to the top of this mountain peculiar shallow depressions were met with from two to three feet in diameter, which completely resembled well-polished giant cauldrons (jättegrytor). If it be taken as settled that such cauldrons have always been polished by currents of water, these showed clearly that even this mountain, which was at least 1,500 feet high, lay under water in former days and was perhaps covered with glaciers.

The following day the party landed on Scoresby's Island, where Nordenskiöld had an unpleasant adventure. "Without being provided with any weapon," he writes, "I ascended the island, in order from its highest point to measure angles between the neighbouring promontories. When I had reached a distance of fifty to sixty paces from the top I saw that a bear had occupied that place before me, probably that he might thence see what prey the surrounding ice-fields had to offer. He had also observed me, and I did not venture to return to the boat, but went straight towards him, supposing that he would be frightened and run away, as I had always previously seen Polar bears do when a man approached them. I had miscalculated; the bear came nearer, advancing slowly in a half circle, and we were soon so close together that I could have touched him with a stick. He stood somewhat higher up on a block of stone, hissing and tramping with his fore-feet; I stood somewhat lower, crying and hooting all I was able and threw big stones at him, with little apparent effect. At length a big stone hit one of his fore-paws resting on a stone, and the pain or perhaps satisfied curiosity induced the animal to retreat. I followed him for a short distance till he was concealed behind a projecting rock and then made my way as fast as I could to the boat. I had not finished relating the adventure to Torell, when he interrupted me with the exclamation, 'See, there he is!' and pointed to a rock about four hundred feet distant, from the top of which the white sovereign of the island was surveying us. Two of our men were sent after him, but when they approached the bear he immediately took to flight and we saw him no more."

On the 11th August the party continued their eastward course, landing on a new point, the third of those that project from the north part of North East Land. Here they found a beach, eight to ten feet high, formed of sand and rolled stones, in which a large quantity of driftwood was imbedded, a peculiar circumstance, showing that in a rock formation matters that are altogether foreign to it may become incorporated. A similar phenomenon is met with in Norway, where beds of clay have been found containing, along with fossil shells of high northern varieties, tree stems which probably grew elsewhere than in the regions where they are now found.

In the afternoon of the same day the stretch of coast marked by Parry "Distant High Land," was reached and named Prince Oscar's Land. The "ice-foot," which long defies the heat of summer, and like a white girdle encloses the shore long after the snow has disappeared from the heights, was now at last gone, and had, where the beach consisted of sand and gravel, left behind it peculiar indications. Everywhere were to be seen conical depressions in the gravel four to six feet across, which had probably been formed by the ice, when it was loosened and raised by the thaw and flood-tide, carrying with it large blocks of stone of which these hollows were the marks. Driftwood was still to be found here, but no longer any articles of Norwegian origin, only a harpoon shaft or an oar which Petersen recognised as belonging to the whale fishery. Animal and plant life were here alike scanty.

On August 13th another advance was made, and the party landed immediately south of Cape Wrede, ascending afterwards a mountain about 2,000 feet in height, affording an extensive view. Towards the horizon two small islands were seen, the one of which is high and bold, the other low and inconsiderable. They are named Charles XII.'s Island, and Drabanten (The Lifeguard). They were surrounded in all directions by impassable masses of drift-ice, but the sea between was pretty open. The boat party accordingly pushed on past Cape Platen, but finding the sea getting more and more packed with ice they resolved to return. So after making a festive meal of some preserved grouse washed down with some old wine that had circumnavigated the globe in the frigate *Eugenie*, which some Stockholm friends had sent them before their departure, the Swedes turned Westwards on the 15th August, passing Capes Platen and Wrede, and landing for the night on Scoresby's Island. They rested next at Castrén's Islands, passed North Cape on the following day, and on the evening of the next day Depôt Point. On the 18th Brandywine Bay was explored, and found to offer a good harbour for wintering in. On the 19th the Swedes met with a Hammerfest skipper and got from him welcome news of

CHARLES XII.'S ISLAND AND DRABANTEN.

the *Æolus*. Opposite Low Island, walruses, which had not been seen on the north coast of North East Land, were now visible in numbers, and according to the harpooners were preparing to go upon land. On the 20th Depôt Island was reached, and immediately after our party sailed across the Strait and rejoined the *Æolus* in Lomme Bay. Adjoining this bay were splendid hunting-grounds, where Petersen and the harpooners killed nine reindeer.

The *Æolus* had been cruising in Hinloopen Strait during the absence of the boat party, the naturalists on board making observations on the temperature of the water, and carrying on daily dredgings. On the 3rd August flocks of the Greenland seal (*Phoca grœnlandica*) were seen for the first time in the neighbourhood of Foster's Islands. They kept together in compact herds, thirty to forty each, swimming with extraordinary speed, and when they breathed, lifting their somewhat pointed heads out of the water all at the same time and ducking immediately down again to repeat, some few minutes after, the same dexterous manœuvre, but at a considerable distance from the place where they showed themselves before. This species of seal is, in the economy of the Greenlanders, of nearly the same importance as the reindeer in that of the Lapps. It is also of great importance in commerce.

Near Waygat's Islands, where the *Æolus* lay from the 8th to the 20th August, the divergence between the marine fauna of East and West Spitzbergen was very striking. Here were found animals exclusively belonging to the fauna of Greenland, seen exceedingly seldom or never on the west coast.

During an excursion to the south of Hinloopen Strait, in the course of which Chydenius satisfied himself of the possibility of extending the triangulation to Stor Fjord, two "marked" reindeer were killed. "We had previously met with such," says Chydenius, "and it is well known to the walrus-hunters that they are often found on Spitzbergen. They are called "marked" in common speech, but it is not meant by this that they have been marked by the hand of man. On the supposition, however, that this is the real explanation, it has been attempted to found a hypothesis that they have strayed from the peopled regions of the mainland to Spitzbergen, and because the country of the Samoyedes is the nearest where tame reindeer are to be found—for Novaya Zemlya, as is well known, is uninhabited—it has been supposed that the sea between Eastern Spitzbergen and the country of the Samoyedes is filled with hitherto unknown islands, between which the reins may go on the ice during winter, from one island to another until they reach Spitzbergen. This hypothesis was often the subject of our conversation. While the *Æolus* was off North East Land and in Hinloopen Strait, our hunters obtained at least four or five "marked" reindeer, and three skins of these animals were brought home by us to the Riks Museum. The ear-points of all of them were cropped nearly right across at the same distance from the root, but the obtuse angles of the point were not equal but somewhat knobby and rounded, and as thickly covered with hair as the other parts of the ear. All the hunters who have killed such reins steadily assert that both ears are always cropped at the same height, at a greater or less distance from the root, and during the expedition to Spitzbergen in 1864 some reindeer were obtained that were marked in the same way. On the supposition that these marks have been made with a knife by the hand of man—a supposition to which the unevenness of the ear-point does not lend any probability—and that the animals at some past time belonged to a nomade household inhabiting some other country, all the "marked" reindeer hitherto shot on Spitzbergen must have belonged to one owner, for the mark, at least during the last twenty years, has been unalterably the same. And as the number of such marked animals on Spitzbergen is so large that they certainly form a tenth of those that are yearly killed, and as the number of these may be, without exaggeration, estimated at the lowest at one thousand, some seasons up to fifteen hundred, the number of "marked" reindeer must have been a hundred per annum. A nomade household, that can lose a hundred reindeer yearly merely by straying, can perhaps scarcely exist for twenty years and have such considerable herds still remaining as to allow the straying still to go on on the same scale. It is to be noticed, besides, that when the northern races mark their reindeer in the ear they only cut a hack or hole in one of the ears, never in both, and it is highly improbable that any one would mark all his cattle by cropping both ears. The marked reindeer on Spitzbergen are not distinguishable from those that are not marked either by size, the branching of the horns, or in any other way; that is to say, they all belong to the Spitzbergen race, which differs from the reindeer living on the mainland by their size being considerably smaller, and by other striking peculiarities, and their skin never has scars from the *Oestrus* larva, which are exceedingly common in the skins of the north-European reindeer. Finally, another more probable cause of the cropped ears may be found, namely, the sharp frosts that occur in some seasons during the nights in spring while the rein-calves are yet young and their ears impatient of cold. For it is an experience obtained in Finmark and Lapland, according to the statements of trustworthy persons, and confirmed from various quarters, that there, too, in the high fell regions, the young reincalves in the cold spring nights have their ears frozen, which never regain their normal form, but appear in the full-grown animal as if cropped."

In Lomme Bay, the rendezvous of the boat parties, there is abundance of animal life. Reindeer pastured near its shores, and eleven were killed. A brood of beautiful Arctic ptarmigan, which is very uncommon

REINDEER HUNTING.

elsewhere in Spitzbergen, was seen here. The white whale, *Beluga catodon*, tumbled about in the water, and one was captured. These beautiful animals, over fourteen feet long, are inhabitants of the Polar Sea proper. They live, like other dolphins, in shoals, and are so shy that they are only taken with difficulty. The Norwegians catch them with a peculiar harpoon, called a *skottel*, different from that used in the whale fishery. The white whale is frequently found in the neighbourhood of glaciers, where the water is often turbid with the fine rock-powder which the glacier grinds down while in motion, and which is carried out into the sea before it. In such water the white whale cannot see the harpooner and his boat. At a distance it strongly resembles a seal in the water. When fully-grown the animal is milk-white, and exceedingly beautiful. Its young, on the other hand, are dark in colour. If the water is clear it is possible to get near them, but they always go down so fast that they cannot be taken.

When they used to visit these regions, the Russians caught them in a strong net, in the same way as is usual in Greenland, where several hundred are taken yearly. The white whale occurs along the shores of the Polar Sea, and the east coast of Asia as far down as 52° N., and on the coast of America it is taken in St. Lorenzo Bay. It often ascends rivers for great distances to hunt fish, and it is found in the Amoor river upwards of 250 miles from the sea.

The *Æolus* weighed anchor on the 24th August, and after steering first to north-west then to north reached 80° 30′ N., the highest point attained during this voyage. The intention to anchor in Brandywine Bay was given up for fear of being shut in by ice if the wind should be unfavourable. Dredging was next carried on in deep water off Treurenberg Bay, after which the *Æolus* anchored on the west side of Muffin Island where dredging was resumed, and Nordenskiöld, Malmgren, and Chydenius landed to make observations. This low, flat island, which rises only six feet above the sea-level, is a favourite resort of the walrus, when the ice melts on the sea and it is obliged to go on land. Here our party met with a sight so sad that it could never pass from their recollection. A long way off they could distinguish something white, which at a distance resembled a limestone rock. The whole

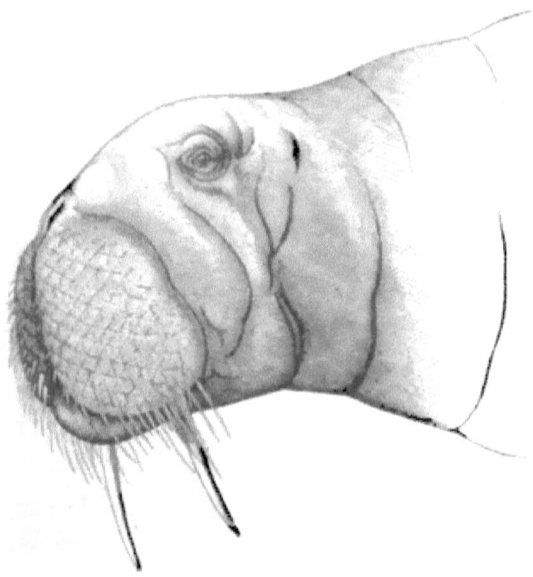

HEAD OF WALRUS.

white mass consisted of walrus skeletons heaped on each other by hundreds, or rather by thousands, and it was evident that many of them had been killed merely for the sake of their tusks, and otherwise left untouched to be destroyed by wind and weather. The walrus-hunters choose the opportunity when the walrus goes on land, steal after them, kill with their lances those lying nearest the sea, and thus form a rampart against the animals lying farther up, which then in desperation endeavour to roll themselves over the bodies of their comrades down the sloping beach, and in the tumult suffocate or cut each other in pieces. The first attack requires a high degree of courage and boldness, but is more a wild slaughter than hunting, for of several hundreds which are killed in this manner, not nearly the whole fall by the hunter's hand. The vessel is now filled with skins and blubber, and when no more can be taken on board, the tusks are hewn from the heads of those remaining, and the bloody field of slaughter, from which the traces of the savage hunt are not attempted to be removed, for years frightens away other walrus herds from the region. Thus for a long period the hunting-ground is destroyed. This mode of walrus-hunting, profitable as it is, ought to be put a stop to, if it were possible to introduce any order or rule into the hunting on Spitzbergen, where every living thing that has any money value —eider, or other fowl, walrus, seal, reindeer, and Polar bear—is now recklessly destroyed out of sheer greed, with the idea, "If I don't kill it, another will." Otherwise there is a strong probability, that in a few decades the walrus will be extirpated on all the accessible parts of the coast of Spitzbergen, as it has been on Bear Island, or that it will become as rare as it now is on the west coast of Spitzbergen, and that the same fate will soon overtake the other animals.

Up to this time ice had been constantly seen in the north, but now the sea was clear, and neither

ice nor ice-blink was visible, and the Swedes would
fain have sailed northwards, thinking it probable that
they might be able to reach the latitude of 82°, but
the seamen and Petersen withheld their approval of
such an attempt on the ground that the *Æolus* was
not a good sailer, and if a storm should come on
she might not be able to avoid the drift-ice, and
might be beset for the winter. The project was
therefore given up, and the *Æolus* sailed for the west
coast, visiting Smeerenberg, perhaps the best harbour

MAINLAND AT SMEERENBERG GRANITE.

of Spitzbergen, which used to be full of shipping
during the flourishing period of the whale fishery, and
was said to have been visited during a single summer
by as many as 18,000 men. Large train-boiling
establishments were erected here by the Dutch, but
almost the only traces remaining from that period
are, as at many other places on Spitzbergen, the
graves which indicate how large a number of men
must once have sojourned on its coasts. On the
31st August, Chydenius went to Norway Island,
searched for the place where Sabine made his famous

observations, and found the inclination there to be 80° 34′ 7″. It was 81° 11′ when Sabine was there.

The snow still lay on a mountain-top on Danes' Island. To judge by the eye it had a position typical for these regions, and Chydenius found by angular measurement that the border of it lay 900 feet above the sea. On the 3rd September, the *Æolus* weighed anchor with the view of going southwards to meet the *Magdalena*, but after cruising off the coast for some

DANES' ISLAND.

days, as the barometer indicated a coming storm, she came to anchor again in Kobbe Bay.

During the 7th, 8th, and 9th September, a furious S.S.E. storm raged with heavy showers of snow and high sea. Autumn had commenced in earnest. The fowl-fells were deserted, and their numerous inhabitants had drawn southwards. The ground was bare, except on the highest fells and in the deepest clefts, where it was still covered with hardened snow, in many places coloured red by a microscopic plant, *Protococcus nivalis*, which has given occasion to "red snow" being spoken of both in the Polar lands and on the highest summits of the Alps. A fresh-water lake, that was covered with ice six feet thick in the end of May had, during the three months that had since elapsed, become ice-free, but its temperature at the surface was only 1·2° C. and at the bottom 2·2° C. It was occasionally visited by a black-throated diver or two, and some Spitzbergen geese. A boat was carried to it, but dredging yielded no new result. Excursions were made in the region, and magnetic observations continued. At last the *Magdalena* was seen entering the bay with all sail set on the morning of the 9th September.

When the *Æolus* parted company with the *Magdalena* on the 9th June, the latter vessel was endeavouring to make her way through the pack past Grey Hook towards the west. While the ice still closed the way, Aldert Dircks's Bay and Wijde Bay were explored by boat parties. The eastern side of Wijde Bay was found to be one of the best hunting-grounds on Spitzbergen. The hunting-boat once returned from a three days' excursion with no fewer than twenty-four reindeer in pretty good condition. Here was found by the side of a fresh-water lake, a dried specimen, three inches long, of the young of the *Salmo alpinus*. Blomstrand and Dunér made an excursion into the interior of Wijde Bay, and there observed the temperature in the shade as high as 16° C. (61° F.), the highest during the whole summer. On the 18th a southerly breeze cleared the sea of ice, and enabled the

Magdalena to leave Wijde Bay. The Norways were next visited, to ascertain whether they were suitable as a starting-point for the triangulation along the west coast. The western Norway Island is well known as a place where the eider breeds in large colonies. The eider lives in great flocks, always on islands where it may be safe from the mountain fox, and there is seldom any bird in company with it except the glaucous gull or the brent goose. The tern also keeps by itself, only single pairs of *Tringa maritima*, or *Phalaropus fulicarius* being permitted to build beside it. The eider when it has not more than one or two eggs in its nest, places a shell, *Buccinum glaciale* beside them.

After various excursions had been made the *Magdalena* sailed from the Norways on the 25th, and after passing Kobbe Bay and South Gat, the sound between Danes' Island and the mainland, anchored in Magdalena Bay. Here, at a height of 2,300 feet above the sea, the following plants were found growing, *Cochlearia fenestrata, Cerastium alpinum, Luzula hyperborea*, and several saxifrages: lower down, small soft tufts of the Arctic willow, *Alsine biflora*, and several grasses. Out of the gravel there rose nearly a foot high here and there the uncommon *Saxifraga hieracifolia* and *Pedicularis hirsuta* with its reddish head, alternating with yellow *Ranunculi* and bright red patches of the graceful *Silene acaulis*, of which, however, a flower here and there had begun to pale under the powerful rays of the sun, which had already caused several *Drabæ* and the here uncommon *Arabis alpina* to go to seed. High up on the fell grew the beautiful *Erigeron uniflorus*. By the side of the small streams that flowed from the top to the bottom of the mountain were mosses, *Saxifraga rivularis, Stellaria Eduardsi,* and two species of *Poa*. It is remarkable that the vegetation diminishes quite inconsiderably with the height above the sea, so that almost all the plants that grow near the beach thrive as well at a height of two thousand feet. The continual sunlight and the insignificant difference in temperature are undoubtedly the causes of this.

The large granite blocks and broken stones, of which is formed the peculiar beach by which the fells are here almost always separated from the sea, are quite concealed by the most luxuriant moss and lichen vegetation. The grey covering, often six inches thick, is for the most part composed of lichens: *Sphærophoron fragile* and *Cladonia gracilis, Stereocaulon paschale, Cetraria islandica*—Iceland moss—*Bryopogon jubatum, Alectoria thulensis, Umbilicaria arctica, Solorina crocea* and many others; and among mosses of *Racomitrium lanuginosum,* with stalks nine inches long, *Encalypta rhaptocarpa, Gymnomitria* and *Bryæ, Polytrichum alpinum* and *Dicranum fuscescens,* &c. While the sloop lay in Magdalena Bay Cape Mitre was visited, a promontory which Scoresby ascended one of the few times he landed on Spitzbergen. When he had reached the summit, he was obliged to sit astride the ridge in order to keep his place. On the 31st of July the *Magdalena* again put to sea, and the same day anchored in Cross Bay. In this neighbourhood the first known fern on Spitzbergen was found—*Cystopteris fragilis*.

Cross Bay is remarkable for an immense glacier in the bottom of its north-western arm. From this glacier large blocks of ice are unceasingly detached, having not unfrequently a height above the water of 40 to 50, and a length and breadth of 150 to 200 feet. They may reasonably be considered veritable icebergs, with which the masses of ice that break off from the considerable glaciers in Wijde Bay, Magdalena Bay, the seven glaciers, &c., cannot stand the remotest comparison. The reason of this clearly is the greater depth of the fjord where the glacier enters the sea. When they enter the sea most of the glaciers of Spitzbergen rest on the sea-bottom, as on a firm foundation; on which account, for evident reasons, only comparatively small pieces can be broken off. If the water, on the contrary, is so deep that the front of the glacier is entirely borne up by it, very much larger masses may break off at once, the glacier wanting the cross-fractures which are apt to occur under such circumstances. In this way are produced the enormous icebergs which float out to sea from the deep fjords of Greenland, and those, in some degree comparable with them, which are to be found in and off Cross Bay, the depth of which was measured by the zoologists of the expedition up to two hundred and fifty fathoms. That icebergs proper are so seldom heard off from this region of the high north, is thus, perhaps, caused less by the glaciers being small and the inland ice inconsiderable, than quite simply by the water round the coast being too shallow. The larger masses from Cross Bay probably never reach the open sea as they are too deep in the water to get over the coast shallows. They are stranded here and there on the shores in the form of ground-ice.

In the neighbourhood of King's Bay, where the

Magdalena next anchored, Blomstrand found a seam of coal, together with impressions of leaves and other parts of plants, showing that there was a period in the development of the globe when spreading forests, composed, it would appear, chiefly of broad-leaved trees, resembling our maples, everywhere covered the valleys

IN THE INTERIOR OF KING'S BAY.

and mountain-slopes, where now, if they be not entirely filled with thick beds of ice, the Arctic willow, creeping inch high along the ground, is the only representative of plants of the nature of trees.

The *Magdalena* being detained in King's Bay by contrary winds and calms, Blomstrand and von Ylen started in a boat for Ice Fjord, which they reached on the 23rd, finding Mattilas in Green Harbour, by whom they were hospitably entertained.

Ice Fjord is, with the exception of Stor Fjord, which is to be regarded as a sound, without question the largest fjord on Spitzbergen, and with its widely-extended water surface, without taking into account the surrounding mountains, it offers a truly splendid prospect. With a breadth of thirty or forty miles it runs deep into the land, with a number of arms—Green Harbour, Coal Bay, Advent Bay, and the yet larger Sassen Bay on the south; and finally with two, Nord Fjord and Klaas Billen Bay, separated by a high mountain ridge.

While Blomstrand and von Ylen were examining Ice Fjord the *Magdalena* left King's Bay on the 23rd of August, and arrived at Advent Bay on the 27th. The mountains exhibited the peculiar forms of immense temples and buildings which distinguish the interior of the fjord. "Here and there a rich green on their dark slopes met the eye, and as we steered towards evening into Advent Bay we were agreeably surprised by the vegetation, lively for Spitzbergen, which clothed to their tops the hills of the western shore, and grew luxuriantly in the valleys. Nearest the beach was a field of stone and fragments of slate sparingly mixed with mould with *Stellaria humifusa* and the modest strand plant *Cochlearia fenestrata*. The green and yellow carpet upon the hills was watered by small streams from the glacier spots on the higher hills, and offered the botanist a special interest in its varied composition, as at least two-thirds of the phanerogamous flora of Spitzbergen were to be found there. There grew luxuriant grasses—*Poa pratensis, cenisia,* and *stricta; Aira alpina, Alopecurus alpinus, Calamagrostis stricta,* and *Trisetum subspicatum,* with the here large-flowered *Polygonum viviparum, Andromeda tetragona, Dryas octopetala* and broad yellow bands of *Saxifraga hirculus* and *flagellaris,* together with *Potentilla emarginata, Ranunculus sulphureus;* and besides the whole multitude of the plebeians of the Arctic flora, *Draba alpina* and *hirta, Salix polaris, Luzula hyperborea, Juncus biglumis, Eriophorum capitatum,* with many others. The moist places were occupied as usual by mosses, *Polytrichum alpinum, Pottia latifolia,* &c., and among them stuck up *Chrysosplenium tetrandrum,* and our childhood's acquaintance, *Cardamine pratensis,* certainly somewhat altered in size and form, yet easily recognisable."

Advent Bay is one of the best harbours on Spitzbergen, affording protection both from the swell from the sea and from all winds. It is about eight English miles long by five broad. While sailing into its mouth, which is about two and a half English miles wide, it is necessary to avoid going too near the projecting low ground on both sides, which extends some distance as reefs under water, but when the point on the western shore with the Russian hut on it is passed the vessel may be steered along the low ground towards the mouth of a mountain stream, which falls into the bay between the low ground and the bold rocks which lie to the south. Three cable lengths from the land there is excellent anchorage in six to ten fathoms water. The bottom is quite different from the other fjords, where it is nearly everywhere newly formed of mud from glaciers still in action. Such is not the case here, where the glaciers have in great part disappeared, and the bottom gets only a slight addition of inorganic matter from the mountain streams; it is, so to say, old, and its dark grey colour and muddy appearance are caused by the large quantity of decomposed organisms which it contains. Here a luxuriant if also somewhat monotonous animal and plant life has been developed—Mussels—*Cardium, Astarte, Tellina, Crenella*, and Univalves—*Natica* and *Tritonium*, here reach a comparatively colossal size, and an incredible abundance, and such was the case also with the other lower animal groups and with the algæ, among which are to be found an uncommon number of high northern fishes of the families *Cottus* and *Lumpenus*, together with the young of *Gadus æglefinus* and *Drepanopsetta platessoides*. The surface of the water swarmed with the high northern *Beroe* and *Cydippe*, exhibiting a beautiful play of colour. Towards autumn they attain completeness in size and colouring, and with them are found a multitude of smaller forms.

The naturalists of the *Magdalena* after making a survey of Ice Fjord would gladly have examined Bell and Horn Sounds, but time did not permit. The *Magdalena* sailed for Kobbe Bay, where the *Æolus* was found at anchor, having arrived some days before. Preparations were now made for the homeward voyage, which was commenced on the 12th September. In the course of it deep dredgings were carried on. Torell had previously dredged at depths of from 1,500 to

1,700 feet in the mouths of Omenak and Upernavik Fjords, on the coast of Greenland, where, in a bottom of fine mud produced by the action of glaciers on the rocks of the mainland and carried into the sea by the glacier streams, he found a fauna, so rich that no diminution of the number of animals with the increase of depth could be observed, and at the same time full of variety, embracing all the different classes of invertebrate animals. He had found also at Omenak and Upernavik two faunas very different with respect to species at the same depth and on a bottom where no difference could be perceived. He had made careful preparations for the dredgings he now proposed to carry on, and had got a "Bulldog" machine constructed, with some improvements by Chydenius. After two unsuccessful attempts with Brooke's apparatus the Bulldog machine struck bottom at a depth of 8,400 feet. The temperature in the middle of mass of matter brought up by the machine was found to be $0\cdot3°$ C. The temperature at the surface of the sea at the time was $5°$ C. ($41°$ F.), and of the air $0\cdot6°$ C.

At this considerable depth, where the temperature is always near the freezing-point, where the only motion of the sea is a flowing from the pole towards the equator, where the pressure of the water on every point is more than the weight of 200 atmospheres, where light is absent, but where the air and salt contained in the water are probably the same as at the surface, there was found on the few square inches acted on by the scoops a number of animals as large and rich in species as could have been expected at a smaller depth on the same kind of bottom. The bottom was found to be covered with a fine sediment, greasy to the touch, of a yellowish-brown or grey colour, which, with the exception of some few and small fragments of stone and grains of sand, consists of finely-divided remains of microscopic calcareous shells of *Polythalamia* or siliceous parts of *Radiolaria*, diatoms, and sponges. The section of the raised mass, sixty-four cubic decimal inches, showed five layers of different thicknesses, from two inches to one-third of an inch, clearly distinguishable by difference of colour, perhaps a sign that periods probably of lengthened duration succeeded each other in the motions of the currents and other circumstances determining the progress of the deposit, and perhaps also in some degree in the conditions of animal life. In this mass there lived *Radiolaria* and numerous *Polythalamia*, among them many very large and well developed specimens of *Globigerina*, *Biloculina*, *Dentalina*, *Nonionina*; of Annelids, a *Spiochetopterus* and a *Cirratulus*; of Crustacea, a *Cuma rubicunda*, Lilljeborg; an *Apseudes*; of Mollusca, a *Cylichna*; of Holothuria, a fragment of *Myriotrochus Rinki Steenstrup*, and an allied form, apparently a new species; of Gephyrea, a *Sipunculus*, like *S. margariticus*, Sars; finally a *Spongia*, in which were found three species of *Crustacea*. The success with which the dredging was carried on awakened a strong desire to prosecute it, but the wind rose and water got scarce and Torell determined in consequence to return to Tromsoe where the *Æolus* anchored on the 23rd and the *Magdalena* on the 27th of September.

COST OF THE EXPEDITION.

The expenses of the expedition (not including the travelling expenses of the members to and from Tromsoe) amounted to 51,967 rix-dollars and 63 ore,[1] which were defrayed thus:—

	Rix-dollars.
Grant by the Swedish Government	12,000
Additional grant by the Swedish Estates	8,000
Gift by His Royal Highness Prince Oscar	4,000
„ Baron S. Adelsvärd	1,000
Contributions from members of the Expedition	5,400
Sale of remaining effects, &c.	4,210.83
Supplementary grant by the Swedish Estates	17,356.80
	51,967.63

[1] About £2,887 sterling.

FOX AND DEAD REINDEER.

CHAPTER III.

THE SWEDISH ARCTIC EXPEDITION OF 1864.

The preliminary survey to ascertain the possibility of measuring an arc of meridian having been left unfinished by the Expedition of 1861, the Swedish Academy of Sciences made a representation to the Government of the desirableness of completing it, and the Estates, on the proposition of the Government, voted a sum of 10,000 rix-dollars (about £550) for this purpose. The new expedition was placed under Nordenskiöld's leadership. Chydenius was to have accompanied him, but he died a few weeks before the departure of members of the expedition from Stockholm, and Dunér, who had also taken part in the work in 1861, was appointed in his stead. In order that the opportunity of studying the botany and zoology of the polar regions might not be lost, Count B. von Platen provided funds to enable a naturalist to accompany the expedition; Dr. Malmgren from Finland acted in that capacity. All the members of the expedition were familiar with Spitzbergen and with the peculiar difficulties that there meet the observer.

An old and strongly-built gunboat of only twenty-six and a quarter tons burden, newly-schooner rigged, named the *Axel Thordsen*, was chartered at Tromsoe, fully equipped and manned with nine men, for four months, for 1,400 specie dollars. This small vessel was provisioned for five and a half months, without counting some sacks of Russian meal which had been laid in, in order that, in case of an involuntary wintering, there might be a supply of *some* vegetable food. There was neither room nor funds for provisioning the vessel for a whole year, as ought always to be done in these waters. The *Axel Thordsen* carried four boats, and, to enable three of these to be manned at once, three additional hands were hired in Tromsoe, so that the crew consisted of twelve persons, of whom the sailing-master, Hellstad, and the dredger, Joachim Lorenz, had taken part in the Expedition of 1861, and Uusimaa, the harpooner, in the Expeditions of 1858 and 1861. The little schooner got to sea on the 15th June, and on the 17th had Bear Island in sight.

When Nordenskiöld passed Bear Island in the spring and early summer of 1858 and 1861 its coast was quite blocked up with closely-packed masses of drift-ice, and, in the autumn, landing was rendered impossible by storm and the thickness of the atmosphere. On this occasion Bear Island was indeed concealed by its winter covering, but the sea round it was free of ice. As no drift-ice had been met with in sailing from Norway, it was supposed that the south coast of Spitzbergen was yet surrounded by "spring ice," that Stor Fjord was not yet accessible, and that a few days' stay at this known little island would not be prejudicial to the main object of the expedition—the preliminary survey in Stor Fjord. Nordenskiöld and his companions with some difficulty effected a landing near what is called the South Harbour, but which does not deserve the name of harbour, being quite open to the south, and therefore not affording the least protection against southerly or south-easterly wind or sea. The shore nearest the anchorage is composed of perpendicular rust-coloured cliffs, whose weathered sides were on this occasion nearly free of snow and covered with sea-fowl and their nests. Farther inland the island had an unbroken covering of snow which extended to the foot of the enormous fell masses of Mount Misery. The rocks on the shore were hollowed out by the waves at innumerable places into gigantic grottoes and arches, which gave the whole the appearance of a once mighty city now in ruins.

A landing was effected on the sandy beach of a bay near the southern Russian hut, the only convenient landing-place in the quarter. Nordenskiöld made an excursion to Mount Misery, Malmgren to the south part of the island, while Dunér, after taking solar observations, went towards the centre of the island. Later in the day Nordenskiöld, stopping up the door, window, and chimney of the Russian hut with tarpaulins, converted it into a photographic studio, and took several photographs of the neighbouring coast. Next day the Swedes rowed to the west coast, into the sound between Bear Island and Gull Island, the rocks on both sides rising boldly out of the sea, so that there was no possibility of landing except here and there where there was a small sandy beach at the foot of them. The party had almost reached the pillar of rock which, pierced by two immense arched openings, rises at the southern extremity of the island to a height of about 500 feet above the level of the sea, when a heavy swell compelled them to return to the harbour. Here they found their skipper very uneasy lest the wind should freshen and their vessel, having an insecure anchorage, be driven on land. While he was weighing anchor and cruising off the island, Nordenskiöld rowed back to fetch his photographic apparatus, and to insert a water-mark at the Burgomaster Port. "This mark consists of an iron wedge driven into the rock, the middle of the wedge on the 19th of June, 1864, at four o'clock, p.m., being four feet (3·896 feet English) above the surface of the sea. When one rows out from the boat harbour near the Russian hut, this mark lies directly to the left, before the Burgomaster Port[1] itself is reached." This mark will afford a means of measuring the elevation of the land which is believed to be going on at a rapid rate in these Arctic regions.

Not satisfied with the hasty and incomplete examination they had been able to give to the island, nor deterred by Hellstad's warnings, our party again landed on the west coast, but finding that the ground was covered nearly everywhere with snow, and that the bare patches showed no sign of any vegetation and consisted only of loose angular pieces of limestone, seldom fossiliferous, as the wind was freshening they returned to their vessel, regretting that they were unable to reach and even cursorily examine the thick coal-seam near North Harbour.

The greater part of Bear Island consists of a nearly level plain, 100 to 250 feet above the level of the sea. There are two terrace-formed mountains, of which the larger, well named Mount Misery, lies in the north-eastern part of the island and rises to a height of 1,200

---

[1] An arch of rock so named by Nordenskiöld from the abundance of these birds.

feet. The coast is rocky and bold with a small sandy beach at some few places, where the herds of walrus, at the seasons when they visit the island, find a convenient resting-place. Immense heaps of walrus bones lie spread about, and bear witness to the grim sport for the sake of which Bear Island was frequently visited in former times, and even colonised for short periods. Two huts remain as memorials of these visits. One we have already mentioned; the other was built near the North Harbour in 1822 by a Hammerfest merchant, who for several years sent men to winter on the island for the purpose of hunting until the whole colony died of scurvy, perhaps in consequence of an unusually unfavourable winter.

Leaving Bear Island behind, the *Axel Thordsen* now sailed northwards, the course being shaped for the middle of Stor Fjord. On the 20th June, a belt of ice was seen in the north, which was found at first to be quite open, but afterwards became so closely packed that any farther progress was impossible. The wind fell and a thick mist came on. The hope of reaching Stor Fjord had to be given up, and after fighting their way through the ice for three whole days, the Swedes succeeded in getting out of it in the neighbourhood of Charles' Foreland, and as an impenetrable belt still surrounded the whole southern coast of Spitzbergen, they anchored in Safe Haven, one of the many harbours of Ice Fjord, there to await a more favourable state of things. Safe Haven is a little bay on the north shore of Ice Fjord, well protected from most winds, with a soft clay bottom, and consequently good anchorage. The innermost part of Safe Haven is occupied by an immense glacier, from which large blocks often detach themselves. The eastern shore is bounded by a perpendicular belt of rock, 50 to 100 feet high, which rises nearer the glacier to a pointed ridge, not very high, consisting of vertical strata, belonging to the mountain limestone formation, and containing abundance of fossils, mainly large species of the families *Spirifer* and *Productus*. On the west side is a mountain about 1,500 feet high, which from the hundreds of thousands of auks which frequent it was called Alkhornet (the Auk-horn). Some small islands on both sides of the mouth of the fjord are breeding-places for eiders and burgomasters. The eiders are there, after the ice has broken up, protected from the attack of the fox, as are the auks and smaller gulls, by the inaccessible rocks where they breed. The pink-footed goose (*Anser brachyrhynchus*) on the other hand requires no protection, and therefore breeds on the mainland, by preference on the edge of the rocks, which on the north-east side of the harbour rise perpendicularly out of the sea.

As the drift-ice still lay in compact masses at the mouth of the fjord, Nordenskiöld, Hellstad, and three men went on a boat excursion to the fells which divide the fjord into two arms, and which like many other similar promontories on Spitzbergen have been called Middle Hook, but which Nordenskiöld re-named Saurie Hook. The first day they reached a low promontory, to which they gave the name of Cape Boheman. Next day finding it impossible to penetrate to the bottom of Nord Fjord, the party landed at the mouth of a stream which falls into the sea between Nord Fjord and Klaas Billen

Bay. This stream flows through a valley which from its being frequented by reindeer is called Rendalen (the Reindeer Valley). Here Nordenskiöld collected a large number of fossils from the interesting Triassic strata which occupy a considerable extent on Ice and Stor Fjords. The following day he found yet finer fossils, among them large nautilus-like shells, and fragments of bones, some of which appeared to have been four feet long, belonging to crocodile-like animals, such as are now found only in the warm countries in the neighbourhood of the equator. In the meantime Hellstad killed seven very fat reindeer, which were carried to the boat with some difficulty, one of the sailors who was fording a rapid stream, with a rein-cow and calf on his back, being carried off his feet and narrowly escaping drowning. Nordenskiöld, returning to the vessel on the 30th of June, sketched the pleasures of his boat journey in such lively colours that his comrades came unanimously to the conclusion that the best thing they could do under the circumstances was to undertake another boat expedition to the inner part of the fjord. Leaving therefore the key of the cabin in which the stock of wine and spirits was kept in the hands of Johansson, a trustworthy Stockholm man, and appointing Uusimaa skipper in the absence of master and mate, the party started, Malmgren, Nordenskiöld, Hellstad, the cook, and two men in one boat, Dunér, the mate, and two apprentices in another. The former party landed first at Coal Bay, and then rowed on through a tolerably ice-free channel to the mouth of Sassen Bay. During the row Malmgren shot a pink-footed goose and collected some of its eggs. Hellstad also shot some reindeer. The following day after landing at a rocky hat-formed hill, which at a distance was seen to consist of hyperite, and taking angles there, they explored some islands off Gips Hook, also consisting of hyperite and covered with eiders' nests. The sailors, who now had considerable experience, had strict orders to collect only fresh eggs, and, the test being applied of putting them into a vessel containing salt water, most of them sank, showing that they had been selected with great skill. Gips Hook was the next landing-place.

Here the scene was magnificent. The headland itself consisted of a low, much disintegrated hyperite rock, from which at some distance from the shore rose a high fell, below consisting of horizontal, grey strata of gypsum interspersed here and there with white nodules of alabaster, resembling strings of pearls; higher up was a black band of hyperite with a perpendicular face, and above it again were grey fossiliferous strata and snow-fields blinding white. Farther up Sassen Bay was Temple Mount, rising directly out of the sea, and perhaps grander still. The thick band of hyperite, forming the top of the fell, has been very regularly cut by the streamlets into forms, which at a distance strongly resemble enormous Gothic arches, and give the whole the appearance of a colossal Gothic dome fallen into ruin. At the foot of the mountain the fjord was strewn with innumerable, fantastically shaped pieces of drift-ice, and lay so calm and still that it mirrored every fragment of ice and every rock along the shore. Innumerable sea-fowl, breeding partly on the sides of the mountain, partly on the hyperite islands circled in the air or swam among the ice seeking their food in the sea, and giving animation to the otherwise calm and silent nature of the high north. After collecting fossils and shooting some reindeer here, the party started to row to the opposite shore and narrowly escaped having their boat nipped between the fast-ice and drift-ice that was carried up the fjord by the tide. Surrounded at first by small ice which could carry neither their boat nor themselves, they managed to follow in the wake of a large block of glacier ice which at first threatened to destroy them by its whirling motion, and reaching the edge of the fast-ice succeeded after several attempts in drawing up their heavily-laden boat on it, so that they could in safety witness the collision between the drift-ice and the fast-ice, by which large pieces of drift-ice were forced upon the fast-ice, forming a wall along its border, the fast-ice at several places itself being broken up. After some hours' waiting, openings appeared in the drift-ice which gradually extended to the land. The boat was again launched, and the north shore of the South Fjord safely reached on the 7th July. The provisions that had been brought along being now nearly exhausted, it was determined to return. After several days' delay, occasioned by the state of the ice, and meeting with a party of Englishmen who had been employed in hunting on the east shore of Advent Bay, Nordenskiöld and his companions rejoined their vessel in Safe Haven.

Dunér in the meantime had visited Coal Bay and Green Harbour, going as far westward as Cape Staratschin, named after the Russian hermit who lived in its neighbourhood. Here he was obliged to turn, and passing Coal Bay he came to Advent Bay, where he was informed by some shipwrecked Norwegians, who were hunting reindeer, that Nordenskiöld and his party had gone to Safsen Bay. He then crossed over to Cape Thordsen, finding there a fine waterfall 700 feet in height. The ice in the North Fjord being closely packed, Dunér returned to the *Axel Thordsen*, and finding that Nordenskiöld and his comrades had not come back, though the time fixed for their return had long passed, started again to search for them, and landed first at Cape Boheman, then at Advent Bay, where he was informed by the Norwegians that Nordenskiöld and Malmgren had left it a few hours before.

Immediately after their return the Swedes were invited to dinner on board the yacht *Sultana*, where they made the acquaintance of the Englishmen on board, Mr. E. Birkbeck, owner of the yacht, Mr. Graham Manners Sutton, Mr. Alfred Newton, now Professor of Zoology at Cambridge, Dr. W. W. Wagstaffe, and, finally, Herr H. Lorange, a Norwegian and interpreter to the party. The Englishmen and Swedes often visited each other, and, says our author, "we had the opportunity of admiring the elegance and comfort, uncommon in these latitudes, with which the *Sultana* was fitted up, and at the same time of being astonished at the idea occurring to any one of sailing in this beautiful but fragile nutshell through seas bestrewn with drift-ice, without serviceable boats or other proper equipment. A collision with the smallest ice-floe had been sufficient to drive a hole in the vessel's side."

The mouth of the fjord had been free from ice for

some days before the return of the boat parties, but on account of a persistent calm the *Axel Thordsen* could not sail before the 16th of July. Before leaving an iron bolt was placed as a water-mark on the outer side of the island off the eastern shore of Safe Haven. On the 15th of July at 4 P.M. the mark was 1·4 metre above the level of the sea.

On the 17th, while the *Axel Thordsen* was off Bell Sound, a violent storm came on, compelling the Swedes to anchor in the sound. It continued with undiminished force during the 19th and 20th, but notwithstanding it Nordenskiöld betook himself to an island off the mouth of the North Fjord that he might photograph a glacier which had filled up a harbour that a few years previously had been one of the best and most frequently visited on Spitzbergen. Malmgren and Dunér landed at Midde Hook, finding there an uncommonly luxuriant vegetation, remarkable for the abundance of plants otherwise rare on Spitzbergen; for instance, the beautiful blue and white flowered *Polemonium pulchellum*. On the 21st the storm was followed by a calm so complete that there was no possibility of a sailing vessel making any progress. Dunér embraced the opportunity to map Van Keulen Bay, while Nordenskiöld went to Van Mijen Bay, returning on the 26th to the *Axel Thordsen*, which again put to sea on the 27th. After passing Dunder Bay an impenetrable fog came on, which did not lighten till midday of the 29th. As it dispersed the most majestic picture that Spitzbergen has to offer, the white tops of Horn Sounds Tind glancing in the sun, became visible. These mountains rise in three steep and pointed summits to a height of 4,500 feet above the sea, and

Scoresby names them as the highest and stateliest of the mountains of Spitzbergen. To Nordenskiöld and his comrades, though they had often sailed past this stretch of coast, the view was altogether new. During the greater part of the year mists conceal them from view. The wind dying away, the *Axel Thordsen* anchored at the Down Islands on the 30th of July. The islands are all low and flat, with numbers of freshwater ponds. They are thus specially suitable breeding-places for eider, the rather because the ice round them breaks up sooner than round most of the other islands on Spitzbergen. The walrus-hunters often visit them in the month of June and luxuriate on the eggs and birds. Hatching time was past, and the eider were now swimming about the shores accompanied by their newly-hatched young. On landing on the islands great flocks of terns were met with, which sought with wild cries to protect their eggs or only down-clad young. If they had not in this way shown where their eggs or young were, it would have been often difficult to discover them among the gravel on which they lay, which was often pricked out in yellow by a species of lichen on account of their greyish-yellow colour. The terns, however, now flew round the observer in flocks with such violence that it is only in case of necessity that any one would visit their breeding-places.

The sides of the fells on the mainland next the sea were formed of coarse *débris*, which up to a great height was covered with a lively green. Here were found innumerable flocks of Spitzbergen's smallest natatory bird the rotge (*Mergulus alle*). These birds choose for their breeding-places the enormous stone heaps, which at many places are found on Spitzbergen on the sides of the fells, and are possibly the remains of old lateral moraines. Here they occur in incredible numbers. Part fly about in the air in flocks so dense that at a casual glance they may be taken for clouds; others sit packed so close on the blocks of stone that it is possible with a single shot to kill ten to twenty of them, or creep under ground like rats in holes among the stones.

When Torell and Nordenskiöld visited Spitzbergen in 1861, they anchored off these islands in the middle of June. They wished to collect some rotges' eggs, and for this purpose searched for them without success in the openings between the stones. They were on their way to return with their errand unaccomplished when the cackling sound, which came from a greater depth, drew their attention. They now began to lift the stones, and they captured several living birds and found some eggs lying on the ice between them. Probably the proper hatching-time had not begun. It was curious to hear the sounds that came from among the stones when one counterfeited the cry of the rotge close to the ground. Without any bird being visible ready answers were heard from underground in all directions, and these answers called forth cackling again and again renewed, so that a single question gave occasion to a very long-continued conversation between the feathered but rat-like inhabitants. The flesh of the rotge is exceedingly savoury, with no flavour of train-oil. During the stay of the expedition at Horn Sound a great many were shot. A shot was thought unsuccessful if it did not kill seven to ten birds at once.

Nordenskiöld and Dunér, each in his boat, set out to

survey Horn Sound, but were obliged to return by contrary strong winds and an exceedingly high sea, after lying to near the north shore of the fjord, and there by triangulation obtaining some considerable contributions to their map. During their return they visited the innermost island at the harbour, and found there in a little heap nine skulls of Russians said to have been robbed and murdered by an English crew who went unpunished. Another similar deed of blood done on the coast of Spitzbergen was discovered in a wonderful way and the actors brought to punishment. On their return to Archangel, the crew of a Russian bodje stated that they had lost their captain and two men at Spitzbergen by an accident. This did not of course attract any special attention, but some years after, in 1853, a Norwegian who was still living in 1867, found a gun-barrel lying beside a human skeleton. The gun-barrel was covered with inscriptions scratched on it, stating that the owner along with two men, who before the writing was finished had died of hunger, had been intentionally left on land by his crew. This remarkable journal closes on the 3rd of March. The Norwegian who found the gun-barrel sent it to Archangel, the crime was discovered, and the perpetrators sent to Siberia.

The *Axel Thordsen* put to sea again on the 3rd of August, sighting, and after a long chase overtaking, a Norwegian vessel, the skipper of which in an "ungentleman-like" way, uncommon on the coasts of Spitzbergen, disregarded the signals made by the Swedes. They got no letters or newspapers from him, but coaxing him on board by the offer of a glass of spirits, an unusual luxury, as no liquor is allowed on board the

Norwegian vessels that frequent Spitzbergen, they extracted from him as best they could some idea of the state of matters in Europe. On the 6th of August South Cape was passed, but it was impossible, on account of ice, to anchor as had been intended. The position of the drift-ice also prevented Whales' Bay from being reached. After sailing some time in a north-easterly direction open water was found along the south part of Stans Foreland. The course was therefore set for Whales' Point, where the vessel anchored on the morning of the 9th.

The proper goal of the expedition was thus reached, but the short polar summer was already so far advanced that at most three weeks' working could be reckoned on without exposure to the risk of a winter passed without the necessary equipment. It was therefore necessary to use every favourable moment, more especially because, from the accounts which they obtained from visitors to Spitzbergen, the weather in Stor Fjord did not promise to be very good. Fortunately it appeared that the discouraging descriptions of the fogs prevailing here were properly applicable to the Thousand Islands, comparatively clear weather being really general in the inner part of the fjord. Here, as at many other places on Spitzbergen, may be found cloudless skies and sunshine, while an impenetrable fog lies at the mouth. The cause of this is to be sought for in the course of the marine currents. While an arm of the Gulf Stream, as the masses of driftwood heaped up at South Cape and the Thousand Islands show, flows past the southern part of West Spitzbergen and Stans Foreland, at least during a portion of the year, it is the Arctic current entering from Helis Sound and Walter Thymen's Strait which principally prevails in the interior of Stor Fjord. There is, therefore, no driftwood to be met with on the shores of this fjord, on which account it is necessary to carry a supply of fuel on boat voyages. During boat voyages along the north coast of Spitzbergen one may, however, nearly always reckon on finding dry and excellent material in the neighbourhood of the resting-place even for a large log-fire. At Whales' Point there still stand ruins of some Russian huts, remains of one of the largest Russian settlements on Spitzbergen. These were described by Keilhau as they existed during his visit in 1827.

From the top of Whales' Point, which was ascended with difficulty, a very extensive view was obtained. On the east Deevie Bay lay open, bounded at the horizon by a black precipitous fell. "To the right of this mountain we could," says Dunér and Nordenskiöld, "with the help of a glass count twenty-eight islands belonging to the Thousand Islands, and gathered, it appeared, into two groups, one near Deevie Bay and the other right to the south of Whales' Point. They were in general small and low. In the sound between them three vessels were seen, among which, as we afterwards found, was that of our English acquaintances from Ice Fjord. We could not on the other hand see Hope Island, and it appears very probable that, as Lamont remarks, it lies considerably farther to the east than is shown on the chart. We cannot state this with complete certainty, however, because Hope Island might have been concealed in a fog that lay on the horizon. On the contrary, the whole west coast of Stor Fjord, the extreme point of which, South

Cape, could with certainty be distinguished, lay in the most glorious sunshine. It appeared to consist of a confused assemblage of snowy summits of nearly equal height, among which only a few were so remarkable as to be easily recognised, as for example the mountains at Whales' Head and Agardh's Bay. But over all those thousands of fells there rose like the tower of a cathedral over the houses of a great city the mighty Horn Sounds Tind, with an angular height at least double that of the other mountains. It was easy to see from this that this stately mountain is the loftiest in South Spitzbergen."

Whales' Head being inaccessible, Agardh's Bay was next visited, and on the 13th the *Axel Thordsen* anchored near Lee's Foreland. Here, as at the former place, the Swedes landed and ascended the neighbouring mountain where they found a Russian cross at a height of 1,000 feet above the sea-level. The west coast of Stor Fjord is occupied by enormous glaciers, which go down to the sea, and are only interrupted by black, often conically-shaped mountain tops. On the east coast, on the contrary, between Whales' Point and Helis Sound there is only a single considerable glacier, the coast being formed of a continuous rocky wall, which rises almost directly from the sea to a snow-free plateau of about 1,000 feet in height. At the foot of this wall there are here and there grassy slopes, which form the finest reindeer grounds on Spitzbergen. Walter Thymen's Strait was right below, and appeared from the many sandbanks which are found in it to be very shallow and foul.

After anchoring near the only glacier, remarkable for its immense moraine, which is to be found on the east coast of Stor Fjord, and shooting an immense Polar bear, our party proceeded on the 16th August to the western extremity of Barentz Land. Along the shore here there is a low plain, during the latter part of summer free of snow, without any proper turf, indeed, but affording excellent summer pasture, and therefore known as excellent reindeer ground. Dunér and Nordenskiöld landed here to take observations, Malmgren to botanise. Dunér shot a fine reindeer, and the cook, who was with them, was sent to the vessel for a boat, with orders to row round to the point which lay nearest the place where the reindeer lay, and fetch it and the party on land. By a series of misadventures Nordenskiöld and Dunér were unable to rejoin their vessel until after a twenty-four hours' fast and sixteen hours' continuous wandering and climbing. To commemorate these the promontory was called Förvexlings Udde or Mistake Point. Weighing anchor again during a complete calm the *Axel Thordsen* was driven backwards and forwards by the current, and for some time moored to an iceberg, or rather to an immense block of ice, which was forced along by the current through the other ice leaving a broad ice-free path behind it. It often happens that the ice moves in two different directions, the low shallow fjord-ice going in one, and the high glacier-ice deep in the water in another. During a calm the Spitzbergen skippers often make an iceberg driven forward by an under-current tow their vessel through the surface current running in an opposite direction.

When icebergs are spoken of in the region of Spitzbergen, it ought to be remembered, that what is meant is large blocks of ice which fall down from the perpendicular sea faces of the glaciers. Though these blocks are often exceedingly large, they cannot in any way be compared with the icebergs in the Greenland waters, which are said to reach a height of 1,000 feet. The glaciers on Greenland near the sea are indeed higher than those on Spitzbergen, but this dissimilarity is not sufficiently great to explain the great difference in the dimensions of the glaciers at the two places. There is much probability in Professor Edlund's hypothesis that the larger icebergs are formed by blocks of ice falling down from a glacier coming in contact in their lower parts with an over-cooled stratum of water which, as is well known when in contact with actual ice, immediately assumes the solid form. On account of the Gulf Stream any such over-cooled stratum of water can occur only exceptionally on the coasts of Spitzbergen, while the contrary is the case in the waters of Greenland, which are taken up almost exclusively by the Arctic current. The ice seeds which have fallen from the glaciers thus find a suitable soil for their further development only at Greenland, it is only there that they grow to those enormous ice-masses which are so often the cause of the navigator's astonishment and alarm.

The *Axel Thordsen* was next anchored near Edlund's Mount, from which an excellent view was obtained. An excursion was made to the inland ice, which was found to be quite level, and as easy to walk on as a floor. Helis Sound was next visited. On reaching their destination, the party drew up their boat on a low piece of land, between the sound and the glacier near White Mount. After the necessary interval of rest, they proceeded to ascend White Mount. The ascent was difficult on account

of the frozen crust by which the snow was covered often
giving way under their feet. The view from the top is
the grandest to be found on Spitzbergen. In the east
at a distance of 120 miles there was visible a very high
land with two rounded cupola like mountains surmount-
ing the others. This was the westernmost part of a
large, nearly unknown Arctic land, which though discovered so early as 1707 by Commander Giles, has been
completely forgotten and left out of the newest maps.

Between this land and Spitzbergen the sea was covered
with large unbroken ice-fields, among which it was
certain that no vessel could make way. A visit was
planned to this inaccessible country after the conclusion
of the survey, but the plan had to be given up. In the
north and north-east were visible, as far as the eye could
reach, the mountains of North East Land and Hinloopen
Strait, and the Strait itself, with its islands, which now
appeared to be surrounded with quite ice-free water.
Nordenskiöld recognised Lovén's Mount visited by him
in 1861. Between it and White Mount rose the high
snow-covered fell-tops of Thumb Point, and right behind
these ran a long, very crooked sound, into which several
glaciers fell. The interior consisted of an endless
desolate snow-wilderness, broken only here and there
by some black, solitary stone masses, strongly contrasted
with the blinding white ground. Far away in the
west and north-west more continuous mountain-chains
appeared. The whole of the west and north coast of
Stor Fjord was also visible as far as Whales' Head,
and the whole north part of Barentz Land, the northern
extremity of which consists of a considerable glacier,
much split up, projecting into the sea. "Under our

feet lay the little sound discovered by Norwegian walrus-hunters in 1858, which we marked with the name Helis Sound, already occurring on Dutch charts. Mr. Lamont mentions it in the account of his voyage under the name of Ginevra Sound, but from his statement it appears that he was not farther than the point of Förvexlings Udde, and that he accordingly did not see the sound proper. Lamont is guilty of another mistake, through not being acquainted apparently with the sketch-map of north-eastern Spitzbergen in Parry's famous voyage, and not having himself determined the latitude. He makes his Ginevra Sound open out about where Lomme Bay is, and places it in 79° 30′ N., while it is in fact in 78° 40′, his latitude being thus no less than 50′ wrong." After taking a number of angles the party returned and found that the men had been hunting reindeer, and had succeeded in killing two very fat ones, and that a bear had taken advantage of their absence to pay a visit to the boat, creating such confusion that it required a whole hour to gather the articles scattered about and put everything to rights. The bear was believed to have been frightened by the noise, to him unusual, made by a bagful of biscuits as he emptied them out, for the marks on the sand showed that he then took to flight. In the course of the night the bear, as was expected, paid another visit to the boat, but he was obliged to make a rapid retreat, unhurt by the bullets which were sent after him, to the great disappointment of our party, who had already by anticipation divided his skin, and were looking forward to bear-steaks, having found those of the bear they had formerly shot very good. Their men, on the other hand, would eat none of it, though it tastes very well, resembling fat and coarse-grained beef, with perhaps a little flavour of pork. This prejudice is thought to be grounded partly on the statement, possibly correct, that the liver is poisonous, partly on the fact that the flesh of the bear, when he has eaten too much blubber, becomes ill-tasting and ill-smelling. The younger sailors fear that they will be grey-haired before their time by eating bear's flesh.

The boat party returned to the vessel, arriving on the 24th of August. The survey being now completed, the question arose how the short remaining working time should be employed. Instead of proceeding to Giles Land, which was clearly impracticable, it was resolved to sail as far north as possible, with the view of ascertaining the position of the ice on the coast of Spitzbergen in the first half of September. Two ways were open, one by South Cape, the other by Helis Sound and Hinloopen. The latter was the more tempting as shorter and affording an opportunity of circumnavigating Spitzbergen, as the Norwegian, Captain Carlsen, had done in 1863, but it was considered too dangerous for a sailing-vessel so late in the season on account of the probability of being frozen in. The former way accordingly was chosen, and on the morning of the 25th the *Axel Thordsen* sailed southwards, after killing six very large and fat reindeer. On the 26th Hellstad shot a bear, and Malmgren and Dunér a number of seals, which followed the vessel from curiosity. They were so fat that they floated, and thus were not lost, as is otherwise generally the case when they are killed in the water. Passing South Cape without landing, as had been intended, they sailed northward with a fresh wind, and by the morning of the 30th had reached the latitude of Charles Foreland, when a boat full of men, with a large flag in the fore, was seen rowing as fast as they could towards the vessel. As they were clearly shipwrecked men the ship was put about, and they were soon on board. They stated that there were six other boats, containing altogether thirty-seven men, belonging to

PHOCA BARBATA.

three vessels, among them the yacht *Anna Elizabeth*, of which Mattilas was master, which had been beset by the ice on the coast of North-East Land. They had traversed in their boats a distance of 100 geographical miles in fourteen days. Another of the boats was picked up in the afternoon, and, on the night between the 2nd and 3rd September, four boats more. After searching for some time for the seventh boat, the *Axel*

Thordsen was anchored in Ice Fjord, whither the missing boat also arrived on the morning of the 4th. Fortunately places could be found for ten men on two small yachts which still lay in Ice Fjord. There thus remained twenty-seven men on board, making in all forty-two men on the little *Axel Thordsen*. There was of course no question now of going farther north. Ice Fjord was left on the 4th of September, South Cape was passed on the night between the 7th and 8th. On the 10th, in 72° 54′ N., the temperature of the water rose almost at once from 3° to 8° C. (37° F. to 46° F.), a proof that the Polar Sea proper had been left behind. On the 13th they reached Tromsoe, and the expedition came to a termination.

DRAGGING BOAT OVER ICE.

CHAPTER IV.

THE SWEDISH POLAR EXPEDITION OF 1868.

THE aim of the previous Arctic expeditions which had started from Sweden had been the exploration of Spitzbergen. The main object of the expedition of 1868 was to penetrate as far northwards as possible. In order to raise funds for this expedition Nordenskiöld, finding the prevailing opinion of Stockholm society to be that enough had already been done in the way of Arctic research, turned to the commercial community of Gothenburg for assistance. He addressed a memorial setting forth the plan and objects of the expedition to the Governor of Gothenburg, Count A. Ehrensvärd. In this document he pointed out that autumn is the most favourable season for sailing northwards, because the old ice has then been partly melted by the heat of the sun, partly broken up and carried away in a southerly direction by the polar current, and the formation of new ice is not yet begun. He also enumerated the varied objects which were to be kept in view during the progress of the expedition. The list included an examination of the flora and fauna of Bear Island, the single remaining fragment of an extensive polar territory which probably at one time connected Scandinavia with Spitzbergen, the flora and marine fauna of which was still almost unknown, though fitted to throw important light on the animal life not only of the Scandinavian peninsula, but also of the northern shores of Britain which are washed by the Gulf Stream; a careful examination of the strata on Bear Island and at Ice Fjord and King's Bay which contain fossil plants, and a search for Post-miocene strata on the peninsula between Bell Sound and Ice Fjord, which might afford some information as to the transition from the warm climate of the Miocene period, which produced a luxuriant forest vegetation, to the ice masses of the present time; a more thorough examination of the Saurian strata at Cape Thordsen; an examination of the fragments of skeletons of whales found on the shores of Spitzbergen; a continuation of the collection and examination of the land and marine fauna and flora; dredgings at the greatest depths; magnetic and meteorological observations; geographical determinations of position, &c. The plan sketched by Nordenskiöld was to start from Tromsoe in the beginning of August in a little sailing vessel, to remain for a couple of weeks at Bear Island, and for three or four weeks at Ice Fjord, and after visiting King's Bay to wait at Kobbe Bay for a favourable opportunity in the end of September or during October for sailing northwards *without, however, making any childish attempt to force the drift-ice.* "Such an attempt," wrote Nordenskiöld, "would not only be attended by unnecessary risk, but would certainly result in the expedition being beset in the ice, and thus prevented both from going forward and from turning back. If, on the other hand, we adopt the principle of *only* going forward when the sea is open and nearly free of ice, we do not incur much greater risk than that which always accompanies navigation during late autumn, and there is besides the probability, indeed, if no accident happens, almost the certainty, of being able to penetrate further towards the north than any one has ever done before." Unless beset in the ice, a contingency for which due preparation was to be made, the expedition was to return to Norway by the middle of November. The expenses were estimated at the very modest sum of 15,000 rixdollars, about £825. The memorial was dated April, 1868, and a few days after it was made public the subscription-list showed a total of 21,300 rixdollars, contributed almost exclusively by Gothenburg merchants. The project met with so favourable a reception in various quarters, that Nordenskiöld was encouraged to approach the Swedish Government with a request that some small steamer belonging to the state might be placed at the disposal of the expedition. The *Sofia*, a small weak steamer, as Petermann says, which was used for carrying the mails during winter between Sweden and Germany, was accordingly ordered to be fitted out and provisioned, and to be placed under the command of Count F. W. von Otter, then captain in the Royal Swedish Navy, now Swedish Minister of Marine, with Lieut. L. Palander as second in command, and Dr. C. Nyström as medical officer. The *Sofia* was manned by volunteers, the inferior officers and crew numbering fourteen, and so great was the eagerness of the Swedish seamen to take part in the expedition, that more than 150 men immediately gave in their names. The *Sofia*, a schooner-rigged iron steamer 135 feet long, twenty-three feet

broad, and drawing eight feet of water, of about sixty
H.P., had been strengthened and prepared for the
voyage, and was provisioned for seventy weeks, without
including the supply of food that might be obtained by
hunting. Nordenskiöld's scientific staff consisted of
A. E. Holmgren, A. J. Malmgren (who had taken part
in the expeditions of 1861 and 1864), and F. A. Smitt
(a member of the expedition of 1861), zoologists;
Sv. Berggren and Th. M. Fries, botanists; S. Lemström
physicist; G. Nauckhoff, geologist and mineralogist.

THE "SOFIA."

The *Sofia* sailed from Gothenburg on the 7th July,
and after calling at Aalesund to take on board coal
and provisions, reached Tromsoe on the 16th. Here
a short stay was made to complete the necessary
equipment, and from this, the usual starting-point
of the Swedish expeditions, the *Sofia* sailed on the
morning of the 20th July, ploughing the waters of
the Gulf Stream, which wash the shores of northern

Norway, and the colour of which is a very clear blue, almost as beautiful as that of the Lake of Geneva. The Polar current coming from the east and running in an opposite direction, is of a dirty grey colour. The sea off the north of Norway is in summer enlivened by numerous vessels, most of which are English, employed in the Archangel trade. Small Russian craft besides visit Finmark every summer to exchange their

SHARK FISHING.

meal bags for dried fish, and a number of Norwegian bank-fishing vessels lie scattered about catching sharks. Such a bank-fisher was visited, and the crew found employed in hauling on board a shark somewhat over eight feet in length, a "foul fish," with an unpleasant expression in its emerald-green deep-set eyes, which lay passive on deck, everybody, however, taking good care to keep at a respectful distance from its dreaded jaws.

After its liver had been extracted, it was handed over to the Swedish zoologists, by whom it was taken on board the *Sofia* and dissected, its dark ash-grey skin being salted for preservation.

Bear Island was sighted on the 22nd July, and on the evening of the same day the scientific staff and their assistants landed with provisions for a week's stay. Five days were employed in an exploration of the island, which forms a pretty level plateau, two to three hundred feet above the sea, rising here and there into inconsiderable elevations and furrowed by small valleys, in the bottoms of which little streamlets seek their way among the naked stones. In the south-east the appropriately-named Mount Misery rises perpendicularly from the sea to a height of about 1,200 feet, and in the south the Fuglefjeld is about the same height. On neither of these, however, is there any glacier or perpetual snow.

It is not the formation of the island which gives it so desolate and forbidding an appearance, but the monotonous grey colour of the whole landscape. No trace of any grass turf is to be found in the interior, far less of any trees or bushes; only the Polar willow (*Salix polaris* and *herbacea*) with its thread-like stalks creeping in the moss, and two or three leaves, scarcely the size of a finger-nail, raised above it. Green patches, in hollows where water has collected and formed a sort of marsh, consist principally of mosses with scattered specimens of the Polar ranunculus (*Ranunculus sulphureus*) and a few other plants and grasses sparingly mixed with them. Except in these marshy places, the ground is nearly everywhere without the slightest trace

of covering. By the combined action of water and frost
the rocks have been literally frozen asunder, the limestone to small angular fragments, and the sandstone to
larger or smaller blocks heaped one upon another. Such
collections of stones cannot, of course, afford nourish-
ment to higher plants, the more especially as any little
mould that may be formed is immediately swept
away by the wind or washed away by the rain. At
long intervals in this wilderness of gravel and limestone there are found solitary specimens of the Arctic
poppy (*Papaver nudicaule*), *Saxifraga*, *Draba*, *Sa-
gina*, &c. Lichens, especially the larger species, occur
here very sparingly and badly developed, though in
spots the ground is almost covered by species
which are exceedingly rare in the flora of Scandinavia.
Where sandstone is the prevailing rock, the view is
still more unpleasing. There is a considerable extent
of surface where the only method of progression is
by jumping from one block of stone to another, from
which blocks all the higher plants, with the exception of
a grass or two, are banished. The exterior of the island
is more attractive. The rocks rise perpendicularly out
of the sea, and as they consist of the looser formations,
they have, in course of time, been shaped by the waves
into the forms of arches, grottos, towers, columns, &c.
The projecting rocky promontories are in some places
found to be clothed with turf, and the perpendicular
cliffs are richly hung with luxuriant *Cochlearia*. The
explanation is easy. It is only the ledges where the sea-
fowl sit that are thus ornamented, and it is only in the
rich mould originating from these fowl that the plants
can attain such luxuriance. This leads us to the most

remarkable thing about Bear Island, its fabulous richness in sea-fowl. Indeed it may be said that the fowl are the proper inhabitants and owners of the island. There are, it is true, some mountain foxes, but they are very scarce, and the greater number only make a visit during winter; resembling in this the Polar bear, from which the island is named, as it cannot, at least now, support itself here in summer. During that season the walrus, which soon after the discovery of the island was found upon its shores in unheard-of numbers, and a little flock of which Keilhau had an opportunity of observing, is now sought for in vain. Even in winter, according to the latest observations, the Polar bear is an unusual guest. The more amazing is the number of the sea-fowl, which build their nests and live upon the perpendicular precipices on the islands and projecting cliffs. One may sail along the coast for stretches of several leagues, during which all the ledges, clefts, and corners of the mountain sides to a height of 400 or 500 feet above the sea are seen to be literally covered with sea-fowl, whose white breasts show against the dark rocks as if they were closely sprinkled with chalk-white specks. Thousands of others fly far out to sea, innumerable flocks float on the waves, and the air near and far is, so to speak, thick with fowl.

The number of plants found by the botanists of the expedition was thirty-three, which, with the other five formerly observed, but not now found, makes the whole number of phanerogamous and higher cryptogamous plants found on Bear Island thirty-eight. The number of species of insects found was twelve. The number of marine animals was unexpectedly small in

consequence of the unsuitable nature of the bottom.
A great part of the island consists of strata belonging
to the Mountain Limestone, in which are found in abundance mussel shells, corals, &c., showing that in times
long past quite a different animal world lived in an almost
tropical ocean. Two and a half centuries ago seams of
coal were discovered on the north coast of the island,
showing as black parallel bands on the perpendicular
cliffs facing the sea. As the coal that occurs on Spitzbergen had been proved by the preceding Swedish expeditions to belong to the comparatively recent Tertiary
period, it had been considered probable that this was
the case also with that found on Bear Island. But on
examination being made impressions of plants were
found, partly in the coal, partly in the sandstone separating the seams, which afforded indisputable evidence
that the strata here belong to the true Coal Formation.
Splendid *Sigillaria, Lepidodendra, Calamites,* and other
characteristic fossils of the Coal period were taken, not
without danger to life, from the perpendicular sea-cliffs
on the north side of the island, and it was with deep
regret that others had to be left behind because there
was not time to cut them out of the rock.

The *Sofia,* whose steam horses had been fed during
part of the time she was cruising off the island with
coal collected here, received the naturalists and their
collections on board on the 27th July, and the course
was shaped right for Spitzbergen, with the intention of
landing on South Cape, but on approaching this headland on the 29th it was found surrounded by an impassable barricade of ice. The course was then shaped
towards the east, but it was soon found impossible to

make any progress in that direction, and the *Sofia* turned westwards, and on the 31st anchored in Green Harbour in Ice Fjord.

In Green Harbour were found three fishing vessels, the crews of which were hunting reindeer in the neighbouring valleys. A party of white-whale fishers had erected a tent on the other side of the Bay, and awaited the arrival of a shoal of these animals. On paying a visit to the party twenty-four white whales, of various sizes, the largest 14 to 16 feet long, were found laid in a row on the beach, most of them already deprived of their blubber, and the rest waiting similar treatment. It was stated that a single animal may yield a barrel of blubber worth in Norway 25 specie dollars, and as a large number (in former times as many as 150) can be taken at once, it is evident that the profit from this branch of industry is not inconsiderable. The skin, when properly prepared, yields a soft and pliant leather. The state of the carcases on the beach afforded evidence of a peculiarity of the climate of Spitzbergen. Although exposed day and night to the direct action of the sun's rays, there was no sign of putrefaction, and the entomologist of the expedition could not capture a single fly or other flesh-loving insect upon them. The gulls, on the other hand, did not neglect to feast on the abundant layers of flesh.

Near Green Harbour is the grave of the Russian hermit, Staratschin, who died of old age in 1826. The ruins of his hut are still to be seen on a promontory which bears his name. He wintered on Spitzbergen thirty-two (some say thirty-nine) times, fifteen consecutively.

The *Sofia* removed to Advent Bay on the night between the 3rd and 4th of August, having on board the brothers Palliser, who had the day before arrived at Green Harbour in a vessel they had chartered for a hunting expedition to the Spitzbergen waters. In Advent Bay lay three walrus-hunting vessels, and one laden with coal for Lord Hastings's pleasure yacht. Lord Hastings made only a very French visit, and having a boil in his finger returned home again with a few reindeer and auks and other sea-fowl.

MUSHROOMS AT ADVENT BAY.

The *Sofia* lay in Advent Bay till the 11th August. Vegetation was uncommonly luxuriant, and the animal world afforded abundant material for collections. In the fjord four salmon were taken, one of them about three feet long. They were all of course preserved in spirits.

On the 6th August, Nordenskiöld, Palander, Malmgren, and four men started in a boat to explore Nord Fjord, lying opposite to Advent Bay on the other side of Ice Fjord. Here was found a splendid field for geological observations, both in the Saurian Mountains, upwards of 1,000 feet high, and in the steep banks of a stream, which offer to the observer sections of beds of earth and rock, which are specially instructive with respect to the changes which the Polar regions have undergone. Lowest in the valley there is found a phenomenon which is exceedingly uncommon on Spitzbergen, namely, an alluvial formation consisting of peat-moss, in some places twelve feet deep.

Although deposited during a comparatively recent period, when the forests of pine and broad-leaved trees could no longer thrive, and containing, in consequence, only the remains of more northern plants, these peat-mosses and the beds of earth which accompany them afford evidence of a climate in which the ice had not yet attained the nearly unlimited sway which it has on Spitzbergen in our days. The river has washed out of the earthy strata on which this peat rests various large and well developed shells of species (*Mytilus edulis, Cyprina Islandica*) which do not now live on the shores of Spitzbergen, but are found in northern Norway. The remarkable Triassic formation discovered here in 1864, containing the remains of animals resembling crocodiles, was re-examined, and a number of fragments of vertebræ were found, but no cranium, though a reward of ten specie dollars was offered for the discovery of one. Among other remarkable *finds* which were made here far up the Reindeer Valley, was a large bone of a whale, which, however, could not be wrenched from the surrounding ice and frozen snow, and had to be left behind. After exploring both the western and eastern arm of

Nord Fjord (the latter was named Dickson Bay), and collecting a large number of fossils belonging to the Mountain Limestone, the party rejoined their comrades; and on the 13th August the *Sofia* steamed out of Ice Fjord, leaving Nordenskiöld, Palander, Berggren, and four men in a boat to survey Prince Charles' Foreland Sound, while the party on board surveyed the seaward side of the Foreland, and carried on dredging to a depth of 1,250 fathoms in the sea off it. The *Sofia* anchored

KING'S BAY — WESTERN SIDE.

in King's Bay on the 16th August, and was rejoined by the boat party on the 17th, remaining there until the 19th, after taking on board about seventy cubic feet of coal from the neighbouring seams. The presence of coal on Spitzbergen has been long known. Keilhau states that in 1826 sixty barrels were brought to Hammerfest. Besides King's Bay small seams have been found at several other places, chiefly at Bell Sound and Ice Fjord, all belonging to the Tertiary period.

On the 20th August a small vessel arrived with letters and a cargo of coal from Sweden. This was taken on board while the *Sofia* lay off the site of Smeerenberg, the old whale-fishing station. On the 23rd August the *Sofia*, leaving a number of the naturalists on land at Kobbe Bay, started on a cruise to ascertain the state of the ice. By noon of the following day the pack was

BEDTIME DURING A BOAT VOYAGE.

encountered, and the *Sofia* followed the edge of the ice. After cruising two days the Seven Islands were sighted, but they were completely surrounded by ice, and for the time inaccessible. The course was next shaped for Brandywine Bay, which was found filled with packed drift-ice, extending several leagues out to sea. This proves that 1868 was a bad ice year, for in 1861 the

Bay was free of ice by the middle of August. Another harbour had to be found, and on the 28th the *Sofia* anchored in Liefde Bay, whence Nordenskiöld, Malmgren, Nyström, and three men started the next day in a boat on a surveying expedition, crossing the bay to Middlehook (Cape Roos), where, by the discovery of a fossil shell, the Red Bay shale or Hekla Hook formation was ascertained to belong to the Devonian period. Their work accomplished they were again taken on board, and the *Sofia* returned to Kobbe Bay, where a violent snowstorm had almost put a stop to the work of the party that was left behind, but did not prevent a series of magnetic observations from being taken and some hitherto unknown insects discovered. The colony immediately went on board, and on the 31st August the *Sofia* steered for Smeerenberg to load coal, and next for Liefde Bay to dredge, with satisfactory results. Brandywine Bay was next visited, the vessel being able to make her way through ice-floes to the north headland, Depôt Point. In 1861 the fjord was quite free of ice in the middle of August; now there was a continuous covering of ice, though it was pretty much broken up. It was everywhere sprinkled with black spots, which by a glass were seen to be seals, resting by their holes, whence they could make food excursions into the deep. Neither walrus nor Polar bear, which were common in 1861, could be seen, but they did not seem to have altogether disappeared, for traces of the latter were found, and the walrus-hunters, who had made a little excursion among the drift-ice, reported that they had got a glimpse of the former. The object of visiting Brandywine Bay was

to take on board a little iron boat, with oars and other
equipment, ten boxes of pemmican, and various other
articles that had been deposited there in 1861. Boat and
provisions were found safe; the latter were very necessary, in view of a possible wintering. On the 5th September the *Sofia* left Brandywine Bay and shaped her
course for the Seven Islands, but was compelled to anchor
at North Cape, the northernmost promontory of North-
East Land. An unbroken belt of ice, several leagues
wide, stretched from North-East Land, south of Castrén's
Island, towards the north and east, where the mountain
masses, 1,500 to 1,800 feet high, of the Seven Islands,
raised themselves defiantly. Only near North Cape the
drift-ice floated in different directions, according to
current and the wind, and in the field between it and
the more southerly of the Seven Islands lanes of open
water were visible. But behind the belt of ice which
blocked the way to the north and east, there stretched
an open and ice-free sea—how far? At last the ice
was so broken up and scattered by the fresh south-east
winds, that an attempt could be made to reach the
Seven Islands, and giving and receiving blows the *Sofia*
got within a mile and a half of Parry's Island, but
like the other six it was surrounded by a girdle of ice,
so that there was nothing for it but to make the vessel
fast with an ice anchor and walk to the land. The
greater part was covered with snow and ice, only in
some depressions in the rocky slopes a lively green was
visible, produced by thickly-growing tufts of moss,
among which—especially at places frequented by sea-
fowl—a small number of higher plants sought a settlement. The animal world was poor, and the number

of insects had so diminished that only some half-frozen specimens of a single species of gnat were found, and numerous swarms of bluish-grey small *Poduræ*, which here, as everywhere else on Spitzbergen, moved amongst the sand or crawled on the snow-fields. A Polar bear, which had left recent traces on the shore, was tracked, but made his escape, sliding down a steep slope of snow on his hind-quarters—a mode of locomotion the animal seems to fancy—plunging into the sea and swimming to the neighbouring Phipps' Island. This point (80° 40′ N.L.) was the most northerly reached by the *Sofia* on this cruise. After Loven's Mountains had been visited and a couple of barrels of very fine Mountain Limestone fossils dug from beneath the snow, the course was shaped for Smeerenberg, where a small coal-laden vessel was waiting with letters from Sweden and new potatoes, both of which were highly appreciated. By this vessel, the *Severine*, Fries, Holmgren, Malmgren, Nauckhoff, Smitt, Svensson, and four Norwegians, returned to Norway, and on the 16th September the *Sofia*, after towing the *Severine* out to sea, shaped her course for the Seven Islands, meeting Tobiesen's vessel near the entrance to Hinloopen. From Tobiesen important information was obtained as to the state of the ice in the Strait, and the movements of the German expedition which had that year visited Spitzbergen. The southern part of Hinloopen was blocked with ice which was considered quite impassable. By the 18th the *Sofia* was among the ice. The Seven Islands could not be approached within twelve nautical miles, but open water was visible to the northward, and hopes began to rise, not indeed, of reaching the Pole, but perhaps a higher latitude than any vessel had hitherto attained. Scoresby's 81° 30' had up to this time been the *ultima Thule* of Arctic voyages. Great accordingly was the joy of the Swedes when on the morning of the 18th the latitude reached was found to be 81° 32', with open water still ahead. In the afternoon bottom was found at a depth of 1,300 fathoms. The following day, after many doublings among ice of variable nature, the latitude of 81° 42' was attained, the longitude being 17° 30'.

"We reached the point," writes Captain von Otter, "just at eight o'clock in the morning. I notified the victory to our scientific men by firing a Swedish salute, and when they came on deck they found the Swedish flag flying from the tops in honour of the memorable day. According to the dead reckoning we would only have been 81° 39', but an altitude which I there took of the sun and a double sight of Spitzbergen which we got the following day, showed us that on this occasion we had the current in our favour. Farther to the west, however, it was found to set regularly twelve to twenty minutes per twenty-four hours towards the S.W., which is also an old experience."

Captain von Otter adds, after expressing his views as to the impossibility of reaching the pole *by open water*, views confirmed by the result of the voyage of the *Sofia:* "I consider the honour of the flag—as it was flying on the steamer—to have been maintained, when we reached a point where none with *clear papers* can show that he has taken an altitude from the deck of his vessel, viz., within 400 nautical miles of the pole. Scoresby, who previously had penetrated farthest, states with the authority he possessed after seventeen years' experience, that the open belt he found there in 1806 was of very rare occurrence, and when such men as Phipps and Franklin had to be content with reaching 80° 48′ and 80° 28′ N., more ought not to be required even of one having the advantage of a steamer with a good iron bow than to go a degree farther. That the altitude we gained could not have been reached without at many places charging ice-floes, where no sailing vessel would ever have dreamed of making its way, need not be said; for when we had advanced some distance there was not a lane or any sign of 'water-sky' to the northward that was not attempted, and when the *Sofia* reached her place of honour in the latitude of 81° 42′, I venture to affirm that there was not a point of the compass towards which a man might not with the help of a boat-hook have walked a league on pieces of ice."

The Swedes had thus gained one of the frost-bitten prizes in the international race to the pole, but here there was a limit to their progress. The ordinary scientific work went on. The physicist made magnetic observations on the ice, specimens of water were taken, and the "Bull-dog" machine brought up from a depth of 1,370 fathoms a sample of the bottom which as coming from that latitude was naturally regarded with more than common interest. As it was impossible to advance in a northerly direction, the course was shaped towards the west, where the sea appeared most free of ice. The current here was southerly. In the evening the depth was found to have diminished to 370 fathoms. The *Sofia* was now surrounded by ice, and some labour was required to work out of it, but on the 20th September

Spitzbergen was sighted. There was no intention of seeking a harbour. Instead of that, the *Sofia* followed the edge of the pack or sailed through drift ice of varying form and dimensions, trying every opening that appeared to lead to the north. The blocks of ice varied in several respects from those seen during the August voyage They were harder, larger, and higher, and seen at a distance with their size surprisingly magnified, appeared formidable enough. Here and there some of them were blackened with adhering earth and gravel, a sign that in some unknown region they had been in contact with land. Pieces of drift-wood were found in the sea, and one of the glass balls already mentioned, speaking witnesses in the question of marine currents. The cold was pretty intense, but the Swedes were acclimatised by their stay in the high north, and found a temperature of $-8°$ or $-9°$ C. quite agreeable and their cabins sufficiently warm. The greatest mischief produced by the cold was the increase of the ice; the surface of the sea where it was diluted by the addition of fresh water from the melting masses of ice, froze, the mist also froze as it touched the water, and the old blocks of ice became hard as steel. Animal life was still abundant; several birds—the glaucous gull and the lumme (*Mormon Arcticus*—were seen; and dredging steadily added to the zoological collections.

After for several days following the edge of the ice, which was found, as in August, to trend southwards, it was determined on the 23rd September, as the stock of coal was pretty well exhausted, to return to Spitzbergen. At this date the *Sofia* was in 78° 26′ N. Lat. and 2° 17′ W. Long. The weather was splendid, with clear sunshine. The vessel lay in an ice-field surrounded on all sides by large and small blocks of ice, some lying flat, others raised up against each other, hollowed into grottos, from whose interior the most beautiful clear-blue *nuances* of colour were reflected. Most of the inhabitants of the *Sofia* were employed on the ice. Some of the crew filled the water-tanks from

MORMON ARCTICUS.

a little fresh-water lake which had been formed on the surface of a large piece of ice, and a skater had found a suitable field for the display of his art. Animal life was found in quite unexpected abundance, and dredging especially became highly interesting. For the depth was 2,650 fathoms, and from this depth there was brought up a mass which consisted almost entirely of brown and

white *Foraminifera*, among which, however, there was
found among other things a crustacean (a species of
Cuma). It was besides surprising to find, among the
ice in the middle of the Atlantic and at a place where
the depth was so great, such an abundance of the higher
animals—seals, glaucous gulls, fulmar petrels, guillemots (scarcely recognisable in their speckled winter
dress), auks, and rotges. In the water near the surface
swam *Pteropoda* and *Copepoda*, their forms and colour
sharply defined against the clear "ice feet" (the extensive under-water parts of the swimming blocks). An
attempt was made to blast a block of ice with gunpowder. A cavity was produced which, however, did
not extend through the whole thickness of the ice,
which was not considered successful.

The return was commenced on the evening of the
23rd. After getting into open water the course was
shaped towards the east; on the 24th bottom was
found at 1,400 fathoms, and on the 25th Spitzbergen
was seen in its white winter shroud (an abundant
fall of snow having taken place during the night),
looking like a gigantic snowdrift. As the coast was
neared great flocks of rotges were seen. The *Sofia*
anchored in South Gat, between Danes' Island and
the main land. After lying here four days preparing
for another cruise, the *Sofia* again started on the 29th
September for Kobbe Bay to take on board the remainder of the coal lying there, and on the 1st October
weighed anchor and commenced another attempt to
penetrate to the north of Spitzbergen, with the hope
of discovering land, the existence of which there was
reason to suspect. If this was found impossible it was

intended to make for the Seven Islands, and thence to undertake excursions to the north and east (to the alluring Giles' Land, "das sagenhafte Land im Osten," as it is called by the Germans). It might be necessary on this account to winter, and preparations were made for doing so. Parry's Island was chosen for the purpose, and it was calculated that provisions and other necessaries for sixty days' travelling on the ice could be carried along, and that within this period it would be possible to reach the 84th degree of latitude and return, leaving time for another excursion to Giles' Land in spring. But the programme was not to be carried out.

Before night ice was visible, and the vessel was moored to an ice-field to await the dawn. On the 2nd, auks, guillemots and fulmar petrels were seen, and a walrus, one of the few observed during the expedition. The cold, which on the 1st had been $-7°C.$, was now $-13·3°$. The new-formed ice was several inches thick, and the vessel could make no more rapid progress through it than two knots per hour. The ice to the northward getting closer and more difficult, the *Sofia* steered towards open water, and so southwards; but on the 3rd, followed the edge of the pack eastwards and northwards till, in the afternoon, ice was seen in the N. E., which appeared likely to bar further progress. On the morning of the 4th, as the *Sofia* was working her way among the masses of ice by which she was surrounded, she came into collision with one of them, and sprang a large leak, through which water rushed into one of the coal-bunkers. The door was immediately made fast so as to confine the water within the bunker. The collision had not only bent and cracked a plate on the starboard side amidships, but also fractured two ribs and driven out several bolts, and broken up the deck above the coal-bunker. It was only by the most strenuous exertions of all on board, that the *Sofia* was kept afloat and safely anchored, 11 hours after the accident, off Amsterdam Island. Next day, the vessel, lightened as much as possible on the leaky side, was brought to King's Bay, where she was beached and the damage made good. On the 11th, King's Bay was left, and the *Sofia* sailed southwards, passing through, on the 12th and 13th, a belt of floating ice, 60 nautical miles broad. On the 14th South Cape was reached, and an attempt was made to penetrate eastwards towards Giles' Land, but on coming within 30 minutes of the Thousand Islands, ice was met with, which, though at first open, soon became of so difficult a nature, that it was impossible to advance. The attempt had therefore to be given up, and after weathering a storm near Bear Island, the *Sofia* reached Tromsoe on the 20th October, Gothenburg on the 15th November, and lay in the harbour of Carlskrona on the afternoon of the 26th, the members of the expedition being welcomed everywhere with unbounded hospitality.

Of this expedition, the distinguished *savant*, Professor Oswald Heer of Zürich, declared—" In my opinion the Swedish Expedition, by the rich collections it has brought home, has achieved more, and more widened the horizon of our knowledge, than if it had returned merely with the information that the *Sofia* had hoisted her flag at the North Pole."

After the close of this expedition, Nordenskiöld

obtained from the Royal Geographical Society, its large gold medal (Founder's medal), and soon after a similar distinction (the Rochette medal), from the Société de Géographie of Paris.

THE "SOFIA" CROSSING THE ARCTIC CIRCLE 14TH JULY, 1868.

CHAPTER V.

EXPEDITION TO GREENLAND, 1870.

THE result of the expedition of 1868, had been to convince Nordenskiöld and the Swedes, of the impossibility of reaching the Pole, or indeed of advancing much farther northwards by means of a vessel. The comparative want of success which attended the expedition by no means diminished the interest that was taken in the question in Sweden. So far was this from being the case, that, almost immediately after the return of the expedition, steps were taken, principally in Gothenburg, to raise funds to send out another Polar expedition, which was intended to push forwards as far as possible in the direction of the Pole by means of sledges, and in the course of a twelvemonth, the greater part of the funds considered necessary for the new expedition was subscribed.

The sinews of war having been procured, it was necessary to fix on a plan for carrying out the new attempt. We find Nordenskiöld accordingly enumerating and comparing the different routes to the Pole thus:—

I. The way east of Spitzbergen. This he considered impracticable, from the fact that an unbroken ice-belt stretches between Spitzbergen and Novaya Zemlya as far down as 78°, only in 'favourable' years leaving a broad channel running up to 80° along the east coast of the former, and the west coast of the latter island.

II. The way along the east coast of Greenland. To this route, although, like the former, recommended by Petermann, there is the objection, that a broad and almost always closely packed ice-stream is swept by the North Polar current, not only along the whole east coast of Greenland, but also during a great part of the year, past Cape Farewell into Davis Strait.

III. The way through Behring's Straits, proposed by Gustave Lambert. Here, however, ice in impenetrable masses meets the navigator, in latitudes where, north of Europe, traces of it are scarcely to be met with in midwinter.

IV. The way by Spitzbergen, and

V. The way by Smith's Sound. These Nordenskiöld considered the only practicable routes. Rejecting the hypothesis of an open polar sea, and believing that the only practicable method of reaching the Pole was by sledge-travelling over the ice, he pointed out the importance of choosing as a starting point for such a journey, some easily accessible place as near the Pole as possible. The choice lies between Spitzbergen and Smith's Sound, and Nordenskiöld preferred the former, as lying near to Europe, and being every year accessible a little north of 80°. By Smith's Sound, on the other hand, he considered it scarcely possible to reckon with certainty on being able to advance with a vessel much farther than 78°.

Spitzbergen was therefore fixed upon as a starting

point for the expedition of 1872. It was determined to erect a building in which to pass the winter, if possible, on one of the Seven Islands, and to advance next spring towards the Pole over the ice by means of sledges. In order to form a judgment, on the spot, of the fitness of Greenland dogs as draught animals for such a sledge journey, and, if it seemed advisable, to procure the necessary number, Nordenskiöld determined to visit Greenland in 1870, and having sailed from Copenhagen accompanied by Dr. Sv. Berggren of Lund, and Dr. P. Öberg, and Dr. Th. Nordström of Upsala, he landed at Godhavn on the 2nd of July. During the voyage, he made observations on the colour of the Arctic Seas, which is in some places greyish-green, and in others indigo-blue, these areas being frequently so sharply distinguished, that a ship may sail with one side in blue, and the other in greyish-green water. Water is also to be found in the Greenland Sea with a decided shade of brown. These colours, green and brown, are caused by a slime which is absent where the blue colour prevails. This slime, which is formed of various species of *Diatomaceæ*, inconsiderable as it is, but spread over hundreds of thousands of square miles, forms an indispensable condition for the existence, not only of the swarms of birds that frequent the northern seas, but also of the giant of the animal creation, the whale, and all branches of industry dependent on whale-fisheries.

On arriving at Godhavn, Nordenskiöld found it impossible there to man the whale boats, in which it was intended to visit the shores of the Waygat, Disco Bay, and Omenak Fjord, and to explore Auleitsivik Fjord, which had not previously been visited or surveyed by

Europeans. After remaining for a week at Godhavn he proceeded to Egedesminde, where, by the assistance of the resident manager Mr. Bollbroe, he was able in a few hours to make the necessary arrangements for beginning the work of the summer.

Öberg remained at Egedesminde for the purpose of carrying on dredging and other geological work. Nordenskiöld, Berggren, and Nordström started on 12th July, and halting at night on the 12th at Manermiut, on the 13th at Kangaitsiak, on the 14th, 15th, and 16th on islands at Auleitsivik Fjord, arrived on the 17th at the northern side of the glacier which projects from the inland ice, and occupies the northern arm of Auleitsiviks Fjord, the spot they had selected for a journey over the ice.

Of this inland-ice the natives entertain a superstitious fear, an awe or prejudice, which has, in some degree, communicated itself to such Europeans as have resided long in Greenland. It is only thus that the curious fact that in the whole thousand years during which Greenland has been known so few efforts have been made to pass over the ice farther into the country can be explained. There are many reasons for believing that the inland-ice merely forms a continuous ice-frame, running parallel with the coast, and surrounding a land free from ice, perhaps even wooded in its southern parts, which might perhaps be of great economical importance to the rest of Greenland. In 1728 a Danish expedition was fitted out for the purpose of rediscovering the lost (East) Greenland by an overland journey. The horses intended for the attempt died either during the journey or shortly after their arrival in the country, and the expedition, which was really magnificent, but equipped in entire ignorance of the nature of the country, was abandoned. Another attempt was made by Dalager, a Danish merchant, in 1751, in about 62° 31' latitude to advance in the beginning of September over the inland-ice to the east coast. Dalager only succeeded in penetrating about eight English miles to some mountain summits rising above the ice-field. He was then obliged to return along with five natives who accompanied him, partly because their boots were worn out, partly because the cold at night was so severe that their limbs became stiff after a few hours of rest. In 1867, Mr. Whymper accompanied by Dr. R. Brown, three Danes and a Greenlander, endeavoured to make their way upon the inland-ice with dogs, immediately to the north of the ice-fjord at Jacobshavn, but they turned back again on the second day, after having proceeded only some few miles. It was Nordenskiöld's original intention to renew these attempts, but on conversing in Copenhagen with Mr. Rink and Mr. Olrik, who had formerly been Inspectors in North Greenland, as also with several other persons who had visited Greenland, he found them all so unanimous in considering further advance over the ice as impossible, that he determined not to risk the whole summer on an undertaking that was beforehand disapproved by everybody. He was, however, unwilling entirely to abandon his plan, and determined to make a journey on the inland-ice of only a few days' extent. The starting-point was selected because the ice there was believed to be freer from crevasses and clefts than in the neighbourhood of the ice-streams.

On the 17th July, the party pitched their tent on

the shore north of the steep precipitous edge of the
inland-ice at Auleitsivik Fjord. After having employed
the 18th in preparations and a few reconnoitrings, they
commenced their journey on the 19th. They set out
early in the morning, and first rowed to a little bay
situated in the neighbourhood of the spot occupied
by their tent, where several muddy streams debouched.
Here the land assumed a character varied by hill and
dale ; and further inward it was bounded by an ice-
wall sometimes perpendicular and sometimes rounded,
covered with a thin layer of earth and stones ; only
a couple of hundred feet high near the edge, but then
rising at first rapidly, afterwards more slowly to a height
of several hundred feet. In most places this ice-wall
could not possibly be scaled ; a place, however, was
found where it was cut through by a small cleft, sufficiently deep to afford a possibility of climbing up
with the means at the disposal of the party, a sledge
which in case of need could be used as a ladder, and
a line originally 100 fathoms long, but which, proving
too heavy a burden, had before arriving at the first
resting-place been shortened one-half. The whole party,
with the exception of an old and lame boatman, assisted
in the by no means easy work of bringing over mountain, hill, and dale, the equipment of the ice expedition
to this spot and, after our mid-day rest, a little further
up the ice-wall. Here the party separated, and only
Nordenskiöld and Berggren, and two Greenlanders,
Isak and Sisarniak, went on.

The inland-ice differs from ordinary glaciers, among
other things, by the almost total absence of moraine-
formations. The collections of earth, gravel, and stone,

with which the ice on the landward edge is covered,
are in fact so inconsiderable in comparison with the
moraines of even very small glaciers, that they scarcely
deserve mention, and no large, newly-formed ridges of
gravel running parallel with the edge of the glacier
are to be met with, at least in the tract visited. The
landward border of the inland-ice is, however, darkened,
it can scarcely be said covered, with earth and sprinkled
over with small sharp stones.

Here the ice was tolerably smooth, though furrowed
by deep clefts at right angles to the border—such as
that made use of to climb up by. But in order not
immediately to terrify the Greenlanders by choosing
the way over these frightful and dangerous clefts,
Nordenskiöld and his companion determined to abandon
this comparatively smooth ground, and at first to take
a southerly direction parallel with the crevasses, and
afterwards turn to the east. They gained their object
by avoiding the chasms, but they fell in with extremely rough ice. They now understood what the
Greenlanders meant, when they endeavoured to dissuade
them from the journey, by sometimes lifting their hands
up over their heads, sometimes sinking them down to
the ground, accompanying their gestures by talk un-
intelligible to the Swedes. The Greenlanders meant
by this to describe the collection of closely heaped
pyramids and ridges of ice that had now to be sur-
mounted. The inequalities of the ice were seldom
more than forty feet high, with an inclination of 25
to 30 degrees; but one does not get on very fast
when he has continually to drag a heavily-laden sledge
up so irregular an acclivity, and immediately afterwards

to descend at the risk of getting broken legs, occasionally losing one's footing on the slippery ice in attempting to moderate the speed of the sledge in its downward rush. The component parts of the sledge were not nailed but tied together, and it lasted at least for some hours. Had it been an ordinary sledge it would have been immediately broken to pieces.

Next day, Nordenskiöld and his party, found it impossible to continue dragging with them the thirty days' provisions with which they had furnished themselves, especially as it was evident that, if they wished to proceed further, they must transform themselves from draught to pack-horses. They therefore determined to leave the sledge and part of the provisions, taking the rest on their shoulders, and to proceed on foot. They now got on quicker, though for a considerable time over ground as bad as before. The ice gradually became smoother, but was broken by large bottomless chasms, over which it was necessary either to jump with a heavy load on the back (in which case woe to him who made a false step) or else to make a long circuit. After two hours' travelling the region of crevasses was passed. In the course of the journey portions of similar ground were frequently met with, though none of any very great extent. The party had now reached a height of 800 feet above the level of the sea. Further inward the surface of the ice, except at the occasionally recurring regions of crevasses, resembled that of a stormy sea suddenly bound in fetters by the cold. The rise inwards was still quite perceptible, though frequently interrupted by shallow valleys, the axes of which were occupied by several lakes or ponds with no apparent outlet, although they received water from innumerable streams running down the sides of the hollows. These streams presented hindrances to the progress of the party, not so dangerous, but causing quite as great a waste of time as the crevasses; they did not occur so often, but the circuits to avoid them were much longer.

During the whole of the journey on the ice the weather was fine, frequently there was not a single cloud visible in the sky. To the travellers, clad as they were, the warmth was quite sensible; in the shade, near the ice, of course a little over the freezing point; higher up in the shade as much as 7° or 8°; but in the sun 25° to 30° C. After sunset the pools of water froze and the nights were very cold. The travellers had no tent, and, though the party consisted of four, they had only two ordinary sleeping sacks, open at both ends, so that two persons could, though with great difficulty, squeeze themselves into one sack with their feet in opposite directions. With rough ice for a substratum, the bed was so uncomfortable that after a few hours' sleep the sleeper was awakened by cramp; and as there was only a thin tarpaulin between the ice and the sleeping sack, the bed was extremely cold on the side resting on the ice, which the Greenlanders, who returned before the rest of the party, intimated to Dr. Nordström by shivering and shaking throughout their whole bodies. The nights' rests were therefore seldom long, but the mid-day rests, during which a glorious warm sun-bath was enjoyed, were taken on a proportionately generous scale, affording opportunities for taking observations both for altitude and longitude.

M

On the surface of the inland ice no stones were met with at a distance of more than a cable's length from the border; but everywhere there were to be found vertical cylindrical holes, a foot or two deep, from a couple of lines to a couple of feet in diameter, and so close to one another that it was impossible to find between them room for the foot, much less for a sleeping sack. The travellers had thus always a system of ice-pipes of this kind as a substratum when they rested for the night, and it often happened in the morning that the warmth of their bodies had melted so much of the ice that the sleeping sack touched the water, of which the holes were always nearly full. But as a compensation, when they rested, they had only to stretch out their hands to obtain the very finest water to drink.

In these holes in the ice, filled with water and in no way connected with each other, Nordenskiöld found everywhere at the bottom of them, not only at the border but in the most distant parts of the inland ice which he visited, a layer, some few millimetres thick, of grey powder, often conglomerated into small round balls of loose consistency. Under the microscope the principal substance of this remarkable powder appeared to consist of white angular translucent grains. There could also be observed remains of vegetable fragments; yellow, imperfectly translucent particles, with, as it appeared, evident surfaces of cleavage, possibly felspar, green crystals (augite), and black opaque grains, which were attracted by the magnet.

"The substance," says Nordenskiöld, "is not a clay, but a sandy trachytic mineral, of a composition (especially as regards soda) which indicates that it does not originate in the granite region of Greenland. Its origin appears to me, therefore, very enigmatical. Does it come from the basalt region? or from the supposed volcanic tracts in the interior of Greenland? or is it of meteoric origin? The octahedrally crystallised magnetic particles do not contain any traces of nickel. As the principal ingredient corresponds to a determinate chemical formula ($2 \mathrm{R Si}^2 + \mathrm{\ddot{A}l Si}^3 + \mathrm{H}$), it would perhaps be desirable to enter it under a separate class in the register of science; and for that purpose I propose for this substance the name Kryokonite (from κρύος and κόνις).

"When I persuaded our botanist, Dr. Berggren, to accompany me in the journey over the ice," he continues, "I joked with him on the singularity of a botanist making an excursion into a tract, perhaps the only one in the world, that was a perfect desert as regards botany. This expectation was, however, not confirmed. Dr. Berggren's keen eye soon discovered, partly on the surface of the ice, partly in the above-mentioned powder, a brown polycellular alga, which, small as it is, together with the powder and certain other microscopic organisms by which it is accompanied, is the most dangerous enemy to the mass of ice, so many thousand feet in height and hundreds of miles in extent. This plant has no doubt played the same part in our country, and we have it to thank, perhaps, that the deserts of ice which formerly covered the whole of northern Europe and America have now given place to shady woods and undulating corn fields. Of course a great deal of the grey powder is carried down in the rivers, and the blue ice at the bottom of them is not unfrequently concealed by a dark dust. How rich this mass is in organic matter is proved by this circumstance among others, that the quantity of organic matter in it was sufficient to bring a large collection of the grey powder, which had been carried away to a distant part of the ice by several now dried-up glacier streams, into so advanced a state of fermentation or putrefaction, that the mass, even at a great distance, emitted a most disagreeable smell, like that of butyric acid.

"At our mid-day rest on the 21st," continues Nordenskiöld, "we had reached latitude 68° 21' and 36' longitude east of the place where our tent was pitched, and a height of 1,400 feet above the level of the sea.

"Later in the day, at our afternoon rest, the Greenlanders began to take off their shoes and examine their small thin feet—a serious indication, as we soon perceived. Isak presently informed us, in broken Danish, that he and his companions now considered it time to return. All attempts to persuade them to accompany us a little farther failed; and we had, therefore, no other alternative than to let them return, and continue our excursion without them.

"We took up our night-quarters here. The provisions were divided. The Greenlanders, considering they might, perhaps, not be able to find our first depôt, were allowed to take as much as was necessary to enable them to reach the tent. We took cold provisions for five days. The remainder, together with the excellent photogen portable kitchen, which we had hitherto carried with us, were laid up in a depôt in the neighbourhood, on which a piece of tarpaulin was stretched upon sticks, that we might be able to find the place on our return, which, however, we did not succeed in doing, though we must have passed in its immediate vicinity.

"Dr. Berggren and I then proceeded on our way. The Greenlanders turned back.

"At first we passed one of the before-mentioned extensive bowl-shaped excavations in the ice-plain, which is here furrowed by innumerable rivers, often obliging us to make long détours; and when, to avoid this, we endeavoured to make our way along the margin of the valleys, we came, instead, upon a tract where the ice-plain was cloven by long, deep, parallel clefts running true N.N.E.—S.S.W., quite as difficult as the rivers to get over and much more dangerous. Our progress was accordingly but slow. At twelve o'clock on the 22nd we halted, in glorious warm sunny weather, to make a geographical determination. We were now at a height of 2,000 feet, in latitude 68° 22' and in the longitude of 57' east of the position of our tent at the fjord.

"During the whole of our excursion on the ice we had seen no animals except a couple of ravens, which on the morning of the 22nd, flew over our heads at the moment of our separation. At first, however, there appeared at many places on the ice traces of ptarmigans, which seemed to indicate that these birds visit those desert tracts in by no means inconsiderable flocks. Everything else around us was lifeless. Nevertheless silence by no means reigned here. On bending down the ear to the ice, we could hear on every side a

peculiar subterranean hum, proceeding from streams
flowing within the ice; and occasionally a loud single
report, like that of a cannon, gave notice of the
formation of a new glacier-cleft.

"After taking the observations we proceeded over
comparatively better ground. Later in the afternoon
we saw, at some distance before us, a well-defined pillar
of mist, which, when we approached it, appeared to
rise from a bottomless abyss, into which fell a large
glacier-river. The vast roaring water-mass had bored
for itself a vertical hole, probably down to the rock,
certainly more than two thousand feet beneath, on
which the glacier rested.

"The following day (the 23rd) we rested in latitude
68° 22′ and 76′ of longitude east from the position of
our starting-point at Auleitsivik.

"The provisions we had taken with us were, however,
now so far exhausted, that we were obliged to think
of returning. We determined, nevertheless, first to
endeavour to reach an ice-hill visible on the plain to
the east, from which we hoped to obtain an extensive
view; and in order to arrive there as quickly as possible,
we left the scanty remains of our provisions and our
sleeping sack at the spot where we had passed the
night, taking careful notice of the ice-rocks around,
and thus we proceeded by forced march without
encumbrances.

"The ice-hill was considerably farther off than we
had supposed. The walk to it was rewarded by an
uncommonly extensive view, which showed us that
the inland ice continued to rise towards the interior,
so that the horizon towards the east, north, and south,

was terminated by an ice-border almost as smooth as that of the ocean. A journey farther (even if one were in a condition to employ weeks for the purpose—which want of time and provisions rendered impossible for us) could therefore evidently furnish no other information concerning the nature of the ice than we had already obtained, and even if want of provisions had not obliged us to return, we should hardly have considered it worth while to add a few days' marches to our journey. Our turning-point was at the height of 2,200 feet above the level of the sea, and about 83′ of longitude, or more than thirty miles east of the extremity of the northern arm of Auleitsivik fjord.

"On departing from the spot where we had left our provisions and sleeping sack, we had, as we supposed, taken careful notice of its situation; nevertheless, we were nearly obliged to abandon our search as vain— an example which shows how extremely difficult it is, without lofty signals, to recover objects on a slightly undulating surface everywhere similar, like that formed by the inland ice. When, after anxiously searching in every direction, we at last found our resting-place, we ate our dinner with an excellent appetite, made some further reductions in our load, and then set off with all haste back to the boat, which we reached late in the evening of the 25th.

"At a short distance from our turning-point, we came to a large, deep, and broad river, flowing rapidly between its blue banks of ice, which here were not discoloured by any gravel, and which could not be crossed without a bridge. As it cut off our return, we were at first somewhat disconcerted; but we soon concluded that—as in our journey eastwards we had not passed any stream of such large dimensions—it must at no great distance disappear under the ice. We therefore proceeded along its bank in the direction of the current, and before long a distant roar indicated that our conjecture was right. The whole immense mass of water here rushed down a perpendicular cleft into the depths below. We observed another smaller but nevertheless very remarkable waterfall the next day while examining the neighbourhood around us with the telescope after our mid-day rest. We saw, in fact, a pillar of watery vapour rising from the ice at some distance from our resting-place, and, as the spot was not far out of our way, we steered our course by it in the hope of finding—judging from the height of the misty pillar—a waterfall still greater than that just described. We were mistaken; only a smaller yet tolerably large river rushed down from the azure-blue cliffs to a depth from which no splashes rebounded to the mouth of the fall; but there arose instead, from another smaller hole in the ice, in the immediate vicinity, an intermittent jet of water, mixed with air, which, carried hither and thither by the wind, wetted the surrounding ice-cliffs with its spray. We had thus here, in the midst of the desert of inland-ice, a fountain, as far as we could judge by the descriptions, very like the geysers which in Iceland are produced by volcanic heat.

"In order, if possible, to avoid the district of ice-rocks, which on our journey out had required so much patience and exertion, we had chosen a more southerly route in returning, intending to endeavour to descend from the ice-ridge higher up to the strip of ice-free land which lies between the inland-ice and Disco Bay. Here, with the exception of some ice-hillocks a few feet high, the ice was in most places as even as a floor, but often crossed by large and dangerous clefts, and we were so fortunate as immediately to hit upon a place where the inclination towards the land was so slight, that one might have driven up it four-in-hand.

"The remainder of the journey along the land was more difficult, partly on account of the very uneven nature of the ground, and partly on account of the numerous glacier streams we had to wade through, with the water far above our boots. At last, at a little distance from the tent, we came to a muddy glacier stream, so large that after several failures we were obliged to abandon the hope of finding a fordable place. We were therefore obliged to climb high up again among the shining ice, in order to effect a passage, coming down afterwards; but the descent on this occasion was far more difficult than before.

"Laborious as this journey along the land was, it was, nevertheless, exceedingly interesting to me from a geological point of view. We passed, in fact, over ground that had but lately been abandoned by the inland ice, and the whole bore such a resemblance to the woodless gneiss districts in Sweden and Finland, that even the most sceptical would be obliged to admit that the same formative power had impressed its stamp on both localities. Everywhere occur rounded, but seldom scratched, hills of gneiss with erratic blocks in the most unstable positions of equilibrium, separated by valleys with small mountain-lakes and scratched rock-surfaces. On the other hand, no real moraines were discoverable. These, indeed, seem to be commonly absent in Scandinavia, and are, generally speaking, more characteristic of small glaciers than of real inland ice.

"As indicated in Figs. 1 and 2, the border of the ice is everywhere sprinkled with smaller boulders, partly rounded, partly angular; but the number of these is so inconsiderable that when the ice retires they give rise only to a slope covered with boulders; not to a moraine similar, for example, to that which the little Assakak glacier in Omenak Fjord drives before it. The small earth-bank which collects at most places at the foot of the glacier is frequently washed away again by the glacier streams and rain. At the foot of the glacier we often find, as in Fig. 2, ponds or lakes in which is deposited a fresh-water glacial clay, containing angular blocks of stone, scattered around by small icebergs.

"It is a common error among geologists to consider the Swiss glaciers as representing on a small scale the inland ice of Greenland, or the inland ice which once covered Scandinavia. The real glacier bears the same relation to inland ice which a rapid river or brook does to an extensive and calm lake. While the glacier is in perpetual motion, the inland ice, like the water of a lake, is comparatively at rest, excepting at those places where it streams out into the sea by vast but short glaciers. If one of these glaciers, through which the ice-lake falls out into the sea, pass over smooth ground where the bottom of the ocean gradually changes into land without any steep breaks, steep precipitous glaciers are produced, from which indeed large ice-masses fall down, but do not give rise to any real iceberg. But if the mouth of the

fjord be narrow, the depth of the outlying sea great, and
the inclination of the shore considerable, the result will

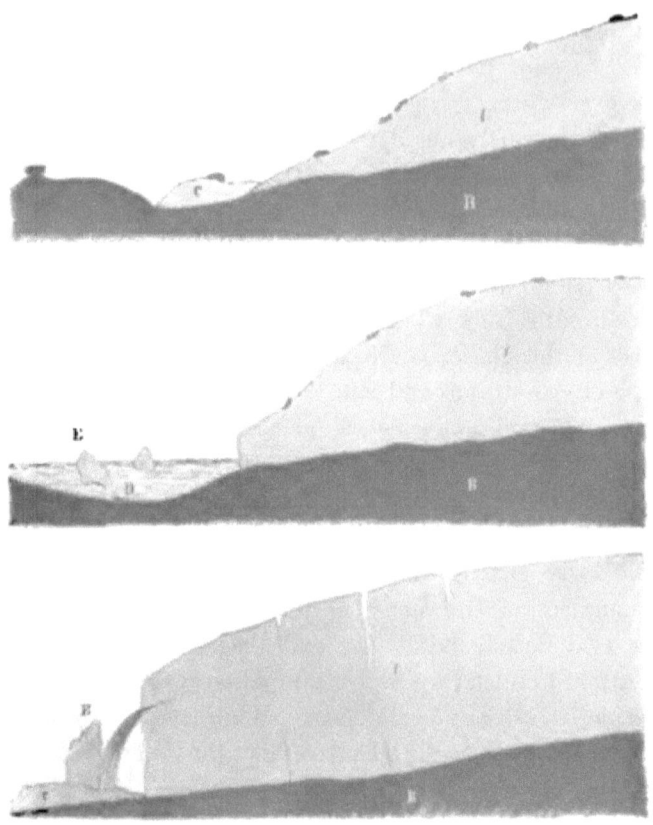

FIGS. 1, 2, AND 3.—INLAND ICE ABUTTING ON LAND.
A Inland Ice; B. Solid Rock; C. Small collections of Earth at the foot of the Glacier; D. Lake; E. Separate Blocks of Ice.

be one of those magnificent ice fjords which Rink so
admirably describes. The following diagram will illustrate this more clearly.

"True icebergs are formed only in those glaciers which terminate in the manner indicated in Fig. 5, though

Fig 4.—Inland Ice (A) extending into the Sea (D) and terminating in a steep front, 100 to 200 feet high.

pieces of ice of considerable dimensions may fall from a steep precipice (Fig. 4). These various kinds of glaciers

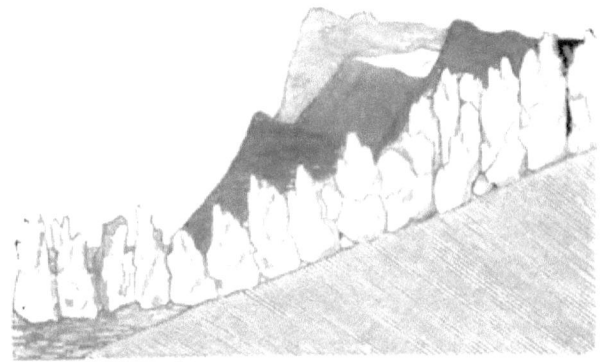

Fig. 5.—Inland Ice abutting on the bottom of an Ice-fjord, i.e., a Fjord in which rea Icebergs are formed.

occur not only in Greenland, but in other ice-covered polar lands, e.g. in Spitzbergen, though on so much smaller a scale than in Greenland that one never meets in the surrounding waters with icebergs at all comparable in magnitude with those of Davis Straits.

"In Spitzbergen, and probably also in some parts of Greenland, the ice passes into the sea in the following manner."

Fig. 6.— Inland Ice abutting on a Mud-bank.

After his return from this excursion on the inland ice Nordenskiöld spent some time in a geological survey along the coast, examining at the same time the kitchen-middens and graves of the old Greenlanders. The results of this survey are given in detail in Vol. IX. of the *Geological Magazine*, to which we must refer the scientific reader. We shall here confine ourselves to the account which he gives of the discovery of some very remarkable meteorites.

"During our involuntary stay at Godhavn, I made an excursion, in company with some comrades, in a boat manned by Greenlanders, to the spot whence the Rudolph meteoric iron was supposed to have been taken, namely, the old whaling station of Fortune Bay, in the neighbourhood of Godhavn. On arriving there, I ordered the Greenlanders to look after *heavy, round, rusty brown stones, which I knew would certainly be found somewhere thereabout.* It was in vain. No meteoric stones, or rather pieces of meteoric iron, were on this occasion found; but before leaving the spot I again repeated to the Greenlanders that pieces of iron of the nature described were *most unquestionably to be met with somewhere in that neighbourhood*, and I promised them a reward if they could discover them against my return in the autumn.

"When, at the end of August, we returned from Omenak to Godhavn, one of the Greenlanders communicated to me with many lively gestures to express their size, shape, &c., that they had certainly hit upon the stones I had described. A small specimen was shown, which confirmed the statement.

"The place where the iron masses were found was not however, at Fortune Bay, but at one of the shores most difficult of access in the whole coast of Danish Greenland, namely, Ovifak, or the Blue Hill, which lies quite open to the south wind, and is inaccessible in even a very moderate sea, between Laxe Bay and Disco Fjord.

"The meteorites lay between high and low water, among rounded blocks of gneiss and granite, at the foot of a vast basalt slope, from which, higher up, the horizontal basalt-beds of Mount Ovifak project. Sixteen metres from the largest iron block a basalt ridge, a foot high, rises from the detritus on the shore, and could be followed for a distance of four metres and is probably part of the rock. Parallel with this and nearer to the sea is another similar ridge, also about four metres long. The former contained lenticular and discoidal blocks of nickel-iron, like meteoric iron in external appearance, chemical nature and relation to the atmosphere (weathering). On being polished and etched the iron exhibited fine Widmanstädtian figures. The native iron lay imbedded in the basalt, separated from it at the most by a thin coating of rust. Moreover, in that basalt, in the neighbourhood of the blocks of native iron, nodules of hisingerite were found, evidently formed by the oxidation of the iron, as also small imbedded particles of nickel-iron."[1]

The meteorites were found, as has been stated, between high and low water, and within an area of about fifty square metres. There were twelve large and many small iron masses. The following year (1871) the Swedish government sent the gunboat, *Ingegerd*, Captain F. W. von Otter, and the brig, *Gladau*, under the command of Lieutenant G. von Krusenstjerna, to bring these remarkable meteorites to Europe. The largest mass, the weight of which is estimated at nineteen tons, was placed in the Riks Museum of Stockholm, and the second largest, weighing about nine tons, in the Museum of Copenhagen, the capital of the country to which Greenland belongs.

[1] For an account of these remarkable meteorites see *Geological Magazine*, vol. ix. pp. 419 and 516, and vol. ii. New Series, pp. 115 and 152.

CHAPTER VI.

THE SWEDISH POLAR EXPEDITION OF 1872-3.

THE main object of Nordenskiöld's visit to Greenland had been to find out by personal inquiry whether it was advisable to employ Eskimo dogs as draught animals in the projected Polar Expedition. The result he arrived at was a negative one. The advice which he received from the experienced Greenlanders whom he consulted was against their employment, the main reason alleged being that the necessary number could not be obtained unless purchases were made at all the settlements of North Greenland, in which case it was almost certain that the contagious dog-sickness, which had recently raged at several of the settlements among the Greenland dogs, would break out among those bought for the expedition. If this should happen the money spent in the purchase would not only be lost, but the expedition would also be deprived of an important means of assistance on which reliance would have been placed.

Having thus broken with the once prevailing Arctic tradition, it was natural that the Swedes should turn to the reindeer, which is exclusively used in the north of Scandinavia as a draught animal in travelling over trackless regions deeply covered with snow.

In order to obtain materials for judging of the fitness of the reindeer for being employed for the purpose in question, a circular was sent by Mr. Oscar Dickson to persons acquainted with the management of this animal with inquiries on a number of points relating to the subject. As the answers to these questions may be expected to interest our readers we offer no apology for inserting here the main drift of them.

First question: *How much can a reindeer draw upon ice covered with deep, packed snow?* Answer: 160 to 200 Swedish lbs., not including the weight of the sledge. If the rein is to travel fast this is sufficient weight, that is to say, not much more than the weight of the person who sits in the sledge behind him. But if the rein is in good condition so that he has sufficient marrow in his bones, he can with this weight get over 10 Swedish (66 English) miles in the course of twelve hours. He does not go at his full speed until his tongue begins to hang well out of his mouth, for the rein has no pores for the escape of perspiration, which must all pass out through the mouth. He requires no food during the day if he is only allowed to have his freedom to go loose during the night at places where it is certain that reindeer moss is found under the snow, and that the ice crust has not frozen fast to the ground. The reindeer may be foddered with the greyish white reindeer moss, which is collected carefully, so that no dirt adheres to it, with the lichen both of the pine and fir, and with hay (especially of river horsetail or so-called star fodder, but not with meadow hay, which he does not eat). If the reindeer be allowed to go at his usual pace, led by a man, the sledge ought not to weigh more than 60 lbs. nor the load placed in it more than 300 Swedish lbs.

Second question: *How can the reindeer be arranged most advantageously?* Answer: Eight to ten reindeer are fastened together so that the first rein, which has no sledge to draw, is fastened by traces to the saddle of the following rein, to whose pulka or sledge the next in order is fastened and so on. The last rein which has nothing to draw is tied with a rein to the pulka of the one preceding him. These eight or ten draught reindeer thus fastened together the Lapp calls a *rajda* and when thus arranged they can be managed by a child of ten or twelve, at least when the leading rein is tame. The last rein, with no pulka to draw, may be unbroken, and he is obliged, notwithstanding all the resistance he may make, to follow the rajda. If the weight to be conveyed is greater than six or eight reindeer can draw, a new rajda is started, and so on.

Third question: *How far can such a reindeer caravan travel daily?* Answer: Two to five Swedish (thirteen to thirty-three English) miles according as the reindeer are good and the attendants quick-footed. If the snow is two or three feet deep, it does not hinder the reindeer in travelling with a load, but the men in charge must have suitable snow-shoes, broader and lighter on loose, than on packed, frozen or hard snow.

Fourth question: *How many draught reindeer can one man manage on such a journey?* Answer: One person, man or woman, even a child, commonly manages six reindeer or a rajda during the march.

Fifth question: *What food is most advantageous during a journey, when pasture cannot be counted on, and what quantities of different kinds of food does the reindeer require daily?* Answer: The pine lichen is best, next, the river horsetail, but the fodder must be collected and dealt out with the hands covered with Lapp gloves.[1] The reindeer, however, cannot altogether want reindeer moss without falling off. Three to four pounds of reindeer moss together with five pounds of barley, or still better, oats coarsely ground, may be considered a good daily allowance. The rein besides eats every possible thing, even butter, but above all, he requires a little reindeer moss daily.

Sixth question: *Is there any difficulty in getting the reins over lanes or other openings, which may be occasionally formed in an extensive icefield?* Answer: If the edge of the ice does not project over the water and the current is not strong the reindeer can cross any stream openings whatever. Wherever a man can cross there is no difficulty in getting across reindeer. The rein is an excellent swimmer and not at all afraid of the water. It is besides very agile, so that if not too heavily loaded it jumps without hesitation over openings four to six feet wide.

Seventh question: *How great a distance can a reindeer sledge be reckoned to last without other repairs than those which can be executed during rests in uninhabited places?* Answer: A new and strong pulka (reindeer sledge) will last during a journey of 250 to 300 Swedish (1,650 to 1,980 English) miles, probably longer. When tarred or greased so as to run easily in the snow it ought to last three or four winters.

---

[1] This was shown by experience to be an unfounded prejudice, as were other similar statements.

Eighth question: *Is there any difficulty in feeding reindeer during a winter on collected reindeer moss, grain, &c., at a place where no proper pasture is to be had?* To this question the following different answers were obtained. A. considers it impossible, unless by felling a broad-leaved tree and dragging it to the herd, or by strewing the fodder that had been collected over the snow field. B. No, not the smallest. C. Some reindeer can certainly be kept within inclosures and fed with reindeer moss and other fodder, but with great trouble, and, perhaps, at considerable expense, but not a great number, for in order to thrive the reindeer must be free in a large inclosure. The fence must be at least eight feet high above the surface of the snow, for if a snow drift be formed within the inclosure the rein immediately climbs over. The reindeer's excrements in a few days make the place unhealthy for this very cleanly animal.[1]

Ninth question: *Is it the best plan to keep the reins within an inclosure, and if so of what nature should the inclosure be, and how many reins could one Lapp attend to?* Answer: The best way is to allow the reins to go at large with a herdsman, for the inclosure would require to be very large, otherwise the reindeer would not thrive long. The Lapps have in the fjells milking yards, the fences of which consist of parallel bars supported to a

---

[1] The fears, shown by experience to be ill-founded, which are expressed in two of these answers, induced Nordenskiöld to allow the reindeer herd that was transported to Spitzbergen to go at large as long as possible, which again led to the loss of all the reins with a single exception. This one was afterwards kept bound during the greater part of the winter; it notwithstanding throve well, and became fat and quite tame.

height of six feet by posts or branches of trees. When
the reincows are milked the whole herd is turned out and
may then, even if it consist of 500 to 1,000 animals, be
taken charge of by a single person and a good dog. If
the ground is covered with ice so that the reindeer cannot
get sufficient food, it may happen that the herd separates
even if never so many herdsmen try to prevent it. But
if, while they are thus scattered about, they are not
attacked by any beast of prey, they come back of their
own accord to that region of the fjells where they were
reared, and the Lapp gets back his whole herd.

Tenth question : *Is there any danger of disease attacking and destroying the reindeer herd during the course of the winter?* Answer : If there is good pasture or other food to be had, the danger of disease among the reins is not great. The hoof disease indeed sometimes causes great destruction among the herds, but this is in most cases occasioned by insufficient or inferior pasture. There also occur two other diseases, one of the liver and the other attended by a stretching of the neck.

Eleventh question : *Where can the best draught reindeer be bought, and at what price?* Answer : The best draught reindeer are bought with the greatest ease and certainty in Jockmock parish, but good draught reindeer can also be bought in Arvidjaur and Arjeploug parishes. The price of exceedingly good draught reindeer cannot be stated lower than forty Swedish crowns (£2 4s. 6d.) A pulka and harness of the best quality cost together about the same sum. The largest and strongest reindeer are found in Arvidjaur in Pite Lappmark where a tribe of Lapps is found, consisting of twenty to thirty families, who have not allowed the

agricultural population to drive them from the forest
region. Their reindeer accordingly have not been compelled, like those of the common fjell Lapps, to seek
their food on the bare fjells, but have kept to the woods
where the pasture is better.

Twelfth question : *How much eatable flesh, blood,
&c., does a draught reindeer yield on an average when
slaughtered?* Answer: An average reindeer yields—

2 roasts of 18 lb. each	36 lb.
2 shoulders of 8 lb. each	16 ,,
1 brisket of 7 lb.	7 ,,
2 sides of 9 lb. each	18 ,,
1 neck of 17 lb.	17 ,,
Feet	8 ,,
Head	8 ,,
Total.	110 ,,

As the answers were in general favourable, the
necessary measures were taken for the purchase of
reindeer and reindeer moss ; the reins, to the number
of forty, from Kautokeino, after an attempt to procure
Samoyede reins from the east side of the White Sea
had been found attended with too great difficulties ; the
reindeer moss partly from Norway, partly from the
district of Örebro in Sweden, the latter costing one
Swedish crown (about 1s. 1d.) per sack when well
compressed. The number of sacks was about 3,000.

The new Polar Expedition obtained from the Swedish
Government, on an application being made by Nordenskiöld, not only a grant of 15,000 Swedish crowns, but
also the use of the mail steamer *Polhem* and the brig
Gladan suitably manned and equipped. The large

quantity of reindeer moss that had to be conveyed to Spitzbergen necessitated the hiring of another steamer, the *Onkel Adam* of Gothenburg. The *Polhem* was built for carrying the mails in the Baltic during the winter, of excellent Swedish plates, and had a high pressure engine of sixty horse-power. On board this vessel, which was under the command of Lieutenant L. Palander and was manned by sixteen man-of-war's men from Karlskrona, were, along with Nordenskiöld,

THE POLHEM.

chief of the expedition in its entirety, Dr. A. Envall, medical officer, E. Parent, lieutenant in the Italian marine, who took part in the expedition at the special request of the Italian Government, A. Wijkander, physicist, from the University of Lund, and F. R. Kjellman, botanist, from the University of Upsala. The expedition was well provided with meteorological, magnetic, astronomical, and physical instruments, together with sounding and dredging apparatus, an abundant zoological equipment, three observatories made at Stockholm, and a library of about one thousand volumes, of which part was provided by the Governor of Gothenburg, Count Ehrensvärd.

The *Polhem* and the *Gladan* started from Gothenburg together on the 4th July. The former, which

VIEW OF GOTHENBURG ROADS.

called at various Norwegian ports, reached Tromsoe on the 13th July. The latter sailed direct to Spitzbergen. On the arrival of the *Polhem* at Tromsoe, the *Amiral Tegetthoff*, the vessel of the Austrian-Hungarian polar expedition, was found lying in the harbour, from which it sailed the following night.

They remained for more than a fortnight at Tromsoe, for the purpose of completing the preparations which the prolonged absence contemplated rendered necessary. During their stay was observed the thousand year festival of Norway—the thousandth anniversary of the battle of Hafrsfjord, which had as its result the union into one community of the various more or less independent tribes which previously possessed the kingdom of Norway among them. The *Polhem* started on her voyage on the morning of the 21st July, and on the evening of the 23rd was off Bear Island, which however was concealed by a thick mist, so that a contemplated landing could not be carried out. On the 25th, South Cape, the southernmost point of Spitzbergen, was sighted, and Nordenskiöld and some of his companions landed on this little visited spot, but without being able to fix its exact position by taking a solar observation as he had intended. On the 26th the *Polhem* anchored in Advent Bay, which *rendezvous* the *Gladan* had reached three days before, and fell in besides with the *Mimer*, a steamer belonging to a Swedish company that had been formed for the purpose of working a coprolite bed at Cape Thordsen.

After exploring Dickson Bay, the most easterly of the two arms into which North Fjord, one of the two main divisions of Ice Fjord, divides itself, the *Polhem* with the *Gladan* in tow left Advent Bay and on the 2nd August both vessels anchored in Green Harbour. Here Nordenskiöld was disappointed in finding that the stratum containing tertiary fossils which had been found here during preceding expeditions was so disintegrated and washed away that it was impossible to collect any remains worth speaking of without removing considerable quantities of earth. He found instead a number of fossil plants belonging to the chalk formation. Kjellman and Wijkander, in the meantime, visited Coal Bay, the former with the view of finding the place where the Dwarf Birch had been discovered in 1870 by Nathorst and Wilander. After a long fruitless search, after all hope of finding it was given up and the return to the boat commenced, its dark green leaves were at last observed projecting from the surrounding moss. The dwarf birch found here, the *Betula nana, var. relicta*, TH. FRIES, is believed to be a survival from the time when Spitzbergen possessed a finer and warmer climate than now. Its height, as found here, did not exceed two feet, the thickest stem being from two to three lines in diameter. After the return to Sweden it was found by the help of the microscope that a stem of this thickness was about eighty years old. The yearly rings were exceedingly thin and faintly marked in several specimens, and in some parts of the stem, altogether indistinguishable. A well-grown beautifully flowering specimen of the *Cardamine pratensis* also rewarded the search of the botanist, a *find* which was specially welcome, because this plant, though pretty widely distributed, is seldom found in flower on Spitzbergen.

Leaving Green Harbour on the 4th August, the *Polhem* proceeded on her voyage with the *Gladan* in tow, passing through the sound between Prince Charles Foreland and the mainland and anchoring on the 7th in Fair Haven for the purpose of regulating the chronometers at the place where Sabine and his companions spent three weeks in 1823, carrying on a series of physical and astronomical observations. The place which is situated on the south-western shore of the inner Norway island still bears the name of Sabine's observatory, and is distinguished by a great number of stones collected in a circle. Next day Fair Haven was left and the course shaped for Parry Island, but an impassable belt of closely packed drift-ice was met with, and the vessels had to turn southwards.

In the neighbourhood of Welcome Point, on the morning of 9th of August, they fell in with a Norwegian vessel, from the crew of which they received the unwelcome news that the state of the ice to the north of Spitzbergen was worse than it had been for many years, that their vessel had lain three weeks shut up in Liefde Bay, and that the sea to the eastward was filled with closely-packed drift-ice, through which it was impossible to force a passage. The *Polhem* and the *Gladan*, fearing to be frozen in, returned to Fair Haven to await the dispersion of the ice by a favourable wind. During this enforced delay, Wijkander carried on a series of magnetic observations at Sabine's observatory. Astronomical observations were also made, and two and sometimes three boats were at work dredging from morning till night. It ought also to be mentioned that on the drift-ice which the *Polhem* had encountered a short time before, Nordenskiöld had found small quanties of dust similar to that which he had discovered in the snow during a snow-storm at Stockholm in December 1871. This dust, which he believes to be of cosmic origin, contains metallic iron, cobalt, nickel, phosphoric acid, and a colloid organic substance. "However small and inconsiderable the quantity of this substance may be in proportion to the snow or water falling at the same time," he writes, "it may yet play an important part in the economy of nature, for example, by means of the phosphoric acid which it contains it may restore the fertility of the soil impoverished by repeated harvests. This observation ought also to be of great importance for the theory of meteors, of the aurora, &c. Perhaps we should inquire whether in this phenomenon we are to seek the explanation of the abundance in which magnesia, which occurs plentifully in meteorites, is found to exist in certain distinct geological districts, and if an increase of the earth's mass, which is certainly minute, but which is going on continuously, ought not to produce very considerable changes in the geological theories now prevailing, which proceed on the supposition that the globe is as nearly as possible unaltered in mass since the first occurrence of plants and animals, and that the geological changes have always depended on changes of distribution in the mass over the surface of the earth, never upon the arrival from without of new constructive material for our globe."

On the 13th August the *Onkel Adam* arrived from Tromsoe, laden with coal and reindeer moss, and having on board the forty reindeer for the journey over the ice and four Lapps, Nils, Mickel, John, and Anders, who had been hired to take charge of the reindeer and who had with them two dogs, Ruun and Kepp. The reins had stood the voyage well.

All the three vessels of the expedition being thus assembled, another attempt was made to penetrate the ice, but without success. Returning to Fair Haven,

the reindeer were landed on the inner Norway, the
Lapps accompanying them and pitching a tent. The
reins appeared to thrive well on their scanty provender
of lichens mixed with a few stalks of grass.

The weather continuing unfavourable, calms alternating with northerly winds, part of the lading of
the *Onkel Adam* was discharged, and she was sent to
meet the Swedish company's steamer *Mimer*, that had
been despatched to Tromsoe to bring stores for the expedition from thence to the so-called Swedish colony
Cape Thordsen. On the 17th August a Norwegian
fishing steamer, named the *Spitzbergen*, on her way
south from Liefde Bay, where she had lain shut in
by ice five weeks, arrived. The captain reported that
towards the east the ice still lay packed close along the
coast, and that six fishing vessels were shut in by it in
Hinloopen Strait and Wijde Bay.

Another attempt was made on the 27th August by
the *Polhem* and *Gladan*, to force a passage eastwards,
but off the mouth of Red Bay a fishing steamer was
met with, whose captain reported that the state of the
ice was almost unchanged, and that he had required
fourteen days to come from Hinloopen. The expedition
accordingly returned to Fair Haven, landing the reindeer which had previously been taken on board, but
this time on the mainland, where the pasture was
better, and they were less exposed to the danger of
falling down the mountain sides.

On the 29th August, a schooner-rigged vessel arrived
in Fair Haven, which turned out to be the *Samson*
belonging to Mr. Leigh Smith who was on board,
and returning from his second voyage of exploration

and sport to the high north. The vessel came now from Wijde Bay where she had lain five weeks shut in by ice, and had required twelve days to come to Fair Haven, though the distance between the two places is only a few English miles. Mr. Smith received his visitors from the *Polhem* with great kindness,

THE GLADAN.

and next day himself visited the vessels of the expedition, showing a deep interest in the undertaking, and expressing his approval of the plans and equipment. Before he parted from the Swedes he gave them to understand that he would be among the first who would look for them next summer. Thus they separated from the man "who," says the narrator of the expedition, "was to render it so great a service, and bind its members to him for ever in the bond of gratitude and attachment." The same day (30th August) the *Samson* sailed from Fair Haven to the north-west for the edge of the ice to hunt seals and Polar bears.

It appeared now impossible to reach the Seven Islands according to the original plan, but still some advance towards them might be made. Leaving Lieutenant von Holten and four men behind to assist in taking the reindeer on board the *Onkel Adam* when she should arrive, the two consort vessels again left Fair Haven on the 1st September, passing Verlegen Hook and affording those on board a view of the cold, icy glacier-filled, stormy Hinloopen Strait, a broad sound between the two largest islands of the Spitzbergen group, West Spitzbergen and North-East Land. The course was now shaped to the northward and at the latitude of Low Island, viz., 80° 5′ N., the edge of the ice was met with and its nature was found to be such as to extinguish all hopes of reaching the Seven Islands. The ice formed a continuous sheet of considerable thickness which appeared likely to stand many a storm, before it was broken up and dispersed. After an unsuccessful attempt to enter Murchison Bay, and finding that Treurenberg Bay was partially filled with ice, Mussel Bay was chosen as the winter quarters of the expedition, and was entered by the vessels on the 3rd September. No sooner had they anchored than Nordenskiöld and Palander went on shore to choose a site for the building that was to be erected. A suitable one was soon found, flat, high-lying, dry, gravelly, and of a sufficiently large area. The work of unloading the vessels and of erecting the wooden building in which the expedition was to winter immediately commenced. This building was fifty feet long, thirty-eight feet broad, and nine feet high in the

GLACIER IN FAIR HAVEN.

side-walls. It was completed on the 10th of September, by which date the observatories were also finished. These were three in number, magnetical, meteorological and astronomical. Observations on the tides were also to be carried on.

On the 6th September the *Onkel Adam* arrived,

bringing with her various rarities, such as newspapers a month old, potatoes of the year's growth, and some salmon newly taken in Ice Fjord, but also the unwelcome news that the leader of the colonisation project had found himself compelled by unforeseen circumstances to stop all work there, to give up the idea of wintering, and to return with all his men to Norway or Sweden, after a dwelling-house had been erected at Cape Thordsen and partly furnished, and various other work completed. Part of the stock of provisions, a quantity of coal, wood, &c., had been left behind. Captain Clase had providently purchased on account of the *Onkel Adam* a considerable quantity of provisions, and the whole stock of medicines. The *Onkel Adam's* cargo was now discharged with all speed, the reindeer being first placed on the island on which the building was erected, and afterwards on the mainland, where according to the Lapps' statement, there was good and pretty abundant pasture for them for a considerable time. The Lapps were furnished with fowling-pieces, and promised a fixed sum for every ptarmigan they brought in. Several members of the expedition also went out shooting, and before the polar night began and darkness put an end to all sport, from 150 to 200 ptarmigan were killed.

The time for the return of the *Gladan* and the *Onkel Adam* had arrived. The preparations were complete. The members of the wintering expedition had written their home letters, the botanist had packed his collections, the geologists had sent their specimens to serve as ballast, the warmest wishes that their returning friends might have a pleasant voyage had been expressed, when on the morning of the 16th of September, the time fixed for the departure, a violent storm commenced. It came on so unexpectedly, without previous warning, and nearly from its beginning in so full strength that there was no possibility of the vessels getting out to sea and there contending with it. There was nothing else to be done but to keep the ships from driving on land, and to wait till the storm should subside. But soon, and not unexpectedly, the cry was heard from the crow's nest, "The ice comes," and in a short time the vessels lay in its cold embrace; by noon of that unfortunate day no opening big enough for a yawl, much less for a vessel of ordinary size, could be discovered, either in the sea or in the bay; everywhere there appeared the white, closely-packed ice.

Was this ice to be speedily dispersed, or was it to imprison the vessels the whole winter? This was the question now eagerly discussed, and the experience of the expedition of 1868 was relied upon in support of the more favourable conclusion. A very unpleasant period of suspense followed. Much snow fell, and the temperature of the air went down on the 29th September at 4 o'clock p.m. to $-27 \cdot 5°$ C., and on land to nearly $-29°$ C. The snow that had fallen, converted into sludge by contact with water, froze and cemented the ice-blocks into a coherent mass which it did not appear likely could be broken up before the spring equinoctial storms. The necessary preparations for the wintering of all the vessels had begun to be made, when on the 30th September, just as the sun went down, six men were seen approaching. In other circumstances, this would have occasioned gladness, now the meeting was looked forward to with apprehension. For it was not very difficult to divine who the visitors were, and what was the object of their visit.

The reality surpassed the worst foreboding. It was not that one or two vessels had been overtaken and shut in by the ice; this hard fate had befallen no fewer than six. The men sent from these vessels, one from each, stated that they and their comrades had been employed during the later part of the summer, in Hinloopen Strait, in hunting seals, walruses, and bears with fair success. Some of them had left Hinloopen before the 16th September, and betaken themselves to Wijde Bay to hunt reindeer, for which this was the best season. The rest had left Hinloopen on the 16th, but had been overtaken by the ice. Four of the vessels lay shut in at Grey Hook, two in the neighbourhood of Welcome Point. The crews of the vessels numbered fifty-eight men, among whom was the veteran Mattilas, who had now ploughed the waves of the Arctic Ocean for forty-two summers. In 1864, he, along with thirty-six like himself — shipwrecked walrus-hunters, were rescued by the Swedish expedition of that year from an enforced wintering on Spitzbergen, and carried to Norway. His great age and occasional ill-health had prevented him from visiting, as he wished, the expedition, with whose chief he had long been acquainted. The walrus-hunters had a quite inconsiderable stock of provisions, which they hoped to be able to eke out by hunting, so as to keep them alive till the beginning of December. After that, death by hunger stared them in the face if they could obtain no assistance from the expedition.

The position was most heartrending. The Swedes numbered sixty-seven men, and it was ascertained, that by reducing the rations to two-thirds, the provisions might be made to last till relief could come from Sweden. To refuse help was impossible, but the attempt to feed one hundred and twenty-five men with provisions which were too scanty for sixty-seven could scarcely have but one result, to involve the whole in a common fate. From one quarter, however, help seemed possible. Captain Clase had brought information that at Cape Thordsen in Ice Fjord there was a stock of provisions. It was accordingly proposed to the walrus-hunters that a number of them should attempt to reach Cape Thordsen, either by land or sea. To this they agreed. But if a third should go and succeed in reaching their destination, the number of those left behind would still be too great. There was little to be hoped for from hunting. Perhaps in their extremity, the reindeer moss might be converted into a substitute for bread. The Swedes did not conceal from themselves, nor from the walrus-hunters, that their prospects were exceedingly gloomy, and the result beyond calculation. "But the requirements of reason and humanity," says the narrative, "were met. It remained to us all only to meet our fate like men, with trust in the guidance of a higher power, and with vigorous efforts on our part to endeavour to conquer our difficulties."

A council was held by Nordenskiöld, von Krusenstjerna and Palander, and they agreed to send to the captains of the imprisoned vessels, a document promising them all the assistance in their power. This document was first read to the six men who had been sent as a deputation, and the reading of it caused a gleam of hope and satisfaction to spread over their countenances. They left on the 1st October with hearts visibly lighter than when they arrived.

As misfortunes never come single, the storm of the 16th September, and the shutting in of the vessels consequent upon it, were soon followed by another, which was fatal to the carrying out of the original plan of the expedition. During a violent snowstorm, while the four Lapps were drinking coffee in their tent, the reindeer made their escape and were never seen or heard of more. The storm prevented the sound of the bells which some of them bore from being heard, and their footprints in the snow were immediately effaced by the furious blast. The Lapps were exceedingly grieved at what had happened, and declared their willingness to do all in their power to recover the runaways. But not the slightest trace of them could be discovered either then or afterwards. The only supposition that could be hazarded was, that they had perished in the crevasses of the inland ice. One indeed returned after a week's absence quite unexpectedly, with a large gaping wound in his back, supposed to have been caused by a piece of rock rolling down some mountain side. The rein was tied to the corner of a house and fed with reindeer moss. The wound was washed and covered with a piece of reindeer skin and speedily healed. The loss of the reindeer was not only regretted as deranging the plan of the expedition, but as depriving it of a supply of fresh meat, of the greatest importance if scurvy should break out.

On the 1st October the building on land was occupied, and next morning, Palander after a short religious service, addressed his men mustered in the hall, reviewing the occurrences that had taken place, telling them that on their behaviour depended the saving of many lives

LAPP WITH REINDEER.

from death by starvation, impressing on them the necessity of patiently submitting to unavoidable privations, and of carefully observing the winter regimen that had been fixed upon, on which observance a fortunate issue in great part depended, concluding with a "God save King and Country," in which all joined with one accord. All were now busy in getting their new dwelling in order, and the bustle was so inspiriting, that the merry jests and salvos of laughter could scarcely have been believed to come from men whose prospects of surviving the winter were exceedingly doubtful.

Soon after the removal, two wild reindeer were shot. Their forms appeared colossal when contrasted with those of the tame reindeer to which the Swedes had been

POLHEM — WINTER STATION.

accustomed. They were reins in winter dress. The whole body was covered with a very close winter coat of hair, several inches thick. The head nearly indistinguishable from the neck, was short and thick, with broad nose, and eyes only visible on careful scrutiny. The trunk appeared shapeless, and the legs short and clumsy. This peculiar shapeless appearance is owing not merely to the coat of long hair, but also to the thick layer of fat by which at this season the whole mass of muscle in the rein is surrounded. It is indeed surprising how this animal can collect such a mass of fat in Spitzbergen, where the vegetation is so scanty and the summer so short. In spring, even in the end of June, they are only, as people say, skin and bone; but in autumn, by the end of August, and throughout September, they resemble fat cattle, and have their flesh so surrounded and impregnated with fat, that it is for many nearly uneatable.

Other three wild reins were soon after shot by the Lapps when out searching for the tame reindeer. They saw no other animals but some ptarmigan, a mountain-fox, and an eider.

On the 22nd October, Palander with five companions, started on an excursion with the view of visiting the imprisoned Norwegian vessels. They took with them an ice-boat, a sledge, and provisions for fourteen days. On the third day they reached Grey Hook, and found four of the frozen-in vessels lying close together near the beach, with a close broad belt of blocks of ice five to six fathoms high thrown up on a shallow; beyond this, the ice was of comparatively inconsiderable dimensions. The walrus-hunters were of opinion that even if storms during winter should break up the rest of the ice, this belt would withstand them all, and not be dispersed till the summer sun exerted its consuming power upon it. Before then they thought that the vessels could not be liberated. The other two vessels lay about sixty-six miles west at Welcome Point. On the 17th October, seventeen men from the vessels' crews taking a boat

with them, had gone over the ice, hoping to find open
water at the Norway Islands. In that event they intended to proceed in the boat to Ice Fjord, and take
up their quarters in the house that had been built at
Cape Thordsen and was now unoccupied. The men who
remained, stated that their provisions would not last
longer than to the middle of November, and asked to
be allowed to join the expedition a fortnight sooner
than the time agreed on, promising to leave a fortnight earlier in spring, when they might more easily
support themselves by hunting, than in the dark month
of November. To show how unusual the state of the
ice was, it may be stated that Mattilas, the Spitzbergen
veteran, whose forty-second visit this was, in every
previous visit had returned to Norway in autumn, and
this, notwithstanding that he frequently started on his
homeward voyage later than this year. In 1871, for
example, he did not leave North East Land till the 16th
October.

The party left Grey Hook on the 25th October, and
reached Polhem (for so the settlement on land was called,
after the ship) on the 26th, making the journey homeward in fifteen and a half hours, the outward journey
having occupied twenty.

Winter began to set in now with severity. The
flocks of birds had gradually diminished in number;
some cider ducks, whose young were not sooner strong
enough to undertake the long journey southward, being
the last to leave. They maintained themselves in a
lagoon, at the bottom of Mussel Bay, which, in consequence of the strong current, was still partially free of
ice. By the end of October the only winged creature

visible were a few guillemots, which now and then were
seen flying singly over the bay, coming from the north,
where probably every opening between the ice-blocks
had not yet been frozen over. They began, however,
day by day, to be more rare. Occasionally there was
heard the cry of an ivory-gull, "which" says the writer
of the narrative, "though not melodious, was pleasant to
us, because it was a token of life, showing that we were
not altogether deserted, and because it broke the silence
which had begun, and which the seldomer it was broken,
was all the more remarkable and impressive." The temperature
now became pretty steady, the thermometer in
general showing about $-20°$ C $-4°$ F. The 13th October
was the last day for four and a half long months on
which a glimpse of the sun was visible. Reckoning
for refraction, the sun should have been visible till the
20th of October, but the mountain-chain to the south of
Mussel Bay, cut off seven days. On the 26th of October,
artificial light was required the whole day long, but out
of doors it was still possible to distinguish one's way.

The long dreary Polar night having thus set in, it was
of the greatest importance that the resources at the command
of the Expedition should be husbanded in the best
way possible, and every precaution taken to preserve the
health of its members. The first question was that of
food. When the *Polhem* left Sweden there were on board
provisions for twenty-two men for eighteen months. The
Gladan having on board two officers, two subordinate
officers, and twenty-one seaman and boatmen, had provisions
for about six months on leaving Sweden. The
steamer *Onkel Adam*, with twelve persons on board besides
the captain, one of whom was a stewardess, Amanda, had,

when she came to Spitzbergen in September, provisions for only a few weeks. These were supplemented by the purchase made by Captain Clase from the Ice Fjord Company, which included about six months' provisions. It was resolved to give the *Onkel Adam* in addition from the *Polhem's* stock, a certain quantity of provisions, chiefly preserved, as only a small quantity of these could be obtained at Ice Fjord. The crews of the *Polhem* and the *Gladan* were regarded as a unit. In the end of September a calculation had been made and a like ration fixed on for the crews of both vessels to be in force from the 1st October. This was of course considerably smaller than that which had been originally settled on.[1]

If the Norwegians, as was daily expected, were to make their appearance, a further reduction must be made, and it was determined to prepare for such an emergency by experimenting on the reindeer moss, of which there was a large stock which was now useless for its original purpose. An attempt was made to bake bread of the moss mixed with flour. The moss was picked and carefully freed from all foreign matter. It was then boiled some minutes to get rid of its bitter taste. In this way part of its nutritive value was lost, but this was unavoidable. It was then dried, ground, or powdered, and mixed with rye-flour and water. The dough thus obtained was fermented, baked in thin loaves and fired. The bread looked very well, had the colour of common ryebread, was well fermented, &c. But it had a very bitter taste, though not in so high a degree but that it was quite eatable. After being a little

[1] See Dr. Envall's Report in Appendix.

accustomed to it, and especially when very hungry, a person could eat it with relish.

The stock of suitable clothing was amply sufficient not only for the wintering party, but for all on board the imprisoned vessels.

The ordinary routine of a man-of-war was observed on board the *Gladan*, and also on land as far as the scientific character of the expedition permitted.

The scientific work carried on during the winter was the following :—Complete meteorological observations every hour both day and night; hourly magnetical observations and in addition five minute observations twice a month on the 1st and 15th, in correspondence with similar observations at the physical institution at Upsala; refraction, pendulum, and other astronomical observations; observations of the aurora, and its spectrum, of atmospheric electricity, and the temperature of the earth and of the sea, and tidal observations; zoological researches by dredging under the ice, and in connection with these, algological studies.

The leisure time of the crew was principally occupied with reading, but also with various games, as draughts, chess, and dominoes. The last game was much liked by the Lapps, who, at the beginning, had amused themselves much by playing cards, and who soon picked up the simpler rules of chess, and became afterwards assiduous and very ingenious chess-players. They also occupied themselves much with a game with the exact nature of which the Swedes did not become acquainted. The apparatus for it consisted of dice, a board divided into squares like a draughtboard, and a number of small wooden figures somewhat resembling cones, which were placed on the outer squares of the board and moved according to the throw of the dice. The whole—dice, cones, and board—were made by the Lapps themselves. Song, music, and sometimes dancing, shortened many leisure hours for the men. In spring there were also games in the open air, as skating, though skating-ice was not so common as might have been expected.

November began with a furious storm, and during nearly the whole month violent storms raged from the south, south-west, and south-east. On the 24th, for instance, there was a snow-storm, the like of which no member of the expedition could remember having seen. The observations were completely stopped, and it was a little time before they could be resumed, as the damage done had first to be repaired. These storms, though rather unpleasant, were welcomed by the Swedes as tending to open a way for the release of the Norwegian vessels. The direction of the wind was the most suitable for driving from land the masses of ice collected along the coast, and it appeared almost certain that in the beginning of the month, there was still open water north and west of the Norways, and that the ice shutting in the two vessels lying at Welcome Point could not be of any great extent. The fear which walrus hunters generally have of wintering in Spitzbergen led to the conclusion that if both, or even only one, of these vessels could be worked out into open water, the crews of the other vessels would abandon them, if they were still shut in, and find a passage in one or both of the others to Norway. In the meantime all necessary preparations were made for their reception. The steamer *Polhem* was assigned to them, and all available means were used to make their quarters as convenient, warm, and wholesome as possible.

In the beginning of November there was found to be open water at a distance of about four miles from the house. By the 8th and 9th the edge of the ice could be reached in a quarter of an hour. The arrival of the Norwegians was awaited with the greatest interest. They were to arrive on the 10th according to the agreement made with Palander at Grey Hook, but they did not come. When some days had passed and the weather continued favourable for the breaking up of the ice, and the open water came still nearer the coast, the apprehensions of the Swedes began gradually to subside, and most of them became convinced that the imprisoned vessels had got out to sea, and were so far on their way back to Norway.

The question now began to be eagerly discussed whether the *Gladan* and the *Onkel Adam* should return if opportunity offered. The difficulty of navigating in the darkness, which was now almost continuous and complete, and the danger of being again beset with ice possibly in a more unfavourable position, were urged against the return of the vessels, but preparations began to be made to take advantage of a favourable conjuncture of circumstances, such as the bay being free of ice, the weather steady, and the moon above the horizon.

During nearly the whole of November the weather was very mild. The temperature seldom sank to -20° C. and was often, especially on stormy days, a degree or two above the freezing point. In September the winter promised to be very severe, but now the contrary appeared probable.

"With the polar night in all its dreary length," says Kjellman, "we first became acquainted during the last days of the month. Towards the end of it the sun was indeed far below our horizon, but the mild light of the moon dispersed in some degree the darkness of the night. Never had this heavenly body been so dear to us, and never had her light appeared to us so strong and beautiful as when she now held back the darkness that was to settle over the region where we had fixed our dwelling. Long shall we remember, if indeed we ever forget, the moonlight November days at Mussel Bay. Certainly we shall never again see a heaven so beautiful as that which we occasionally had an opportunity of gazing at with deep admiration. It was specially at noon that it was finest. One day Nordenskiöld and I walked out to the edge of the ice to enjoy near at hand the sight of the waves dancing in joyous motion and the ice blocks quietly swimming about. Our way was over the ice, and walking was exceedingly difficult. When we reached the farthest part of the archipelago we threw ourselves down to rest and take a view of our surroundings. They were surprisingly grand. The south-western part of the vault of heaven was lighted by the circumpolar full moon. In the flood of light which streamed out from her there swam some few long drawn out clouds. Right to the south near the horizon there was visible a faint reddish glimmer, clearly and sharply distinguishable from the white moonlight. Here the sun had gone down, when the long polar night began; it was the last glimpse of his light that we now saw. In the south-east some few rays of light changing every moment in strength, colour, and position—in fact, the aurora in the form it commonly takes here, raised themselves towards the horizon. Above our heads glows the pole star, everywhere over the sky sparkle stars, darting stronger or weaker, differently coloured lights, and on the north or north-eastern horizon rests the deep darkness of the polar night. I will not try to paint the rich changing play of colour and the *chiaroscuro* full of effect. Add to this glorious heaven a wide-stretching sea glittering in the moonlight, the white surface of Mussel Bay with the three vessels standing out against it, the dark precipitous fell sides that surround it, and the little building on land from whose every window lamplight streams—and the main points of the panorama are enumerated. It is difficult to believe that noon is approaching; it might rather be taken for evening, a quiet winter evening in the country. A grave stillness and tranquillity hangs over the neighbourhood. Only now and then the deep silence is broken by a low grating sound. It is heard in the direction of the edge of the ice, and is produced by the rubbing of the ice blocks against each other, when they are moved by the swell."

By the 25th November there were only about 100 feet between the *Gladan* and open water, but on the 27th the moon went down and complete darkness supervened. Indeed, at this time, and during the whole of December and January, and part of February, the aurora was very common, but in general its light was too feeble to diminish the darkness in any appreciable degree. It appeared at all hours of the day, and towards all points of the compass, but principally in the south. It seldom occurred in the form most common in Sweden, that of a how formed of a bundle of illuminated rays resting on a dark bed of cloud or mist, but most frequently as a feebly-lighted border on the cloud edges, or as long fine rays, now few in number and scattered, now numerous, and in that case generally combining in the zenith to form a more or less complete corona. Occasionally, again, there occurred auroral bands, broad, strongly illuminated, differently coloured, and folded as it were elegantly, and exceedingly beautiful. They lasted only a little while. They were specially suitable for examining the grand phenomenon in question by spectrum analysis, and this was done as often as possible. The results were given by Wijkander on his return, in a paper entitled "Our Norrskenets Spektrum," published in the Öfversigt of the Transactions of the Royal (Swedish) Academy of Sciences.

Another phenomenon also attracted attention at this time. The beach was in general covered with snow drenched with water, the temperature of which occasionally fell to $-10.2°$ C. In this snow-sludge a large number of almost microscopic crustacea maintained themselves, giving evidence of their existence by an intense bluish-white light, which was given out by the sludge when it was touched, and which, on a closer examination, was found to proceed from the small organisms in question. "It produced, indeed," says our author, "a very peculiar impression to walk along the strand on a dark and stormy day, for at every step a man took there burst out on all sides bluish-white flames, so that one was apt to fear that his shoes and clothes would take fire.

"Not less peculiar was it on a quiet day, when the sea was open and calm, to walk along the girdle of ice which always ran along the strand. For every wave as it rolled forward slowly against the ice girdle emitted, at the moment of contact, a sharp bluish-white flash, which for a moment lighted up the part of the dark water-mirror lying nearest.

"We collected some of these small phosphorescent animals, which have been examined after our return by Professor W. Lilljeborg, who found them to consist of several species belonging to the crustacean order, *Copepoda*. The observation is certainly of great interest, that so-called cold-blooded animals—for such all crustacea are known to be—can retain their vital power unimpaired, when the temperature of the surrounding medium has gone down to 10° C. below the freezing point. It may be remarked, however, that their stay in the cold snow sludge may certainly be considered occasional. They lived principally in the sea-water, and with it, when it rose at flood, they were carried up among the snow along the shore, in which they were left when ebb began, to be carried away with the next flood-tide, or at least warmed up by the relatively warm sea-water. If in this way these crustacea do not maintain themselves during the whole winter in a medium whose temperature is several degrees under the freezing-point, they must, however, be supposed to have the power of enduring for some time a comparatively considerable cold, whence it seems to follow that, if they continue in a medium whose temperature is considerably lower than that in which they commonly live, they must be able for some time to retain in their interior the temperature they have in normal circumstances."

On the 30th November the *Gladan* lay in open water, but the other vessels were still fast. New ice soon began to form, and rapidly increased in strength. On the 8th December the first attack of scurvy happened. The patient was an old seaman, who, not having been accustomed to preserved provisions, had eaten only salt meat. With change of diet and proper treatment the disease abated. On the 11th there was again moonlight, which was very agreeable after a period of darkness so deep that it was impossible for a man to choose his way, and avoid the objects that lay in his path out of doors. Advantage was taken of the moonlight by the *Polhem* towing the *Gladan* to a new anchorage. The *Onkel Adam* had previously been moved, and the vessels were now all within a few feet distance from each other. When the ice broke again they would all undoubtedly be free at the same time. Another attack of scurvy having taken place, Dr. Envall enjoined on all the necessity of taking exercise in the open air, and of using the preserved provisions, which were thought in general not to be much relished. On the 20th one of the boatmen, who had been ill some days, died of pleurisy, which was believed to be due to scurvy and of pneumonia concurring with it. He was buried with due solemnity on the 22nd. On the morning of the 23rd the ice, which some hours before had been so strong that artillery might have been run over it, broke up, and the three vessels were again free, but in the absence of the moon all thoughts of an immediate return home had to be given up.

Christmas or Yule Eve, as it is called in Scandinavia, was celebrated by observing the customary festivities. A Christmas tree, "Yule fir," or rather "Yule pine," grandly decorated, with the Swedish, Norwegian, and Italian flags in fraternal combination occupying its top, and nearly overloaded with the "yule gifts" that hung from its branches, was the principal object of attraction.

BURIAL IN 80° N.L. DURING THE POLAR NIGHT.

The yule gifts consisted of knives, brushes, books, pieces of tobacco, cigars, pieces of soap, &c. Lotteries were held for their distribution, every person having three or four lots, and as many prizes, the lotteries causing the greatest excitement. The Lapps, who had never seen the like before, and who honoured the occasion by appearing in holiday attire of variegated colours, were beside themselves with gratification at what had fallen to their share. After this came supper with the national "lutfisk," and the "julgris," which was eaten by most with good appetite, notwithstanding its strong train oil flavour. After the merriment was over and silence had succeeded the merry din, the thoughts of all went home to Sweden, to the comrades and friends in whose company Christmas eve was wont to be spent, and whom they knew to be full of concern for the disaster that had overtaken them. Christmas was observed with due solemnity, as was also the second day of Christmas, according to the national custom.

New year's eve was celebrated with a supper on land, to which the officers of the *Gladan* and the *Onkel Adam* were invited. When it was over some fireworks were let off, and a parting salute was fired to the year 1872, which had been so eventful to the members of the expedition.

Meanwhile the men were employed building a bath house with material furnished by a Russian hut at some distance, but this turned out to be insufficient, and the house was never completed. Then an exercise house was to be built of the bags of moss, but as often as it neared completion some alteration required to be made and the nearly finished house had to be pulled down and begun anew. It was next determined to inclose the building with a wall of snow, and it was soon found to be superior as a building material to moss sacks. Several snow houses were afterwards built, one of which, called the crystal palace, from the splendour of its architecture, was long used as a second magnetic observatory.

During the whole winter the dredgings carried on without intermission, sometimes in open water, sometimes under the ice, gave sufficient occupation to Christian and the four Lapps. Without doubt the constant employment in which all thus shared contributed greatly to keep them in good spirits, and to prevent them from suffering so much from the reduced rations as might have been expected. The repeated outbreaks of scurvy, amenable as it was to treatment, showed that if the Norwegians had been obliged to join the expedition the result would, in all probability, have been that the greater number, if not the whole, would have found their graves on the desolate shores of Spitzbergen. For the insufficiency of rations must be considered the main cause of scurvy breaking out so early and attacking so many members of the expedition, although great weight ought also to be given to the depressing effect of the long darkness and the predisposing influence of the Arctic regions.

On the 8th January the thermometer rose in the morning from $-30°$ and $-32°$ up to $-7°$ C., and soon after a violent S.E. storm began to blow, which in a few hours cleared Mussel Bay of ice and set the vessels free. Preparations were now made for the *Polhem* going northwards to find out where the edge of the ice was, but before they could be completed a N.W. storm came on and the vessels were again frozen in. During the rest of January the cold was inconsiderable, the wind mostly from the south, and the ice in the bay was breaking up. It was now settled that as soon as the vessels were free they should all leave Mussel Bay, the *Polhem* to go northwards, the other vessels to return home. On the 29th January the whole of the bay was free of ice, and the evening of that day was fixed for the departure, but the wind rose to such a height that it had to be deferred. On the 30th the storm continued and increased in violence. The *Polhem*, *Gladan* and *Onkel Adam* were all like to drive on land, the *Polhem* actually running aground on a sandbank but being got off without much difficulty. Soon the storm subsided and the members of the expedition congratulated each other on their escape from the dangers that had threatened them, the greatest of which was the loss of the provisions that were on board the vessels. For if the vessels had stranded, the greater part of the provisions would, in all probability, have been lost or damaged, and the Swedes would thus have become a prey to starvation and to death.

On the 6th February lamp light could first be dispensed with at noon, but only for a short time. It was not until the 13th March that the sun was visible. On the 20th February the cold reached its maximum, the mean temperature of the day being $-36°$, the minimum $-38°$ C. This was welcome to Wijkander, who intended to make observations on refraction at a very low temperature. Preparations had been made for them, and the instrument stood waiting the opportunity that now offered. Fortunately the cold was accompanied with a calm and clear atmosphere. Wijkander remained whole nights in his observatory bravely defying the cold and patiently overcoming the many difficulties attending astronomical observations made in such circumstances. In the cold weather the work out of doors was not stopped and the dredgings still went on, it being of great importance to ascertain whether the severe cold and the long darkness exercised any special influence upon the marine animal and vegetable world. The sea was now covered with ice as far as we could see, and the ice in Mussel Bay increased in thickness every day. On the 3rd March, however, the arrival of some glaucous gulls led to the supposition that there was open water at no great distance. This was rendered

ASTRONOMICAL OBSERVATORY.

more probable during the following days by a heavy swell in Mussel Bay, and on the 4th a small bow-formed, open channel was seen from a neighbouring height stretching from the mouth of Hinloopen Strait to the little Muffin Island, and from that down to the Norways. Another lane went from Hinloopen along the west coast of North East Land towards Low Island and Brandywine Bay. The same day the Lapps went up on the western fells to look for ptarmigan. They also saw open water and found ptarmigan, but could not shoot any. They saw besides a not inconsiderable number of

DREDGING UNDER THE ICE IN WINTER.

glaucous gulls and guillemots hovering about the tops of the rocks and settling on the ledges.

On the 6th March a large polar bear was shot, and his flesh afforded a welcome change of diet to the Swedes who had been so long confined to the tasteless preserved provisions. It was hoped that another bear would soon make his appearance, but none came.

About the 10th March it was determined that two parties should start on the 16th, one led by Nordenskiöld and Palander to Giles' Land, the other headed by Von Krusenstjerna and Parent to explore North East Land. Fate, however, seemed to be set against the expedition, for by the 16th a violent storm, accompanied by snow, had come on from the S.E., and it was impossible to start. The weather for a long time was bad. It stormed and snowed almost daily, and was comparatively very cold, between $-25°$ and $-35°$ C. Before any alteration of the weather took place the greater part of March was past, and it was too late to carry out the plan that had been formed, because the polar journey proper was to be begun in the middle of April.

On the 3rd April a snow-bunting made its appearance, and was welcomed as the messenger of spring. The sun now remained so long above the horizon that there was in fact no more night. Short but pleasant and invigorating the time was felt to be during which night and day succeeded each other. During the first part of the "dark time" a nearly unconquerable sleepiness had been experienced. Men felt as if they could sleep without difficulty the whole twenty-four hours. Towards the end of the "dark time" sleeplessness succeeded, and it was difficult for almost all to obtain the needed rest. The sun returned, and the interchange of day and night began. Now all fell asleep the moment they went to bed, slept undisturbed till morning, and rose refreshed and strong. With the unbroken polar day the sleeplessness returned, but not in the same degree as before.

In the end of March part of the sea off Mussel Bay was open, but during the cold days about the middle of April all the ice-free places froze again, so that as far as could be seen from the island on which the house was situated, the sea was covered after the 15th April by a continuous sheet of ice.

The month of April was occupied by preparations for the ice journey towards the north, of which we shall now give an account in the words of Professor Nordenskiöld.

"The situation of Mussel Bay is exceedingly unfavourable for an expedition in which sledge journeys northwards are proposed to be undertaken. Although partly in consequence of this, partly on account of the greatly diminished strength of our men from the insufficiency of their rations during the winter, and finally on account of the unfortunate accident of the escape of the reindeer, we had given up thoughts of reaching so high a degree of latitude as we had previously reckoned upon, we were unwilling to let our abundant sledge equipment remain altogether unemployed. Independently of the latitude that could be reached, a sledge journey northwards was of great interest, because only in this way could we obtain a knowledge of the state of the Polar ice during this season of the year, founded on actual observations. My intention was, if possible, to arrange that the main party should be attended by two smaller ones, of which one should bring with it provisions to the Seven Islands and then return, and the other the same, after coming some distance to the north of this group of islands. With the help of three Lapps (the fourth had fallen very ill, as it afterwards appeared, of scurvy, just as the expedition started), two

Norwegians hired for the expedition at Tromsoe, and a volunteer, Christenson, a mate from the *Onkel Adam*, the main party and the returning party, which was to accompany it farthest towards the north, could be manned from the *Polhem*. The third party the commander of the *Gladan* had promised to organise from the vessel under his command.

MUSSEL BAY.

"The departure was fixed for the 23rd April, but had to be postponed till the following day, because one of the sledges broke down immediately after it was set in motion. We started, therefore, on the 24th April with three sledges, each provided with its boat. We went over the chain of hills, about 1,000 feet high, which divides Mussel Bay from the entrance to Treurenberg

Bay. At the beginning nearly all the men who were in good health helped to draw the sledges up the high but gently sloping acclivities wherewith the chain of hills sinks towards the starting-point of our journey. Notwithstanding the acclivities and the heavy loads on our sledges, we accordingly made pretty rapid progress. At the summit our companions left us, and we continued our journey down the hill, which here slopes pretty gently towards Verlegen Hook.

"During our downward journey, however, a new misfortune befell us, inasmuch as the sledge which was set apart for the main party was smashed, and when farther forward we met with Von Krusenstjerna who had taken another way over the hills, we received the unwelcome intelligence that one of the men belonging to his party had fallen ill, on which account he considered himself obliged immediately to return. One of our own men, too, complained of what afterwards appeared to be a pretty severe attack of scurvy. Everything thus appeared to be in league against us.

"In any case it was our intention immediately to proceed with the two parties from the *Polhem*, after having exchanged the broken sledge for that which was intended for Von Krusenstjerna's party; but on a close examination that too was found to be broken. It was now clear that our sledges, made with the greatest care at Copenhagen after patterns from England, were not sufficiently strong to bear upon rough ice or uneven ground the heavy loads (2,000 to 3,000 lbs.) which were here required, and that it would be necessary, in case we made another journey, to provide new sledges, or sufficiently strengthen the old ones, with the materials available at our winter station. For this purpose Palander and part of the men returned to the *Polhem*.

"It was of course unnecessary that all the men should return, and I accordingly determined to employ the time required for getting ready the new sledges in forming a depôt as far on our way northwards as we could, consistently with the possibility of allowing the necessary number of men to meet at Verlegen Hook. For without the help of a portion of the men whom I required for this expedition, the equipment of the principal party left behind at Verlegen Hook could not be brought on.

"Accompanied by ten men I started on the 24th April from our encampment at Verlegen Hook, going over Hinloopen Strait towards Shoal Point. The smallest boat was carried by four men on their shoulders, the provisions, the tent, and other equipments were loaded on two sledges and a pulka (reindeer sledge), to which our sole remaining reindeer was attached, which was accompanied and observed by me with a quite special interest, chiefly to obtain a knowledge fully to be depended on and grounded on experience, of the fitness of this animal for such journeys as these. I can safely say *that it surpassed our expectations. The reindeer drew, although the Lapps declared it was not one of the best, upwards of* 200 *lbs.* (a good reindeer draws 300 lbs.), *was quiet and easily managed as an old work-horse, ate with relish the moss we brought with us, and when slaughtered, after the moss was finished, afforded excellent flesh.* With forty such draught animals and Parry Island for a starting-point, we might certainly have reached a very high latitude, even with so unfavourable a state of the ice as prevailed this year north of North East Land.

"The distance from Mussel Bay to Verlegen Hook was, reckoning by the circuitous route we had taken, nearly two Swedish (about thirteen English) miles. So far had we advanced the first day, notwithstanding that a height of about 1,000 feet had to be passed. On the other hand, on account of the extremely unfavourable state of the ice, I required three days to cross Hinloopen Strait, which, at the place where I passed it, is at most eighteen miles broad. The weather was at first favourable, but by the second day there descended over the mouth of Hinloopen an ice fog, which made it impossible for us to choose a way for our sledges among the fields of rough ice. This fog, however, was speedily dispersed by an easterly and south-easterly wind, which swept before it along the ground a stream of driving snow, consisting of fine ice-needles glittering in the sun, which in a few minutes filled a hole more than six inches deep in the snowdrifts so that no trace of it was left. The rest of the sky was still indeed quite clear, so that not only the sun, but also numerous fine mock-suns and halos, produced by the refraction of the solar rays by the ice-crystals, were visible. On the other hand, all near the horizon was concealed in an impenetrable mist. The mountain tops, surrounding Treurenberg and Lomme Bays, lying at a distance of several Swedish miles, showed contours so clear and sharp, that they seemed close at hand, while objects near the ice or ground at a distance of only a few hundred paces, either could not be distinguished at all, or appeared, when the wind and driving snow lessened for a few moments, as high snow-covered mountain ranges, looking as if they lay at a much greater distance than the mountains at Lomme and Treurenberg Bays. These circumstances, so different from those to which we are accustomed at home, gave occasion to the only accident accompanied by loss of human life which the expedition has to record.

"Before referring to this I shall, in a few words, give an account of the beautiful halos produced by the ice-fogs, which were constantly visible at this time. Unfortunately I had already, the day after we left Verlegen Hook, in consequence of my imprudence in not immediately using snow-shades, been attacked by incipient snow-blindness, so that even the slightest strain on the eyes was attended with the most severe pain. It was therefore impossible for me to carry out any measurements, and I can consequently only give here a description of these beautiful phenomena, without a statement of the angles, which is indispensable for their complete explanation.

"The halos appeared, as has been said, almost constantly, but of variable brightness and extent. Sometimes they consisted only of a single ring with faint mock-suns, but occasionally it was possible to follow the phenomenon round the whole horizon. Even when it was brightest the halos were coloured only at the part of the horizon lying towards the sun. They did not consist of circles, but of beautiful curves of very various forms, which *to a certain extent also underwent variation in their relative position.* Thus, the one nearest the sun was of a pear-shaped form, pointing downwards. In its border three mock-suns were visible, two particularly fine at the same height as the sun, and another less developed below. When the sun was on the horizon the lower mock-sun was not visible. When up on the inland ice I observed it touching the horizon on the 7th June at 6 o'clock p.m. We were then in the latitude of about 79° 50′, from which it is possible to calculate the angle between the sun's centre and the lower point of the pear-shaped halo of $22\frac{1}{2}°$. When the halo was complete, the pear-shaped figure was surrounded by two others, the inner like an Ω, and the outer bell-shaped, the latter at its uppermost point being touched by an arc of a basin-shaped rainbow.

"Of these two outer halos, however, there were commonly visible only the bows which touched the inner pear-shaped halo, and that just referred to which touched the outer one at its highest point. A line drawn through these two points of contact by no means always corresponded with the vertical plane, but oscillated, often within a short time, and, as I believe, with the wind, which probably had a very considerable influence on the position of the ice-crystals, now to the right, now to the left. All the lines which have been described were coloured with the colours of the rainbow, which were sometimes intense, but generally only faint. Through the sun and the two horizontally placed mock-suns there went a band of light, which, though faint, was continued round the whole horizon with clearly-marked brighter points of light here and there. The halos visible opposite the sun consisted of circle-like or pear-shaped curves of the same dimensions as the pear-shaped figure already described. Right opposite the sun, upon the other side of the horizon, two such curves touched each other without showing any trace of mock-suns at the point of contact, while, on the other hand, two luminous points were visible where the curves in question touched the curves next to them on their other sides. The whole vault of heaven was besides, as it were, marbled by regularly grouped lighter and darker spots, whose position however I could not further clear up. All these lines were uncoloured.

"The forms which I have described, and which were also visible, although less clearly developed, farther on during our journey over the inland ice-field of North East Land, differ considerably from the halos which have previously been sketched. This depended perhaps on the circumstance that the stratum of air filled with ice-needles which gave rise to the phenomenon of diffraction lay in this case close to the surface of the earth along which the ice-dust was driven at a furious rate by violent winds.

"The halos originate, as is well known, in the diffraction of the solar rays by, and their reflection from, the ice-crystals with which the air is sometimes filled. For the theory of this phenomenon the knowledge of the crystalline form of ice is of the greatest importance. This I had previously endeavoured to investigate, and during this year's stay among the ice and snow of the Polar lands I had besides on several occasions opportunities to make observations, which show that the statements found in most scientific handbooks are in some respects very incomplete, in others altogether erroneous. These are generally founded on the form of snowflakes, which has been described by Kepler, De Mairan, Wilke, Scoresby, &c. These writers, and many others, have shown that snowflakes and similar crystals artificially produced from water are composed of six-sided star-like figures, more or less complex, consisting of fine long crystal-needles disposed at angles of 60° and 120° to each other. From this the conclusion has been drawn, that the fundamental form of ice is a regular six-sided pyramid. Although twin formations of the kind which occurs in the case of snowflakes do not absolutely exclude the possibility of an hexagonal crystalline form, they are so much the less an evidence of it, as such twin-groups seldom occur in the true hexagonal system, but are much more frequent in the case of rhomboidal crystals with a fundamental prism of about 120°.

"In order to settle the question of the true crystalline form of ice, it is necessary to examine single crystals of sufficiently large size to be determined crystallographically. By such an examination I have found that ice is dimorphous, for it crystallises—

"1. *Hexagonally*—Short six-sided prisms optically uniaxial, seldom truncated by pyramidal surfaces, and not showing any particular disposition to form double crystals. I observed crystals of this variety, strongly resembling crystals of colourless apatite, several years ago upon certain minerals which had been packed in moist blotting-paper, and had been exposed to a temperature under the freezing-point, and in old snow which had several times been alternately exposed to mild weather and to a low temperature. The finest crystals of this kind were, however, found during our journey over the inland ice of North East Land. They form here a separate stratum, of which the passage from the loose snow to the firm ice is composed, and are often of a singularly regular formation, especially on the walls of the cavities of which this stratum is full. The crystals are commonly bounded by a terminal plane forming the base, and a six-sided prism. The base is smooth and glazed, the prism surfaces are streaked. The angles are seldom truncated by pyramidal surfaces, which commonly occur only at one end of the crystal. Ice accordingly is believed to crystallise hemimorphously, a circumstance which is of importance, because all substances which crystallise hemimorphously are commonly also pyro-electrical, that is, become polar-electrical during warming or cooling. This pyro-electricity of ice is probably the reason why the ice-needles in the air are often parallel, which again is a condition of a portion of the beautiful phenomena of refraction and reflection now under discussion.

"2. *In the Rhombohedral System*—The ice which is deposited on the inner side of window-panes, and on metallic objects, stones, &c., which stand out in moist air, does not crystallise in six-sided plates, but in right-angled parallelopipeds, probably belonging to the rhombohedral system. I have not found any truncated angles on such crystals, and therefore I have not succeeded in determining the constants of the axes. We may, however, conclude from analogy with other substances which crystallise both in the hexagonal and rhombohedral systems, that here also the faces of the fundamental prisms have an inclination to each other of about 120°. The crystalline needles, of which the snowflakes are composed, belong probably most frequently to this, and not to the hexagonal system.

"The third day after our departure from Verlegen Hook I supposed that we must be near the shore at Shoal Point, and when we rested at noon I ordered two of the Lapps to go forward, without loads, a little farther, in order to see whether we were so close to land that driftwood could be obtained for cooking our dinner. They returned very soon, one with the report that he had seen land quite near, the other with a piece of wood from the strand itself. They were now ordered, together with the Quane Christian, to go to land for wood with one of the sledges. Two of the seamen besides, from mistaken zeal, without any order from me, took upon themselves to leave the encampment with the other sledge for the purpose of fetching wood, but without following the party sent by me, or asking a single question about the direction. One of them, however, soon observed that they were going the wrong road, and returned, after having in vain urged his companion, the boatman Snabb, to do the same. Snabb, a serviceable but stubborn man, given to religious scruples, however held on the way he had begun to take, and never returned. The same afternoon, along with one of the Lapps, I attempted to follow the traces left by Snabb and the sledge he drew, but all marks in the snow were again filled up, so that all trace was lost, and the drifting snow did not admit of any proper search without traces. Equally fruitless attempts for his recovery were made in the course of the following days, attempts that were rendered unusually difficult by the drifting snow that prevailed at the time, and the state of our eyes, which were suffering from an exceedingly severe attack. The Lapp John, for instance, was so blind that he required to be led, and many others of us were in nearly as bad a condition.

"This accident prevented us from going farther, so that unfortunately I was obliged to relinquish my intention of forming a depôt farther up opposite the Seven Islands; for it was not possible to leave this quarter till we had done what we could for the recovery of Snabb, and while there remained a possibility of his return. Before this the time was already arrived when, according to the agreement we had made, men should be sent to meet Palander at Verlegen Hook.

"On the 2nd May six men were sent thither over the ice. I remained with three at Shoal Point, where at the appointed time, the 5th May, Palander made his appearance with the sledges, the equipment of the main party, &c. As the greater part of the men walked along the border of the ice, Palander was enabled to make use of an opening in the ice-field which the high winds had made a few days before for the transport of the boats and provisions, and thereby succeeded in avoiding the rough ice which detained my party so long. In this way he had been able to pass the mouth of Hinloopen Strait in eighteen hours. With Palander were the men I had sent to meet him. On the other hand, von Krusenstjerna had been obliged in the beginning to give up his intention of accompanying the expedition, and in this way a considerable diminution was caused in the number of the days for which the main party could carry provisions with it after leaving the Seven Islands.

"The sledge party was now composed as follows:—

"1. The main party, consisting of Palander, myself, and nine men. We carried with us a boat, a tent, the necessary equipment of clothes, sleeping-bags, fowling-pieces, instruments, medicine, cooking apparatus, tallow for fuel, and finally, provisions for fifty days. The equipment was loaded on two sledges, which now, after the alterations Palander had caused to be made, victoriously withstood the severe trials to which, during the remaining part of the journey, they were exposed.

2. A party of six men, who were to accompany us only to the Seven Islands, to assist the main party during its journey thither, and bring on provisions to a depôt we intended to make there.

"Our normal manner of life and marching order during the sledge journey was the following : Two hours before the start the cook (occupying a not very agreeable post, which went in turn round the men so that each held it but for a day at a time) was wakened to get coffee ready. The fuel employed was driftwood, when it could be had, otherwise tallow, and, as in the latter case, the cooking required for the sake of economy to be carried on for the most part within the tent, it was thereby speedily filled with abundance of sooty smoke, which gave the skins of the inhabitants a uniform black colour difficult to get rid of, and not unlike that of the tribes inhabiting the burning deserts of Africa. When coffee was ready the cook loudly called our attention to the fact, and immediately afterwards dealt out the beverage in equal portions in large tins which served at the same time for coffee-cups and soup-basins. When the coffee-pot came off there was next set on the fire a pan containing half a pound of pemmican for every man. In the morning a quarter of a pound of bread and one-fifth of a pound of butter were also dealt out to each of them. When the meal was finished we started. After five hours' march, with intervals of fifteen minutes' rest every hour and a half, we rested at noon for an hour, when a quarter of a pound of bread, a piece of pork, and a cubic inch of brandy were dealt out to each person. We then proceeded on our journey for five hours, when the tent was pitched for the night. In the evening one cubic inch of brandy, a quarter of a pound of bread, and half a pound of pemmican were again dealt out to each man. This was made into a strong and highly relished soup, which would certainly, if it could have been partaken of twice a week during winter along with suitable vegetables, have protected every one who took part in the expedition from scurvy. After coffee (or tea) our india-rubber mattresses were inflated and spread out, we all crept into our sleeping bags, a grey felt covering was spread over us, and in a few moments we were fast asleep. No night-watch was kept, although we daily fell in with bears during our journey along the north coast of North East Land. They never troubled us at night.

"On the morning of the 6th of May we started from Shoal Point, and, favoured by a good wind which permitted us to use sails on our sledges, we reached the southern point of Low Island, thirteen miles from our starting-point. Next day there was a great fall of snow, the wind at the same time increasing in violence, which after a few hours' advance compelled us to stop and seek protection in our tent. Both the following days the wind and driving snow with a cold of $-19°\cdot5$ C. continued, so that we were obliged to lie unemployed in our tent, where our stay became very unpleasant, partly on account of the snow-dust, which the wind forced in

through the thin cotton-duck and the seams, partly on
account of the abundant fall of snow which took place
within the tent when the blast shook loose the hoar-
frost which during the severe cold was continuously
deposited on the inner side of the tent, packed full as
it was of human beings. We were therefore very glad
when, on the 10th of May, with splendid weather, and a
temperature of $-17°·5$ C., we could again start and resume
our journey. We went past Cape Hansteen, over Brandywine Bay and the low point, now nearly free of snow in
consequence of storm and wind, which divides this fjord
from the bay at Extreme Hook. On the 12th of May
we reached Castrén's Island.

"The ice in Brandywine Bay was even and smooth,
and there were no very large blocks of drift-ice along
the shore,.a proof that this bay was covered with ice
before the severe winter storms began. But from the
rocky heights at Cape Hansteen we could see that
the ice farther out was exceedingly uneven. This was
caused there probably by masses of drift-ice which
had been piled up during the course of the winter against
the west coast of North East Land by the severe storms
then prevailing, and been afterwards frozen together.
The point over which we advanced was nearly free of
snow and without vegetation. It was formed of low
granite rocks, strewn with numberless loose blocks, of
precisely the same kind as the underlying granite, which
has a strong inclination here to disintegrate under the
action of frost. They clearly lay *in situ*, notwithstanding their resemblance to *rullstenar* (rolled stones), and
had been formed by the splitting-up of the surface of the
rock to a certain depth by the action of the frost after

the glacier had receded. Here also, as is the case with the sandstone stratum between the South Harbour and the English river on Bear Island, the rock which was split up into large blocks has been afterwards displaced to a considerable extent by the frost and further disintegrated, being thus changed in part to rullsten-like blocks rounded but rough on the surface, and in part to a coarse angular granite gravel. In consequence of this no sign of striæ could be anywhere observed on the rocks, which were exposed at innumerable places. These facts are of the greatest interest in a geological point of view, because similar pseudo-rullsten formations, as Igelström and Gumælius have shown, often occur in Sweden. The height of the promontory above the sea, at the place where we passed it, was, according to measurement with the aneroid, thirty-four metres.

"One of the Lapps had become completely snow-blind, so that it was necessary to leave him and one of the tents on Castrén's Island. In the hope of reaching Parry Island in a single day we also left behind us at the same place the greater part of the equipment of the returning party, the provisions required for the return, &c. During the rest-day that was occupied with these arrangements two Lapps were sent out to hunt for reindeer. They returned without having seen any reins, but reported quantities of their traces and dung. Besides, they informed us that right opposite the inner part of Castrén's Island another considerable island was to be found. On further inquiry, however, it was believed that the island spoken of by the Lapps was formed of the rocky masses whose north point is designated North Cape on the map, and that Beverly Bay is not a bay but a sound.

If this be so, however, a bridge of ice must have covered this sound when in 1861 I made angle measurements from the top of the neighbouring Grytberg.

"Early on the 14th of May we continued our course towards Parry Island, the south point of which is only eleven miles distant from our resting-place on Castren's Island. But the sea lying between was now covered not with level ice, but with hummocks so close to one another that, although we put forth our utmost efforts, we required nearly three days to accomplish that inconsiderable advance.

"On the 16th at noon we reached Parry Island, on whose shores the ice was again quite level and smooth. We had now one of the few fine days we had to record during the whole of our sledge journey. The driftwood, so important for comfort in the tent, was found on the shore in abundance; and an occasion for its use, specially welcome for the sake of variety, was afforded by a rein that was seen when we landed at the place appointed for laying down the depôt on the south-eastern side of the island. It was immediately hunted and killed. Numerous traces and remains showed that even these islands lying in the neighbourhood of 81° are inhabited in great numbers by very large animals, which, if the facility of procuring the necessaries of life were the only condition of their choice of habitat, ought to betake themselves to far more southerly regions. Numerous footprints of bears, often following the traces of the reins for long distances, showed that a dangerous enemy to the reindeer lives in its neighbourhood. The principal food of the bear, during that part of the winter when he does not hybernate, consists however of seals, perhaps also in case of necessity of mosses and lichens, as we may conclude from the fact that the number of seal-holes that we discovered in the course of our journey was much smaller than the number of bears we fell in with in the same time. In the stomach of a bear shot in Stor Fjord during the expedition of 1864 there was found nothing but earth mixed with remains of plants.

"After a small depôt had been formed here, and, to protect it from bears, covered with large stones, the mate Christenson and the men hired at Tromsoe were sent back. We started on the 17th of May, going along the sound lying between Phipps' and Marten's Islands, which at the time was covered with level and good ice, so that in a few hours we reached the south-eastern point of the former island. Here we stopped in order to take a view of the state of the ice from a rocky height, and perhaps discover some level ice-field between the masses of hummocks that now from the foot of the mountain appeared to bar our way northwards.

"When we reached the top we had an extensive view, which showed that the sea north of the Seven Islands was covered with confused masses of ice, piled up close to each other, interrupted neither by open water nor level ice-fields, so that there was no possibility of pushing forwards with our heavily-loaded sledges. This was the more surprising to me, as on two former occasions I had an opportunity of viewing just the same part of the polar basin and then found an unbroken level sheet of ice which did not appear to offer any serious obstacles to a long sledge journey, although it would have been necessary to be prepared to meet here and there with places that were difficult to pass. This belief is also thought to be strengthened by Parry's and Scoresby's experience as well as our own, in 81° 42' north latitude. *In the existing state of the Polar ice north of Spitzbergen, it was, on the contrary, clearly impossible to advance over it a single degree, and a continuation of our sledge journey northwards was thus altogether objectless.*

"If we had succeeded in erecting our winter house on Parry Island instead of on the shore of Mussel Bay, we might, even in present circumstances, have been able, by means of previous reconnoissances in various directions, to find out a more favourable field for our journey towards the north without the necessity of diminishing the stock of provisions set apart for the sledge journey proper. Now, however, it was impossible, because a continued stay at Seven Islands for this purpose would have caused so great a diminution in the stock of provisions with which our sledges were yet loaded, that what remained would not have been sufficient to enable us, even under the most favourable circumstances, to make any very considerable advance northwards. Besides, taking into consideration the state of the ice during the winter, and the open water which was already visible east off Shoal Point, I hoped, with the steamer *Polhem*, to be able, somewhat later in the summer, to discover another starting-point early enough and situated far enough to the north to enable us, with fully-loaded sledges, to begin our journey at least a degree of latitude to the north of the Seven Islands. These circumstances induced me to refrain from continuing a journey northwards the result of which, in any case, was certain beforehand.

"In order, however, that the labour we had expended

on our sledge journey might not be altogether lost, I chose for our return not the direct way we had come, but the way round North East Land, with a view to settle its disputed eastern boundary and to clear up its geology, the nature of its inland ice, the extent of the groups of islands lying to the north-east of North East Land, &c. Even with this very considerable circuit we hoped to be again at our winter quarters in twenty or thirty days, and so in time enough for making preparations for the second attempt to force a passage northwards. However, although the original plan of our journey was not carried out in its entirety, the return took up more than forty days, and was attended by much greater obstacles, difficulties, and dangers than we had anticipated; but the scientific results were also greater than we had expected, especially in respect of the knowledge we obtained of the nature of the inland ice of Spitzbergen, which differs in more than one particular from the inland ice in the regions of Western Greenland visited by me, situated 10° farther south.

"Leaving behind us the boat and various other effects that were not now absolutely necessary at our resting-place on Phipps' Island, in order to lighten our sledges, we started on the 18th May, going south of Marten's Island, towards Cape Platen. At first we had good ice, so that we went quickly forward, but as we neared the longitude of the south-eastern point of Marten's Island we met with exceedingly difficult hummocky ice, over which we could only advance very slowly. This unfavourable state of things, with a piece of level ice here and there, continued as far as Cape Platen, which, in consequence we did not reach till the 23rd of May.

The distance we had come from our starting-point was, however, only twenty-three miles.

"The ice we thus passed is formed not of colossal blocks or icebergs, but of angular blocks of ice, *not waterworn*, piled loosely over each other, so as to form pyramids, or walls of ice, up to thirty feet high, which were so close to each other that the space between them was frequently not large enough for our tent.

"The cause of the formation of these ice-walls, which were also observed by Wrangel on the north coast of Siberia, is probably to be sought for in the changes of volume which ice undergoes when its temperature is changed. According to Plücker and Geissler the linear expansion-coefficient of ice is $=0.0000528$. If, therefore, ice of $0°$ C. be cooled to $-15°$ C., cracks must arise which, for 1,000 metres, have a breadth of thirty-two inches. The cracks naturally freeze together immediately afterwards, and when the ice is again warmed, for instance to $-5°$ C., a piling-up must take place of twenty-one inches per kilometre. During the course of the winter this phenomenon is repeated innumerable times, one layer of ice being piled upon another, till the whole ice-field forms a confused mass of blocks of ice heaped up against each other. Similar forces are also in operation in the crust of the earth, with less intensity, indeed, in consequence of the smaller expansion-coefficient of the rocks which compose it, and the inconsiderableness of the changes of temperature which occur in them, and the cracks thus formed may here come together again, provided no chemical or mechanical sediment has been deposited in them, as is, perhaps, often the case. On the other hand, the forces operate in the earth's crust during millions of years, and I doubt not that in the circumstances here noticed the cause of the strata being contorted, dislocated *and thrown over each other*, is to be sought for. This last, perhaps, to judge by the observations I had the opportunity of making on the polar ice, happens far oftener than we commonly suppose, and when it takes place there often occurs no considerable disturbance in the original horizontal position of the stratum. Certainly in most cases the veins filled with foreign minerals, by which the upper strata of the earth in particular are intersected in all directions, derive their origin from similar causes; that is to say, from cracks which have, in consequence of changes of temperature, many times over opened and come together again, *provided they were not prevented by the falling in of débris.* This has, however, often taken place, considerable masses of sediments, formed chemically or mechanically, have frequently collected in the cracks, and during the immense duration of geological ages they have hardened and been metamorphosed to solid crystalline rocks—limestone, quartz, felsite, pegmatite, &c.

"The sides of the ice-blocks themselves were covered with beautiful crystals of ice, falling down at the slightest touch, loosely connected like the crystals which form hoar-frost, but here in the home land of the ice often above an inch in diameter. Between the blocks of ice lay larger or smaller quantities of snow, which was of little depth and exceedingly loose at the places where the rough ice had been formed *during the present winter;* in other places again, *where the rough ice had been formed the preceding year*, it was deep and pretty well packed, but not hard enough to carry a person on foot; and in consequence exceedingly difficult and tiresome to walk over. In order to prepare a way for the sledges, axe and spade had to be constantly used, and even with the greatest exertions it was impossible on many days to advance the length of a single geographical mile. During nearly the whole of the time that we wandered over this ice-field, and during the greater part of our sledge journey, so thick an ice-fog prevailed, at least close to the horizon, that we generally had to advance at random without choosing our way. It happened several times, for instance, that we went forward hour by hour over exceedingly difficult ground, although, when the air happened to clear, we discovered that we had an even ice-field in our immediate neighbourhood.

"A number of bears were seen during our journey over the ice and nearly everywhere it was crossed by their traces. Even this desolate region thus forms a haunt for vertebrate land animals, and it is difficult to understand the reason why the bear prefers to live here where neither seals nor other living animals which could form the object of his pursuit are to be seen. It was singular to observe the care with which the bear chooses the fittest and least troublesome way, avoiding large hummocks and deep snow-drifts, provided they are not sufficiently packed to carry his body, which is heavy but supported on broad paws. When, as was often the case, the ice mist prevented us from ourselves choosing the most advantageous way and bear tracks were found in the direction of our journey, we frequently followed them for long stretches and found it for our advantage to do so.

"East of Cape Platen the ice was good, at least in the neighbourhood of the coast, so that we could go on very fast, though our journey was delayed by the necessity of going out of our way for the purpose of mapping the country and of stopping at various places to take astronomical observations. The weather too was generally pretty good, some days in the end of the month were even warm, so that the snow melted and small collections of fresh water could be found in holes and hollows along the sides of the hills. On 29th May we thus obtained for the first time during the year natural drinking water. We were now set free from the time-and-fuel-wasting ice melting; only for a couple of days however, for we soon after went forward over the inland ice-field where during the first half of the month of June all was yet frozen and the snow quite dry. On the other hand *evaporation of snow* takes place during the whole winter, and that on so extensive a scale that a covering of snow so closely packed that it cannot blow away speedily disappears by evaporation under violent and dry winds even at a temperature considerably under the freezing-point.

"At many places the fjords were surrounded by beautiful mountains whose precipitous slopes now already, notwithstanding open water was not to be found in their near neighbourhood, formed the haunt of millions of sea-fowl breeding in these fells, while the fell foot was formed of immense quantities of débris, richly clothed with black lichens. Sometimes there also appeared grass, or, more correctly, moss patches of a lively green derived from the previous year, particularly at the foot of the fowl-fells. These tracts lying so far to the north, in which probably no sportsman ever before disturbed the peace, offered very excellent and secure pasturage to a number of reindeer. Veritable footprints of reindeer and bears were also visible at innumerable places above all along the shore and off the promontories. Naturally several reins were also shot, and these were, remarkably enough, fatter than those formerly shot by us in spring in the parts of Spitzbergen lying more to the south.

"The journey along the north coast of North East Land took up the whole of the remaining part of the month of May, a considerably longer time than we expected. The reason of this was that North East Land, as the accompanying map shows, extends considerably farther towards the east than the distance given in most of the sea charts, a circumstance which was first pointed out by Mr. Leigh Smith, who, as is well known, has visited Spitzbergen in summer, partly for sport, partly to carry on researches in geography and natural history. We had now an opportunity of confirming his observations in the main points by means of astronomical observations accurately made with an artificial horizon, and of making a complete map of the north coast of North East Land lying east of the turning-point of the expedition of 1861.

"For some days a dark sky had showed itself in the east and north-east, which was thought to be a sign that there was already open water on the east side of Spitzbergen. In order to make certain of this and to get a view of the state of the ice both on the sea and the inland ice, Palander and I ascended the highest summit of von Otter's Island on the 31st of May, the most easterly on the north coast of North East Land, with the exception of some small islands. According to aneroid observations, the height was 105 metres.

"We had an extensive view from this point, which showed that a considerable stretch of open water *surrounded on all sides by ice* was to be found along the east coast of North East Land as far as Brock's and Föyen's Islands. On the other hand no land was seen in the north-east, so that it is to be supposed that the land again placed in these regions in the more recent maps will meet the same fate as King Carl Wilhelm's Land.

"For several years back the question of a land east of Spitzbergen has been the subject of various discussions in which German, English, and Scandinavian geographers have taken part, and as several erroneous statements on this point have crept in and almost obtained a foothold in the literature of geography I may be permitted to dwell a little longer on the subject.

"A land east of Spitzbergen is given in the old Dutch charts, for instance in that published in Holland by van Keulen founded on Giles' and Utger Reps' observations. In this chart the land in question is delineated immediately north of 80° N.L., and about 50′ east of the east coast of North East Land, which, however, is placed too far west. The land is marked 'Commandeur Giles Land entdekt 1707, is hoog Land.' Afterwards this land was left out of the recent maps of these regions, until Norwegian walrus-hunters again asserted the existence of land east of Spitzbergen, the position of which, however, was more southerly than that given in the Dutch chart. At all events, the Norwegians called the land Giles' Land. In 1864 the Englishmen Birkbeck and Newton came in sight of the Norwegians' Giles' Land, and in the same year the same land was seen and sketched by Dunér and myself from the top of White Mount, immediately

north of Helis Sound. The land is named Giles' Land
in the map published by us. When Count Zeil and
Baron von Heuglin some years afterwards visited Stor
Fjord they sighted the same land from some high hills on
the north-eastern side of Edges' Land, but they believed
that they ought to give the land a very great extension
towards the south. The land was treated as if new and
obtained the name 'König Carl Wilhelm's Land.' At
first the observation by Dunér and me was neglected
entirely. Afterwards it was declared that the land seen
by both of us was only a plateau-shaped island or a foreland, 'Schwedisches Forland,' which lay in the front of the
newly discovered land, a statement, the incorrectness of
which is shown both by the sketch of the land seen from
the top of White Mount, published in the account of the
expedition of 1864, and by the description given in
that account.

"To avoid loading the map unnecessarily with new
names, we had continued to mark the land with the
name Giles' Land, and, on the ground of our measurements made from the White Mount under favourable
circumstances, we had called in question the extension of
the land so far south as von Heuglin supposed. We were
violently attacked on the subject by Petermann, who expressly declared that our remarks originated in envy and
other discreditable motives. The great extension which
von Heuglin gave the land to the south led the English
also to wish to identify it with that marked Wiche's
Land in Purchas's map to the east of Spitzbergen and to
claim it accordingly as an English discovery. This claim,
however, was also resisted in the most positive manner
by Petermann. Finally the question of the extent of

the new or old land was completely settled in 1872, when three Norwegian whalers, Altman, Johnsen, and Nilsen sailed round it and determined its extent. The observations of the Norwegians were arranged by Professor Mohn of Christiania, who, to put an end to the dispute about the name, proposed at the same time to call the land after the King of Sweden, *King Carl's Land*, a settlement of the name question against which people in Sweden, at least, can have no remark to make. In various maps published during the last few years Petermann has marked with the name Giles' Land, a land far to the north-east of the north-eastern point of North East Land, situated as far to the north of van Keulen's Giles' Land as King Carl's Land is situated to the south of it. It is reserved for futurity to show whether this land does in fact exist. From the top of von Otter's island, as I have already stated, no land could be observed in the direction given by Petermann.

"The geology of the region east of Cape Platen is exceedingly monotonous. The rock consists everywhere of a mica-schist mostly stratified horizontally, here and there gneissoid, resting on greyish white granite, in outward appearance strongly resembling Stockholm granite, but wanting orthite. *Strata* of a granite of similar nature, alternate with the schists, which though in the main horizontally stratified are both much folded. Nearly everywhere the underlying rock and the low islands lying off the coast consist of granite and the hills of mica-schist. Well-marked striæ are seldom met with here; they have been destroyed by the action of the atmosphere and of lichens wherever the receding glacier has left an exposed stone surface not covered by water or clay. But innumerable other signs show that the inland ice of North East Land in former days extended many miles farther north, and that it is the denuding action of the ice that has determined the present distribution of the land.

"The power of resistance of the mica-schist has in this case been clearly much less than that of the hard granite, and the existing rock surface on the low promontories and islands therefore consists of the stratum of contact between the two rocks. Here, for long stretches, we may walk forward over horizontal granite rocks, into which, to judge by the surface, angular pieces of gneiss are as it were kneaded. A geologist of von Buch's school would here doubtless believe that he saw an immense eruptive mass of granite, everywhere interspersed with fragments of gneiss mechanically transported. On a closer examination, however, it is found that there is no true inclusion of gneiss in granite but that the whole effect depends on the denudation having stopped just at the boundary between the two rocks, in which however all the bends of the waved strata have not been followed, the consequence of which is that a fold of the gneiss descending here and there into the granite has been left behind. It therefore appears, judging from the surface, as if the whole rock consisted of granite interspersed to a great extent with angular blocks of gneiss. That the granite and the gneiss stand to each other in the same relation as the layers of sand and clay in the later rocks I consider a settled truth.

"That in Sweden, too, inclusions of gneiss in granite have a similar origin, I consider highly probable, though many cases occur (for example, the inclusion of gneiss and magnetite blocks in pegmatite) where this explanation is not admissible.

"Before we discovered, from the summit of von Otter's Island, the open water channel mentioned above I was very doubtful which way should be chosen for our further advance, whether *upon* the sea ice along the east coast of North East Land, in which case there would be a possibility of accurately determining the extent of the inland ice in that direction,—and this, if repeated after several decades of years, would be of great importance for establishing the rate at which the ice advances or recedes,—or *over* the inland ice itself towards Cape Mohn or Cape Torell, which offered abundant opportunities for observations of a formation which is exceedingly interesting in a geological point of view. But the open water which we saw from the summit, no longer left any choice open to us in this respect. If, as was to be supposed, some considerable opening or water channel extended from the open water to the precipitous impassable border of the glacier, it would form an insurmountable obstacle to our advance in case the way along the east coast was taken, as we had left the boat provided for the sledge journey behind at the Seven Islands. Seen from a distance, on the other hand, the inland ice of North East Land was level and free from clefts.

"North East Land forms the most northerly of the four large islands, into which Spitzbergen is divided. Its extent from north to south is seventy-five and from east to west about ninety-two geographical miles. The whole interior is occupied by an ice-sheet 2,000 to 3,000 feet thick, to which the fall of snow (and rain) during summer and winter brings new material, and which accordingly would be unceasingly increased, if the mass of ice did not, as is the case with all glaciers, flow out into the sea slowly, but without intermission. The principal direction of the ice-stream in North East Land is towards the east, and the whole of the east coast is therefore occupied by a single precipitous ice-wall, insurmountable from the sea, which, being nowhere interrupted by rocky heights or tongues of land, forms the broadest glacier or skridjökel known to man. It is, for instance, considerably broader than the Humboldt glacier in Greenland described in such lively colours by Kane. Northwards, however, the ice-sheet of North East Land terminates with an even and gentle slope, which sometimes reaches the sea, but generally leaves a small stretch of ice-free land along the coast. On this side there is no obstacle to an advance into the interior, at least from precipitous slopes.

"After a halt of twenty-four hours at our last resting-place on the north coast, for the purpose of taking observations and for short excursions in various directions we started again on the 1st of June. We now went no longer east but southwards to a point where the ice-field was believed to terminate towards the sea with a slope sufficiently gentle for the up-transport of our sledges. This went on more speedily and with less difficulty than we expected, but we had scarcely advanced a few hundred yards before our journey was interrupted for a little by a hazardous adventure, which showed us that we had now entered a field full of dangers, certainly not unexpected, but much more serious than we had supposed.

"Like the glaciers of Switzerland, of Greenland and of Scandinavia, the glaciers of Spitzbergen are interrupted by clefts or fissures which often extend perpendicularly through the whole mass of ice several thousand feet thick. The occurrence of these fissures stands in close connection to the motion of the glacier, and there is therefore a smaller number to be met with where the glacier is spread over an extensive level field without interruption from rocky heights. Accordingly we had reason to suppose that clefts or fissures would not in any specially great number intersect the way we had chosen, and I hoped besides that all the crevasses would have been filled with snow during the snow-storms of winter. This supposition was so far correct, inasmuch as fissures do not here occur in such numbers or of such size as in that part of the inland ice of Greenland which I examined along with Dr. Berggren in 1870—but deep, almost bottomless openings do nevertheless occur in numbers sufficiently large to swallow up us and our sledges. They were the more dangerous as they were for the most part concealed by a fragile vault of snow, so that even when we stood on the edge of the cleft, it was only by boring with an ironshod stick, very often first by ourselves falling in, that we could assure ourselves of neighbourhood, direction, and extent.

"Already before we had got up our sledges a hundred feet or so we met with a wide but not particularly deep crevasse, open in many places, that is to say, not covered with snow, which, however, was easily passed upon a snow bridge, formed during some snow-storm, sufficiently strong to carry us and our sledges, but as it was impossible to distinguish any more crevasses with the eye, I supposed that the North East Land inland ice which, as I have mentioned, is quite level in the direction in which we were going, would be continuous and safe, at

least till we reached the other side. But scarcely had
we advanced two thousand feet farther before one of our
men disappeared, at a place where the ice was quite
level, and so instantaneously that he could not give even
a cry for help. When we, affrighted, looked into the
hole made where he disappeared, we found him hanging
on the drag-line, to which he was fastened with reindeer
harness, over a deep abyss, previously completely concealed by a thin snow vault. A few moments afterwards
he was hoisted up again unhurt and not terrified, but
somewhat surprised at his adventure, as he had had no
warning of the existence of such pitfalls. If his arms
had slipped out of the rein-harness, which consisted of a
single belt, suspended from the shoulders, he would
have been lost.

"For safety's sake the drag-harness was now altered so
that no slipping out of it need be feared—in a case like
that which had just happened a man would hang se-
curely in it; and the foremost man was provided with a
boat-hook with which to examine suspected places as
far as was possible. During the remaining portion of
our journey innumerable crevasses were passed, the
greater number of which were first discovered by the
snow-vault giving way under our feet, or by some of us
falling in with the foot or half the body. Commonly,
however, we succeeded in time in getting the other foot
on a more secure foothold, or in catching hold with the
hands of a sledge or some of our comrades' lines, and
so were kept from falling down altogether. This, too,
happened often; yet, thanks to the strength of our
drag-lines, without occasioning any further mischance.
I cannot sufficiently praise the intrepidity which our
sailors showed, or the cheerful and mirthful spirit in

which they took these adventures, new to them, and foreign to their profession.

"During the first day of our wandering on the inland ice-field the air was pretty clear, so that we had a good view, which showed that the streak of open water east and north-east of us had increased in size. The inland ice extended to the south and west without interruption by any ridges of hills, or so-called glacier islands, raising itself evenly and imperceptibly to a plain, the farther side of which we could not see, lying 2,000 to 3,000 feet above the sea, along whose level surface every puff of wind drove along a stream of fine snow-dust, which, from the ease with which it penetrated everywhere, was as troublesome to us as is the fine sand of the desert to the travellers in Sahara. By means of this fine snow-dust steadily driven forward by the wind, the upper part of the glacier, which did not consist of ice, as in Greenland, but of hard packed blinding white snow, was glazed and polished so that we might have thought ourselves to be advancing over an unsurpassably faultless and spotless floor of white marble, or perhaps rather over a white velvet carpet. At the resting-places there was nearly always dug a deep hole in the surface of the glacier for the use of the cook, whereby I had an opportunity of closely examining the way in which the glacier is formed of snow.

"The snow, at a depth of four to six feet, passes into ice, being changed first to a stratum of ice-crystals, partly large and beautiful to the eye of the crystallographer, then to a crystalline mass of ice, and finally to a hard homogeneous glacier ice, in which, however, there could still be observed numerous cavities filled with air, compressed by the pressure of the overlying ice. When the ice-wall becomes, on the melting of the ice, too weak for the pressure of the inclosed air these holes break up with a peculiar crackling sound which in summer is continually to be heard from the pieces of glacier ice floating about in the fjords.

"With the exception of the first day there prevailed during the whole of our wanderings over the inland ice-field (1st to 15th June) either a snow-storm, which in case the wind was high and contrary, hindered our advance and compelled us to pass several days in complete inactivity, closely packed in a thin tent of cotton duck, or so thick an ice-mist that we could only see a few yards before us. As the ice, with the exception of the fissures before mentioned, which in all cases were covered with snow, was at first completely level, this mist did not particularly hinder our journey, the direction of which was determined by the compass. When the ice farther forwards began, however, to be intersected by broad *canals* (which ought not to be confounded with the fissures previously mentioned), which were too broad and deep at most of the places, and bounded by walls too steep to be passable with sledges, this ice-fog became exceedingly troublesome. It was not only a hindrance to us to have to choose the ground least interrupted by *canals*, but it was a special disadvantage that it was impossible to distinguish by the eye whether we had before us a deep impassable channel or only a depression a couple of feet deep. It was therefore necessary at suspected places to lower a man for the purpose of finding out the depth. Often he had to be hoisted up again without having reached the bottom, but it happened sometimes that the bottom was reached at a depth of some few feet, often enough after we, on account of that inconsiderable depression had made a circuit of several hours, which we found out too late to have been altogether unnecessary. Another time it happened that we were so deceived by an ivory gull, which had alighted in our neighbourhood, and in the mist resembled an immense Polar bear, as to make the common preparation for a bear-hunt, by ordering all the men to the tent or behind the sledges, so that the bear might not be frightened beforehand and so escape us.

"The table below exhibits a comparison between the temperature on the inland ice-field and at the sea-shore, and shows that there was a not inconsiderable difference between them.

Comparative Table of Observations of Temperature on the Inland Ice and at Mussel Bay.

	Mean Temperature at Mussel Bay.	Approximate Mean Temp. on the Inland Ice.	Height[1] above the Sea.
June 1	+ 0·71 C.	− 3·2	0 − 98 metres.
,, 2	+ 1·26	− 2·3	98 ,,
,, 3	+ 1·68	− 4·4	98 ,,
,, 4	+ 1·90	− 5·6	98 ,,
,, 5	− 1·58	− 1·2	78 − 307 ,,
,, 6	− 1·45	− 3·5	308 − 454 ,,
,, 7	− 2·99	− 7·5	454 − 495 ,,
,, 8	− 3·09	− 7·1	495 ,,
,, 9	− 1·98	− 7·1	495 − 488 ,,
,, 10	+ 0·45	− 5·9	490 − 407 ,,
,, 11	+ 0·35	− 5·5	407 − 473 ,,
,, 12	+ 0·26	− 4·6	468 − 492 ,,
,, 13	+ 3·83	+ 0·4	477 − 480 ,,
,, 14	+ 1·72	− 4·8	480 − 550 ,,
,, 15	+ 1·40	− 1·6	550 − 553 ,,

[1] Reckoned by comparing the barometrical observations on the inland ice and at Mussel Bay.

"During our journey over the inland ice we several times had a highly peculiar fall of—

"1. Small round snowflakes, sometimes resembling stars, of a woolly appearance.

"2. Grains falling simultaneously, of about the same size as the snowflakes, but formed of a translucent irregular ice-kernel, surrounded by a layer of water, which, however, froze in a few moments after the fall to ice, and in a short time covered our sledge-sail, &c., with a thin and smooth crust, or fastened itself on our hair and clothes as small translucent ice-drops. During one such fall on the 5th June there was seen *simultaneously* a faint halo and a common rainbow, the temperature being 4° to 5° C. under the freezing-point. That a fall of ice mixed with water can take place with so low a temperature is clearly due to the fall being derived from a stratum of cloud formed of over-cooled watery vapour, that is to say, formed in part of small drops of water cooled under the freezing-point, but still fluid. A similar fall is perhaps also very common even in more southerly regions. For instance, such a fall is the cause of the crust of ice which during the late autumn so often fastens on all the tackle and rigging of a ship, and forms the worst obstruction to winter navigation. The thin covering of ice had probably also a similar origin which, when Torell and I, during the expedition of 1861, ascended the hill on Marten's Island, covered all rocks and stones thereabouts with a translucent crust of ice so loosely fastened that it fell down with the least motion.

"In many respects there is a very essential difference between the ice-field over which we now travelled and the inland ice-field in Greenland, which was visited by me in 1870. The reason of this may perhaps be in a great degree the fact that in North East Land we wandered over a kind of *névé region*, that is to say, over a part of the glacier where the surface is occupied by a layer of snow which does not melt away during summer, while in Greenland at the beginning of the month of July the snow upon the surface of the glacier was on the contrary already nearly completely melted. No trace of the glacier lakes, the beautiful and abundant glacier streams, the fine waterfalls and fountains, &c., which occur everywhere on the Greenland inland ice, could be observed here, and the configuration of the surface showed that such forms never occur, or only to a very limited extent. The melting of the snow clearly goes on upon Spitzbergen on too inconsiderable a scale for such phenomena to arise.

"As might have been expected, the crevasses of the Greenland inland ice were much larger than those of North East Land, but, at least at the time of our visit, they were much less dangerous because they were open, not covered with snow. On North East Land almost all the fissures were so much concealed by a thin arch of snow, partly loose, partly hardened, as to be quite indistinguishable. Here, therefore, a man must be prepared every moment for an abyss opening at his feet. Over the Greenland inland ice, Dr. Berggren and I could advance unbound and even without having a rope with us; during our wanderings in North East Land, however, prudence required us to keep all the men bound to the sledges, carefully to examine the ground where the tent was pitched, and to stake off at night with poles stuck into the snow, the area within which the men had leave to go unbound and without special permission.

"The fissures in general run parallel with each other, in straight lines, but they are also sometimes bent, and at some places there occur two different systems of fissures which cross one another. Here the danger is multiplied. If a man glances down from an opening in the snow vault he sees how the fissure is, as it were, lost in a bluish-black darkness. Upward comes the glitter of innumerable loosely-fastened table-shaped ice-crystals, like those that are to be seen on the sides of the blocks of which the hummocks are formed. The surface of the snow was, as has been already mentioned, quite level, generally hard packed by the storms, and completely glazed and polished by the stream of snow which even the gentlest breeze of wind carried forward along the ground. This stream of snow, or more correctly of air mixed with snow, had, however, in the absence of a downfall, and provided the wind was not all the more violent, only a depth of a few feet. It threw fragile bridges of snow over the crevasses, but did not fill them; formed, where there were great precipices, true snow-cascades; and filled up in a few minutes all shallow holes and depressions. Thus, for instance, when we emerged from our tent in the morning all trace that the snow had been trampled down the evening before had generally disappeared, and the sledges were concealed in a large drift. Accordingly, no such cylindrical water-filled holes, one or two feet deep, as were met with everywhere on the Greenland inland ice, were to be met with here, at least at this time of the year, and in consequence it was impossible to observe either the remarkable dust, the origin of which is such an enigma (kryokonite), which I found on the Greenland inland ice, or the microscopic algæ which Dr. Berggren discovered there.

"On the *Greenland inland ice*, a little distance from the coast, there were to be found shallow basin-shaped depressions, whose middle was occupied by one or several small lakes or ponds, without visible outlets, though they received water from innumerable streams which ran down the sides of the hollows. *Here* occurred, as I have already said, no such depressions, but instead, on the 10th June, as we approached Cape Mohn, we came upon an area which was intersected by *canals* which for the most part ran parallel with each other, at some places at a distance of only 300 feet. The depth was up to 40 feet, the breadth 30 to 100. As it was impossible to get our sledges drawn up a bank of some few feet in height without unloading, this part of the glacier would have been completely impassable if, after going for a little along the sides of the glacier *canal*, we had not always fallen in with some place where the *canal* had been almost completely filled with snow, and was therefore passable with sledges. These passable places, however, *always* lay in a capricious zigzag, which compelled us to take circuitous courses many times longer than the direct line. The passage was besides always accompanied with danger and risk because the *canal* was bounded on its sides by deep snow-covered crevasses running in the same direction, sometimes of considerable size. Nor could a man at any time be quite certain that the snow-drift which he passed over was not a fragile arch of snow. Once, for example, such an arch over a *canal*, large enough to swallow us and our sledges for ever, gave way before our feet just at the moment when we were about to use it as a bridge. Dangerous cross fissures also occurred, which also were generally covered with snow above, but towards the wall of the canal itself presented a dark open gap. In

CLEFT IN THE INLAND ICE (CANAL).

order to obtain protection from the wind we often used the bottom of a *canal* as a place to pitch our tent, as the accompanying sketch shows.

"Sometimes, also, there occurred other depressions, bounded in all directions by precipitous sides, of greater depth than the glacier *canals*, but of limited extent; these, perhaps, may most fitly be called by the name given them by the sailors—*docks*, or *glacier docks*.

"The inland ice of North East Land was at the time of our visit too much covered with snow for me to make out with complete certainty the way in which the glacier *canals* originate. That they were not river channels was clear. For they were much deeper than the river channels on the Greenland inland ice, where, however, the melting of the snow must proceed on a much more considerable scale than on Spitzbergen, and they occur in too close proximity at certain places (while at others they are completely absent) for them to be the beds of the channels of the streams, certainly very inconsiderable, which are produced here during the height of summer. There is a strong probability, on the other hand, that they originate from faults in the ice, strongly resembling those that are observed in the solid strata of the earth, and which, there as here, derive their origin from the alternate expansion and contraction of the strata or the ice in consequence of variations of temperature.

"If, for instance, the cracks, which arise in consequence of a slight depression of temperature in a solid mass, come together downwards so as to include a wedge-shaped piece, it naturally sinks a little with every contraction of the solid mass, without being able to raise itself when the mass expands by a new rise of temperature. The friction is too great for this. The expansion must therefore cause an upthrow at some other place, perhaps far from where the sinking took place. With every change of temperature the same phenomenon is repeated, so that it is not surprising if in the end the wedge sinks several score feet. If the cleavages are not quite regular there remain always at those places irregular fissures which give rise to crevasses at the edges of the glacier *canals*, or to the openings filled afterwards with débris or chemical sediment, which are nearly always found in connection with faults in the solid crust of the earth.

"From the point on the inland ice where we turned to the west we could clearly see, when the ice mist cleared up for a few moments, that the ice-field farther south was subjected to more considerable dislocations than were to be observed at the places over which we travelled. For from our turning-point, which was situated at a height of 407 metres, the inland ice sank gently to an ice-plain lying considerably lower, from whose southern side it again rose rapidly in steep terraces, and with the assistance of glasses it was possible to distinguish immense angular ice-blocks, which lay strewn over the ice-plain at the foot of the terrace-formed shelves from which they had tumbled down. It is possible that the height of the ice-plain itself over the sea is very inconsiderable, and that we had before us an arm of the sea opening out on the east coast of North East Land, and covered by a continuous ice-field.

"This was the rugged ice-terrain which compelled us to give up our plan of going from von Otter's Island down to Cape Mohn, and thence along the coast to Cape Torell, then over Hinloopen and the inland ice of West Spitzbergen, past Mount Chydenius' to Mussel Bay. Instead we turned to the west towards Wahlenberg Bay. Here, too, we came to an exceedingly rugged terrain 1,500 to 2,000 feet above the sea, which detained us till the 15th June, when we quite unexpectedly came down to the most easterly part of Wahlenberg

Bay, which extends considerably farther to the east than we supposed.

"In this bay, named after the renowned botanist and glacialist, we found on the 15th June the first plant in flower of the year, a beautiful red saxifrage. The first plant in flower was found in 1861 in Treurenberg Bay on Midsummer eve.

"The ice-field does not terminate towards the bottom of Wahlenberg Bay with any steep slope, but with a gentle declivity interrupted by no precipices or crevasses, over which our sledges made rapid progress. In the proximity of the lower part of the bay some low granite rocks projected out of the mass of ice at a height of 280 metres, and further on were to be seen extensive moraines formed of clay and angular gravel of the same type as those which I observed in 1858 at Axel's Islands in Bell Sound, and in 1864 at the bottom of Stor Fjord. I consider it highly probable that the moraines here, like those on Axel's Islands, have been forced up by the glacier, and that its border at this place is not receding but advancing.

"When we came to Wahlenberg Bay on the 16th June numerous openings were visible in the ice-covering of the fjord, especially near the shore, so that it was only with difficulty that we could come down upon it, and go up again at the opposite shore near the mouth of the fjord, where, on account of the way in which the sea-ice was broken up, we were again compelled to take our course over the glacier that occupies the southern part of the peninsula between Murchison and Wahlenberg Bays. Here, too, the glacier close to Wahlenberg Bay was completely cut to pieces by dangerous gaps,

but farther forward it became quite level and free from
fissures, and terminated northwards and westwards with
an even slope without any cross terraces. A heavy
snowstorm detained us here too, so that it was only at
midnight between the 23rd and 24th June that we
reached Shoal Point. From the high ice ridge which
we crossed during our wandering between Wahlenberg
and Murchison Bays, we could see a small vessel cruising in tolerably ice-free water in the north part of
Hinloopen. We tried in vain, by firing shots, waving
flags, &c., to attract attention, and we therefore, to our
great disappointment, missed the news that this, the first
messenger from home, could have given us.

"With a little boat left at Shoal Point on our outward journey, Palander with three men immediately
crossed over to Mussel Bay, in severe weather and
with a high sea. I was obliged to remain at Shoal
Point with the rest of the men till Palander could send
a sufficiently large boat for us. Before it could arrive,
however, I had got on board a fishing-vessel lying at
anchor near Low Island, which brought me and my men
to Mussel Bay, where the whole expedition was thus
again assembled on the afternoon of the 29th June."

For the members of the expedition that remained at
Mussel Bay the time which followed the departure of
the exploring party was the dreariest of all. The month
of May was come, but winter continued. The temperature of the air occasionally rose to $-5°$ or $-6°$, but was
in general about $-10°C$. The sun had been long
circumpolar, but was seldom visible. A cold thick mist
lay for the most part over Mussel Bay, or the sun
was concealed by heavy, low-lying clouds. The ice lay

undisturbed, and increased instead of diminishing in thickness. No speck of open water was visible. The stock of provisions got very low. Some indispensable articles, as vinegar and lime-juice—two of the most powerful antiscorbutics—began to grow scarce. A great and general lowering of strength took place, especially among the men, and showed that an increase in the rations was highly necessary. But it was to be feared that a still greater reduction than that which had taken place would have to be made. On the 6th May it was found that all on board the *Onkel Adam*, with one exception, were scorbutic, and some so ill that Dr. Envall thought it best to remove them to land. On the *Gladan* the sanitary state was far from satisfactory, and even in the case of several on board the *Polhem* symptoms of scurvy began to show themselves. Daily a number of scurvy patients from the vessels came to land, some on crutches, others supporting themselves with a staff, and others again carried by their comrades. A more sorrowful sight could scarcely be seen. Home-sickness or at least a desire to get away from Mussel Bay, began to seize the greater number, and concern for their absent comrades made the lives of those that remained behind anything but pleasant. The cold, the ice, the want of food, the scurvy, were the common subjects of conversation, but the scurvy was regarded with the greatest apprehension. This dreary time, however, was not without its pleasant moments. These were chiefly the few days when the sky was cloudless, when the sun shone and the temperature neared the freezing-point. Then the imprisoned Swedes sunned themselves, enjoyed the warmth and drank in the fresh air, listened to the pleasant spring twitter of the snow-bunting, and bethought themselves that summer was coming when the air would be warm and the sea open, when many birds might be shot, and the walrus-hunters would bring letters and newspapers from home, and, best of all, when they could leave Mussel Bay, some of them steering their course direct for home, and others to visit unknown regions of Spitzbergen and make great discoveries of various kinds.

Attempts were made to shoot game for the sick, but only a brace of ptarmigan and a few snow-buntings fell to the guns. Seal-hunting was attended with the same want of success, though a considerable number were seen daily, and strenuous efforts were made to get within shot of them, but in vain. This was the more tantalising, as dislike to the preserved, and even to the salt provisions, had become general, and a seal steak was looked forward to as a luxury.

The observations still went on. Soon after Nordenskiöld's departure Wijkander commenced a series of pendulum observations. The tidal observations were also extended. Five minute observations were carried on at least a whole hour twice a day, at ebb and flood.

After the first half of May was past an agreeable change took place in the weather. The sun shone in a cloudless sky and the air was pure as it can be only on Spitzbergen. The birds became more numerous, small pools of water began to appear here and there, and the damp reindeermoss which lay before the house began to reek in the sunshine. A "water sky" was visible.

On the 20th of May, von Krusenstjerna, Parent, and seven men set out for the Norways to deposit there information as to the position occupied by the expedition, &c., but had to return without effecting their purpose, the canvas boat on a wooden skeleton and the sledge they had taken with them requiring alteration.

On the same day another party, consisting of Clase, Stjernberg and one of *Onkel Adam's* crew, started for Verlegen Hook, where they built a cairn and deposited papers.

On the 23rd May a part of Nordenskiold's party returned in good health and highly delighted with their journey. After this the *Polhem* became more lively. The dredgings now went on with new spirit. They were very troublesome on account of the thickness of the ice, which was now from six to seven feet, but were of great importance and interest. The Lapps always took guns with them. One day two of them went up to the Ptarmigan Fell—so the place was commonly called where ptarmigan were first discovered by the Lapps—and succeeded in shooting three ptarmigan and thirteen guellemots, on which some of the most severely-attacked scurvy patients made a good meal.

Some plants of scurvy-grass were found with beautiful green leaves from the former year, but which, having been protected by a covering of snow, remained, it was thought, quite fresh. The day after, *Saxifraga ricularis* was found opening its leaf-buds. At the same time a little black spider was seen busily engaged in spinning its web in a cleft of a rock, but no small creatures that could be caught in the net were yet visible.

On the 29th May open water was reported in the neighbourhood, and the ice off Mussel Bay was soon seen to be broken up to a great extent and in drift. On the

30th the barometer began to fall rapidly, and in the afternoon a fresh south-easterly breeze sprang up which set the ice in motion off Wijde Bay, and before night an extensive surface of water was visible glittering in the sunshine and extending from Verlegen Hook towards Welcome Point.

The 31st May was the first day that the average temperature rose above the freezing-point. At noon the thermometer showed 4° C. In the afternoon, Christian and one of the Lapps who had been out at the edge of the ice returned, bringing with them a number of birds and a young seal. The seal beef was in great demand and much relished.

On the 5th June, von Holten and four men of the *Gladan's* crew started for the Norways in a boat which had, the day before, with sail set, been driven over the ice on its sledge by a stiff south-easterly breeze, the canvas-boat, intended only for narrow openings in the ice, not being used on this occasion.

At length the long-looked-for moment arrived. On the 6th June a sail was visible, and up went the flag at the flag-staff on the house, the *Gladan* and the *Onkel Adam* also showing the blue and yellow. The house is almost deserted. All make for the edge of the ice and arrive in good time, the vessel yet being far off and seeming to move as slowly as if she sailed in tar. At last she reaches the edge of the ice, and before the ice-anchor is fast her deck is crowded with visitors, gathering in compact circles round the crew, who are stormed with questions from all directions. What was learned was, in short, that the vessel, a little sloop, was named the *Solid*, and hailed from Hammerfest; that King Charles XV.

was dead, and another of the royal family, they knew not which; that they had not heard of any vessel being sent to the relief of the expedition; that several fishing-vessels had been seen on their way northwards— two of them at a short distance from Mussel Bay; that the greater number of the walrus-hunters who had been shut in the previous winter had returned to Norway after a very difficult passage, but that many had wintered on Spitzbergen, their fate being as yet unknown. The Swedes tried to purchase some provisions from the master of the *Solid*, but he could only spare a few potatoes, a little salt meat, and some coffee. Immediately after noon the two vessels were seen, and one of them bore down on Mussel Bay, having on board letters and papers for the expedition, and some provisions which the agent Ebeltoft, at Tromsoe, had had the thoughtfulness to send. Her walrus-hunters brought the sorrowful news that Mattilas and his Quane cook, who had stayed behind to look after the four vessels which were shut in by the ice at Grey Hook, were dead. There was no news of the seventeen men who had gone to Cape Thordsen before the opportunity of escape by means of the vessels at Welcome Point had occurred.

On the 9th June von Holten and his men returned, having only gone to Grey Hook, where at the place where Mattilas ended his days they found a document stating that a vessel had gone from Grey Hook to Mussel Bay with provisions "for the Swedes."

Notwithstanding this supply the situation was exceedingly serious. The lowering of strength was great and general, and the scurvy threatening. Every effort was made to obtain fresh food, and a great number of fowl were shot, but they were insufficient for nearly sixty men, and ammunition began to fail. The reduced rations were sufficient to last only at farthest to the end of July, and the Swedes were by no means certain of reaching, by that time, a place where a fresh stock could be obtained.

Such was the state of things when, on the 12th June, a large vessel steamed into the bay. It had been observed far out at sea, and was at first taken for a Swedish gunboat. It turned out to be the *Diana*, belonging to Mr. Leigh Smith, who, along with several young Englishmen, was on board. The Swedes hastened to the edge of the ice and were very hospitably received by Mr. Smith, in whose countenance they saw expressed the greatest satisfaction with the way in which they had contended with the dangers of the Arctic winter—dangers in which he was by no means inexperienced. On being informed of the state of the expedition as to provisions, Mr. Leigh Smith stated that he had a large stock, and offered to give the Swedes all that he could spare—an offer that naturally was most gratefully accepted. Next day he came to visit the settlement of the expedition, inspected the building and the observatories, and received an account of the wintering and of the scientific work that had been carried on. The same day the promised provisions were received; fresh potatoes, preserved vegetables, and soups and preserved meat of various kinds, "all of excellent quality, and much better," says the Swedish account, "than the preserved provisions we brought with us," lime-juice, wine, tobacco, &c. All was handed over as a gift to the expedition. "May we here be permitted," says the author of the Swedish account, "publicly to express the deep gratitude of all of us to Mr. Leigh Smith for the costly and welcome gift, and to assure him that it will be long before the members of the Swedish Polar Expedition of 1872–3 forget the *Diana's* visit to Mussel Bay."[1]

The Swedes could now look forward without apprehension. The weather, too, became exceedingly favourable for the breaking-up of the ice. That which covered Mussel Bay diminished gradually, but perceptibly, day by day. When about the half of the bay was free of ice von Krusenstjerna determined to saw a channel through that which still lay between the ships and open water. The sawing commenced on the 20th June, and was carried on with the greatest eagerness. Release was now at hand. Cold, wet, and snow-blindness mattered little.

Spring had commenced. The temperature was not unfrequently a couple of degrees (centigrade) over the freezing-point. The wind from the south began to be mild. Day by day the covering of snow on the lowland diminished. Snow still sometimes fell, but there were also occasional heavy showers of rain. The lagoons were freed from their ice covering and the mountain streams began to rush down the fell sides. Snow-free places became green with vegetation, and by the 14th June the beautiful *Saxifraga oppositifolia* had decked its branches with young fresh leaves and opened its blossoms, whose red-violet colour showed agreeably against the luxuriant green of its leaves. The whole of the Spitzbergen bird-world had returned. Auks,

---

[1] This timely relief was the saving of a numb r of lives. See Dr. Envall's report in Appendix.

guillemots, and eider-ducks swam in thousands in the sea or sat in large flocks on the ice-floes. Geese, looms, and snipes frequented the lagoons and small fresh water-ponds. By the 13th of June geese had begun to lay eggs. On the 15th two long-tailed ducks were shot—a rare occurrence, as these birds are very seldom met with on Spitzbergen.

The hope of the vessel's speedy release, the increase of the stock of provisions and the consequent increase of the rations, exerted a powerful influence on all the dwellers at Mussel Bay. The scurvy began to disappear, the cripples laid aside their crutches and staves, and gladness and cheerfulness drove away the low spirits and the depression which had overcome almost all of them in the hard and threatening days of May and the beginning of June.

Midsummer day came, and with it Palander and some of his companions. It was a day of rejoicing. The travellers were so changed as to be almost unrecognisable. Their hair and beards were long and matted, their faces darkened with smoke, soot, and sun-burning. But they were welcome. It was indeed a disappointment that the Polar excursion had to be broken off at Phipps' Island, but the Swedes consoled themselves with the thought that all that was possible had been done, that the journey over the inland ice of North East Land, rich in dangers and difficulties as it had been, was unique, and that the observations of various kinds made in the course of it would form an important contribution to our knowledge of the nature of the Arctic lands.

On the 29th Nordenskiöld returned with most of his

party, and the same day between four and five o'clock p.m. the channel was finished, and an hour later the *Gladan* and the *Onkel Adam* anchored with hurrahs in open water. At eight the same evening the *Onkel Adam* started on her home voyage, followed by the *Gladan* early the following morning. The *Polhem* was to remain some time on the coast of Spitzbergen, and left Mussel Bay on the 1st July, leaving Wijkander together with some men to complete his magnetical and meteorological observations, and to put everything in order for the return home. The *Polhem* shaped her course for Grey Hook, where the mournful duty of burying Mattilas and his companion was performed. A fishing-vessel lay at Grey Hook commanded by Fritz Mack from Tromsoe. With him the agent Ebeltoft had sent provisions, letters, and newspapers. Captain Mack was employed in saving what he could of the cargo of the vessels that had been run ashore, and had made some preparations for the burial which took place the following day. Mattilas and his companion had turned two boats together with the keels outward, and covered them with sails and skins. This formed their dwelling, in which they had a little stove.

"Mattilas," says Kjellman, "indeed deserves the name of an Arctic veteran. For two-and-forty summers he had ploughed with his little skiff the cold billows of the Icy Sea, defying all dangers and sufferings. A period of success and good fortune had made him a prosperous man, one of the richest of the Norwegian walrus-hunters, but he had afterwards met with many misfortunes. His vessel was wrecked and sport was bad. In this way his property was diminished, and what now remained was a small share in the vessel of which he was master, and in the proceeds of the summer's hunting and fishing. It was the hope of being able to save his small property which induced him to remain on Spitzbergen, and not to accompany his comrades and countrymen on the return home. There perhaps conduced—so we have at least been informed—

MATTILAS' WINTER QUARTERS AT GREY HOOK.

to this unfortunate determination a long cherished desire to pass a winter in the land whose coasts he had visited so many summers, and where he had successfully escaped so many dangers and survived so many adventures.

"It was with reverence that we stood beside the grave of these men. They had struggled manfully and

T

suffered much. Affecting were the simple words they had written in their journal. They tell us how both of them had at first striven, with the elements in uproar, unceasingly and energetically to save the vessels and their cargo, which formed the whole of their property, and the loss of which would bring them to poverty. They failed in the endeavour. The vessels had to be abandoned, and were thrown up on the beach, where wind and waves worked with success at their destruction. Now the struggle for life begins. Disease unites itself with the elements. They exert themselves to keep at a distance the murderous scurvy, but in vain. When no other work is left, one of the unfortunate men draws round their wretched dwelling a sledge which they had made, loaded with stones. Disease weakens them more and more. Drawing the sledge becomes too difficult. In a short time they can no longer walk. One is completely helpless; the other is compelled to crawl out for a little fuel, with which he warms up their quarters once a-day. But this, too, becomes too troublesome; indeed they are not able even to write down, as was their wont during the last period, a prayer to God in the journal. The death-struggle begins—and relief comes."

Mack had also the sad news to give us that the seventeen men who had gone the previous autumn to Ice Fjord to pass the winter at Cape Thordsen had perished of scurvy. He had been among those who first landed at their winter quarters. Fifteen of them were found dead, and two were supposed to have been buried by their comrades, but, the ground being covered with snow, their graves were not visible. The men had unfortunately not understood how to avail themselves of the resources at their command. There were provisions in superabundance. Even to the last they had lived principally on salt-beef and pork, using little of the preserved and dried vegetables and of the potatoes, of which a large quantity still remained. None who ever wintered here before have had so great resources as they—the necessaries of life of all kinds in superabundance, an excellent house, sufficient fuel, tools of all possible kinds, a carpenter's bench, &c. It was plain that they had given themselves up to inactivity, and believed that the abundance of provisions which they had would keep them free from scurvy. Instead of using two rooms for sleeping in, they had all seventeen packed themselves into one. They seemed to have thought of nothing else but eating and sleeping. The last entry in a journal which they kept was dated 19th April. At that date there were supposed to have been three men still alive.

Leaving Grey Hook late on the morning of the 2nd, the *Polhem* sailed northward towards the Seven Islands, and at 9 o'clock p.m. on the 3rd was in 80° 42′ N. lat., and close to the ice, which stretched in a curve east and south of the Seven Islands and then towards the N.W. or W.N.W. There was now abundance of provisions. The walrus-hunters provided the expedition with abundance of eggs, fowl, and reindeer flesh, and were generally unwilling to accept anything in return. After dredging for some time near Muffin Island, the *Polhem* steered eastward, and passing Mussel Bay, entered Treurenberg Bay, falling in there with Mr. Leigh Smith and his vessels, the steamer *Diana* and the schooner *Samson*.

After visiting Hinloopen Strait, where unbroken ice was found near Dim Point, the *Polhem* returned to winter quarters, where the observations were now concluded, the instruments packed, and everything in order for starting. The *Polhem*, however, first conveyed Nordenskiöld to Ice Fjord, and then sailed northward, passing west of Charles' Foreland, dredging every other hour. On nearing the Norways the ice was found to have drawn southwards, which occasioned some fear of

NORTH POINT OF PRINCE CHARLES' FORELAND.

being again shut in; but after tedious delays from fogs, the *Polhem* anchored in Mussel Bay on the 17th, and, after taking on board everything that could be removed, finally left the bay on the 18th July. At Grey Hook it was only with the greatest difficulty that the *Polhem* could force her way between the land and an ice-field about two English miles long. After visiting Smeerenberg Bay and Kobbe Bay, and taking on board Nordenskiöld and his companions at Cape Staratschin, the *Polhem* entered Ice Fjord and anchored in Skans Bay on the 21st, and lay there eight days, during which time the botanical and zoological collections were greatly increased, the former by *Tofieldia borealis*, a phanerogamous plant, new to the flora of Spitzbergen. On the 28th the *Polhem* left Ice Fjord, and was compelled to anchor in Green Harbour, where six Norwegians, who had formed part of the crew of a Norwegian vessel that had been nipped by the ice on the east coast of Spitzbergen about a month before, were taken on board. The *Polhem* proceeded the following day to Recherche Bay in Bell Sound, finding there the remainder of the crew of the vessel just mentioned, and on the 1st August weighed anchor on her return voyage, arriving at Tromsoe on the 6th, and, after some delay at Bergen, on the 29th August at Gothenburg, where the expedition was broken up.

WINTER DRESS AND HUNTING WEAPONS.

CHAPTER VII.

VOYAGE TO THE YENISSEJ IN 1875 AND ASCENT OF THE RIVER.

SPITZBERGEN having now been pretty thoroughly explored, Professor Nordenskiöld turned his attention to that part of the Polar basin which lies to the north of Siberia. The Sea of Kara, lying to the east of Novaya Zemlya, had long been considered impenetrable, an "ice cellar," as von Baer called it; but this had been shown to be a mistake by the voyages of Johannesen, Carlsen, and other Norwegian walrus-hunters who had circumnavigated Novaya Zemlya, sailed into the Kara Sea, and even pushed their way beyond White Island, at the mouth of the Gulf of Obi. The natural history of this sea and its shores was still completely unknown, and this Professor Nordenskiöld proposed to investigate. It also formed part of his plan to penetrate to the mouth of Yenissej—thus solving a commercial problem of the first importance—and to ascend that river.

The *Proeven*, a little Norwegian sloop of only about 70 tons burden, 55 Norwegian feet long, and manned by 12 Norwegian walrus-hunters, all of whom had previously taken part in voyages in the Arctic seas, had been fitted out at Tromsoe for the expedition of 1875, at the cost of Mr. Oscar Dickson, of Gothenburg, who defrayed all the expenses of the expedition. Professor Nordenskiöld was accompanied by two botanists, Dr. F. R. Kjellman and Dr. A. N. Lundström; and two zoologists, Dr. H. Théel and Dr. A. Stuxberg.

"After the *Proeven* had been towed out from Tromsoe free of cost by a little steamer of the same name," says Professor Nordenskiöld, "we were compelled by contrary winds to lie at anchor for five days in the sound between Carlsoe and Renoe. At length, on the 14th, we were able to weigh anchor and get to sea through Fugloe Sound. The course was then shaped past North Cape, which was passed on the 17th, for the southern part of Novaya Zemlya.

"During spring and the early part of summer the west coast of this double island is surrounded a little from the land by a compact ice-girdle, impassable at most places, which disappears later in the season, and in which, according to the experience of the walrus-hunters, two sounds are early formed, which are only covered with thinly-scattered navigable drift-ice, and through which the ice-free belt of water along the coast is placed in communication with the open sea westwards. One of these open channels is commonly to be found off Matotschkin Schar, and is caused by the strong currents which prevail in that sound; the other is near the latitude of Severo Gusinnoi Mys (North Goose Cape.) The latter was chosen by me for the *Proeven*, and passed without any special difficulty on the 22nd June. Seven days after leaving Carlsoe the *Proeven* thus anchored for the first time on the coast of Novaya Zemlya, in a little ill-protected bay immediately north of North Goose Cape.

"During the voyage sounding and dredging had been carried on when the weather permitted; the surface of the sea was examined for animal and diatom life, and the temperature was observed at different depths. The reward of our labours was often abundant, showing that in this sea rich harvests in natural history are to be reaped. We also made repeated trials at different depths of an instrument for taking specimens of the bottom, constructed for the expedition by Dr. Wiberg, which proved very suitable for its purpose, and easily managed.

"After remaining two days at our first anchorage, we sailed northwards, anchoring here and there along the coast where opportunity offered: from the 25th to the 28th June in Little Karmakul Bay; from the 2nd to the 6th July in Besimmenaja Bay; from the 7th to the 13th at different places in Matotschkin Schar. To this point the sea along the coast was nearly free of ice; but north of this sound, which connects the Kara Sea with the sea between Novaya Zemlya and Spitzbergen, the ice extended to the land, so that, at least for the present, it was impossible to sail along the coast northwards, as was the original plan of the expedition. Instead, the ice in the western part of Matotschkin Schar being broken up, it appeared at first as if we would soon be able to sail through this sound eastwards. After having penetrated into it for this purpose as far as Tschirakina, I went thence in a boat towards the interior to examine the state of the ice. Lundström at the same time ascended a neighbouring mountain, from which he had an extensive view, and at the top of which he placed a minimum thermometer. It now appeared that the eastern part of the sound was still covered with an unbroken sheet of ice, which was thought strong enough to defy for a considerable time longer the influence of the Polar summer. I therefore did not consider it advisable to await the possibility of a passage here; and as any advance in a northerly direction was also for the time out of the question, I determined to try my fortune at one of the two sounds, the Kara and Jugor Straits, which on both sides of the Great Waygats Island lead into the Kara Sea.

"We left Matoschkin Schar on the 13th of July, and arrived after having anchored on the 14th at Skodde Bay, where we made a rich collection of Jurassic fossils; on the 16th at North Goose Cape, on the 18th at South Goose Cape, on the 21st at Kostin Schar, and during storm at the Kara Gate on the 25th. The strait was completely blocked with ice, and the wind was too violent for us to endeavour to anchor here. I sailed on therefore, and was fortunate enough to find, during the furious north-east storm, which raged in these regions from the 26th to the 30th July, protection for the vessel on the south-west coast of Waygats Island, where we anchored on the 26th of July off Cape Grebeni. The storm was now so violent, that although we lay at anchor quite close to and in lee of the land, we could not until the 30th July put out a boat for the purpose of landing on the island. Here we made a rich collection of Upper Silurian fossils, resembling fossils from Gotland, and therefore of special interest to Swedish geologists. Here we met for the first time with Samoyedes, who, when they saw the vessel, drove down to the beach in peculiar high sledges intended for use in summer as well as in winter, and drawn by three or four reindeer. They let us know immediately that they wished to come on board, whither they accompanied us, and where they soon after were very hospitably entertained.

"During our stay on the west coast of Novaya Zemlya we were of course continually engaged in examining the geology, fauna and flora, &c., of the regions visited by us, and the great number of places along the coast where we landed made it possible for the scientific staff of the expedition to bring together a large mass of materials relating to their natural history. On the other hand, in consequence of the high north-east winds which had been blowing lately, and which, as we had reason to suppose, had driven the ice down to the southern part of the Kara Sea, there appeared to be little probability of our being able to push forward in an easterly direction this year. Notwithstanding this, I determined as soon as possible to make an attempt in this direction, and therefore again weighed anchor on the 31st July, in order to sail into Jugor Sound. I was, however, compelled by a calm to anchor the *Proeven* right in the mouth of it, in the neighbourhood of a place where a large number of Russians and Samoyedes from Pustosersk are accustomed to live during summer for fishing and hunting, and which on this account is called 'the Samoyede town.' The day after I rowed in a boat farther into the sound, having ordered the vessel to follow as soon as possible. On the very next day, the 2nd of August, the *Proeven* weighed anchor, and with the help of a gentle breeze and a favouring current sailed over to my encampment on the other shore. I immediately went on board, and, carried forward almost entirely by a strong south-westerly current, we advanced towards the Kara Sea. The sound was passed successfully, and on our entering the Kara Sea we found it completely free of ice. The course was shaped towards the middle part of the peninsula which separates the Kara Sea from the Gulf of Obi, and which is called by the Samoyedes Yalmal. The wind was exceedingly light, so that we only went forward slowly, a circumstance which certainly tried our patience severely but had this good result, that while navigating these waters, visited for the first time by a scientific expedition, we could daily undertake dredgings, hydrographic work, &c. The dredgings yielded an unexpectedly rich and various harvest of marine animals, among which I may here specify some colossal *Isopoda*, peculiar *Cumacea*, masses of *Amphipoda* and *Copepoda*, a large and beautiful *Alecto*, uncommonly large *Ophiurida*, finely marked *Asterida*, innumerable *Mollusca*, &c. The peculiar circumstance occurs here that the water at the surface of the sea, which, in consequence of the great rivers debouching in these regions, is nearly free of salt, forms a deadly poison for the animals which live in the salt water at the bottom. Most of the animals brought up from the bottom therefore die in a few moments if placed in water from the surface of the sea.

"Here also, when opportunity offered, there were made, as on the west coast of Novaya Zemlya, determinations of the temperature of the sea, not only at the surface, but also at different depths under it, with thermometers by Negretti and Zambra and Casella. These researches yielded a specially interesting result, and may be considered as settling a number of questions much disputed of late years regarding the marine currents in these regions, the direction of which, in the absence of other data, it was sought to determine by the indications of the surface-temperature of the water. By numerous observations along the west coast of Novaya Zemlya from Matotschkin Schar to Jugor Sound, thence past Cape Greleni to $75\frac{1}{2}°$ N. Lat., and $80°$ E. Long. and on to the mouth of Yenissej, I have obtained indisputable proofs that the temperature of the surface water of this sea is exceedingly variable and dependent on the temperature of the air, on the neighbourhood of ice, on the flowing of warm fresh water from Obi and Yenissej, but that the temperature of the water at a depth of only ten fathoms is nearly quite constant, between $-1°$ and $+2°$ C. There are thus no deep marine currents here. An exception to this was observed in Matotschkin Schar itself, where the water near the bottom at a depth of seven to fifteen fathoms was about $+5°$ C. Possibly the southern part of an arm of the Gulf Stream here strikes Novaya Zemlya, and even passes through Matotschkin into the Kara Sea. A large number of specimens of deep water have been taken with Professor Ekman's apparatus, which is excellently constructed for the purpose, and I am convinced that at the bottom the salinity is also constant.

" On the 8th of August we landed for a few hours on the north-west side of Yalmal to take an astronomical observation. Traces of men, some of them barefooted, and of Samoyede sledges, were visible on the beach. Close to the beach was found a sacrificial altar, consisting of about fifty skulls of the Polar bear placed in a heap, bones of walrus, reindeer, &c. In the middle of the heap of bones there stood erect two images roughly-hewn of driftwood roots newly besmeared on the eyes and mouth with blood, and two hooked sticks, from which hung bones of the reindeer and bear. Close by was a fireplace and a heap of reindeer bones, the latter clearly the remains of a sacrificial meal. After some hours' stay at this place I sailed farther north until unnavigable masses of large level ice-fields in 75° 35′ N. Lat. and 79° 30′ E. Long. prevented farther progress in that direction. Afterwards I followed the edge of the ice towards the east, and finally shaped the course for the north side of the mouth of the Yenissej, where the Swedish flag was hoisted and the anchor let go on the afternoon of the 15th. We had now attained a goal which great seafaring nations had for centuries striven in vain to reach.

"Already during our approach to the harbour a bear was seen *pasturing* along with some reindeer close to the shore. The bear, an aged male, however, soon after slowly departed from the reins and finally laid himself to sleep on the beach quite near to our anchorage. Before the anchor fell Dr. Théel went out in a boat to try to kill him. Having reached the shore, Théel approached the reclining bear, which in a few moments became aware of his approach and immediately rushed forward, as was supposed, to attack him. He was, however, soon hit right in the face by a Remington ball discharged at a distance of twenty paces, which, however, did not penetrate the skull but cut a deep and long channel right between the eyes along the face. The bear now sought to take to flight, but fell immediately after to a new shot which pierced the lung and the upper part of the heart. I consider this a good omen that the many thousand years' reign of the bear in these regions will speedily come to an end, and that numerous vessels will here carry on communication between Europe and the colossal river territory of the Irtisch, the Obi, and the Yenissej."

The place where Nordenskiöld anchored on his arrival at the mouth of the Yenissej he named Dickson Harbour. It affords very good anchorage. Here preparations were made for an ascent of the Yenissej by Nordenskiöld, Lundström, and Stuxberg, and three walrushunters, in a Nordland boat which had been specially built for the purpose in Norway. The *Proeven* returned to Tromsoe under the charge of Dr. Kjellman, who endeavoured to sail round the northern extremity of Novaya Zemlya but found the ice impassable to the north of Cape Middendorff. He therefore sailed southwards to Matotschkin Schar, which he reached on the 4th of September after various delays by calms. The passage through the sound was protracted by storms, calms, headwinds, and the unfavourable current. At length on the 10th of September the western entrance was reached, and on the following day the *Proeven* left Matotschkin and steered her course homewards, meeting with fearful gales on the way, and reaching Hammerfest on the 26th of September and Tromsoe on the 3rd of October.

The *Anna*, as the boat was named, in which Nordenskiöld and his companions were to ascend the Yenissej, left Dickson Harbour on the 19th of August, sunk almost to the gunwale with the provisions and equipment with which she was laden, and not in a condition to stand any heavy swell. "I must, therefore," writes Nordenskiöld, "consider it a very fortunate circumstance that during our sailing up the mouth of the Yenissej we had always a sufficiently strong wind from the land.

"The course was taken along the shore inside the numerous low, bare, rocky islands which, to the north, bound the Gulf of Yenissej, and are marked in the Russian maps with the long name Severo-Vostotschnoi-Ostrov (North-East Islands). The Sound between those islands appears to be sufficiently deep even for large vessels, though perhaps rendered foul by rocks. With a favourable wind and smooth water we sailed on, without any long rest, in forty-two hours to Cape Schnitanskoi, where we arrived on the night before the 21st, wet through, and worn out by want of sleep. On the way we landed only at two places, the first a point near Jevremov Kamen, the last rocky promontory on the eastern bank of the Yenissej, for a distance of nearly 600 miles. .

"Jevremov Kamen itself is merely a peculiarly formed dolerite rock fifty to sixty feet in height. In the neighbourhood of the place where we landed three Polar bears were seen peacefully pasturing among the rocks, not allowing themselves to be disturbed by the log-fire which we made in their proximity, or, as we hoped, to be attracted towards us by curiosity. We had no time for hunting, and after drinking the coffee we had made ready at our immense log-fire, we sailed on. At the beach we collected still, but for the last time during our journey up the Yenissej, true marine animals; *Appendicularia, Clio*, large *Beroidæ*, various *Medusæ*, &c. A land excursion here yielded a *Harpalus*, two species of *Staphylinidæ*, two species of spiders, a number of *Acaridæ* and *Poduridæ*, a *Lumbricus*, and, as at the vessel's anchorage, vegetation

had a character differing greatly from that of Novaya
Zemlya. Large bushes, even dwarf birch, were still
completely wanting, and the ground was not covered by
any carpet of grass.

"The second place where we landed was Krestovskoj,
a now deserted *simovie* (place inhabited both summer
and winter), but which, to judge by the number of the
houses and the style in which they were fitted up, must
at one time have had its prosperous period. Three
houses with flat turf-covered roofs still remained, each by
itself forming a veritable labyrinth of rooms—living-
rooms, bake-rooms, bath-rooms, store-room for blubber,
with long troughs for blubber hollowed out of immense
tree-stems, cisterns for blubber, with remains of white fish,
&c., all in one. All household articles were taken away,
and literally there was not to be found a nail in the
wall, a sign that the inhabitants had not died out but
removed. We learned at Dudinka that this had taken
place some years ago, and was caused by the difficulty of
procuring meal in that remote situation, otherwise well
adapted for fishing. Now, since the traffic on the
Yenissej has increased, a new settlement is said to be
under consideration. The vegetation in the neighbourhood of the place was extraordinarily luxuriant, the
grass and other plants rendering walking difficult, an
effect, without doubt, of the quantity of animal manurial
substances which had been collected during the former
fishing period of the history of the place.

"Two miles and a half from Krestovskoj a sandbank
shoots out far into the river, on which account we were
compelled to keep farther from the side and sail between
some small islands occurring here, between which the

river had a depth of five to six fathoms. Taken overhead, the north-eastern side of the Gulf of Yenissej does not appear to be rendered particularly foul by shallows. The depth a little from the shore reaches six to eight fathoms, sometimes even twelve and upwards.

"The surface temperature of the water was, on our arrival at the mouth of the Yenissej, 7°·8 C., but sank during the storm of the following days to 1°·5 C. At Jevremov Kamen it was 2°·5 C., but rose afterwards, in the neighbourhood of Krestovskoj, to 11°, a temperature which it retained afterwards during nearly the whole of our boat journey. The water was of a brown colour, but was often, near the banks, coloured by muddy streams.

"A little south of Jevremov Kamen the eastern bank of the Yenissej is occupied by sand-banks having a height of about twenty or thirty feet, and a steep slope towards the river. From the river bank stretches the *tundra*, an endless, slightly undulating plain, full of low marshes and small shallow pools, and overgrown with a scanty vegetation, the flowering season of which was now almost concluded. We found instead, at our first night-quarters (Cape Schaitanskoi), masses of ripe cloudberries, the taste of which, in itself delightful, was on this occasion heightened by the circumstance that they were, for us, the first of the summer's fruit. The red and bog whortleberry are also found here, if in small quantity. Cape Schaitanskoi was the most northerly point on the Yenissej, where we found dwarf birch, and at the same place also Dr. Stuxberg found a species of *Physa* which had been found previously by Middendorff as far north as 73° 30'.

"After having rested at Cape Schaitanskoi we sailed

on with a favourable breeze to Sopotschnaja Korga, where the high wind, and a sand-bank lying off it,—th extent of which we could not make out during the dusk of the night,—compelled us to lie to earlier than we otherwise intended.

"Sopotschnaja Korga (the toe of the boot) forms a low promontory projecting far into the Yenissej, which, as numerous remains of buildings show, was formerly inhabited, but now stands deserted. Fishermen and hunters, however, still settle here occasionally, to judge by the numerous fox-traps still in good order which are found everywhere along the banks. We found one of these traps set. The place is the least agreeable I have seen on the banks of the Yenissej. For a great part the promontory is occupied by masses of driftwood, immense stems with branches and roots broken off, piled over each other in an endless chaos, among which it was only with difficulty and care that any progress could be made. The logs that lie nearest the sea are quite fresh. Others, lying farther from the strand, and cast up thither decades or centuries ago, are in all possible intermediate stages between fresh and decayed wood. Between the logs are often deep holes full of black, stinking water. Similar masses of driftwood, though perhaps not so extensive, are found nearly everywhere farther down nearer the mouth of the river, but higher up there occur only scattered pieces of driftwood, and at some places even these are almost completely wanting. The promontory was strewn besides with a large number of other fresh-water pools, more or less grown up with water mosses and swarming with a small species of fish (*Gasterosteus oculeatus*), *Branchiopoda* and other sweetwater *Crustacea*, and yielding to the botanist various *Carices* not observed farther north; and water plants (*Carex chordorrhiza, Hippuris vulgaris, Juncus castaneus* &c.). Higher up on the drier places the ground was sparingly covered with *Empetrum nigrum* and *Andromeda tetragona*, and on the steep slopes inwards from the promontory there was a luxuriant vegetation of grass and herbaceous plants a couple of feet high. On the other hand, the place was exceedingly poor in mammalia and birds, as well as in insects, and even the holes and paths of the lemming, with which the coast land of Novaya Zemlya is crossed in all directions, are found here only to a limited extent.

"Hard gales and a high sea compelled us to remain at this place nearly two days. But on the afternoon of the 23rd August we were at last able to sail on. The course was shaped for Goltschika, which for the present is the most northerly inhabited *simovie* on the eastern bank of the Yenissej, but as we approached the bank where we supposed the *simovie* was situated, under the darkness of night we came with a pretty high sea on an extensive shoal, over which we did not consider it advisable to row forward in the darkness. I therefore shaped the course with a fresh breeze towards Sverevo on the west bank of the Yenissej, where a *simovie* is still inhabited, but on arriving at the western shore, we could not distinguish in the darkness any dwelling-houses here either. We sailed therefore again across the river, in order, when the day dawned, to find a more convenient landing place farther up. While we thus sailed along the strand, looking for houses, in a very high and rough sea, we found ourselves suddenly among furious breakers.

After several unsuccessful attempts to row the boat back against wind and sea, during which it nearly foundered, we had no other resource left us than again to hoist the sail and shape the course right through the dangerous surf. Fortune favoured us. Just at the shallowest place the boat was lifted over a high breaker and we found ourselves again in deep water. We soon saw a little hut on the bank which we supposed to be inhabited, without however being able, as I wished, to lie to there on account of the heavy swell. We sailed on therefore, till at last we succeeded in finding a suitable landing-place in the neighbourhood of Mesenkin, a little river falling into the Yenissej on the right bank.

"During the excursions which were undertaken in all directions immediately after our landing at Mesenkin, we observed two persons, who, attended by a large number of dogs, searched for cloudberries on the bogs. At first they appeared to wish to avoid us, but in the end approached and informed us that they were Russians in the employment of a merchant from Yenisseisk, who had a hunting station at Goltschika. After a little conversation I proposed to the younger of them, a Cossack, Feodor, who appeared to be well acquainted with the region, to accompany us to Dudinka as guide, a proposal which he, after a little negotiation, agreed to on condition of receiving fifty silver roubles and obtaining the permission of his master who was settled at Goltschika, thirty versts farther north. In order to procure this permission he started immediately, promising to return the following evening.

"The delay was of course employed by us to the best of our ability in examining the natural history of the place, in taking solar observations, &c. It appeared thereby that our resting-place was situated only about twenty-five miles to the south of our former landing-place. The low river valley of the Mesenkin is however far better protected from the winds of the Polar sea than the low promontory at Sopotschnaja, and the influence of this is plainly apparent in the vegetation being much richer.

"What immediately strikes one on landing is the dark green thickets about four feet high, which appear to consist of alder (*Alnus fructicosa*). Between the alder bushes and protected by them our botanists found a number of well-grown herbaceous plants : *Sanguisorba, Galium, Delphinium, Hedysarum, Neratrum,* &c. The *Salix* bushes too were taller here than before, the turf finer, and the slopes of the sandy hills in the interior of the country were now adorned with a number of new forms : *Alyssum, Dianthus, Oxytropis, Saxifraga, Thymus,* &c.

"As I have stated previously, we found at the places we visited on Jalmal neither small stones nor sub-fossil shells ; in the fine sand east of the mouth of the Yenissej the sand is coarser, and contains both sub-fossil shells and stones large and small. The sub-fossil shells, according to information obtained at Dudinka, occur in some places in such masses as to form true shell-banks. At the places which we visited, the shells however were not found in proper beds, but only scattered in the sand. Immediately at the first glance it appeared that the shells collected by us here belonged in preponderating numbers to species with which in the living state we had before become acquainted in our dredgings in the Kara and Obi-Yenissej Sea.

"A collection of specimens of the stones which occur in the sandy layers of the *tundra* was always to be found along the river bank, where they lay still, after the lighter particles of the sand-bank had been washed away, and we could here obtain many important contributions to a knowledge of the way in which the *tundra* is formed, and the nature of the rocks which yielded the material of the masses of sand here collected. No erratic blocks, comparable in size with those found in Sweden, occur here, a circumstance which I look upon as a proof that the sand-beds of the *tundra*, at least in these regions, are not of glacial origin. I ought however to observe that on some small blocks of stone there are to be seen scratches and grooves quite like those found on moraine blocks. But in this case these grooves must have been formed either by the slipping of the earthy layers or through the agency of river ice.[1]

"In the north part of the *tundra* I could never distinguish among the stones washed out from the sand any blocks of granite or gneiss. For the most part they consisted of different kinds of basalt with numerous cavities containing calcspar and zeolites. Besides, there occurred especially at Cape Schaitanskoi a not inconsiderable number of blocks of marl and sandstone containing fossils, partly of marine origin, partly containing tree-stems more or less carbonised or petrified. Pieces of brown and common coal were also found here in considerable numbers.

[1] Nordenskiöld is of opinion that Siberia, during the European Glacial period, had about the same climate as at the present time, and that the former great extension of the glaciers in Europe depended only on local circumstances.

"On the 26th August, early in the morning, our future pilot arrived, accompanied by five other Russians settled in that quarter. Naturally the guests were entertained immediately in our tent as best we could, and the conversation was lively. They informed me that at Goltschika there lived a 'prikaschik' together with three labourers for hunting and fishing, and at Sverevo only an old man and his son; the old *simovies* farther to the north were now abandoned. Natives (Samoyedes, Dolganes, Yakuts,) on the other hand often come down from the *tundra* to the strand, but their numbers had of late years been considerably diminished by a severe small-pox epidemic, which raged especially among the Samoyedes.

"After talking for a while with our guests, who were friendly and exceedingly interested in our journey, we went on, the weather being calm and exceedingly fine, to Cape Gostinoi, where we halted at noon. While sailing along we observed, for the first and last time during our voyage up the Yenissej, a remainder of the winter's enormous snow-covering in a deep cleft cut out of the *tundra* near the strand. At our resting-place was found the first granite block among those washed from the sandy stratum of the *tundra*. The bush vegetation on the banks of a river debouching here was specially luxuriant, and among the bushes was found a raspberry leaf (*Rubus Arcticus*) and plants of *Angelica*, *Cortusa*, &c., four feet high.

"Having rested for a while at this place we sailed on, and after various deviations in the darkness and fog of the night landed on a low promontory near the mouth of the Jakovieva river. A close mist compelled us to pass the night here, although the place was nearly bare of vegetation, and driftwood was found in so limited quantity that the wood required for cooking could scarcely be found. To judge by the quantity of remnants of fish found on the strand, an abundant catch of sturgeon appeared to have been lately made by the inhabitants of the neighbouring *simovie* Jakovieva, which was said to be inhabited by two Russians and two Samoyedes.

"We halted next at a specially attractive fishing station on a small sound among the Briochovski Islands, the most northerly in the island labyrinth which occupies the channel of the Yenissej between $69\frac{1}{3}°$ and $70\frac{1}{3}°$ N.L. The fishing was, however, finished for the season, and the place accordingly deserted. But two small houses and several huts, all in good condition, stood on the bank, and, together with a number of large boats and wooden vessels intended for salting fish, gave evidence of the employment that had been carried on here.

"On the 28th of August we rowed on between a number of islands, covered with a luxuriant vegetation, and commonly ending towards the river with a bold escarpment from which large masses of peat had tumbled down here and there. At such places it could be seen that the island originally formed a sand-bank thrown up by the river, which in course of time was covered first with masses of driftwood, and afterwards with a luxuriant vegetation which gradually gave rise to a thick layer of peat not yet completely decayed, of which the part of the island lying above the surface of the water is for the most part formed.

"Towards evening we lay to at the Nikandrovska Islands near a fishing-station still occupied, the inhabitants of which were engaged in drawing a net as best they could. For a silver rouble I bought here nine fat muksuns and tschirs, weighing together 25 lbs., yet the price demanded of a foreigner was naturally twice as great as the common one. The Yenissej is famous for its richness in large eatable varieties of fish, and I was much disappointed that my own and my comrades' complete unacquaintance with the art of fish culture prevented us from bringing to Sweden, as I wished, impregnated roe at least of the giant-like Njelma of the Yenissej, probably the largest and finest of its family. During our voyage up the Yenissej I caused specimens of all the varieties of fish I could obtain to be carefully placed in a barrel filled with spirits.

"Like most of the dwellers on the lower course of the Yenissej the inhabitants of the Nikandrovska fishing-station kept a number of dogs, which appeared to be of the same race as those used in Greenland for draught. The dogs are used in summer to tow boats along the banks up the river, and during winter for general traffic. The dog, however, is considered, for reasons already stated in the introduction to Middendorff's *Siberische Reise*, quite useless for long journeys over uninhabited tracts if no opportunity of fishing or hunting occurs in the course of the journey. In such cases reindeer are always employed.

"Early next day we sailed, or more correctly, rowed on, the weather being calm and very fine. We halted at noon at a now deserted *simovie* on the southern part of the island Sopotschnoj. Thence we proceeded first to Cape Maksuninskoj, where we visited a Samoyede family who had here set up their skin tent in order to collect the necessary winter stock of fish, then to Tolstoj Nos, a still inhabited, well built *simovie*, where the people received us in a very friendly manner and with great interest and surprise informed themselves regarding our journey. About two miles north of the settlement there was a beautiful chapel-like monument over one of the many who during the last century had been exiled hither for political reasons. He had, according to the inscription, first been hanged in the neighbourhood of the place where he lies buried, by the order of the authorities, but was afterwards declared innocent. This memorial was, singularly enough, the first indication which met us of a class of society which is so important in Siberia in all social respects.

" We were informed here that the last steamer had passed the place five days previously, and was now lying some leagues farther up the river. I was therefore compelled to go on without delay, and after twenty-six hours sailing and rowing, interrupted only by short visits to land, at length on the 31st of August, at nine o'clock in the morning, we came up with the steamer, *Alexander*, which we had been eagerly pursuing for the previous two days. Of this steamer the merchant, Ivan Michailovitsch Jarmenieff, was master, and we were received by him with all conceivable good will, as indeed we were during the whole of our Siberian journey continually by all classes, high and low alike.

" We were yet far to the north of the Arctic circle, and as many perhaps imagine that the little known region we were now travelling through, the Siberian *tundra*, is a desert wilderness covered either by ice and snow, or by an exceedingly scanty moss vegetation, it perhaps may not be unsuitable to state that this is by no means the case. On the contrary, we saw snow, as has been mentioned before, during our journey up the Yenissej only at one place, in a deep valley cleft some fathoms in breadth, and the vegetation, especially on the islands which are overflowed during the spring floods, is distinguished by a luxuriance to which I have seldom seen anything comparable.

"Already had the fertility of the soil and the immeasurable extent and richness in grass of the pastures drawn forth from one of our walrus-hunters, a middle-aged man, who is owner of a little patch of ground among the fells in northern Norway, a cry of envy at the splendid land our Lord had given 'the Russian,' and of astonishment that no creature pastured, no scythe mowed, the grass. Daily and hourly we heard the same cry repeated, and in even louder tones, when some weeks after we came to the grand old forests between Yenisseisk and Turuchansk, or to the nearly uninhabited plains on the other side of Krasnojarsk covered with deep *tcherno-sem* (black earth); equal without doubt in fertility to the best parts of Scania, and in extent surpassing the whole Scandinavian peninsula. This judgment formed on the spot by a genuine though an illiterate agriculturist is not without interest in forming an idea of the future importance of Siberia.

"In the summer of 1875 three different Russian expeditions traversed Siberia with the view of inquiring into the possibility of an improved river communication within the country. These expeditions have, according to unofficial communications made to me in Yenisseisk, arrived at the result that it is possible for an aggregate sum of 700,000 roubles to render the Angara, a tributary of the Yenissej, the navigation of which is rendered difficult by cataracts, or more correctly rapids, navigable to the Baikal Lake and to connect the Obi with the Yenissej and the Yenissej with the Lena. How great an extent of territory the river communication thus provided would embrace may be seen from the fact that according to the calculation of the academician von Baer the Obi-Irtisch and the Yenissej drain an area larger than the combined river territories of the Danube, the Don, the Dneiper, the Dneister, the Nile, the Po, the Ebro, the Rhone, and all the rivers which flow into the Black Sea, the Sea of Marmora and the Mediterranean. Part of the territory in question indeed lies to the north of the Arctic circle, but here too there are to be found the most extensive and the finest forests on the globe ; south of the forest region proper, level, stone-free plains covered with the most fertile soil stretch away for hundreds of leagues which only wait for the plough of the cultivator to yield the most abundant harvests, and farther south the Yenissej and its tributaries flow through regions where the grape ripens in the open air. As I write this, I have before me a bunch of splendid Siberian grapes.

"The steamer *Alexander* was neither a passenger nor a cargo boat, but formed a movable warehouse propelled by steam, the master of which was not a seaman, but a friendly merchant, who clearly did not take much concern with navigation, but more occupied himself with goods and trade, and was also seldom styled by the crew captain (*kapitan*), but generally master (*hosain.*) The equipment of the vessel itself corresponded to this state of things. The whole fore-cabin was fitted up as a

store, with shelves for the goods along the walls, a
common desk, &c. The after-saloon was employed as
a counting-house, writing and bedroom for the master,
and was besides also over-filled with various kinds of
goods, spirit casks, &c. There was thus no place for
passengers, and at the first instant, after we lay alongside the steamer, with the Swedish flag hoisted, the
'master's' reception of us was by no means specially
friendly. At the beginning he was even not disposed to
take us along. But I had scarcely succeeded in explain-
ing to him, by the help of our pilot, Feodor, and a
Swedish-Russian dictionary, what sort of people we
were, and what journey we had made, before all was
completely altered, and from that moment we had in
our 'master' the most agreeable and accommodating
host we could desire. In order to make ready a place
for us on board, a cabin before the wheel-house was
emptied and arranged as a room for passengers. Its
extent, however, was by no means great. At night
we could, for instance, with difficulty lie across it on a
bed made of boards, which took up nearly the whole
cabin. Our walrus-hunters at first found room where
they could in the engine-room, and they were well
taken care of by the engineer. Afterwards we obtained
another somewhat more roomy cabin, and our walrus-
hunters got that which we had at first.

"The nautical command on board was in the hands of
two mates of stately and original appearance, clad in
long caftans, who each during his watch sat on a chair
at the wheel, generally smoking a cigar, and, with the
most careless appearance in the world, exchanging
jokes with people descending the stream. A man stood

continually in the fore trying the depth with a long pole. For in order to avoid the strong current of the deep main stream, the course was never taken on the deepest part of the river, but as near the bank as possible, often so near that it was almost possible to jump ashore, and that our Nordland boat, which was towed by the side of the steamer, was occasionally drawn over land. The *Alexander* had besides in tow at first one, afterwards two, *lodje*, almost of the same size as the steamer itself, intended for the reception of the fish bought during the voyage, which generally were salted and prepared on board. The whole way between Yenisseisk and the sea there was not a single jetty, and therefore both steamer and *lodje* had in tow a number of large and small lighters and boats intended for communication with the land.

"Siberia, and especially the river territory of the Yenissej, possesses rich coal-seams, which probably extend under a great part of the Siberian plain, but as yet are not worked, and are little valued. Like all the other steamers on the Siberian rivers, the *Alexander* on that account was fired not with coal, but with wood, of which, if I recollect right, 180 measures went to the voyage up the river. The steamer could, however, carry but a small part of this quantity at one time, for which reason frequent halts became necessary, not only for trade, but also for taking fuel on board. The weak engine too, notwithstanding the safety-valves were, when necessary, overloaded with lead weights, was often enough unable to take all it had in tow up the stream, which at some places was very rapid, and in the endeavour to find water without a current near the banks we often went too near land, and ran aground, notwithstanding the steady 'laduo' cry of the poling pilot posted in the fore. Our advance was therefore so slow, that it was only after the expiry of a whole month that we reached the steamer's destination, the town of Yenisseisk, situated about 1,000 English miles from Dudino.

"Under such circumstances most steamboat passengers would have been impatient and annoyed. To us, on the contrary, the delay was welcome, inasmuch as we thereby had an opportunity of extending our examination of the flora and fauna of the Yenissej river valley beyond the 60th degree of latitude. It is easy to see that part of these researches will be of practical interest; for instance, those made by Dr. Lundström on the flora of northern Yenissej.

"Our knowledge of it is founded hitherto on observations made by scientific men (Middendorff, Schmidt, &c.) who have visited these regions for other purposes, and had opportunities of directing their attention to the flora only in passing. Dr. Lundström's main object, on the contrary, was exclusively botanical (he had previously made himself familiar with the Arctic plant world by tours in Lapland, and in his native district Norrland), and as during the journey up the river he came from the northerly regions, poor in species, to the southerly, rich in species, it was easier for him than for one who travelled in an opposite direction to fix the limits of a large number of species of general occurrence, common to Siberia and Scandinavia. Abundant botanical and climatological material has been collected in this way, and when it is worked out it is easy to see what new light a comparison of the distribution of plants towards the north within our own cultivated land and the desert regions of Siberia will spread over the question of the possibility of cultivating the latter country. I may here be permitted to state that, contrary to what might have been supposed beforehand, the northern limit of many plants in Siberia *is situated farther to the north than in Sweden.* To a certain extent this may indeed depend on the transport of seeds with the great river from more southerly regions; but it shows too that the severe winter of Siberia has by no means any specially unfavourable influence on the summer's growth.

"Immediately after we came on board, the steamer weighed anchor and steamed to the church village Dudino, situated some leagues farther up the river at the mouth of the tributary Dudinka. The village consists of some few houses, inhabited by an influential merchant, Sotnikoff, two priests, a magistrate (*smotritel*), a couple of exiles, some labourers, and natives. Sotnikoff carries on an extensive and profitable trade with the natives in the whole of the surrounding district, bartering grain, cloth, tea, sugar, iron goods, powder, lead, brandy, &c., for furs, fish, and mammoth tusks, &c., which are afterwards sent by steamer first up the Yenissej and afterwards, by different means of communication, to China, Moscow, Petersburg, &c. He is much praised by the academician Schmidt in his well-known account of his expedition for the exhumation of a mammoth found near the mouth of the Yenissej, for the liberal and energetic way in which he furthered the work of the expedition. Even to us the simple, straightforward merchant was particularly accommodating and hospitable, and I must add that we met with the same reception from all the other notabilities of the place. The friendly clergyman, who was much interested in our journey, even performed a short thanksgiving service on board the steamer for the successful issue of our expedition, without accepting any special honorarium.

"As in the *simovies* situated farther to the north, the houses in all the villages on the Yenissej are built of logs in much the same style as the dwellings of the well-to-do peasants in Russia, pretty close together, with the richly-carved gable to the street or lane. Except for the cockroaches that crawled round everywhere, the interiors of the houses were very clean, and the walls were adorned with numerous, if not very artistic, photographs and engravings, for the most part of the imperial family, remarkable Russian notabilities, often in generals' uniform, scenes from Russian history, &c. Richly decorated sacred pictures were always found placed in a corner, and before these there hung some small oil-lamps or little wax-lights, which were lighted on festivals. Sometimes the floor, at least in the principal room, was covered with furs. The bedstead was generally formed of a couch near the roof, so large that it occupied a third part or a half of the room, and so high from the floor that a man could go upright under it. Food was cooked in large ovens which were fired for that purpose daily, and at the same time warmed the houses. Fresh bread was to be had every day, and even for the household of the poor a large brass tea-urn was a necessary household article. One was certain to meet with a hearty and friendly reception wherever he stepped over the threshold, and if he stayed a short time he generally had to drink a glass of tea with his hosts, whatever time of day it might happen to be. The dress was everywhere somewhat similar to the common Russian dress; for the well-to-do, for instance, wide velvet trousers stuck into the boots, a shirt grandly embroidered with silver in the breast and a wide caftan often trimmed with fur; for the poor, provided they were not too ragged, the same cut, but inferior, dirty, and torn materials. In winter, however, we were informed that for going out of doors the Samoyede pesk was common to high and low, Russian and native, settled and nomad.

"At present there are only very few in these regions who have been exiled thither for political reasons, but there are many exiled criminals, and among them also some few Finns and even a Swede, or at least one who, according to his own statement in broken Swedish, had formerly served in the King's Guard at Stockholm. Security of person and property was in all cases complete, and it was remarkable that there appeared to be no proper distinction of caste between the Russian-Siberian natives and those who had been exiled to these regions for breaches of the law. Little interest appeared to be taken in finding out what crimes had caused the exile. On making inquiry on this point I commonly got the sufficiently elastic reply, 'for bad behaviour.'

"I have already stated that mammoth tusks here form an important article of commerce. They appear also to occur in great numbers on the *tundra*, though the badness of the communications often renders their removal impossible. Though this is the proper mammoth region, it is believed that large pieces of the skeleton are very uncommon, especially such as still have the flesh, hide, and hair upon them. It was for instance on the peninsula between the Obi and the Yenissej that the famous Trofimoff mammoth *find* was made, and in the neighbourhood of the same place was found the mammoth which gave occasion to Schmidt's expedition. It is besides probable that the nomad native here has the same indisposition to inform the Tchinownik (official) of a large mammoth *find* as the Swedish peasant had in former times, and still has in certain districts, to give information of the discovery of a supposed vein of ore.

"On the 4th September, the weather being splendid, the *Alexander* again weighed anchor and steamed southwards.

"The landscape now began by degrees completely to alter its character. On most maps indeed the limit of trees is drawn at that considerable bend which the Yenissej makes immediately west or north-west of Dudino, and here for the first time are found numerous pines, seldom more than twenty feet high. They covered the heights with a scattered and by no means specially striking vegetation which completely lacked the luxuriant character which marked the willow and alder thickets farther to the north. Some few leagues to the south of Dudino, however, the pine-forest was already magnificent, although the place is north of the Arctic circle. It is here that the forest proper commences, the most extensive forest in the world, stretching with few interruptions across the whole of Siberia, in one direction from Ural to the Sea of Ochotsk, in the other south of the 58th or 59th degree of latitude and north of the Arctic circle; indeed at several places, for instance at the rivers Chatanga and Lena, beyond it or to the neighbourhood of 72° N. Lat., that is, to the mouths of the Chatanga and Lena, more than sixty miles to the north of the North Cape.

"During our boat and steamer journey up the Yenissej we had hitherto only landed either on the eastern bank of the river, which was everywhere high, or on some of the numerous islands which at certain places occur in the river where it widens almost to a lake. On the 7th September we had an opportunity of landing on the western bank of the river which, like the western bank of most of the rivers running from south to north, consists of ground almost on a level with the water, and of low-lying tracts overflowed in spring. This meadow land was now covered partly with an extraordinarily luxuriant carpet of grass, of course untouched by the scythe, partly by an exceedingly peculiar bush vegetation of equal height, among which we found a great number of herbaceous plants known in Sweden, here from six to eight feet high. Close thickets of a beautiful straight-stemmed willow often alternated with even turf of a lively green, and one small stream of water fell into the Yenissej in such a way that the whole had the appearance of a very beautiful park carefully kept and watered. On the eastern bank again the ancient forest proper commenced at the river bank. Here nature had a quite different character—grand and gloomy. The forest consisted mainly of pines already, from a point north of the Polar circle, often of the most colossal dimensions—but in such cases many times grey and half withered by age. Between these the ground was so covered with fallen branching stems, some of them fresh, others half rotten or wholly changed into mould, held together only by the bark, that one could only force a way with difficulty, and with the danger of breaking his legs, in the thicket of logs. Besides, the fallen stems were everywhere covered, many times even concealed, by an uncommonly luxuriant moss vegetation, while lichens occurred only very sparingly, in consequence of which the pines wanted the shaggy covering common in Sweden, and the bark on the birches which were visible here and there among the pines had an uncommon blinding whiteness. When one goes into this unvaried forest a little way from the river he ought to see that he has a correct knowledge of the points of the compass—a mistake here might carry him in a direction where for a distance of a hundred, perhaps two hundred leagues, there is no chance of meeting with an inhabited place. In speaking of the vegetation of those regions it may be mentioned that in the north forest region along the river bank there is great abundance of wild currants, both red and white, exceedingly well-tasted and of dimensions exceeding even the largest varieties of cultivated fruit I have had the opportunity of seeing.

"Ever since we left Jevremov Kamen, near the mouth of the Yenissej, we had seen no solid rock, but on the 8th we saw, on the eastern bank, rocks *in situ*. Here, as at a number of the other places where we landed, we made a rich collection of land Mollusca. By these collections, which have been handed over to be worked out by our skilful molluscologist Dr. C. A. Westerlund, at Ronneby, the known Mollusc-fauna of northern Siberia will be considerably increased, and many erroneous views concerning the geographical distribution of this interesting animal group rectified. The same holds good of various other land or fresh-water vertebrates, of which considerable collections were made, which have been handed over to specialists to be worked out.

"After halting at about ten different *simovies*, or fishing-places, for a longer or shorter time, we came, on the 12th September, to a *simovie*—Silivanskoj, exclusively inhabited by Skoptzi. The Russian orthodox Church is, as is well-known, tolerant towards foreigners of other religions—Lutherans, Catholics, Jews, Mahommedans, Buddhists, Schumans, &c., but, on the other hand, persecutes, quite in the same way as was formerly done in the Protestant world, sectaries within its own pale with temporal punishments on earth, and with threatenings of eternal suffering in another world. Especially in past times have a large number of sectaries been sent to Siberia; and here, accordingly, are sometimes to be found thriving settlements inhabited exclusively by a certain sect. Such is the Skopt settlement at Silivanskoj, where, however, it may be remarked that the nature of the religious delusion in this case brings upon them the severity of the law or the administration. For on the ground of a text in the gospel of Matthew, interpreted in a surprising way, all Skoptzi subject themselves to a self-mutilation, in consequence of which the sect can only exist by new proselytes; and remarkably enough these fanatics, in spite of all persecution, or perhaps just on account of it, still, in fact, find followers. A number of the Skoptzi are natives of Ingermanland, and so I could, without difficulty, converse with them. They informed me that they had, 'for righteousness' sake,' been torn from their homes, imprisoned, flogged, and sent to Siberia. Here they had, by industry and perseverance, succeeded in attaining a certain degree of prosperity, were hospitable and friendly, and bore their hard fate with resignation, assured that, in another life, they would have a rich compensation for all their sacrifices, sufferings, and misfortunes here below. They did not themselves kill any warm-blooded animal, 'for it was a sin to kill what the Lord had created;' but this did not prevent them from killing and eating fish, nor from selling to us—who in any case were lost beings—for eighteen roubles a fine fat ox, on condition that our own people should slaughter it. Their dislike to animal food had, besides, the good result of inducing them to cultivate the soil. Round the huts, therefore, were to be found patches of land with potatoes, turnips, and cabbages, although the settlement was situated in the latitude of Avasaxa, that is to say under the Arctic circle.

"Later in the day we came to the Troit monastery, in former times renowned and rich, but now inhabited by a single monk, the prior himself. He was an aged and venerable man, and received us in a hospitable and friendly manner. The guest-house was adorned with many paintings of Siberian bishops. There was a portrait of a Russian czar in powdered hair and scanty military uniform, with blue grand-cross riband. It was a likeness of Czar Paul, but, by some mistake, the Skoptzi had got it in their heads that the picture represented their holy prophet, Czar Peter III., whose history the Skoptzi had completely altered in accordance with their idea of the world. An educated man, who belonged to this sect, and was on this account banished to North Yenissej, informed me in all seriousness, that Czar Peter III. was not murdered, but was knouted, and sent to Siberia, all on account of his holiness; and it happens as a result of all this that the portrait of Czar Paul in the Troit monastery has become a sacred picture to which prayer is offered.

"I have already referred to the rich abundance which the Yenissej yields of uncommonly fine varieties of fish, and stated that we made as complete a collection of them as possible during our river journey. The slow voyage of the steamer in search of fish was besides utilised by me in collecting statements regarding the names, selling price to the steamer, and size of the most important varieties of fish. These are to be found in the following table:—

	Common Weight.	Greatest Weight.	Price.
Njelma — Species of Coregonus.	13 lb.	50 lb.	80 kop. per pood.
Tschir	6 ,,	25 ,,	10 ,, each.
Omul	1½ ,,	3 ,,	2 ,, ,,
Muksun	4 ,,	12 ,,	9 ,, ,,
Salmon (Taimen) . . .	16 ,,	80 ,,	
Sterlet	3 ,,	30 ,,	150 kop. per pood.
Sturgeon	16 ,,	280 ,,	
Silj (young of Coregonus)	—	—	40 ,, ,,

"The trade is carried on so that the goods which are to be bought are valued in money, but payment is made in goods after the merchant's valuation, on which account the true price is perhaps considerably lower than that here given.

"After the numerous crew of the *Alexander* and the *lodje* had with great devoutness attended divine service in the church of the monastery and in a neighbouring chapel, where the holy founder's dust is preserved, after we had seen various remarkable things belonging to the monastery, among them an exceedingly well preserved Slavonic Bible from the sixteenth century, and after I had paid a visit, along with the captain, to an old cripple, who in his youth had made a pilgrimage to Jerusalem, we steamed on. As was usual, we went ahead only slowly in consequence of the strong current and the frequent delays, which of course were taken advantage of by us for making excursions, talking with the natives, &c. These consisted partly of Russian settlers, partly of natives, 'Asiatics,' who, some on their own account, others in the service of Russians, had settled here for the summer to fish in the rivers. In such cases they lived in tents of quite the same form as the Lapp *Kota*. The Samoyede tent is commonly covered with reindeer skins, the Ostiak tent with birch bark. There is always to be found in the neighbourhood of the tent a large number of dogs, which are employed in winter for general purposes, and in summer for tracking boats against the current, a means of propulsion on water which highly surprised our walrus-hunters. For this purpose a sufficient number of dogs are harnessed to a long line, one end of which is

fastened to the stem of the boat. The dogs then go
forward on the level strand, where veritable dog-paths
are formed in this way, and the boat, which is not deep
in the water, is kept afloat at a sufficient distance from
the bank, and is managed by a person sitting in the
stern. The boats are often hollowed out of a single
tree-stem, and may be nevertheless, thanks to the
dimensions of the wood in those regions, of very
beautiful form and very large. The dogs have a strong
resemblance to the Eskimo dogs in Greenland, which are
also employed as draught animals. The fact perhaps
may be regarded as a proof that the same climatic
relations and similar ways of employing a species of
animal produce similar races. We are informed that
at the present time most of the natives who come in
contact with the Russians profess Christianity. That
many heathenish customs still survive is shown for
instance by the following incident. At a *simovie*,
where we landed for several hours on the 16th September,
we found as usual a burying-place in the wood near the
houses. The bodies were placed in large coffins above
ground, with a cross nearly always erected beside them.
At one of the graves a sacred picture was affixed to the
cross, which must be regarded as a further proof that a
Christian reposed in the coffin. *Notwithstanding this,
some clothes which had belonged to the deceased were
found hanging on a bush at the grave, together with a
bundle containing food, principally dried fish.* At the
graves of the well-to-do natives we learn that the
survivor even places some rouble notes beside the food,
that the departed may not be altogether devoid of ready
money on his entrance into the other world. But that

grand clothes are not looked upon as any special recommendation by St. Peter is evidenced by the exceedingly dirty, ragged, and mended condition of the garments hung up at the grave.

"Hitherto during our voyage up the river from Dudino we had had very fine, often warm, autumn weather. The first frost south of Saostrovskoj occurred on the night before the 20th September, and from that day the temperature of the nights was generally under the freezing-point. The days, however, were still warm and fine. The fall of rain was slight.

"On the 20th we anchored at the mouth of one of the largest tributaries which the Yenissej receives from the east, namely the Podkammenaja Tunguska. Immediately below a welcome opportunity offered of making soundings right across the river which was here somewhat over a kilometre in breadth. A short distance from the western bank the lead gave four fathoms, the depth then diminished to two and a half fathoms, but afterwards increased to seven fathoms. At many other places soundings were made which appear to confirm the statement of the pilots, that the depth of the river up to Yenisseisk is sufficient even for vessels of considerable draught. In order to establish this with full certainty, however, and to ascertain the most suitable course for navigation, there are wanted far more comprehensive hydrographical surveys than those which we had the opportunity of making in passing.

"As I have already stated, luxuriant patches of potatoes and cabbage were met with at the Skopt colony north of the Arctic circle, and the farther south we came the more did such patches increase in number and size.

There is no proper cultivation of grain at present until
we come to Sykobatka, situated in the sixtieth degree
of latitude, but without doubt in the future, *when the
woods and mosses are diminished*, a profitable agriculture may be carried on much farther to the north.
Already from this point, where cultivation is now carried
on to the southern boundary of Siberia, or more correctly
to the steppe lands of Central Asia, we have at most
places more than six hundred miles, and if we consider
that a belt of land of this breadth, for the most part
covered with splendid, easily cultivable soil, stretches
right across the whole of Asia from Ural to the Pacific,
we may form an idea of the extensive field of conquest
for the plough to be found in these regions, and the future
which, some time, ought to open for them.

"Immediately south of Sykobatka we passed the
church village of Nasimovskoj and a now deserted gold
washing 'residence' situated right opposite to it, called
after the first conqueror of Siberia, Jermakova. It originated from the discovery of sand-beds rich in gold in
a pretty extensive territory situated on an eastern tributary of the Yenissej, which before the discovery of Cali-
fornia was said for a short time to be the richest gold
country in the world. Here, within a limited period
many colossal fortunes were made, and the stories of the
hundreds of poods which were washed one year or another, and the fast, reckless life led by those to whom
the great prizes of the gold-washing lottery fell, still form
a favourite topic of conversation in the region. Many
of the once rich gold-washers have been ruined in the
struggle to win more, and others who succeeded in
retaining their gold 'pood,'—that is the mint unit gold-

washers prefer to use in conversation—have removed to
Paris, Petersburg, Moscow, Omsk, Krasnojarsk, &c. All
the 'residences,' therefore, are now deserted, and on the
eastern bank of the river form a row of half-decayed
wooden edifices surrounded with young trees, after which,
soon enough, only the tradition of the former period
of prosperity will be left standing. In one respect,
however, these gold-washers have exerted a powerful influence on the future of the country. For it is by them
that the first pioneers have been scattered in the wilderness, the first seeds sown of the cultivation of the region.

"At many places along the river there is to be seen
besides another peculiar memorial, dating chiefly from
the time when workmen by thousands were yearly assembled at the gold-washing places—colossal flat-bottomed
boxes formed of logs, here called 'barks,' which lie drawn
up on the banks in a state more or less decayed. They
have been employed for the transport along the river of
the necessaries of life from southern Siberia—and one
may get an idea of the quiet flow of the Siberian rivers
so suitable for water communication, from goods having
been carried in this way as far as to the most northerly
simovies on the Yenissej along the main river from regions lying south of Minusinsk, near the Chinese frontier,
and along its tributary the Angara from the Baikal Lake—
indeed from beyond it, for even the river Selenga, which
falls into it from the south, is navigable for a good part
of its course. In order to render the river navigable
from Yenisseisk there are required, however, as I have
already stated, some operations, inconsiderable in comparison with the importance of the object, for clearing the
channel. 'Barks' of medium size, built in Minusinsk

for the transport of grain, cost 300 roubles, load 130 tons, and are managed during their passage down the river by fifteen men. After reaching their destination they are sold, if a buyer can be found, for a few roubles. Notwithstanding their awkward form they are very suitable for the river traffic in question—and they would be still more so if twenty or thirty such craft were formed into a train and towed by a small tug like those employed in the archipelago of Stockholm. In this way the number of the crew on each 'bark' might be diminished one-third—and the cost of transport, already low, be further reduced.

"Since the 20th September night frosts had often occurred, which naturally diminished the collections made during excursions from the halting-places. We were therefore more impatient than before to reach our nearest destination. The rapid current and the frequent halts, however, still delayed our journey, so that the anchor could not be let go at the town, Yenisseisk, until the 31st September. Here we stayed several days for the purpose of getting news from Europe, inspecting some fine collections in natural history made in the neighbourhood by an exile, Herr M. Marks, settling our affairs, &c., in connection with which I ought to mention Herr Balangin, the owner of the *Alexander*, who declined to receive any fare for our long voyage in his steamer, so that I, instead, handed over to him and the excellent captain, Herr Jarmenieff, as a memorial of it, the Nordland boat in which we had begun our river journey and which had afterwards been brought along in tow.

"Our home journey was afterwards continued over land by Krasnojarsk, Tomsk, Omsk, Tjumen, Ekaterineburg, Tagilsk, Perm, Kasan, Nischni-Novgorod, Moscow, Petersburg, and Helsingfors to Abo, and thence by steamer to Stockholm."

For this voyage, from Norway to the mouth of the Yenissej, whereby a sea route to Siberia was inaugurated, Nordenskiöld received in January, 1876, the thanks of the Russian Government.

CHAPTER VIII.

SECOND VOYAGE TO THE YENISSEJ IN 1876.

THE success of Nordenskiöld's expedition to the Yenissej in 1875 was complete, but there were some who urged that it was dependent on an unusually favourable state of the ice. Nordenskiöld endeavoured to meet this objection by a reference to the voyages of the Norwegian walrus-hunters, of the brothers Palliser in 1869 and of Wiggins in 1874 in the Kara Sea. As it was the case however that the Yenissej had only been reached by a single vessel, and as besides it was desirable to carry on the scientific researches which had been commenced both in the Kara Sea and in the valley of the Yenissej, it was resolved to send out in 1876 two expeditions, one by sea and the other by land, the latter to descend the Yenissej and meet the former near the mouth of the river. Nordenskiöld gave the charge of the land expedition to Dr. Hjalmar Théel, who was accompanied by two botanists, Rector M. Brenner of Helsingfors and Docent H. W. Arnell of Upsala, and by two zoologists, Dr. J. Sahlberg of Helsingfors and Candidate F. Trybom of Upsala.

For the sea voyage the *Ymer*, a strong cargo steamer, built of oak, of 40 horse-power and 400 tons burden, was chartered. In order practically to open this new commercial route, some goods were taken on board, chiefly samples of Swedish manufacture, suitable for North Siberia. The expenses of the expeditions were defrayed by Mr. Oscar Dickson of Gothenburg, and Mr. Alexander Sibiriakoff, a wealthy Siberian.

Nordenskiöld was accompanied in the *Ymer* by Docent F. Kjellman and Dr. A. Stuxberg, both members of the expeditions of 1875, and the former of that of 1872-3.

The *Ymer* left Tromsoe on the 25th July going within the archipelago past Hammerfest to Masoe, a commercial settlement situated some few leagues to the south-west of North Cape. Besides the merchants and some half-score of fisher families, there is here a church, an hospital chaplain, and a medical man, and the place thus forms the farthest outpost of European civilisation towards the north. Here Dr. Kjellman was landed, in order that during the voyage of the *Ymer* to Yenissej he might commence an examination of the marine algæ of north-eastern Norway, which had become highly desirable on account of the similar work which the same observer previously carried out in 1872-3 on Spitzbergen and in 1875 on the coast of Novaya Zemlya.

The *Ymer* remained here only as long as was necessary to land Dr. Kjellman, his travelling effects and scientific equipment, and then steamed on through Mageroe Sound towards the east. The course was shaped for Pervoussmotrennaja Gora, a mountain two to three thousand feet high, situated on the west coast of Novaya Zemlya in 73° N.L., visible far out at sea. By the hunters from the plains of Northern Russia it was considered for some centuries back, and perhaps is still

Y

considered, the forepost of the world's highest mountain-chain, and it obtained its distinctive name, "the first seen mountain," more than half a century ago, from the famous Russian Polar traveller, Admiral Count Lütke.

"With a favourable wind, a calm and completely ice-free sea," writes Nordenskiöld, "we sighted this mountain three days after passing Nordkyn. Immediately after, however, we were detained some hours by a thick fog, which on the 30th dispersed so much that we could enter Matotschkin, the long, narrow, but deep sound which intersects Novaya Zemlya from east to west, immediately to the north of the seventy-third degree of latitude. Near the western mouth, directly opposite the river Tschirakina, two Russian vessels lay at anchor on our arrival. We halted a few moments in order—as is usual at such meetings in the Polar sea—to have a talk about the state of the ice, hunting, &c. The Russian hunters informed us that they were engaged in the capture of white fish, reindeer, and salmon, of which the last occurs at the mouths of the rivers of Novaya Zemlya in extraordinary abundance, and has occasionally been the object of a profitable fishery. Hitherto, however, their success had been inconsiderable. For they had taken only a few salmon, of which they gave us two in token of welcome—a gift which was of course immediately returned. As we had not succeeded during the former year's expedition in obtaining from Novaya Zemlya any full-grown specimens of this noble fish so variable in its types, the gift was specially welcome to the zoologist, and it fell accordingly to his spirit-cisterns and not to the kitchen.

"We soon steamed on to the eastern part of the sound,

where we anchored in Bjeluscha Bay, which is situated on the north side and is well protected from winds. We remained here nearly a day getting the coal out of the hold into the bunkers, the naturalists of the expedition employing the time as usual in dredging, geological excursions, &c.

"The anchor was weighed on the afternoon of the 31st July. Two hours thereafter the *Ymer* left Matotschkin and steamed into the Kara Sea. We had up to this time met with only a few pieces of ice which were driven hither and thither by the current in the eastern part of the sound, but in the offing the Kara Sea was free of ice as far as the eye could reach. It appeared as if we could still reckon on open water. The course was therefore shaped right eastward. Within a short time, however, we saw in this direction the usual sign of ice— a white streak of light in the stratum of air nearest the horizon—and some hours afterwards we fell in with loose pieces of ice, which increased in number until the whole sea at length was so covered with closely-packed drift-ice that it was no longer advisable to force our way farther in that direction. I now endeavoured to go round the mass of ice in a southerly direction, but here, too, the *Ymer* soon met with unnavigable ice. It was therefore necessary to turn and wait at some convenient place near the eastern mouth of Matotschkin for a more favourable state of the ice.

"In order to be in as favourable a position as possible for observing the position of the ice, I anchored on the inner side of the promontory which projects from the southern shore of the sound, about half way between its mouth and Gubin Bay. There is to be seen here a ruined Russian hut, and the place is marked on the map as Rossmyslov's winter station 1768-69.

"The sea is here rich in varying animal types, the land bleak and poor. The mountains for the most part consist of black clay-slates, probably pre-Silurian, and grey dolomite beds, in which I searched for fossils without success. The slates, on the other hand, were full of quartz veins with numerous drusy cavities whose glittering crystalline contents gave occasion to the statement of the unfortunate Tschirakin, that he had found here a block of stone set full of the most beautiful and valuable precious stones—an account for which after his death he was bitterly reproached by his chief Rossmyslov, who sought in vain for the supposed treasure.

"In one respect this part of Novaya Zemlya is of great geological interest. For here are to be seen no fewer than seven distinctly-marked beaches, situated at different heights above each other and showing that the land here has risen during the latest geological period at least 500 feet. With the exception of Greenland, where during the latest centuries a considerable sinking of the land has taken place, a similar raising of the land has been observed in most other Arctic regions, and this elevation has without doubt played a very important part in the great geological changes which have occurred on the surface of the globe since the close of the Tertiary period. For us Swedes the phenomenon is of special interest, because attention was first drawn to it in our country more than a century ago, and it then gave occasion to a violent controversy well known in the history of science.

"On the 5th August at 4 A.M. we again weighed

anchor to steam into the Kara Sea. As there had been no strong westerly or south-westerly winds during the days preceding our departure, there was still no prospect of finding open water right eastward. A broad ice-free belt of water had in the meantime been formed along the east coast. I determined to make use of this in order to endeavour to find a way farther south over the sea, which this year was thought to be fuller of ice than usual. Most of the ice-fields were, however, already quite wasted away, and it was clear that they would be entirely melted during the remaining part of the summer.

"Favoured by splendid calm weather the *Ymer* steamed rapidly forward along the coast, so that on the 6th August the latitude of the Kara Gate was reached. A new attempt was made to sail right across the sea; but this time too our advance was soon hindered, partly by ice, partly by a thick mist which rendered navigation among the ice-fields exceedingly difficult. I was often compelled to let the *Ymer* lie still in the fog several hours on end, and these delays afforded excellent opportunities for carrying on the zoological and hydrographical work. When the fog lightened a little, we steamed on, following the edge of the ice as far as possible. This soon drew to the east, and if the weather had been clear we would probably have been able to reach the opposite shore the following day. Now four days were required for this, so that we first sighted Cape Bjeluscha on the west side of Yalmal on the 10th August.

"The sea along the coast was covered with ice-fields very much wasted, which at first were so scattered that they did not hinder our progress in any noteworthy degree. At many places, however, more compact bands of ice extended from the coast, and the navigation was still rendered difficult by a fog more or less dense, which made it impossible to distinguish the extent and distribution of the floes from the vessel. In the attempt to force a passage through such a belt of only a few hundred fathoms' breadth, the *Ymer*, at noon of the 10th, was beset among some pieces of thick old ice which lay among the thin rotten year's ice. After being beset about twenty-four hours, we again got free, not on the north, but the south side of the ice-belt, however, which therefore still formed an obstacle to our progress. A mist, besides, made it impossible to judge of the extent of the belt from the ship, and thus to sail round it, which would not, probably, otherwise have been attended with any difficulty or great loss of time.

" At noon of the 12th the ice-belt lying before us had at last broken up—so much that we could steam on. The sea became more and more ice-free, so that we could continue our course without any deviations caused by ice, round White Island, past the Gulf of Obi, to the mouth of the Yenissej.

" We sighted land here on the 15th, thus exactly a year from the time when the rocks at Dickson Harbour were first seen from the *Proeven*. It was some hours earlier than the dead reckoning promised which at first was ascribed to the influence of an easterly current in the part of the Kara Sea in which we had been sailing during the previous days. When we came nearer I was surprised to see before me a plain uninterrupted by any ridges (osar), though I knew, from the former year's experience, that an elevated ridge (bergos), low indeed,

but distinctly marked, runs across the *tundra* towards
Jevremov Kamen. Neither could we discover any of the
numerous rocky islands that distinguish Dickson Harbour. In the meantime we continued our course up the
river along the shore, and after the lapse of four or five
hours, obtained a highly unexpected explanation of the
circumstances just mentioned ; for it appeared that the gulf
at the mouth of the Yenissej, which is about seventy miles
wide, is divided in two by an island above thirty miles
long, which appeared to have been unknown both to the
Russian map-makers and to the natives. That it has not
hitherto been observed probably arises from the fact that
it is not visible from the river bank, along which the few
boats which traverse this part of the river appear always
to have kept. The navigable water on both sides is deep
and free from shallows. This large new island ought
clearly to be of advantage to navigation in these regions,
forming, as it does, a welcome protection from north-
westerly winds and sea for the vessels in the mouth of
the river. I intend to name it Sibiriakoff's Island, after
the zealous and generous patron of all the Siberian
expeditions of the present year.

" During our voyage up the river we steamed in the
forenoon of the 16th between Sverevo and Sopotschnaja
where the mouth of the river, for the first time, narrows
Korga, to a breadth of about thirteen miles. Soon after
we anchored at Goltschika, the northernmost *simovie* at
present inhabited on the eastern bank of the Yenissej.
The commercial agent settled there immediately came on
board. He informed us that during the course of the
summer the place had been visited by three river steamers
which had taken away the wares collected during

summer, and had furnished his modest store with a new stock. He had been told that Sidoroff had fitted out a vessel to convey a cargo of graphite to Europe, and that some foreigners had been in Yenisseisk, whence they intended to undertake a journey down the river to its mouth. Nothing more, however, had been heard of this journey.

"Impatient to meet with my comrades as soon as possible, I again weighed anchor and steamed to Mesenkin, in the near neighbourhood, the place which, for the reasons stated below, had been appointed a rendezvous with Théel's party.

"When I travelled up the river the year before I was incidentally informed by the natives that parts of the skin of a mammoth had been washed out of the *tundra* near our halting place at the mouth of the Mesenkin, which I had left some days before. Unfortunately, however, it was too late to make an examination, as the season was so far advanced, and it was only by the utmost exertion that I could get up with the last steamer that left Dudino for Yenisseisk in the autumn of 1875. But of course I wished instead to avail myself of the opportunity which this year's expedition offered to gain some addition to our knowledge regarding one of the most interesting questions of geology, and to obtain for our museums one of those much talked-of remains of a former period preserved from destruction in the frozen soil of Siberia. It was accordingly included in the plan of the expedition that Théel should endeavour to reach Mesenkin in time enough to make excavations at the place indicated. A further reason for fixing the rendezvous so far to the north was the uncertainty of finding water sufficiently deep for the *Ymer* farther south without soundings, which Théel's party were to carry out during their boat journey down the river.

"A couple of hours after leaving Goltschika I anchored at Mesenkin, where some Russians—among them Feodor, my attendant from the previous year—and a number of natives happened to be assembled. We, however, did not meet with our comrades, and none of the inhabitants had heard anything of them."

Nordenskiöld made an excursion to the place where the mammoth hide was said to have been found, and succeeded in digging out of a newly-formed sand-bank a couple of large and a number of small pieces of hide which appeared to have been recently washed by the spring floods to the place where they were found from some point higher up the valley. He also got from the natives some pieces of hide and two fragments of bone, the only parts of the skeleton that had been discovered. On the morning of the 17th August the *Ymer* started in order to proceed farther up the river. In the neighbourhood of Jakovieva the depth, which up to this point had been from five to twelve fathoms, began to diminish. A dense fog rendered navigation very difficult, and after running aground several times in the search for a deeper channel, and being warped off again without damage, the *Ymer* returned to the former anchorage off the Mesenkin.

Nordenskiöld now determined to await the arrival of Théel's party at the appointed rendezvous, and to employ the time in discharging the *Ymer's* cargo at the *simovie* Korepovskoj, situated a little to the south of the Mesenkin, and to leave them under charge of the guide

Feodor, who lived there, and was considered trustworthy. It was necessary to do this because the last steamer for the season had already gone up the river. The landing of the goods was commenced on the 21st and finished on the evening of the 23rd August. There being no return cargo to be had, the *Ymer* was again ready to sail on the 25th, and dropped down the river to the mouth of the Mesenkin. Not finding the overland party there Nordenskiöld made another attempt to ascend the river but did not get so far south as before, anchoring between Orlovskoj and Gostinoi.

"I chose this place," he writes, "on account of some bone *finds*, which during a preceding excursion had been made in a valley on the *tundra* near by. The following days were devoted to excursions which yielded interesting information regarding the geology of the *tundra*, and an exceedingly rich collection of sub-fossil shells which were found in the *tundra* sand.

"By the word *tundra* are denoted, as is well known, the immense plains in Russia and Siberia lying between the limit of trees and the Polar sea. The ground at least in the northern portions of the Siberian *tundra* is constantly frozen at a limited depth, but it bears during summer a vegetation of low bushes, mosses, and grass, which yields summer pasture to numerous herds of reindeer, some wild, others tame, which wander about here.

"On the eastern bank of the Yenissej the *tundra* forms a level or slightly-rolling plain sloping towards the river with an escarpment 50 to 100 feet high. In the interior the plain is not interrupted by any considerable heights, but on the contrary is intersected at many places by deep river valleys, whose precipitous sides offer beautiful sections of the earthy strata. On a cursory examination it is evident that they consist for the most part of enormous masses of sand and mud washed down by the rivers of Siberia. The *tundra* is, however, by no means a common delta formation. Numerous marine shells imbedded in the sand show that the *tundra* plain in former times lay under the surface of the sea, and that therefore a considerable elevation of the land has taken place during the latest geological periods. For the shells imbedded in the *tundra* sand all belong to living types, the most of which have been dredged up by us from the Kara Sea, and are to be found in the post-glacial shell-banks of Uddevalla and Christiania Fjord, and the Crag formation of England. All this shows that the *tundra* has been formed under climatal conditions very similar to the present, which is further confirmed by the geognostic formation of the strata. It has therefore long been difficult of explanation for the geologist that just in those sandy strata is found a large number of remains of mammoths, rhinoceroses, &c., that is to say, of animal types which for the present live only in tropical or subtropical climates.[1] This evident contrariety has indeed obtained an explanation through the researches of Middendorf, Schmidt, and Brandt, the Petersburg academicians. But there still remains much to clear up, and collections from those regions have a peculiar interest from the remarkable circumstance that in the frozen soil of the *tundra* are found, not only skeletons, but also the flesh, hide, hair, and entrails of animal-forms which died out many

---

[1] The mammoth, for instance, is believed to be the progenitor of the now living Indian elephant, but a progenitor considerably larger than the descendant, and provided with an abundant covering of hair.

thousand centuries ago. I therefore availed myself with delight of the opportunities which offered themselves for excursions in the neighbourhood of the places where the vessel was anchored. Among our collections may be mentioned large pieces of mammoth hide found along with some few fragments of bone where the Mesenkin falls into the Yenissej, the skull of a musk ox, remarkable for its size, found along with fragments of mammoth bones in another *tundra* valley south of Orlovskoj, a very rich collection of sub-fossil shells found principally between Orlovskoj and Gostinoi. Various interesting observations regarding the geological formation of the *tundra* were also made.

" During our stay on the Yenissej a close mist with rain was often prevailing, but otherwise we were favoured, as the following table shows, with warm, summer-like weather:—

TABLE *showing the temperature of the air and the direction of the wind at the northerly simovies of the Yenissej from 16th August to 1st September*, 1876.

	Minimum.	Maximum.	Wind.
August 16	13·6° C.	20·4° C.	E.S.E.
,, 17	11·0	12·6	S.E.
,, 18	11·5	14·9	S.
,, 19	7·8	9·9	S.W.
,, 20	9·5	14·4	E.
,, 21	11·4	15·6	S.E.
,, 22	11·0	14·0	S.E.
,, 23	10·3	18·7	Calm, N.N.W.
,, 24	7·9	10·0	N.W.
,, 25	9·3	11·8	N.
,, 26	9·0	16·4	N.
,, 27	11·3	12·9	Calm.
,, 28	11·8	12·5	S.
,, 29	2·2	7·6	S.W.
,, 30	5·2	5·8	N.W.
,, 31	1·3	5·3	N.
Sept. 1	3·0	7·0	N.N.E.

"The ground was quite free of snow, and in many places, particularly in the *tundra* valleys, adorned with a variegated carpet of flowers. The natives stated, however, that the first part of the summer had not been so fine in those regions, and that the previous winter had been exceedingly severe. The temperature of the river water at the surface was almost constantly 12° to 13° C., and even at a depth of nine fathoms the deep-water thermometer showed 11°·1 C.

"It had been settled before leaving Stockholm that in case the *Ymer* did not succeed in reaching the Yenissej, Théel should in no case remain on the northern part of Yenissej so long as to run any risk of missing the last steamer of the year to Yenisseisk. I had now been informed by the natives that the last river steamer was to start from Saostrovskoj about the 7th September (new style). The distance from this place to Mesenkin is about 165 English miles, to traverse which in a boat *up the river* seven or eight days are considered necessary under ordinary circumstances. It was not to be supposed that Théel would continue his boat journey beyond Saostrovskoj in case it appeared that Mesenkin could not be reached before 1st September. I therefore did not consider it necessary to remain with the *Ymer* in those regions after the end of August, and not at all advisable, as in any case there was no certainty that the large quantity of 'year's ice' which we met with in the Kara Sea in the first week of August would be so completely melted away before new ice was formed, that there would be no danger of being beset if our return were too long delayed. For these reasons it was determined to start on the 1st September, however unpleasant it might be to return without the members of the Siberian land expedition, and without bringing with us the very large collections they certainly had made. Before starting, however, I sent off a messenger in a boat for a heavy payment (reindeer were not now to be had) to Saostrovskoj with a letter to Théel informing him of our intention to start for Norway on the day that we had fixed."

This letter reached Théel, who with his party had by the 11th August got as far north as the Briochovski Islands, but found it impossible to get boats and rowers to convey them and their collections farther down the river. Théel's party accordingly returned overland.

The *Ymer* started on her return voyage on the 1st September at seven o'clock A.M., reached Dickson Harbour on the 2nd, and the weather being favourable proceeded without stopping in the direction of Cape Middendorff. The sea was at first completely free of ice, but as Novaya Zemlya was approached in $75\frac{1}{2}°$ N.L. a very compact belt of ice was met with which extended along the coast towards Matotschkin, which was reached on the evening of the 7th September. The *Ymer* remained there until the 13th for the purpose of filling the coal bunkers and taking on board water and ballast. The weather being fine, Nordkyn was sighted on the 16th, and Tromsoe reached on the 22nd September.

"Of all the expeditions," writes Nordenskiöld, "which have gone to Novaya Zemlya and the surrounding sea there were only three, before the two last Swedish ones, that concerned themselves with researches in natural history. These were von Baer's expedition in

1837, Heuglin's in 1871, and the Austro-Hungarian in 1872-74.

"With reference to zoological researches Baer brought home from his journey about seventy invertebrate animals, Heuglin has increased our knowledge of the number of species in some groups, and the Austro-Hungarian expedition in others. But all those collections were from the south-west, west, and north-west coasts of Novaya Zemlya. Of the nature of the animal life in the Kara Sea there was no real knowledge until the summer of 1875. There was also a current tradition among zoologists, grounded on the knowledge of the immense mass of fresh water carried down yearly by the Obi and the Yenissej, perhaps also on some originally loose expressions in literature which afterwards took the form of an axiom, that the Kara Sea is exceedingly poor in animal life.

"The Swedish expedition of 1875 dissipated this misconception, as it also brought from the west coast of Novaya Zemlya and Waygat's Island a collection many times richer in species than their predecessors. But in any case the collections made during a single summer could not be supposed to yield a complete idea of animal life in those regions such as is requisite not only for a comparison with the existing fauna of other Arctic lands, but also for a complete exhibition of its relation to the fauna in the deposits of the Siberian *tundra*. It was for this reason that I gave Dr. Stuxberg, a zoologist, an opportunity of accompanying the expedition for the purpose of continuing the zoological researches. His success has been very great, as will appear from the following short sketch communicated by him :—

"During the voyages to the Kara Sea and back in

1875 and 1876 dredgings have been carried on at fifty places and at different depths from the beach down to 200 fathoms, and good and comprehensive collections of animals have been made in this way. A very large number of species occur locally and in quite incredible numbers. Others again are found at nearly every dredging, but in far smaller numbers. The occurrence of the latter is more uniform, consequently distinctive for the fauna area in its entirety. To these belong first of all two species of the family *Idothea* (*Id. Sabinei* and *Id. Entomon*), both strongly developed, and it may with reason be said that this family is characteristic of the Kara Sea. It is the province of the Idotheæ. To the animal types, again, which are local in their occurrence, belong various species of *Mollusca*, *Hydromedusæ*, and *Bryozoa*, but in the first place all the known representatives of *Echinodermata* from the Kara Sea. Their abundance is often truly surprising, and, what is more singular, when a species occurs in any considerable number it lives almost alone—almost to the exclusion of all others. This is the case, for instance, with species of the families *Cribella*, *Stichaster*, *Ctenodiscus*, &c., which are found here in large and well-developed types. Not unfrequently the swab brought up at the same time hundreds of individuals of the same species. Of the beautiful crinoid *Alecto Eschrichtii* there were obtained many very fine specimens.

"But rich as is the Kara Sea in *Asterida* and *Ophiurida*, it is equally poor in *Echini*. These are there sought for everywhere in vain, except possibly close to the east coast of Novaya Zemlya. This is so much the more surprising, as along the whole west coast a species of the family *Echinus* is one of the most abundant and most frequently occurring animal forms.

"In two respects the zoological work of this summer has been very profitable for our museums. First of all, it has added something new in all groups to the exceedingly rich collections of the previous summer. It has, for example, increased the collection of *Crustacea* by twenty per cent. new species, and a large number of forms of *Echinodermata* has, by oft-repeated swabbing, been obtained in an extraordinary number of individuals. Further, the swab has brought up from the depths of the Kara Sea two animals specially remarkable and important in a systematic respect, one belonging to the *Echinodermata*, the other to the *Pennatulidæ*. The former was swabbed up during the expedition of the previous summer not far from the eastern mouth of Matotschkin Schar. Only a few specimens were then found; now we have brought together a considerable number. It is a hitherto unknown holothurioid, which is distinguished from most others of the same group by its exceedingly perfect bilateral symmetry, but differs from all in its habit and anatomical formation and is unique in its kind, as it combines in itself characteristics from different classes of animals. It has of late been exhaustively described and delineated in detail by Dr. Théel, its first discoverer. The other remarkable animal is one of the greatest rarities within the animal world. It is an *Umbellula*,[1]

---

[1] Two specimens of the family *Umbellularia*, the first of which we have any knowledge, are said to have been found on the coast of Greenland before the middle of last century. The animal was registered by Linnæus in the year 1758 in his *Systema Naturæ*, under the appellation *Isis encrinus*, after a description first given by Ellis and Mylius. What became of the original specimens is

of about a foot and a half in length. It was found in 130 fathoms south of Cape Middendorff and north of the seventy-fifth degree of north latitude.

"From the collections made during the Swedish expedition it appears that the Kara Sea, far from being so poor as was supposed, is really distinguished by an animal life very rich both in individuals and in types, equal to any that Spitzbergen, Greenland, Iceland, or the Arctic regions of North America can show. And it would appear as if a nearly uniform marine fauna stretches round the north pole along the whole coast of Siberia and the Polar archipelago of North America. The mass of fresh water which the great Siberian rivers carry down determines in no small degree the composition of animal life at the bottom of this Polar sea.

"Until the various groups have been worked out by specialists it is difficult to state for certain the number of the lower animal types of the Kara Sea, but it may be approximately reckoned at nearly five hundred species—

---

unknown. The "goat-like animal form" of the descriptions was the subject of many interpretations until Dr. J. Lindahl, during the Swedish expedition to Greenland, succeeded in dredging up in Baffin's Bay two specimens of it, and described its inner formation in the *Transactions of the Academy of Sciences* (Votenskaps Academiens Handlingar). After this time individuals of the same family were found first by the English *Challenger* expedition of 1873 between Portugal and Madeira, and by the same expedition between Prince Edward's Island and Kerguelen's Land, and possibly at some other places in the Antarctic Ocean, afterwards by the Austrian-Hungarian expedition of 1873 between Novaya Zemlya and Franz Joseph's Land, also during the present summer (1876) by the Norwegian Atlantic expedition off the west coast of Norway, and now last of all by us in the Kara Sea. It is thus an animal type extensively distributed but of very infrequent occurrence.

a very considerable number for a sea which was formerly considered as poor in species as the Baltic. This fact, with the addition of about a hundred species of insects from Novaya Zemyla, from which only seven were pre-known, and an extended knowledge of the vertebrate world of the same lands, is the main zoological result of the surveys of the two latest Swedish expeditions in those regions."

By these voyages of Nordenskiöld to the Yenissej there was inaugurated a sea-route from the Atlantic destined to be of incalculable importance for the development of the resources of Northern Asia and for the commerce of the world. Siberia has been declared by M. Ferdinand de Lesseps to be the richest country of the whole world in respect of the produce of the animal, vegetable, and mineral kingdoms. Nor will this estimate appear much overdrawn when we consider the abundance and variety of the wares which Siberia is capable of supplying—gold, silver, copper, iron, graphite, and coal, fossil ivory, timber from boundless forests, wheat and other vegetable produce from illimitable plains of the most fertile soil, in course of time even wines from the warm southern regions, furs from the cold region, wool, tallow, and meat from the grassy prairies, the meat preserved fresh by simple exposure to the severe cold of winter, and finally fish of the finest quality in extraordinary numbers.

A week after Nordenskiöld had left the mouth of the Yenissej it was entered by the steamer *Thames*, commanded by Captain Joseph Wiggins, who had made great personal sacrifices in attempting to open up

communication with Siberia by sea. He ascended the
Yenissej as far as the Kurejka, where he laid his vessel
up for the winter and returned overland. Going back
in spring he found his steamer completely covered with
ice and snow. After getting her in proper trim by the
expenditure of a great deal of labour, he had the misfortune to run aground on a shoal, and was in consequence obliged to abandon his vessel. Herr Bojling had
undertaken to transport the goods landed by the *Ymer*
to Yeniseisk, and, to make himself independent of the
river steamers, had built a peculiar vessel—river-boat
or lighter—for the purpose of getting the goods up the
river, but coming to an arrangement with one of the
river steamers, he found his newly-built vessel superfluous, and sold it to Mr. Seebohm, the well-known
English ornithologist, who wished to sail in it down
the river and join Wiggins in order to carry on his
researches in his company. Seebohm was successful
in finding Wiggins, whom he accompanied until he was
obliged to abandon his steamer.

In 1876, while Nordenskiöld, was seeking to penetrate to the Yenissej, a Russian captain, Schvananberg,
was endeavouring to make his way down the river with
a cargo of graphite belonging to Herr Michael Sidoroff,
a member of the Russian Geographical Society. Schvananberg sailed from Yeniseisk, where his schooner
had been built, but, meeting with several delays, he
was compelled to leave his vessel at the Briochovski
Islands under charge of his mate and four men. He
then travelled overland to St. Petersburg to make
arrangements for next year's voyage. In his absence
the schooner was wrecked and the cargo of graphite lost.

The five men were saved, and took up their residence in a hut on the river-bank, where they died of scurvy, one after the other, with the exception of the mate. In the spring, Schvananberg sent a relief party to his vessel, who found it wrecked, and took up their quarters in the hut with the survivor, waiting an opportunity of returning to Yeniseisk. The spring inundations now came on, and the party in the hut were compelled to take to the roof, where they spent eight days, surrounded by the river now widened to a sea. In the meantime Wiggins and Seebohm with their men had betaken themselves to the river-boat which Seebohm had bought from Bojling; and Wiggins, who is a brave seaman, proposed that in this craft, unfit as it was to encounter the dangers of the sea and of navigation among ice, they should sail down the river, across the Kara Sea, and endeavour to reach some European port. The sailors, however, refused to accompany their captain on such a voyage, and Schvananberg making his appearance at this juncture the river-boat was sold to him. Undismayed by his previous failure, Schvananberg named his purchase the *Zaria* (*Dawn*), and though it was a mere lighter, fifty feet long by fourteen feet wide, flat-bottomed, and drawing only two and a half feet of water, he succeeded in reaching Vardoe on the 30th August, and Cronstadt on the 19th October, 1877. As Schvananberg sailed out of the Yenissej on the 21st August he met a steamer entering the mouth of the river. This steamer, the *Fraser*, had been purchased by Sibiriakoff in Nordenskiöld's name, and, laden with sugar, tobacco, a steam-pump, and other goods, had sailed from Bremen on 25th July under the command of Captain Dallman,

who had gained his experience of ice navigation in the
Arctic waters at Behring's Straits and in the South
Polar Sea. Schvananberg informed Dallman that
Sibiriakoff had a cargo of wheat in readiness for him,
but, after Dallman had landed his goods and waited till
the 11th September without hearing anything more
of the wheat cargo, he considered it unadvisable to
delay longer, and accordingly commenced his return
voyage, leaving the mouth of the Yenissej on the 14th
September. Not reckoning a delay of two days at
Matotschkin Schar, the *Fraser* steamed the whole
distance from the Yenissej to the first Norwegian light-
house near Hammarfest in six days eight hours.

The steamer *Luise*, 170 tons, 60 H.P., Captain C.
Dahl, started from Lubeck on the 23rd June, 1877, and
after touching at London and Hull, reached Tromsoe on
the 28th July, and the southern extremity of Novaya
Zemlya on the 2nd August; and having steamed up the
Obi and its affluent the Irtisch for more than a thousand
miles, arrived at Tobolsk on the 20th September.

Thus not without difficulty, but with the mingled
success and failure which attend the commencement of
all enterprises, is Siberia, with its boundless prairies, its
endless forests, its immense expanse of inexhaustible
"black earth," its rich mineral treasures, and the
finest grain-producing soil known, being opened to the
commerce of the world.

CHAPTER IX.

THE NORTH-EAST PASSAGE EXPEDITION, 1878-1879.

MORE than three centuries have passed since the first North-East Passage Expedition was fitted out. It consisted of three ships, equipped under the direction of Sebastian Cabot by the Company of Merchant Adventurers, afterwards called the Muscovy Company, and placed by them under the command of the ill-fated Sir Hugh Willoughby, who, having attempted to winter on the coast of Russian Lapland, was found frozen to death along with his crew, while his more fortunate companion Chancelor made his way to Moscow and laid the foundation of our commerce with Russia. Willoughby's expedition sailed in 1553. In 1556 the Muscovy Company, without waiting for the return of Chancelor, whom they had sent out on a second voyage, in the course of which he was shipwrecked and drowned, fitted out a small vessel, the *Search-thrift*, for the purpose of making discoveries in the north-eastern seas. Stephen Burrough in command of the *Search-thrift* passed between Novaya Zemlya and Waigatz Island, and entered the Kara Sea, but was stopped by fog and ice.

In 1580 Arthur Pet was sent out by the Muscovy Company in command of the *George*, forty tons, and

Charles Jackman in command of the *William*, twenty tons. Pet discovered the straits between Waigatz Island and the mainland, and the vessels passed through it, but found it impossible to penetrate the heavy pack-ice which filled the sea beyond. The Dutch sent out three expeditions—in 1593, 1595, and 1596—under Barentz, who during the last of these was imprisoned by the ice on the coast of Novaya Zemlya, along with his crew, and died before the return of spring. Henry Hudson was equally unsuccessful in three voyages which he undertook for the discovery of a north-east passage. The first was in 1607, in a small vessel with ten sailors. In the second he reached Novaya Zemlya in 1608. The third voyage, in 1609, from Amsterdam, was at the expense of the Dutch East India Company. In 1653 the Danes made an attempt in the same direction with no better success. At last, after the return of Captain John Wood from Novaya Zemlya in 1676, and mainly in consequence of the descriptions, partly true, partly overdrawn, which he gave of the natural obstacles to be encountered, the search for a north-east passage was given up in despair by the great seafaring nations.

It was now, however, taken up by the Russian government, and from time to time no fewer than eighteen different expeditions were sent out from that country for the purpose of surveying Novaya Zemlya, the Kara Sea, and the Siberian coast lying to the eastward. During these expeditions the attempts to navigate the Kara Sea either totally failed or only partially succeeded under very unfavourable circumstances. Admiral Lütke's voyages, 1821-1824, seemed to prove the impossibility of forcing a passage through this sea;

the academician von Baer expressly declared after his return in 1837 that it was an "ice-cellar," and Pachtusov, who started in 1832 with the intention of penetrating to the Obi and the Yenissej, returned after wintering on Novaya Zemlya with his object unaccomplished.

It was natural that, when the Kara Sea had been explored, and the possibility of reaching the mouths of the great Siberian rivers placed beyond a doubt by the voyages of 1875 and 1876, Nordenskiöld should turn a longing eye to the vast expanse of unexplored sea that skirts the northern coast of Asia, and that the old enterprise of effecting the north-east passage, which in past centuries had so uniformly ended in failure, should be again entertained.

The new expedition was planned on a larger scale than any of the preceding. It was to cost £20,000, of which sum Mr. Oscar Dickson contributed £12,000, the King of Sweden £2,200, and Mr. Alexander Sibiriakoff a similar sum. Mr. Dickson bought for the expedition the steam-whaler *Vega*, built in the years 1872–1873 at Bremen, of oak, with an ice-skin of greenheart. The *Vega* measures 299 register tons, and loads about 500 tons, has a length of keel of 130 Bremen feet, overdeck of 150 feet, the greatest breadth is 29 feet, and the depth in the hold 16 feet. The engine is of 60 horsepower. The *Vega* is fully rigged as a bark, and is considered a good sailer. The Swedish Diet, on the proposition of the government and of Herr Wærn, the president of the Swedish Merchant Navy Society, voted grants for equipping and provisioning the *Vega*, and for the pay of the medical officer. The government also promised those officers and men of the Swedish navy who should volunteer for service on board the *Vega* the same pay and other advantages as they are entitled to in the case of man-of-war expeditions to distant waters.

With this new expedition in view Nordenskiöld had made an exhaustive study of all the attempts that had been made to sail along the coast of Siberia from the mouth of the Yenissej to Behring's Straits. The results of this study he embodied in a memorial addressed to the Swedish government. An English translation of this memorial has been printed, from which we extract the following statement of the conclusions at which Nordenskiöld arrived.

"From what I have thus stated it follows :—

"That the ocean lying north of the Siberian coast from the mouth of the Yenissej to Tschaun Bay has never been ploughed by the keel of any proper sea-going vessel, still less has been traversed by any steamer specially equipped for navigation among ice.

"That the small vessels with which it has been attempted to navigate this part of the ocean never ventured very far from the coast.

"That an open sea with a fresh breeze was as destructive for them, indeed more destructive, than a sea covered with drift-ice.

"That they almost always sought some convenient winter harbour just at the season of the year when the sea is freest of ice, namely late summer or autumn.

"That although the sea from Cape Chelyuskin to Behring's Straits has been repeatedly traversed, none has yet succeeded in traversing the whole extent at once.

"That the covering of ice formed during winter along the coast, but probably not in the open sea, is every summer broken up, giving origin to extensive fields of drift-ice, which are driven, now by a northerly wind towards the coast, now by a southerly wind out to sea, yet not so far but that it comes back to the coast after some days of northerly wind, whence it appears probable that the Siberian Sea is, so to speak, shut off from the Polar Sea proper by a series of islands, of which for the present we know only Wrangel's Land and the islands which form New Siberia.

"I consider it probable that a well-equipped steamer would be able, without meeting with too many obstacles from ice, to force a passage this way during autumn in a few days, and thus that it would be possible not only to solve a geographical problem of several centuries' standing, but also, with all the means now at the disposal of the man of science in carrying on researches in geography, hydrography, geology, and natural history, to survey a hitherto almost unknown sea of enormous extent.

"I am also fully convinced that it is not only possible to sail along the north coast of Asia, provided circumstances are not too unfavourable, but that such an enterprise will be of incalculable practical importance, by no means directly as opening up a new commercial route, but indirectly by the impression which would thereby be communicated of the practical utility of a communication between the ports of North Scandinavia and the Obi and Yenissej on the one hand and between the Pacific Ocean and the Lena on the other.

"Should the expedition, contrary to expectation, not succeed in carrying out the programme which has been arranged in its entirety, it ought not to be looked upon as having failed. In such a case the expedition will remain for a considerable time at places on the north coast of Siberia, suitable for scientific research. Every mile beyond the mouth of the Yenissej is a step forward to a complete knowledge of our globe, an object which some time or other must be attained, and towards which it is an affair of honour for every civilised nation to contribute in its proportion.

"Men of science will have an opportunity in these hitherto unvisited waters of answering a number of questions regarding the former and present state of the Polar countries, of which more than one is of sufficient weight and importance to lead to such an expedition as the present. I may be permitted here to refer to only a few of these.

"If we except that part of the Kara Sea which has been surveyed by the two last Swedish expeditions, we have for the present no knowledge of the vegetable and animal life in the sea that washes the north coast of Siberia. We shall certainly here, in opposition to what has been hitherto supposed, meet with the same abundance of animals and plants as in the sea round Spitzbergen. In the Siberian Polar Sea the animal and vegetable types, so far as we can judge beforehand, exclusively consist of survivals from the Glacial period which next preceded the present, which is not the case in the Polar Sea where the Gulf Stream distributes its waters and whither it thus carries types from more southerly regions. But a complete and exact knowledge of which animal types are of Glacial and which of Atlantic origin is of the greatest importance not only for zoology and the geography of animals, but also for the geology of Scandinavia, and especially for the knowledge of our loose earthy strata.

"Few scientific discoveries have so powerfully captivated the interest both of the learned and unlearned as that of the colossal remains of elephants, sometimes well preserved with flesh and hair in the frozen soil of Siberia. Such discoveries have more than once formed the objects of scientific expeditions and careful researches by eminent men, but there is still much that is enigmatical with respect to a number of circumstances connected with the Mammoth period of Siberia, which *perhaps* was contemporaneous with our Glacial period. Specially is our knowledge of the animal and vegetable types, which lived at the same time as the mammoth, exceedingly incomplete, although we know that in the northernmost parts of Siberia, which are also most inaccessible from land, there are small hills covered with the bones of the mammoth and other contemporaneous animals, and that there is found in that region so-called Noah's wood, that is to say, half petrified or carbonised vegetable remains from several different geological periods.

"Taken overhead, an investigation as complete as possible of the geology of the Polar lands, so difficult of access, is an indispensable condition for a knowledge of the former history of our globe. In order to prove this I need only point to the epoch-forming influence which has been exerted on geological theories by the discovery, in the rocks and earthy layers of the Polar countries, of beautiful fossil plants from widely-separated geological epochs. In this field, too, an expedition to the north coast of Siberia may expect to reap abundant harvests. There are to be found, in Siberia, strata which have been deposited almost contemporaneously with the coal-bearing formations of south Sweden, and which therefore contain animal and vegetable .petrifactions, which just now are of quite special interest for geological science in our own country with reference to the discoveries of splendid fossil plants, which have of late years been made at several places in Sweden, and give us so lively an idea of the subtropical vegetation which in former times covered the Scandinavian peninsula.

"Few sciences perhaps will yield such important practical results as meteorology is likely to do at some future date; a fact, or rather an already partially realised expectation which has won general recognition, as is shown by the considerable sums which in all civilised countries have been set apart for establishing meteorological offices, and for carrying on meteorological researches. But the state of the weather in a country is so dependent on the temperature, wind, pressure of the air, &c., in very remote regions, that the laws of the meteorology of a country can only be ascertained by comparing observations from the most distant countries. Several international meteorological enterprises have already been started, and we may almost consider the meteorological institutions of the different countries as separate departments of one and the same office distributed over the whole world, by whose harmonious co-operation the object in view is one day to be reached. But besides the places from which daily series of observations may be obtained, there are regions, hundreds of square miles in extent, from which no observations, or only scattered ones, are yet to be had; and here, nevertheless, we must seek the key to many meteorological phenomena, otherwise difficult of explanation, within the civilised countries of Europe. Such a meteorological territory, unknown but of the greatest importance, is formed by the Polar Sea lying to the north of Siberia, and the land and islands there situated. It is of great importance for the meteorology of Europe and of Sweden, to obtain trustworthy accounts of the distribution of the land, of the state of the ice, the pressure of the air, and the temperature in that little-known part of the globe; and the Swedish expedition will have in this a subject for investigation of direct importance for our own country.

"To a certain extent the same may be said of the contributions which may be obtained from those regions to our knowledge of terrestrial magnetism, of the aurora, &c. There are, besides, the examination of the flora and fauna of those countries hitherto unknown in this respect, ethnographical researches, hydrographical work, &c.

"I have of course only been able to notice shortly the scientific questions which will meet the expedition during a stay of some length on the north coast of Siberia; but what has been said will perhaps be sufficient to show that the expedition, even if its geographical object be not attained, ought to form a worthy continuation of similar enterprises which have been set on foot in this country, and which have brought gain to science and honour to Sweden.

"Should the expedition however be able to reach Behring's Straits with little hindrance and in a comparatively short time, in that case, the time on the way which can be devoted to researches in natural history will be quite too short for solving many of the scientific questions I have mentioned. But without reckoning the world-historical navigation problem which will then be solved, extensive contributions of immense importance ought also to be obtainable regarding the geography, hydrography, zoology, and botany of the Siberian Polar Sea; and beyond Behring's Straits the expedition will meet with other countries having a more luxuriant and varied nature, where other questions which perhaps concern us less, but are not on that account of less importance for science in its entirety, will claim the attention of the observer, and yield him a rich reward for his labour and pains."

With such motives and views was the plan of the expedition that was to achieve the North-east Passage arranged. In this memorable expedition Nordenskiöld is accompanied by Lieutenant A. A. L. Palander, commander of the *Vega*, Lieutenant E. C. Brusewitz, second in command, Dr. F. R. Kjellman, botanist, Dr. Ant. Stuxberg, zoologist, Dr. Ernst Almquist, medical officer and botanist, Lieutenant Giacomo Bove, of the Italian navy, acting as sailing master, having charge of the chronometers and taking the necessary astronomical observations, Lieutenant Andreas Hovgaard, of the Danish navy, and Lieutenant Oscar Nordquist, of the Imperial Russian family's battalion of sharpshooters, acting as interpreter and zoologist. The crew consists of eighteen seamen of the Swedish navy, selected from 200 who volunteered their services, and three Norwegian walrus-hunters. The *Vega* was provisioned for two years, and provided with a plentiful supply of antiscorbutics, including cranberry juice, preserved cloudberries, horse-radish, pickles, and lime-juice. During winter a cubic inch of the last-named article entered into the daily ration.

The *Vega* was accompanied part of her course by three other vessels; as far as the mouth of the Yenissej by the steamer *Fraser*, Captain Nilsson, and the sailing vessel *Express*, Captain Gundersen; and as far as the mouth of the Lena by a small steamer of the same name, of 100 tons, built at Motala of Bessemer steel, commanded by Captain Johannesen. The *Express* had taken on board in an English port 350 tons of coal for the use of the expedition, and along with the *Fraser* was to carry on Herr Sibiriakoff's account about 40,000 pood wheat, 500 pood tallow, and some oats from the Yenissej, where they were laid up at a *simovie* near the mouth of the river. Besides coal the *Express* had on board a small quantity of salt, intended for the fisheries on the Yenissej. The *Lena's* cargo consisted of sixteen months' provisions and coal. The *Fraser*, laden with tobacco and iron, and having the *Express* in tow, sailed from Vadsoe on the 13th July, and arrived at Jugor Straits on the 20th of the same month, having towed the *Express* the whole way, as there was no wind.

The *Vega* sailed from Gothenburg on the 4th, and from Tromsoe on the 21st July, accompanied from the latter port, where Nordenskiöld joined the expedition, by the *Lena*. The vessels were delayed by a storm and head wind at Masoe until the 25th, when they weighed anchor, shaping their course through Mageroe Sound, past Nordkyn, for Goose Cape. By this detour it was

intended to avoid the drift ice which is generally to be
encountered far into the summer in the bay between the
west coast of Waigatz Island and the mainland. On this
occasion the precaution was unnecessary, as Jugor Straits
were reached without a trace of ice being seen. Novaya
Zemlya was sighted on the 29th July, and on the 30th
the *Vega*, having steamed along the coast to Jugor
Straits, anchored at a Samoyede village called Chabarova,
in the neighbourhood of which the *Fraser* and *Express*
had been lying at anchor since the 20th. On the 31st
the *Lena* came in sight, and the little squadron was
complete.

The stay at Chabarova, while the *Vega* and the *Lena*
replenished their stocks of coal from the cargo of the
Express, was turned to account by the naturalists of the
expedition. Lieutenant Palander took photographs and
Lieutenant Hovgaard magnetical observations. Lieutenant Nordquist endeavoured to collect contributions to
the exceedingly scanty insect fauna of the region, and
Dr. Almquist tested by Holmgren's method the colour
sense of the Samoyedes, which was found to be in
general well developed. Solar altitudes were taken by
Lieutenant Bove and Nordenskiöld. The latter purchased dresses, household articles, &c., of the Samoyedes,
and succeeded, after some difficulty, in persuading an
old woman to sell him some of the idols which are still
worshipped by the tribe, although they are professedly
Christians, and take part in Christian worship. The
idols were all different in appearance. One consisted of
a stone, which by the help of brightly-coloured patches
had been made into a sort of doll; another was a similar
doll with a piece of copper plate for a face; and a third

was a little skin doll ornamented with earrings and pearls. These idols, which are still regarded with reverence by the Samoyedes, in general resemble the rag dolls which peasant children make for themselves without the help of the toy-shops of towns.

On the 31st July Nordenskiöld, accompanied by Dr. Almquist, Lieutenant Hovgaard, Captain Nilsson of the *Fraser*, and a Russian who had entertained them to tea the preceding afternoon, visited a sacrificial altar on which were placed, among a number of reindeer horns still fast to the skulls, a newly-killed bear's skull and paws, and alongside upon a stone two lead bullets which had been used, and with which probably the animal had been killed. The following day the vessels of the expedition weighed anchor and sailed or steamed through Jugor Straits into the Kara Sea. The weather being still calm the *Fraser* towed the *Express*, and the *Lena* steamed in advance to White Island, where Dr. Almquist and Lieutenants Hovgaard and Nordquist landed and remained thirty-six hours, and then proceeded to Dickson Harbour. Till now no ice had been seen, but on reaching the latitude of White Island an extensive field of drift ice was encountered, which, however, was so rotten and so open as not to obstruct navigation. East of White Island the ice entirely disappeared, and on the 6th of August all the vessels with the exception of the *Lena* were anchored in Dickson Harbour. On the following day that small steamer joined her comrades.

On the morning of the 9th August the *Fraser* and *Express* proceeded up the river to Saostrovskoj, arriving there on the 20th and discharging their cargoes.

The *Express* remained there to load, and the *Fraser*
ascended the river to Dudinskoj, about 500 miles from
its mouth, where a full cargo of wheat, rye, and tallow
was taken on board, returning to Saostrovskoj on the
2nd September. After some days' delay here both
vessels started on their homeward voyage, and arrived
on the 9th September at Tolstonosovski where they fell
in with the steamer *Moskwa*, Captain Dahlman, from
Bremen. On board the *Moskwa* the Swedes were informed that her consort, the Norwegian steamer
Zaritza, had stranded at the mouth of the river on the
2nd September, and had been abandoned on the 4th by
her crew who had gone on board the *Moskwa*. The
Fraser and *Express* took the *Zaritza's* crew on board
and proceeded down the river where they found the
vessel afloat but with six and a half feet of water in the
hold. Men were put on board to pump her dry, and
put the engine in repair, which they succeeded in doing
so that the *Zaritza* could go to sea under the *Fraser's*
escort. In the Kara Sea very little ice was seen during
the return voyage. North of North Cape the vessels
parted, the *Express* sailing southwards, and the *Fraser*
calling at Hammerfest and Tromsoe, arriving at the
latter port on the 29th September.

After a day spent in surveying Dickson Harbour the
Vega and the *Lena* on the 10th August resumed their
eastward voyage, shaping their course for the Kamenni
Islands, lying off the mouth of the river Pjasina, and
on the 11th fell in with ice which, however, as it
moderated the high sea which had before prevailed,
was not unfavourable to navigation. The ice consisted
almost exclusively of bay ice, so rotten that it was

rather a sort of continuous slush than veritable ice. It was evident that in a few days it would have entirely disappeared. Notwithstanding the frequent fogs and the numerous islands along the coast that were not laid down on the chart, the *Vega* did not once run aground. As the distance from the Yenissej increased the salinity, which had at first been inconsiderable, began to increase and the temperature to fall. Organic life at the sea-bottom became simultaneously more plentiful. On the night between the 13th and 14th of August, while the *Vega* lay tied to a floe, Dr. Stuxberg brought up a large number of fine purely marine types, for instance, large specimens of the remarkable Crinoid *Alecto Eschrichtii*, a number of Asterids (*Asterias Linckii* and *panopla*), Pycnogonids, &c. Dredging near land also began to yield to Dr. Kjellman several of the larger marine algæ. On the other hand the higher plant and animal life on land was still so poor that the coast here forms a complete desert in comparison with the rocky shores of Spitzbergen and West Novaya Zemlya. Sea fowl were few in number. Only snow-buntings, six or seven species of waders, and some varieties of geese were found on land in any considerable numbers. If there be added a ptarmigan or two, an Arctic owl, and a species of falcon, the whole bird fauna of the region is enumerated, as far at least as it could be investigated on this occasion. Two walruses and some seals (*Phoca barbata* and *hispida*) were seen, and fish appeared to be abundant.

While the *Vega* lay anchored to one of the few pieces of ice which were large and strong enough to carry half a score of men, Nordenskiöld went on the ice, accompanied by Lieut. Nordquist, to search for traces of the cosmic dust which he had found in 1872 on the north coast of Spitzbergen. His search was not attended with success, but his attention was drawn by Nordquist to some yellow specks on the snow, which Nordenskiöld at first supposed to consist of diatoms, and handed over to the botanists, but which on examination proved to be a coarse-grained sand, formed exclusively of very beautiful crystals up to two millimetres in diameter. These Nordenskiöld with the limited time at his disposal could not identify with any common terrestrial mineral, but thought they might perhaps consist of matter crystallised from the sea-water during the severe cold of winter.

From the 14th to the 18th August the *Vega* and the *Lena* lay at anchor, waiting for clear weather, in a splendid harbour, situated in the strait between Taimyr Island and the mainland, which Nordenskiöld named Actinia Haven from the number of *Actinia* which the dredge brought up from the bottom.

The land was free of snow and covered with a grey-green vegetation, consisting of grasses, mosses, and lichens. The number of species of phanerogamous plants was exceedingly small, that of mosses and lichens on the other hand was abundant enough. The reindeer pasture was much better than in the valleys where these animals are numerous on Bell Sound, Ice Fjord, and Stor Fjord on Spitzbergen, but here they were both scarce and shy, which Captain Johannesen ascribed to the presence of wolves, having fallen in with the carcase of a reindeer that had been killed by a wolf.

Nordenskiöld recommends Actinia Haven as a suitable place for a meteorological station, if such a station cannot be established at Cape Chelyuskin itself. The haven is well sheltered from all winds and possesses good anchorage.

Although the fog still continued, the *Vega* and the *Lena* weighed anchor on the 18th to prosecute their voyage towards Cape Chelyuskin, and steamed along the western shore of Taimyr Island, the northern extremity of which was found not to be so far north as shown in the charts. The ice that was met with was only bay ice so broken up that scarcely a piece could be seen strong enough to carry a couple of men. Taimyr Bay was nearly ice-free.

On the 19th the vessels continued their course along the coast of the Chelyuskin Peninsula, the fog being still exceedingly close, though occasionally lightening so that the contours of the land could be distinguished. In the course of the day they steamed past an extensive field of unbroken ice occupying a bay on the western side of the Chelyuskin Peninsula. It appeared, however, on close inspection that this fast ice was nearly as rotten as that which they had met with at sea.

The fog was so dense that Nordenskiöld feared that Cape Chelyuskin would be so closely enveloped in it that it would be impossible to land. Soon, however, an ice-free promontory again glinted out in the north-east, and the *Vega* and *Lena* soon after anchored in a little bay, open to the north and ice-free, that cuts the promontory in two. Flags were hoisted, and a salute fired from one of the small cannon carried by the *Vega*. The first object of the voyage had been attained—the northernmost point of the old world, variously called Cape Chelyuskin, Cape Severo, and North East Cape.

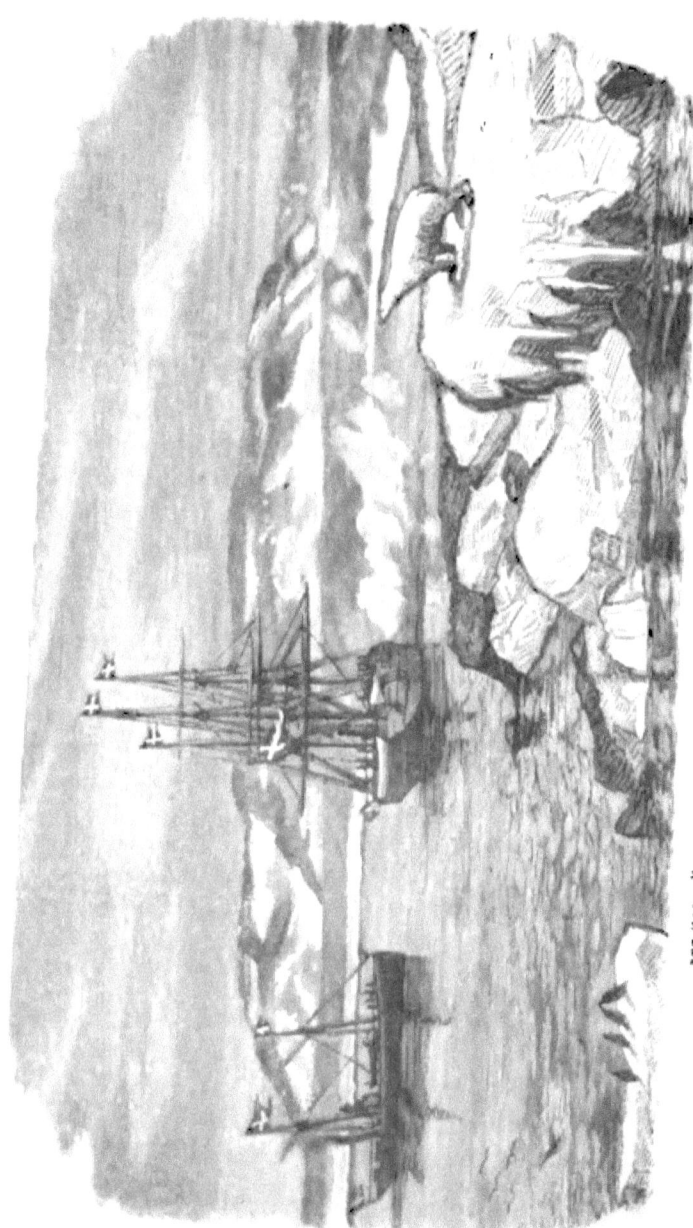

THE "VEGA" ROUNDING CAPE CHELYUSKIN, THE NORTHERNMOST POINT OF THE OLD WORLD.

The air had cleared and the cape lay before them lighted up by the sun and free from snow. A large Polar bear was seen parading the beach with eyes and nose turned towards the bay to inspect the new arrivals. Frightened by their salute it took to flight and escaped the balls of the Swedes. The *Vega* and the *Lena* remained here until noon of the 20th in order to fix the position of the cape by an astronomical observation and to give the naturalists an opportunity of making excursions.

Cape Chelyuskin forms a low promontory, divided into two parts by the bay in which the vessels had anchored. More elevated land with gentle slopes runs parallel with the coast from the eastern shore towards the south. The western promontory was found to be 77° 36′ 37″ N. Lat., and 103° 25′ 39″ E. Long. from Greenwich. The eastern is a little farther to the north, viz., 77° 41′ N. and 104° 1′ E. Inland the mountains appear to rise gradually to a height of 1,000 feet. Both the plains and the high land were nearly free of snow, but the icefoot still remained at the beach in most places.

The plains consist of clay-fields, of which some are nearly bare and split up into more or less regular six-sided figures; some are covered with a mixture of grass, moss, and lichens, resembling that found at the places where landings had previously been effected. The rock here was not granite, but upright unfossiliferous strata of slate, full of pyrites, and crossed at the outer promontory by thick quartz veins. Of phanerogamous plants Dr. Kjellman could only discover twenty-four species, most of them marked by a disposition to form compact, half-globular tufts. Dr. Almquist found the

lichen vegetation monotonous, though luxuriant. It
almost appeared as if the plants of the Chelyuskin
Peninsula had tried to migrate farther north, and when
they encountered the sea had stood still on the outer-
most promontory. For here in very small compass were
found nearly all the plants, both phanerogamous and
cryptogamous, which the land had to offer, and many of
them were sought for without success farther up the
plain. Animal life on land was equally meagre. Of
birds there were seen only a number of sand-pipers,
some species of *Tringa*, a large flock of brent geese, a
few eider ducks, and the remains of an Arctic owl. In
the sea, now nearly ice-free, a single walrus, two shoals
of white whales, and a few seals were observed—and it
was evidently poor in warm-blooded animals. On
the other hand the dredge brought up various large
Algæ (*Laminaria Agardhi*, &c.) and a number of
minute animals, among them very large specimens of
Idothea entomon.

At noon on the 20th the *Vega* and *Lena* left their
anchorage and steered in an eastward direction in the
hope of meeting with a continuation of the new
Siberian islands. Drift-ice was soon met with which
was at first very open, but consisted of larger floes than
had been previously encountered. Navigation was
rendered difficult by a dense fog. After having sailed
through a pretty compact ice-field during the previous
night, the Swedes found on the 22nd that no further
progress could be made. The course was accordingly
altered to a more southerly one, but without better success.
After lying-to for some time anchored to ice-floes, and
searching in vain for a navigable channel leading to the

south or east, the *Vega* and *Lena* worked themselves out
of the ice by the way they entered. This occupied a
whole day, and by the evening of the 23rd they were
again in open water. The depth, which had varied between 33 and 35 fathoms, now began to diminish, and the
north-eastern extremity of the Taimyr Peninsula, situated
in 76° 30′ N. and 130° E., was sighted the same evening.

The air had cleared, and a fresh breeze carried the
vessel rapidly along without the aid of steam over a
perfectly smooth sea. Soon the cliffs along the shore
became high and of that peculiar split-cone formation
which marks the eastern bank of the Yenissej between
Mesenkin and Jakovieva. Picturesque mountains, at
least 2,000 to 3,000 feet high, were seen a short distance
inland. These were free of snow to their highest
summits, though some small collections of ice and what
were thought to be small glaciers could be observed.
Animal life now became very rich. While the vessels
lay anchored to the floes Dr. Stuxberg had dredged up
from a depth of thirty-five fathoms an unexpected
variety of marine animal types, among which were
three specimens of a crinoid, probably young individuals
of *Alecto Eschrichtii*, which besides was found full
grown in excessive abundance, masses of sea-stars, the
extremely rare *Molpadia borealis*, two cuttle-fish, a
colossal Pycnogonid of 180 m.m. diameter, &c. At a
less depth the lower animal life was not less rich, though
the types were partly different.

All the animals found here were clearly of pure Arctic
types, without any migration whatever from southern
seas, as is doubtless the case with the fauna of Spitzbergen. The collections will therefore be of great scientific

interest in connection with the researches which have for a long time back been carried on by the naturalists of the North concerning the glacial animal forms, living and fossil, found on the shores of Scandinavia, and which touch questions of great importance for a knowledge of the latest era of the history of our globe.

Often now no trace of ice could be seen from the vessels and, as they before encountered land where sea was shown on the maps, they now sailed over regions marked as land on the maps.

At 11 a.m. on the 24th August land was sighted, which was identified with Preobraschenski Island, at the mouth of the Chatanga. Landing here, Nordenskiöld found the island to belong to the chalk formation, and its strata were shown by the only fossil discovered (a belemnite) to be contemporaneous with those which occupy extensive portions of the plains of north-western Siberia. After the 23rd the weather was magnificent, and the sea completely ice-free. The depth of water during the rest of the voyage to the mouth of the Lena was from five to eight fathoms. The temperature of the water at the surface was ascertained six times a day, and the temperature and salinity at different depths once or twice daily. It was found that if the depth reaches thirty metres the temperature at the bottom varies between $-1°$ and $-1°·4$ C. The specific gravity of the water amounts there to from $1·026$ to $1·027$, the salinity being little less than that of the Atlantic. At the surface the temperature was exceedingly variable. Thus for instance it was $+10°$ C. at Dickson Harbour, $+5°·4$ a little south of Taimyr Straits, $+0°·8$ among the drift-ice immediately off this strait, $+3°$ off Taimyr Bay,

—0°·1 at Cape Chelyuskin, +4° off Chatanga Bay, and +1°·2 to 5·8 between the Chatanga and the Lena. The salinity of the surface water in a broad channel along this part of the coast never exceeded 1·023, and was generally below 1·01. The latter figure corresponds to a mixture of one part of sea water with two parts of river water.

These figures show incontestably that a warm and only slightly salt surface-current runs from the mouths of the Obi and the Yenissej along the coast in a north-easterly direction, and afterwards, under the influence of the earth's rotation, in a more easterly course. Other similar currents proceed from the Olenek, Lena, Jana, Indigirka, and Kolyma, which all pour their waters, more or less warmed during the hot summer of Siberia, into the Polar Sea, and make it, during a short season of the year, nearly ice-free along the coast. It was a correct apprehension of these facts which led Nordenskiöld to draw up the programme of this expedition.

It was his intention to anchor off the mouth of the Lena, but a favourable wind and an open sea offered so splendid an opportunity of continuing his voyage that he did not consider himself justified in neglecting it. The *Vega* and the *Lena* accordingly parted on the night between the 27th and 28th August, the former to sail direct to Fadeyev, one of the New Siberian Islands, where Nordenskiöld intended to remain some days, the latter to ascend the river of the same name.

A pilot had been engaged to descend the Lena and wait the arrival of the small steamer of the same name, but Captain Johannesen could discover no flag-staff or signal-tower, which, according to the contract that had been entered into, ought to have been visible from Cape Olenek. Left to his own resources, Captain Johannesen, after considerable difficulty, from the shallowness of the water, made his way through the delta of the Lena, and on the 7th September entered the river, where navigation was less difficult. Yakutsk was safely reached on the 21st September. Despatches from the *Vega* were sent on to Irkutsk, and a telegram from that town on the 16th October announced to the civilised world the successful accomplishment of the first part of the programme of the expedition—the rounding of Cape Chelyuskin and the navigation of the Lena by a steamer from the Atlantic.

Nordenskiöld, when parting from the *Lena*, hoped, if he should meet with no extraordinary delay from ice, to reach Behring's Straits by the end of September. He was then to make his way to Yokohama. Weeks and months passed, however, without further news, and it became probable that he had been caught in the ice, the rather because American whalers reported 1878 a bad ice year north of Behring's Straits. At length, on the 11th December, the *New York Herald* published a telegram from San Francisco, dated the previous day, in which it was stated that two American whalers, who had newly returned from St. Lawrence Bay, in the neighbourhood of Behring's Straits, had been informed by two trustworthy natives that they had seen a Russian war-ship frozen in north of East Cape, at a distance of forty English miles from land.[1] This vessel,

---

[1] Other accounts placed the vessel at a distance of only ten miles from the coast in a bay between an island and the mainland west of

supposed by the natives to be Russian, was immediately identified as the *Vega*, and a lively concern for the safety of the expedition, without any proper justification from the facts of the case, was generally felt. Again months passed without further intelligence, and the trustworthiness of the native reports began to be doubted, when, in the middle of May, after Mr. Alexander Sibiriakoff had despatched a steamer, named after Nordenskiöld, and built expressly for the purpose, to his relief, despatches were received from the expedition, from which it appeared that the *Vega* was lying frozen in near Serdze Kamen, a cape situated at a distance of only 100 nautical miles from Behring's Straits, and visited almost yearly by whalers from the Pacific. Later despatches enable us to give the following details.

After parting from the *Lena*, the *Vega* steered in a North-Easterly direction towards the most Southerly of the New Siberian Islands. These islands are very remarkable in a scientific point of view, being very rich in the remains of the mammoth and other animals of the same period, which are found in greater abundance among them than in the *tundra* of the mainland. Some of the sand-banks on their shores are so full of the bones and tusks of the mammoth that the ivory collectors who for a series of years travelled nearly every year from the mainland to the islands in dog-sledges, used to return in autumn, when the sea was again covered with ice, with a rich harvest. According to Hedenström, the only educated person who has examined these islands in

East Cape, and in the neighbourhood of a native village, which, in case of need, would afford shelter and subsistence to the members of the expedition.

summer, there are besides in the interior hills which are covered with the remains of the mammoth, the rhinoceros, horse, aurochs, bison, sheep, &c. In consequence of the inaccessibility of the region, no thorough scientific examination of these remains has yet been undertaken. Nordenskiöld, knowing the importance of even a superficial inspection, wished to lie-to at one of the islands or at least to cruise between them.

The air was calm, but the sky for the most part overcast; the temperature as high as + 4° C., and the sea free of ice. Rapid progress accordingly was made. But after Semenoffski and Stolbovoj, the most westerly of the New Siberian Islands, had been sighted on the 28th August, the shallowness of the sea, which was for long stretches only three and a half to four fathoms deep, and some very rotten ice, or rather sludge, that was met with, prevented the *Vega* from going at full speed. On the 30th Liachoff's Island was reached, and Nordenskiöld wished to land, but had to give up the idea on account of the rotten ice which surrounded the island and the danger to which the vessel would have been exposed in such shallow water if a sudden storm had come on.

In order to ascertain the distribution of the land at the close of the Tertiary Period, to obtain a knowledge of the mammalia that were coeval with the appearance of man on the globe, to collect new contributions to a solution of the difficult problem—how it was possible for the progenitors of the Indian elephant to live in the icedeserts of Siberia, to get some more extended knowledge of the nature of the Siberian Polar sea—a point which now appears to be of great importance for navigation—

a thorough scientific survey of all the islands which lie to the north of the Siberian mainland ought, remarks the Professor, to be carried out as soon as possible. And for such a survey he considers the little steamer *Lena* the most suitable vessel, on account of its light draught of water, the tough Swedish Bessemer metal of which it is built, and the steam-saw with which it is provided.

The sound which separates the most southerly of the New Siberian Islands from the mainland is only 30′ broad. On the south side it is bounded by a promontory which, like many other points on the north coast of Russia which are rounded with difficulty, is called Svjatoi Nos (the Sacred Point). In 1736 the undaunted Arctic explorer Laptjeff declared that it was impossible to sail round this promontory, because according to the unanimous averment of all the Yakuts who lived in that quarter the masses of ice which surround it never melt. Three years after, however, it was rounded by Laptjeff himself—one of the many instances, says Nordenskiöld, of how possible many "impossibilities" are, in fact, found to be. The same feat was performed in 1761 in what appears to have been pretty ice-free water, by the Siberian merchant Schalavroff. Nordenskiöld believes that the sea here is navigable every year not only by a steamer, but also by a common fishing sloop provided it be manned by able seamen. On the 31st August the weather was calm and fine, and the *Vega* sailed through the sound, which was free of ice, without difficulty. The land in the neighbourhood was also free of snow.

Eastward from this point there was an open channel along the coast. The water was slightly salt, and had a temperature rising to $+ 4°$ C. Up to 1st September the weather continued fine with the wind in the south, the temperature of the air in the shade at noon being + 5°·6. On the following night the wind became northerly and the temperature fell to − 1°. Next night there was a heavy fall of snow, so that the deck and the Bear Islands, which were reached at noon of the 3rd, were covered with snow. These are several rocky islands lying off the coast in 71° lat. and 160° long. E. from Greenwich, about 360′ from the southern extremity of Liachoff's Island. This distance was traversed in three days, at the rate accordingly of 120′ per diem, a fact which, if the time which was lost in dredging, taking soundings, and determining the temperature and salinity of the water at different depths, and the caution that had to be observed in navigating unknown waters be taken into consideration, shows how little the progress of the *Vega* was hindered by ice. A few pieces of ice were met with, and further to the north continuous ice-fields were visible which prevented Nordenskiöld from carrying out his plan of sailing northward from the mouth of the Kolyma to ascertain if land or islands could be found between Liachoff's Island and Wrangel's Land. An attempt to steer right eastward to Cape Schelagskoj from the most easterly of the Bear Islands had also to be given up because the course was barred 40′ to 50′ east of the Bear Islands by impenetrable masses of ice. Nordenskiöld accordingly was obliged to betake himself to the narrow open channel along the coast, but that became narrower and narrower. He was compelled to keep closer and closer to the shore though the depth went on diminishing to an extent that was rather unpleasant. There were, however, no serious delays. The *Vega* passed the mouth of Tschaun Bay during the night before the 6th September, and Cape Schelagskoj was reached at 6 o'clock the next morning.

The nights now became so dark and the sea so full of ice, that the *Vega* had to lie-to during the night anchored to a large ground-ice. When it dawned on the morning of the 6th, the Swedes found themselves so surrounded by ice, that it was impossible to advance farther in a due easterly direction. It was necessary to seek opener water either to the northward, or in the still nearly ice-free but shallow channel along the coast. The latter course was chosen. But on this occasion there was no little difficulty in penetrating the masses of ice that surrounded the vessel.

The *Vega* had scarcely neared the land before two boats were seen of the same build as the "umiaks" of the Eskimo. They were full of natives, the first that had been fallen in with since the vessel had left Chabarova at Jugor Straits. A halt was made to allow them to come on board. They met with a friendly reception, but unfortunately none of them could speak Russian or any other language intelligible to the Swedes. Only one boy could count ten in English, a circumstance which shows that the natives have more communication with American whalers at Behring's Straits than with Russian merchants. Since then the Swedes have been in daily communication with the natives along the coast, but they have not in a single instance found one of the pure Tchuktches who travel far and wide capable of expressing themselves intelligibly in any European tongue. Lieutenant Nordquist devoted himself to a study of the language, and Nordenskiöld set free Jonsen, one of the walrus-hunters, from all other employment so as to enable him to live as much as possible among the natives and to become acquainted with their customs and language. The Tchuktche still partly uses implements of stone and bone, and his features have an unmistakable resemblance both to those of the Mongolians of the old world, and those of the Eskimo and Indians of the new.

Beyond Cape Schelagskoj the *Vega* steamed on during the 6th and 7th September in a narrow open channel along the coast, and on the following night was anchored as usual to a ground-ice-floe. The hempen tangles and the trawl-net were used with good effect. Next morning the progress was found to be impossible, and Nordenskiöld and his comrades landed at the invitation of the natives. The beach is low and sandy, running between a small lagoon and the sea; farther from the sea the land gradually rose to bare hills free of snow, or only thinly covered with it from the snow-fall of the last few days. Lagoon formations of the same kind as were here met with for the first time are distinctive of the coast of north-eastern Siberia. The villages of the Tchuktches are commonly situated on the beach which separates the lagoon from the sea. The dwellings consist of large roomy tents, which inclose one or two sleeping-places. These form as it were a special inner tent of warm reindeer-skin, which is heated and lighted by a train-oil lamp. In summer, but not in winter, a wood fire is kept up in the middle of the exterior tent, an opening being made in the top of it for the escape of the smoke.

The Swedes were received in a very friendly manner, and offered whatever the dwelling contained, the supplies of food being then abundant. In one tent reindeer-flesh was boiling in a large *pot of cast-iron*. In another tent, an old woman was employed in extracting from the paunch of newly-killed reindeer, the green, spinach-like contents, and stuffing them into a sealskin sack, evidently to be preserved during the winter as a stock of vegetable matter. Other sacks of sealskin were seen filled with train-oil. These sacks are both air and water-tight. They consist of the whole skin with the exception of that of the head, which is cut off at the neck. Children were met with in great numbers. They were well treated. They all appeared to be very healthy. They were often carried on the shoulder both by men and women, and were so wrapped up that they almost resembled skin balls. In the interior of the tent, on the other hand, they were completely naked, and they might be seen sometimes to run out among the tents on the frost-covered ground, at a temperature below the freezing-point, without shoes or other clothing. Fog rendered further progress impossible until the 10th September, a number of land excursions being made in the interval. The beach is sandy, and immediately above high-water-mark is covered with a luxuriant carpet of grass. Further inland a very high range of hills was visible, and beyond it, at a considerable distance from the coast, snow-covered mountain-tops. The low land consists of layers of sand and clay, evidently raised above the sea-level at a very recent date. It is remarkable that the erratic blocks, which form so remarkable a feature of the loose earthy layers of northern Europe and northern America, are here completely wanting, a circumstance which appears to show that during the latest geological periods, glaciers have not played any great part in this portion of the northern hemisphere. Nor, to judge from the complete absence of erratic blocks from the present seashores, does there now exist in the sea to the northward any such glacial land as Greenland.

At some places the solid rock runs out to the coast and there forms precipitous cliffs fifty to sixty feet high, which consist of magnesian schists, limestones more or less silicious, and silicious schists. The strata run from north to south, and are nearly vertical, but contain no fossils. They yielded Dr. Almquist numerous contributions to the hitherto completely unknown lichen flora of this region. In consequence of the advanced season of the year, the higher land plants collected were few, and Dr. Kjellman dredged in the sea for algæ without success. Animal life was scanty—in the sea were seen only a walrus and some seals, on land no mammalia were visible, but holes and paths of the lemming, crossing the land in all directions. Among birds a species of *Phalaropus* was seen. In the neighbourhood of the place where the *Vega* was anchored there are for the present no dwellings, but at many places along the beach old foundations of houses were visible. At one place at the mouth of a rivulet, Dr. Stuxberg discovered a large number of graves with burned bones. The burning had been so complete that only a few of the remaining fragments of bone could be recognised by Dr. Almquist as human. After the burning, the remains of the bones and the ash had been gathered into the hole and covered first with turf, and then with small flat stones.

This was the first time a vessel had lain off this
coast. The arrival of the *Vega* was evidently a very
remarkable occurrence for the natives, and the report
of it must have spread rapidly. Though there were
no tents in the neighbourhood, the Swedes received
many visits. The correspondence between the household articles of the Tchuktches and the Greenlanders was
remarkable. This correspondence often exists in the
most minute particulars.

The wares most in request with the natives were
sewing and darning needles, knives, preferably large
ones, axes, saws, boring and other tools of iron, shirts
of wool and linen, preferably of bright colours but
also white, neckerchiefs, and tobacco. Of course brandy
also was in demand — an exchangeable article of
which Nordenskiöld had a supply, but which he did
not think it right to use. For this the natives will
offer anything. Otherwise they are shrewd and calculating men of business, and have been accustomed
to it from childhood through the barter which is
carried on between America and Siberia. Many a
beaver-skin that comes to the market at Irbit belongs to an animal that has been caught in America,
whose skin has since gone from hand to hand among
the wild men of America and Siberia, until it has at
length reached the Russian merchant. For this barter
a kind of market is held on the island Ilir in Behring's
Strait. Ilir however is only one of the intermediate
stations. At the most remote markets in Polar America,
according to the Russian traveller Dittmar, a beaver-
skin is sometimes exchanged for a single leaf of tobacco.

Tobacco is here in universal use. All the men, and

the women too when they get an opportunity, smoke
peculiar pipes, and the men always carry a tinder-box
and tobacco-pouch. The pipes are exceedingly small.
The material employed for smoking is sometimes tobacco, at other times some substitute, of which samples
were taken. For producing fire there were used steel,
agate, and tinder formed of woody fibre, by chewing
some suitable kind of tree or bush. Tobacco and its
substitutes are also chewed. The chewed tobacco is
placed behind the ear to dry, and is then used for
smoking. Salt is not in use, but all are very fond
of sugar. They do not care for coffee unless with
a very large quantity of sugar, but they are fond
of tea.

Dr. Almquist examined the colour-sense of a large
number of the natives, and found that nearly all had
normal vision. In order to induce them to submit
themselves to this test, he offered the examined at
the close of the examination a little brandy, amounting
at first to a cubic inch and a half. This made many
of them slightly intoxicated, cheerful, merry, unsteady
on their legs, but not quarrelsome.

Some bore small amulets on the neck, which they
would not part with. One carried a Greek cross on
the neck. He appeared to have been baptized, but
his Christianity did not come to much. He crossed
himself to the sun with much zeal in our presence.
This was the only trace of religion or religious observance that we could discover. The men's dress consists
of one or more "pesks" of reindeer-skin, resembling
those of the Lapps. Upon the "pesk" is worn in
rainy or snowy weather a shirt of gut, or for show

of cotton cloth, which is called by the natives "calico." The main head-dress consists of a close-fitting pearl-ornamented cap, but both men and women generally go bare-headed. The shoes consist of mocassins with soles of walrus-skin, in winter sometimes of bear-skin, in the latter case with the hair outwards. The dress of the women consists of "pesks" which are very wide, not open below, but sewed together, so as to form wide trousers, which go to the knees, in addition to which an outer pesk, resembling the men's, is worn during winter. The lower part of the arm of this garment is wide and open, as was the fashion with ladies at home some decades ago. In the inner tent the women go quite naked with the exception of a narrow girdle, probably a reminiscence of the dress the people wore when they lived in a milder climate. They wear their hair long, parted at the top and plaited. The men generally have the hair shaved off or clipped to the root with the exception of the outer margin, which is left inch-long, and is combed over the face in front. The same custom was so prevalent among the Indians in the interior of North America two hundred years ago, that the famous missionary Hennapin could put himself on good terms with the Indian women and obtain food by combing their children's locks. Most of the men carry pearls or other showy articles in the ears. The women are tattooed with two dark-blue lines bent inwards on either side of the face from the eye to the chin, four lines on the chin converging towards the mouth, and some peculiarly formed markings on the cheek. The men are sometimes, but not always, painted with a black right-angled cross placed obliquely on the cheek-bone, or with some reddish brown colouring matter.

During the night before the 10th September the sea was covered with a very thick crust of newly formed ice. The drift-ice appeared to have broken up somewhat. The *Vega* therefore proceeded on her voyage, but was soon brought up by a belt of old ice so firmly bound together by the ice that had been formed during the course of the night that a channel had to be cut through it. Beyond this belt the sea was pretty open, but the fog became so dense that the *Vega* had to lie-to beside a ground-ice. On the 11th the *Vega* continued her voyage, and on the 12th having passed Irkiapi or North Cape a good way, fell in with ice so compact that it was impossible to penetrate further. It was only with great difficulty that she could force her way towards land. She was at length anchored on the inner side of a ground-ice stranded near the extreme point of the promontory.

Close to the promontory the sea is very deep, but a violent storm drove the ice-floes in the neighbourhood backwards and forwards with such force that it became necessary to remove the *Vega* to a little bay formed by two rocky points projecting towards the north. Here the vessel had to lie till the 18th September waiting a change in the state of the ice. For the name North Cape, given to this promontory because it was the most northerly point of the mainland of Siberia seen by Cook during his voyage north of Behring's Straits, ought, says Nordenskiöld, to be substituted the native name Irkiapi, to prevent it from being confounded with other capes which have a better title to the name.

On this promontory there is a village, consisting of eighteen tents. There are also the ruins of a large number of dwellings which belonged to a race which formerly lived in these regions, and several hundred years ago was driven by the Tchuktches, according to their statement, to islands lying at a great distance in the Polar Sea. Wrangel says the people were called Onkilon, and he narrates several very interesting traditions of their last battles, which are said to have been fought out on this bold headland.

Lieutenant Nordquist and Dr. Almquist made excavations at the dwelling-places of the Onkilon tribe, and collected several old implements of stone and bone. The houses were in groups. They were, at least partly, built of whales' bones and driftwood, covered with earth, and were connected by long passages with the open air and with one another. Probably their method of building resembled that of the Indian race the Indgeletes at Norton Sound described by F. Whymper in his travels in Alaska.

The kitchen-middens in the neighbourhood of these old dwellings contain bones of the whale, walrus, seal, reindeer, bear, dog, fox, white-whale, and several species of birds, together with stone and bone implements. Though they had lain in the earth for 250 years, there were stone implements still fast in their wooden handles, and the thongs with which they had been bound were still remaining. To these old inhabitants, as to the present, the tusks of the walrus furnished a material which in case of need could replace iron in the manufacture of lance-points, arrows, fish-hooks, ice-axes, &c. Whales' bones, and perhaps mammoth bones, were used on a great scale. The former were found in abundance. Several of the old Onkilon dwellings were used by the Tchuktches to keep blubber in, and at others excavations appeared to have been made in the kitchen-middens in search of walrus-tusks.

At the top of the stony *débris* at Irkiapi there were found two old dwellings. These were probably built during the conflicts which preceded the expulsion of the Onkilon tribe. At several places on the slopes of the mountain were seen great collections both of large numbers of lichen-covered bears'-skulls laid in rings with the nose inwards; and of reindeer, bear, and walrus skulls mixed together in a less regular circle, at the centre of which reindeer horns were piled up. Along with the reindeer horns were found the skull and part of the horns of the elk or some other large species of deer. Beside the other bones lay heaped together innumerable temple bones of the seal, which had evidently formed part of sacrificial offerings. As no human bones were found, and the remains were said by the natives to be those of the Onkilon tribe, these were probably old sacrificial places.

The prevailing rock in this region is of a plutonic nature, somewhat resembling gabbro. On the west side of Irkiapi it is intercalated with a black schist containing traces of fossils, possibly graptolites. Kjellman was successful in obtaining some algæ with the dredge, but the collections of the zoologists were scanty on account of the unfavourable nature of the bottom.

From a hill 400 feet high Nordenskiöld had an

extensive view of the sea, which was everywhere covered with the unbroken pack with the exception of the narrow channel along the shore, which however was also at many places interrupted in an ugly way by belts of ice.

Up to the 18th September the state of the ice was unchanged. But if a wintering was to be avoided it was not advisable to delay longer. The *Vega* accordingly steamed along the coast in the open channel, the depth of the water varying from three and a half to four and a half fathoms. The *Vega's* draught of water is from sixteen to seventeen feet. After forcing her way with great difficulty through a belt of ice, the vessel ran aground on a ground-ice foot, and, as the tide was ebbing, she was only got off the following morning after a considerable part of the ground-ice had been cut away with ice-axes. Some attempts to blast the ice with gunpowder were unsuccessful, and Nordenskiöld suggests that dynamite, as being a much more powerful explosive than gunpowder, should be carried on voyages in the course of which it may be desirable to blast a way through belts of ice.

During the 19th the *Vega* continued her course in the same manner as before through smooth and for the most part shallow water along the coast between high blocks of ground-ice which often had the most picturesque forms. No true icebergs were to be found here. Later in the day very low ice that had been formed in rivers or narrow inlets of the sea was met with, and the *Vega* sailed in water which was only slightly salt and whose temperature was over the freezing point. The following day the *Vega* continued her course almost exclusively

between low, dirty ice, which had not been subjected
to much pressure during the preceding winter. It
has less depth in the water than the blue ground-ice
and therefore drives nearer the coast—a great inconvenience for a vessel so deep in the water as the *Vega*.
A point was soon reached where the depth of water was
only from twelve to fifteen feet. The *Vega* accordingly
had to lie-to to wait for more favourable circumstances.
The wind had now changed from W. to N. and N.W.
The temperature became milder and the weather rainy,
a sign that there must have been great stretches of open
water to the north and north-west. During the night
before the 21st it rained heavily with the wind N.N.W.
and a temperature of + 2° C. An attempt was made
to find a place where the pack that was pressed against
the coast could be broken through but it was unsuccessful, probably on account of the very dense fog which
prevailed. On the 21st Nordenskiöld and Palander
took soundings to the eastward and discovered a channel
through which the *Vega* continued her voyage on the
23rd among very close drift-ice, often so near land
that there was only a foot of water under the keel.

The land here forms a grassy plain, still free from
snow, rising to gently-sloping hills or eminences. On
the beach there was a considerable quantity of driftwood, and here and there were to be seen remains
of Onkilon dwellings. On the night before the 26th
the *Vega* lay-to near a pretty large opening in the
ice-field, which unfortunately closed during the night,
so that it was not until the 26th that further progress
could be made, at first with difficulty but afterwards
in pretty open water, to a point called on the maps

Cape Onman, and to which the natives that came on board gave the same name. The ice met with here was larger bluish-white, not dirty.

On the 27th the eastern side of Koljutschin Bay was reached. The following night was calm and the temperature sank back to $-2°$ C. Notwithstanding the limited degree of cold, the sea was covered with newly formed ice, which indeed in the opener places could only delay, not hinder, the progress of the ship, but which bound together the ice-floes lying off the coast so firmly that a vessel, even with the help of steam, could with difficulty force her way. On the following day when the *Vega* had sailed past the point that bounds Koljutschin Bay on the east the narrow channel along the shore became too shallow, and it being found impossible to advance in any other direction the ship was made fast to a ground-ice, the Swedes hoping to get loose and traverse the few miles that separated them from the open water at Behring's Straits, the more confidently because whalers several times had not left the place until the middle of October.

This hope was to be disappointed. For at least a month after the 28th September, a north wind blew, at first with violence, but afterwards more gently, heaping up greater and greater masses of ice along the coast, and by degrees bringing down the temperature to $-26°$ C. By the 25th November the newly formed ice was *nearly two feet thick*, and there was no longer any hope of getting free before next summer.

The *Vega's* winter harbour was situated at the northernmost part of Behring's Straits in the neighbourhood of the tent village Yintlen, a mile from land and only

115′ from the point where Behring's Straits open into the Pacific. "When we were frozen in," writes Nordenskiöld, "there was ice-free water some minutes farther east. A single hour's steaming of the *Vega* at full speed had probably been sufficient to traverse this distance, and a day earlier the drift-ice at this point would not have formed any serious obstacle to the advance of the vessel.

"This misfortune of being frozen in so near the goal," he continues, "is the one mishap during all my Arctic journeys that I have had most difficulty in reconciling myself to, but I console myself with the brilliant result, almost unexampled in the history of Arctic exploration, that has been already won, with our excellent winter harbour, and with the prospect of being able to continue our voyage next summer. A winter's meteorological and magnetical observations at this place and the geological, botanical, and zoological researches which our being frozen in will give us an opportunity of prosecuting, are besides of sufficient interest to repay all the difficulties and troubles which a wintering involves."

"Now that the ice has become so thick," wrote Lieutenant Palander on the 25th November, "I consider the *Vega* perfectly safe from ice pressure. From our southerly position we suffer little from darkness. To-day we have seven hours' daylight, and even on the 21st December we shall have no less than five hours. The temperature is uniform and falls slowly. The minimum to date is $-28°$ C. The average temperature of the month of November is nearly $-20°$ C. The wind during the two months we have been here has blown steadily between N.E. and N.W., mostly from N.N.W.

"We have erected on shore a house of ice-blocks, intended for a Magnetic Observatory. The instruments have been mounted and the observations begin to-morrow. All the way from Cape Chelagskoj the coast is thickly studded with villages, consisting each of from five to fifteen tents, inhabited by Tchuktches, a tribe doubtless descended from the Eskimo of Greenland. The Tchuktche has black hair and eyes, a brownish-yellow skin, and is small of stature. He is very friendly and serviceable, especially if he gets 'kakau,' a common expression for all kinds of food. He will do almost anything for a drop of brandy. During summer a number of American vessels come here and carry on barter with the Tchuktches. These vessels introduce annually large quantities of spirits, notwithstanding the prohibition of the Russian Government. We have made it a rule never to use brandy in barter; only a drop is given them sometimes to encourage them. In our immediate neighbourhood are three villages, Yentlin, Pitlekaj, and Irgonouk. The natives live by fishing, including whale-fishing, and hunting the seal and walrus. They are dressed in reindeer-skins, with which they also cover their tents, procuring them by barter with the nomad portion of the population of the Tchuktch Peninsula, the so-called Reindeer-Tchuktches, who carry on the breeding of reindeer and wander from place to place. During winter, when fishing is impossible, the coast Tchuktches travel along the coast with dog-sledges and carry on barter with the natives of other villages."

Christmas and New Year's Day were celebrated with the usual festivities, the temperature outside being −35° C. The cold was very disagreeable, especially when it was accompanied by a strong wind. The wind continued to blow between N.W. and N.E. except on two occasions, when a southerly and a south-westerly storm brought warm air along with them. On the 30th December the temperature for several hours was as high as + 2° C. During both these storms the ice opened at a distance of several English miles. The average temperature of October was −5·2° C., of November −16·6°, of December −22·8°, and of January −25·1°. The minimum temperature to the end of January was −46°C.

During their imprisonment the members of the expedition enjoyed good health and spirits. The time was spent in busy scientific work and in intercourse with the friendly Tchuktches, who supplied the party with bears and reindeer. Game was abundant and spring brought numbers of wild fowl. The dreaded scurvy was absent, thanks to the thorough precautions taken for its prevention, and in some degree no doubt to the circumstance that there was no dark period, the upper limb of the sun being visible on the shortest day. There was little sickness and no death among the members of the expedition.

At length after 264 days' detention in the ice the *Vega* was released on the 18th July and passed East Cape, Behring's Straits, on the 20th, having thus been the first to accomplish the North-East passage.

Skirting the Asiatic coast the *Vega* entered St. Lawrence Bay, then crossing to the American shore visited

Port Clarence, and recrossed to Konian Bay, dredging carefully all the while, the sea-bottom being particularly interesting on account of the meeting of currents from the Arctic and Pacific oceans. After touching at St. Lawrence Island Nordenskiöld next visited Behring's Island, and discovered there the fossil remains of the gigantic marine animal *Rhytina stelleri*. Leaving the island on the 19th August, the *Vega* had a pleasant voyage till the 21st, when she encountered a severe gale during which lightning struck the vessel, splitting the maintop and slightly injuring several persons. At length at 10.30 P.M. on the 2nd September she cast anchor in the harbour of Yokohama, and in a short space of time the telegraph spread the news of her arrival over the civilised world.

Professor Nordenskiöld considers the voyage from Europe to the east coast of Asia certain of accomplishment and safe with a little more experience. He believes that all the northern seas from Japan to the Lena present no difficulty to skilful navigators, and looks forward to a large prospective trade with Central Siberia.

After a fortnight's stay at Yokohama the *Vega* proceeds on her memorable voyage, in the course and at the conclusion of which the illustrious leader of the expedition and his distinguished comrades will be welcomed with universal acclamations as worthy sons of the old Vikings, and as men who have made their names immortal by breaking the line of innumerable defeats by a splendid and bloodless victory, achieved by human skill and daring over the powers of Nature and the rigours of the Icy Seas.

APPENDICES.

APPENDICES.

APPENDIX I.

OFFICIAL REPORT TO THE (SWEDISH) ROYAL BOARD OF HEALTH ON THE HYGIENE AND CARE OF THE SICK DURING THE SWEDISH POLAR EXPEDITION, 1872-3, BY DR. A. ENVALL, MEDICAL OFFICER.

Appointed, as a volunteer medical officer on the steamer *Polhem* during the Arctic Expedition, 1872—1873, I now proceed to report to the Royal Board of Health concerning the hygiene and care of the sick during the expedition.

For this expedition the Government had granted the use of two vessels, the mail steamer *Polhem*, and the brig *Gladan* as tender, the latter only for the summer months, though from unforeseen occurrences it had to winter.

The *Polhem* is, as is well known, quite a small iron steamer, only 110 feet long. For this voyage the vessel had been completely covered in by building over the deck from fore to aft, which was of extraordinary utility, particularly in bad weather. No other arrangements had been made, as it was not intended that we should pass the winter on board, but should live on land in a house made in Gothenburg. The brig *Gladan*, as has been already mentioned, also stood at the disposal of the expedition, for the purpose of conveying, to the place where it was to winter, the house and other necessaries.

Besides these two vessels, the expedition was obliged to charter a third, the *Onkel Adam*, which brought us coal, forty reindeer, and reindeer moss for them.

The *Polhem's* crew consisted in all of twenty-nine persons, counting in the chief, the medical officer, and three scientific men, but it was intended that during winter this number should be reduced to twenty two, inasmuch as one of the scientific men and six of the crew were to return with the brig *Gladan*. Its crew consisted of two superior and two inferior officers, and twenty one men, in all twenty five.

On the *Onkel Adam* there were thirteen persons, counting in the master and mate. One was a woman acting as cook. The number of those who wintered through the shutting in of both the other vessels in the ice was sixty-seven, in place of twenty-two as had been originally intended. Of these sixty-seven, twenty-nine lived in the house erected on land, twenty-five on board the *Gladan*, and thirteen on board the *Onkel Adam*. On board the *Gladan*, which was not intended to winter, as has just been stated, various arrangements were made for protection against the much dreaded Arctic winter, and to endeavour to maintain a good sanitary state. The whole deck from fore to aft was covered with a tent of sails, so that one could very comfortably take exercise in the open air, protected from bad weather and cutting winds. It was unfortunate that this tent required several times to be moved, in order that the vessel might be navigated during the breaking up of the ice, which repeatedly happened during bad weather. The officers and an inferior officer lived aft in berths which were warmed by a good stove in the little cabin. They protected themselves from draughts from the colder hold below them, by reindeer hides laid on the cabin floor, and the walls were made pretty tight by felt and extra boarding. The crew and an inferior officer lived in the "trossbotten," which for so little a vessel was very roomy, but for the present number of inhabitants, namely, twenty-two, and under these circumstances must be considered too confined, inasmuch as for every man there were only 80—90 cubic feet of space. It was warmed partly by a stove, partly by the galley which stood there, and a comparatively very good ventilation was obtained, partly by the opening downwards, and partly by the opening above the galley. In order to avoid draughts and damp, and make the "trossbotten" as healthy as possible, the tross deck was covered with felt, the deck with boards between the beams of the deck, the floor with tarpaulins and reindeer skins over them, and all iron was covered over with oakum and grease; one of the store cabins was arranged as an excellent sick cabin, and aft the galley a large and roomy washing cabin was fitted up, the latter, in my opinion, a very good arrangement whereby a great deal of damp and dirt was avoided in the rest of the "trossbotten." Besides these arrangements, for which the officers of the vessel deserve all praise, a stove was also, on my proposal, placed in the hold, where fire was kept up day and night. The temperature could there in general be maintained without difficulty many degrees above the freezing point, and even up to 10° C. and higher. The advantage of this was that the crew, whether employed, or in their leisure moments, did not require to live in the confined "trossbotten," but could remain in that large and airy apartment, whereby the deterioration of the air in the "trossbotten" was in no small degree diminished. On board the *Onkel Adam* the master, inferior officers and cook, five persons in all, lived aft in a cabin with berths, the others in a very dark and confined forecastle. Extraordinary arrangements, similar to those on the *Gladan*, were also made here for protection against the storms and the cold of winter, and the hold, which was placed in communication with the forecastle by a door, was kept warmed by an iron stove. The temperature here, however, could not in general be maintained many degrees over the freezing point. The cubic contents of the forecastle were 640 cubic feet, or eighty cubic feet per man. Both these crews were thus in this respect under more disadvantageous circumstances than those who lived on land, where the cubic contents of the men's room were 2,772 cubic feet, or divided among eighteen men, 154 per man.

PROVISIONS.

In this respect the same regulations were in force as during the expedition of 1868, namely, that the ordinary rules for men-of-war being set aside, the chief, in consultation with the medical officer, was entitled to make suitable arrangements for the dietary. In the light of the experience obtained during preceding expeditions, both English and Swedish, two such dietaries were framed, one for summer, the other for winter. I annex these together with the dietary with reduced rations, which required to be drawn up in consequence of the unforeseen increase of the *personnel*, and for the sake of comparison, the dietary that was in force for the *Sofia* in 1868. From 1st October, 1872, to 1st July, 1873, we lived on rations reduced almost to two-thirds, a circumstance which could not have other than an injurious influence on the state of health, of which more below. The *Polhem* was provisioned for twenty-two men for eighteen months, and the *Gladan* for twenty-five men for six months. The steamer *Onkel Adam*, which arrived at Spitzbergen on the 13th August, had then only provisions for some few weeks, but, with a praiseworthy foresight, the master purchased from the Ice Fjord Company, then in course of being broken up, about six months' provisions. The provisions for the *Polhem* and the *Gladan* had been bought in Copenhagen from the well-known purveyor, Beauvais, and taken overhead ; the provisions were of excellent quality. Some remarks, however, I must make, which perhaps will affect the dietaries as much as the purveyors.

The preserved meat,—that of Beauvais consisted of meat and soup together,—like all preserved foods, does not, in my opinion, fully replace the fresh, though from a theoretical point of view the meat at least ought to do that. It soon becomes quite tasteless, so that one gets disgusted with it, and this effect on the taste probably has an influence on the nutrition, and thereby indirectly on the nutritive value of the food. This may appear a somewhat bold hypothesis, but according to my experience, and as far as I have been able to form an impartial judgment, fresh and preserved meat do not appear to me to have quite the same nutritive value. The soup which accompanied the meat was, on the contrary, palatable in a high degree, but I will not say on that account that its nutritive value was particularly great. I have tested preserved provisions from several firms, and to a certain extent this holds good of them all. Such meat as has not had soup made with it is of course much better, and for such journeys only this kind of preserved meat ought to be used, and the soup taken separately. Besides, perhaps, a little variety of beef, mutton, and veal, were useful, such as the Englishmen had in their Arctic expeditions ; one then tires of it less speedily. The preserved vegetables, which consisted mainly of roots in thin dried slices, were of great service as an addition to the soup, but could not be used for other purposes. With respect to them, it is still more problematical in what degree they replace fresh vegetables. Among the preserved foods it was the potatoes which we had in the form of dried slices and meal, which in the opinion of all best served the purpose of replacing the fresh. All the salt meat and pork, as well as the bread, was from Copenhagen, and the quality was such that no fault could be found with it.

From 1st October, 1872, to 1st July, 1873, fresh bread was baked daily by the employment of leaven. Potatoes, in which, as is well known, there is a substance capable of passing into fermentation, were used in preparing it. After being well boiled and kneaded, the potatoes were mixed with a small quantity of warm water, and left over-night in a moderately warm place. After ten to twelve hours, common fermentation had begun in this mixture, and by the addition of flour, an excellent leaven was obtained, which afterwards could be used an indefinite number of times, by adding as much flour every time a portion of the leaven was taken away, to raise the dough. In this way, well fermented and well tasted bread was daily obtained. Various other methods were also tried among others, one with yeast powder from Copenhagen, but they were all more or less unsuccessful, while on the contrary, the above described method was quite certain and reliable. With more or less attention directed to scurvy, there had been placed in the dietary, pepper, vinegar, mustard, extract of meat, sour-krout, raisins, prunes, currants, and dried fruit, and more directly for medical purposes there were stocks of preserved milk, pickles (a large sort), and horse-radish preserved in vinegar. I think we ought not to ascribe to extract of meat any special anti-scorbutic properties, though according to current views of the nature of scurvy, these ought to be very great; in practice this did not appear to be the case.

With respect to the dried fruit, I will only remark that there would have been no harm if the quantity had been somewhat greater. Of preserved milk we had several kinds; two of Norwegian manufacture were exceedingly bad, one of them, adulterated with flour, when dissolved in water, yielded a deposit which gave a reaction with iodine. That obtained for the vessel was from Beauvais, and was also very bad. The best of all the sorts which I have tested, both now and during previous expeditions by sea, is the Swiss. The horse-radish preserved in vinegar might doubtless with great advantage have been replaced by the fresh root from Sweden. The pickles, considering their low cost, were exceedingly good and serviceable for those attacked by scurvy, as was also the lime-juice, which is considered indispensable for such expeditions, and of which of course we had a supply.

Besides the ordinary dietary the gunroom *personnel* had provided themselves with better preserved provisions, some wine, and other extras.

Among these I may specially mention 2,000 eggs, preserved with aseptine by Herr Gahn, in Upsala, but of which scarcely 100 could be used. According to my experience, gained in a foregoing sea-voyage to warmer countries, aseptine is not a suitable means for preserving eggs.

Chocolate was drunk instead of coffee twice a week, and I consider it to be specially suitable in the Arctic regions, although it was not much relished, especially in the beginning, but the taste is far from pointing out always what is most useful. I believe spirituous liquors to be of great use in small and moderate quantities, but exceedingly mischievous and pernicious in the case of the least excess. They consisted of brandy and concentrated rum, the latter specially ordered from London for the ice journeys, and of only middling flavour. For the ice journeys which were projected, and which also were carried out, there had been provided 1000 lb. pemmican—artificially dried meat, mixed with fat, some currants and sugar, and placed in hermetically sealed tins. Of the excellence of this food for such journeys there cannot be two opinions. Some, however, have a dislike to it.

We were unable to obtain any great increase to the stock of provisions during the first summer, because we lay for a long time at a place quite unsuitable for hunting, and during the remainder of the season were too much engaged with preparations for the winter. Two reindeer that were shot in September had uncommonly fine and savoury flesh. They were, however, at that time rather fat, having under the skin a layer of fat nine to ten centimetres in thickness. Those that we obtained earlier in the summer from the walrus-hunters were not so fat, and therefore better. In October were shot about 150 ptarmigan, which formed a welcome delicacy. Several seals were also killed and their flesh eaten under the form of beefsteaks, by most with relish and appetite. The same was the case with the flesh of a bear that was shot during winter under our windows. Of the many sea-fowl that visit Spitzbergen during summer, it is without doubt the *Alca Brünnichi* which has the most savoury flesh. Next in order, perhaps, comes *Mergulus Alle*, though it is exceedingly small, so that a great number of them are required to make a meal for the crew of a vessel. Besides the rest—as black guillemots and eiders—were not neglected, especially both in spring when we were quite tired of preserved meat, and in winter when we had no superabundance of provisions.

We had not taken any great stock of beer because we did not think it could be kept fresh and good any great length of time. Experience, however, showed that this was not the case, for in the gunroom there was a little private stock, of which there remained some in April which was then excellent.

Some other little luxuries, as preserved whortleberries, and other preserves of different kinds, fruit juice, dried apples, prunes, and so-called "drops," had been taken along by private members, and were all in great request.

CLOTHING.

The expedition was as well provided in the way of clothing as in that of provisions, partly from the stores of the Crown, partly through purchase, although the abundant stock was also in this case reduced by the unforeseen occurrences. On board the *Gladan* underclothing was made from felt taken from the naval stores, and it answered the purpose very well, though it was not very strong in wear. Besides, as much of the stock intended for the *Polhem* was handed over as could be spared. I believe none of the man-of-war's men had reason to complain that they needed to freeze. The case perhaps was different with the crew of the *Onkel Adam*, of whom I found some very poorly clad; but after my remarks on this point to the master, the matter was amended in one way or other.

In summer other clothes are not required on Spitzbergen than what are commonly worn in Sweden in spring and autumn.

In winter some increase is of course required. With complete woollen underclothing, and the common thick sailor's clothes, sea-boots, and skin-cap, the men got on commonly very well. During the coldest time there were dealt out to the crew so-called "skallar," a sort of shoes, made of the skin of the reindeer's head, in which was placed a certain kind of dried grass. These shoes are exceedingly warm, and with them a man can defy the severest cold. For the cold season the men had a sort of overcoat of canvas, lined with wool. Under ordinary circumstances, and with constant exercise, no furs were required. There were mittens both of wool and skin in quantity. Besides, for the ice journeys were used "peskar," reindeer-skins with the hair outwards, sewn together both behind and before, so that when put off or on they required to be drawn over the head like a shirt, "bällingar," a sort of overtrousers, also of reindeer-skin, canvas boots, and "komager," or fine boots of soft leather, also with hay inside. Next the foot, over the stocking, were used, during the ice journeys, foot cloths, about two feet in length, with which the foot was draped above the stocking before it was inserted into either the "skallar" or "komager" above described. The excellence of this foot covering is best evidenced by the fact that not a single case of frost bite occurred in the case of those who used them.

During the ice journeys too, gutta percha mattresses, which could be inflated with air, formed part of the equipment. In this way the damp, which otherwise would have arisen from the action of the heat of the body on the snow and ice, was wholly avoided.

ROUTINE AND DISCIPLINE.

A well-arranged routine and proper discipline are, without doubt, of the very greatest importance for the hygiene during a winter in the Arctic regions. Besides the sorrowful fact that seventeen Norwegian walrus-hunters at one place, and two at another, who at the same time with us braved the dangers of the Arctic winter, succumbed, and without doubt just through this want of discipline, the difference in the state of health that prevailed on the two Government vessels on the one hand, and the commercial ship on the other, showed, in my opinion, the effect of this uniform routine and discipline.

On board the *Polhem*, or more correctly on land, the time was divided in the following way :—6.30 A.M., general awakening; 8, muster, after which free gymnastics for ten to fifteen minutes, and breakfast; from 9 to 12, work; from 12 to 1, mid-day rest; from 1 to 5, work, after which the men had leave to employ themselves as they had a mind; 7.30, supper, and 10, to bed. None was allowed to sleep by day without special reason or permission. On the *Gladan* the ordinary routine of a man-of-war was observed. On the *Onkel Adam*, on the contrary, the master was less strict in maintaining proper discipline, and as he himself neglected or transgressed what was useful in this way, the crew also fell into habits of indifference and laziness, and on board great disorder prevailed; and, notwithstanding my injunctions, the men were not kept to cleanliness and neatness.

MEDICAL STORES.

These consisted of the common complete equipment of vessels belonging to the navy, consisting of bandages and instruments, linen, &c.

With attention specially directed to the supposed severity of the winter, there were bought in Gothenburg thirteen respirators, which however did not come much into use.

APPENDIX I.

There were also purchased twenty-four so called "goggles," and they were not only of great use, but absolutely indispensable. As the stock of them was not sufficient, the carpenters had to make such spectacles as the Eskimo and Greenlanders use. They were of wood, and were not so good nor so convenient to go with as the proper spectacles. Of the latter, the soot-coloured are the best, the blue do not diminish the intensity of the light, only change the colour, and are therefore not so reliable for the prevention of snow-blindness. Neither are green or blue veils, which were tried during the English Arctic expeditions, and by several during our expedition, so much to be relied on. Those who use the soot coloured spectacles certainly escape snow-blindness.

The stock of medicines was specially large, because we were to be completely shut out from the rest of the world, and thus, if anything had been wanting, there would have been no possibility of procuring it.

From Medical Councillor Herr Dr. Edholm, I obtained a collection of Professor Almén's *Gelatinæ medicatæ in lamellis*, which he wished to have tested for their practical utility; I had also bought a quantity as medical stores for the projected ice-journey, when the weight and bulk of the equipment were of so great importance, and the *gelatinæ* therefore appeared to me to be of great utility.

Through a very extensive employment of them, I have had opportunities of making observations of their practical utility, during sea expeditions especially, and of their great practical value in general. Excepting that some, as *Gel. acetatis plumbici*, and *Gel. tartratis stibicokalici*, had a fine crystalline powder on the surface, they all, after the fifteen months the expedition lasted, showed themselves unaltered both in their outward appearance and in their therapeutic action. In order to ascertain if different ways of keeping them would affect them differently, they were kept in dry and moist, cold ($-30°$ to $-38°$ C.), and warm ($15°$ to $30°$ C.) places, and I have here only to remark a certain disposition to the formation of mould in those that were exposed to damp, and in two *Gel. lactatis ferrosi*, and *Gel. gummi guttæ aloeticæ*, which lay in a warm place, a certain brittleness and fragility, doubtless caused by a too small addition of glycerine.

For military medical officers and others who are obliged to act as apothecaries, they are on account of the facility of dispensing, so convenient and of so great utility as to be far above my praise.

They ought also to be of great use and practical importance for hospitals and similar institutions, partly for the reason already stated, partly because they appear to remain unaltered nearly for any length of time, and thus what is not consumed on one occasion may be used another time, and long after with advantage, which is not the case with medicines in the form of infusions and decoctions, or even of powders and pills, not to speak of some other common modes of dispensing. Another thing which makes the *gelatinæ* so useful and practical, is the ease with which medicine in this form can be taken by the patient, without his being in the least annoyed by its taste or smell. He takes only the small capsules of gelatine (one or more) into his mouth with a few drops of water and swallows them, and the medicine is carried without the least inconvenience into the stomach, and I have seen patients who said they had the greatest difficulty in taking even the least disagreeable medicines, who could with ease take them in the form of *gelatinæ*. That gelatine preparations act at least as certainly and speedily as medicines under other forms when taken inwardly, I have never had reason to doubt. An advantage of the *gelatinæ* so easily understood that I need not waste any words upon it, is the ease with which one in very small bulk, as in his pocket-book, note-book, or otherwise in his pocket, can carry a very large collection of medicines. Their cheapness, as compared with other forms of dispensing, is also of great importance. In short the utility and practical value of *gelatinæ* are so evident that we can only be astonished at their not having come into general use, to which it has perhaps conduced in some degree that they have not been placed in the list of medicines.

In Tromsoe there was purchased a large vessel containing 130 lbs. preserved cloudberries (*Rubus Chamæmorus*), which, according to the medical men there, are a good antiscorbutic. As such we had besides from Copenhagen, as above stated, two kegs of large pickles, twenty bottles of horse radish finely sliced, preserved in vinegar, and from England, fifty kannor (nearly thirty gallons) lime-juice. There were besides, for hospital use, 200 tins of preserved milk. To the hospital equipment also belonged several articles taken from the naval stores at Carlskrona; mattresses, woollen nightshirts, English hammocks, &c.

CLIMATE AND DISEASES.

The climate of Spitzbergen during the summer months is very good and healthy; the variations of temperature are not very great. As summer we cannot reckon more than the half of June, July, August, and part of September.

According to our experience, which concerns the latter half of one summer and the first half of the succeeding, August and the half of September, as well as the latter half of June and the whole of July, were very fine and pleasant. Yet I believe the weather is very changeable at different places on Spitzbergen. During our stay at the Norways, the north-west corner of Spitzbergen, where cold and warm winds often meet, there was a great deal of fog and violent gusts of wind, now from one direction, now from another. The temperature was sometimes a couple of degrees under the freezing point, but averaged in general from $2°$ to $4°$ C., and even rose to $7°$ C. Rain and snow, though not in considerable quantities, were not uncommon. The first half of September at Mussel Bay, where we were compelled, by obstacles presented by the ice, to settle instead of at Parry Island, as had been intended, was the finest season we had during our stay on Spitzbergen, but the sun was now no longer circumpolar, and the nights began to be dark. In the middle of the month violent snowstorms commenced, and the temperature sank hastily. On the 16th September the vessels were shut in by masses of drift ice. In the last days of the month we had already a temperature of $-29°$ C., not a very good outlook for the winter. During the first four months, however, it was not of any uncommon severity; on the contrary, it was sometimes very mild, as $3°$ C. in the month of January, at the 80th degree of latitude. The temperature was during this period subjected to many frequent and sudden changes; a rise or fall of $10°$ C. in an hour was not uncommon. In the same way the variations of the barometer were sometimes very great. The sun, which disappeared on the 22nd October, was replaced only in an inconsiderable degree by the moon and the frequently recurring aurora. Frequent storms raged particularly during November and January, and drifting snow and fog combined to make the darkness yet more impenetrable. During the darkest period, from the middle of November to about the middle of January, one could not take long walks.

The depressing influence of darkness on the spirits was too evident to escape any one of ordinary powers of observation. There were some persons, indeed, who declared that the darkness did not in any way affect them; the same persons, however, complained, like others, of the difficulty of sleeping at night, &c. Over the most came a certain indisposition to exertion, coupled with a peculiar irritability of temper, and when in February light began to return the countenances also lightened, and the spirits became better and gayer, the difficulty of sleeping at night disappeared when the distinction between day and night returned, to show itself again in some cases when the sun became circumpolar and there was no longer any night.

February and March, and even a part of April, were the winter months proper. In order to avoid repetition, I refer to the tables of temperature in the Appendix. During these months the air was calm and often clear, though fogs of ice-crystals also hung over the ground, and thick snow showers were not absent. During April and May a very severe cold still continued, and few or almost no signs of spring showed themselves.

Towards the end of May, and during the month of June, milder weather commenced, the temperature by day being a few degrees above the freezing point, and by night a few degrees under it. The summer climate of Spitzbergen is, as we have said, without doubt very good, and even healthy, but we must remember that here, as at most other places, one summer is probably very different from another. Of the "continual sunshine," and the "weather always calm and fine," we did not enjoy too much. In this respect we were perhaps unfortunate, as in so many others. Thick fogs often concealed the sun, and rain and sleet with a raw and damp atmosphere greatly preponderated over the clear and glorious days of sunshine, of which so much is said in foregoing accounts. Either some difference in this respect must in fact have been experienced, or it may perhaps be explained by the disposition in the narrators to remember better the pleasant days than the chilly ones; but with the notes before me I must leave the facts as they are without any poetic colouring one way or the other. It must be allowed that when the weather was fine it was so indeed; although the temperature was not high, the sense of enjoyment surpassed all description. One breathed so easily the clear transparent air then; in fact, it appears to be, as a colleague has previously expressed it, "more respirable," and I cannot find any more suitable expression. The winter climate, which is far from equalling in severity that of Siberia or the

Archipelago of North America, perhaps on the contrary ought to be considered as less salubrious, both on account of the long continued low temperature, the frequent storms, and the sudden changes of weather, the great variations of temperature within short spaces of time, and above all, the intolerable darkness. Their effect was exhibited somewhat differently in different individuals. As has already been stated, there occurred in some a disposition to sleep, an indisposition to exertion, and a feeling of indifference; in others an occasional irritability, with a generally deep depression; some complained of sleeplessness by night and great fatigue by day, and all were in a more or less distinctly marked chloro-anæmic condition. On the return of the sun the colour of the face was a pale yellowish green, as of plants reared in darkness, or with an insufficient supply of light. Another effect of the long Arctic winter, which ought perhaps to be ascribed indirectly to the darkness, and more directly to the anæmic condition, was a generally prevailing dyspepsia, a sort of want of tone in the organs of digestion. During the winterings of the English in the Arctic regions, I have found this often remarked. To the general loss of flesh, which occurred with very few exceptions, and in a very great degree, the darkness may also have conduced to some extent, but mainly both the quality of the food, and above all its insufficiency in a quantitative respect. For the sake of comparison I annex a table showing the nutritive value of the rations consumed during several expeditions and in different circumstances. For the figures in this table I do not of course claim any absolute value, but having been calculated according to the same analytical tables, they ought to be sufficiently exact for a comparison.

The rations on the *Onkel Adam* were nearly the same as on the vessels belonging to the navy, but an unfavourable circumstance was their containing a larger quantity of salt meat.

It is exceedingly difficult to say on what the purity of the air on Spitzbergen depends. But with the increasing knowledge of germs, and their relation to a number of diseases, one is very much inclined to suppose that if they are not entirely absent there, they occur under other forms, or to a considerably smaller extent, than elsewhere, a supposition which gains support in the highest degree from several phenomena, as the way in which putrefaction takes place there, the complete absence of some diseases, and the relatively limited number of others, which are either certainly known or are believed to be dependent on these germs.

The life-conditions of these disease-producing organisms must there be very unfavourable on account of the low temperature, but wherever men settle and dwell they may bring with them germs, and favourable conditions for their development may also arise.

I did not consider that I had sufficient experience to settle the question regarding germs, but I naturally had my attention always fixed on all circumstances which might have a bearing on it.

Remarkable indeed is the small number of catarrhs in the respiratory passages which occurred, and of how mild a nature the cases were, and how one might expose himself to chills without bad effects. There was scarcely a single individual who did not during the cold season make acquaintance to a greater or less extent with cold water, and in no single case did any injurious consequences follow the cold bath. Only two cases of bronchitis have been registered in the sick journal, and even these were not of any special intensity. Very many exceedingly mild attacks of catarrh in the respiratory passages indeed occurred besides these. Coryza occurred in not so few cases, but only one or two were of a fully-developed nature. I believe, however, there is no good ground for the proposal to send consumptive patients, and persons liable to repeated catarrhs, to Spitzbergen. A hired Norwegian with chronic bronchitis had, both during summer and winter, several very acute attacks of it, and returned noways improved in health. One case, of course, does not prove much.

The state of things was quite different with disturbances of the digestive organs; acute and chronic gastric catarrhs, indigestion, and occasional diarrhœas were exceedingly common. During the ice journeys, when Lieutenant Palander had the care of the sick on his hands, equipped principally with gelatine capsules, it was diarrhœa that gave most trouble—scarcely any one escaped. They were relieved with ease by a capsule or two of opium or Dover's powder; but it recurred after a day or two, to be again removed in the same way. During these laborious marches the men were very thirsty, and drank eagerly, and Palander, in his notes, is inclined to believe that this was the cause of the diarrhœa. But during a couple of days when Palander and his men were obliged to halt on the inland ice on account of a snowstorm—and it is mentioned in his notes that a very small quantity of water was drunk—diarrhœa occurred. I am inclined to believe that the diarrhœa was caused by the pemmican with the large quantity of fat, the sugar, and the dried meat, almost free of water, which it contained. Rheumatic affections, mainly in the form of muscular rheumatism, were as common as the disturbances of the digestive organs. Only five cases are noted in the sick list, but besides these, there were a great number of mild attacks. Of three cases of articular rheumatism, two of them in the same person, one was complicated with both pericarditis and pneumonia, and it was only with great exertions that I succeeded, after several months, in getting the man well.

Two attacks of pleuritis, both in the same person, of which the second was without doubt a complication of scurvy, have occurred. Here, indeed, were wanting both the affection of the gums and the common purple spots; but the indistinct rheumatoid pains, the profuse repeated bleedings at the nose, the œdema over the ankles, the brawny effusions in the connective tissue over the left ankle, the thrombosis of the veins of the ankle, and the copious effusion in the right pleural sac, found on a *post mortem* examination, appear to me sufficient evidence of scurvy. Pneumonia in the other lung occurring at the same time, with rapidly-increasing pulmonary œdema, brought this patient's life to a close.

There occurred in all twenty-eight attacks of scurvy, of which twelve were on board the *Onkel Adam*, or 92·3 per cent. of the crew; ten on board the *Gladan*, or 40 per cent.; and six among the *Polhem's* men, or 20·6 per cent.

These different percentages appear to me conclusive evidence of the different effects produced by the circumstances in which the crews were placed. As unfavourable for the *Onkel Adam's* men we must consider both their having more salt meat than the others, the inferiority of their quarters, and the comparative absence of order and cleanliness which prevailed there; and for the *Gladan* the confined space in which the men lived; and besides, for both these vessels' crews the psychical effect of finding themselves quite unexpectedly compelled to winter in these desolate and gloomy regions. For the *Polhem's* men all these circumstances, as has been pointed out above, were much more favourable. For all the three there is an additional etiological consideration of great importance with respect to scurvy, namely, the reduced rations. That the Arctic regions specially predispose to the development of scurvy is a fact so generally known that I need not further refer to it. Add to this so important a consideration as the insufficiency of food, and we have only to congratulate ourselves that we were so fortunate as to lose but a single patient.

In the month of June, however, the condition of the sick was such that I am almost certain that if the Englishman, Mr. Leigh Smith, had not kindly presented the expedition with a large quantity of preserved provisions, fresh potatoes, and other refreshments, we should not have got off with less than one or more deaths in addition.

The effect of these supplies was very evident ; in the course of a week or two all were improving, a number of small ailments were, as it were, blown away, and the anæmic and reduced condition that prevailed with most of us had almost completely disappeared. The psychical depression among the men, which was caused by the news that no vessel was coming from Sweden to our assistance, had, I believe, great influence on the deteriorated condition which began in June. It was as if the hope of relief from home, which now all at once came to an end, had hitherto kept them up.

Among the principal symptoms of scurvy were the rheumatoid pains, which occurred very early, and might easily mislead the inexperienced in the diagnosis, and the anæmic and reduced condition. The affections of the gums were wanting in many cases. Large and fœtid sores in the palate and gums were not uncommon. In many cases the teeth were loose and movable in their holes. Bleedings at the nose and effusions in the connective tissue, the latter showing themselves under the form of hard infiltrations under the skin, with or without violet discolourations of it, occurred in the largest number of cases. These infiltrations, which generally were as hard as bone, and were from the size of a walnut to that of the closed fist, were sometimes painless, sometimes tender and painful. Occasionally they extended over the whole leg, from the groin to far below the knee, and again from the toes to above the knee, with all the varieties of colour which are caused by a serious contusion. The leg in such cases was always stiff at the knee, and could not be bent, and the patients were thus obliged to use crutches. The infiltrations were considerably more common in the leg than in the arm, and in the latter only occurred to a limited extent ; they were never found in the trunk. The small purple spots, which are so characteristic, were absent only in two cases ; œdema over the ankle was also seldom absent in the developed cases. Of the whole *personnel* 41·7 per cent., and of the different age-classes under 20, 50 per cent. ; 21 to 30, 43·7 per cent. ; 31 to

40, 36·3 per cent.; above 40, 44·4 per cent.—were attacked by scurvy; but no inference can be drawn from these figures, they are quite accidental. The disease attacked both those who had the worst bodily constitution and those who were strongest and healthiest. Some who had a dislike to the preserved provisions, and exclusively or mainly lived on salt meat, were first attacked.

With respect to treatment, I place first a well-arranged dietary, excluding salt provisions as much as possible; further, the greatest cleanliness and exercise in the fresh air, and regular work, as good for the spirits. Among pharmaceutical means I have with great advantage employed iron and quinine, and specially value the former as antagonistic to, and curative of, the anæmia. Vegetables and the juice of fruits of all kinds have been considered very useful, and certainly with good ground. Lime juice is, without doubt, also a good means of preventing and curing this disease. Best of all, in my opinion, are cloudberries; they were given in quantities of 125 grammes, or three to four large dessert spoonfuls daily. I had several opportunities of observing the difference between such patients as got cloudberries and those to whom I did not at first, for the sake of experiment, prescribe them. The improvement of the former began very soon, and made great progress, while the latter remained nearly at the same point till they got the same treatment as the others, after which they also speedily began to improve. I do not doubt, but am much inclined to believe, that some, and perhaps most other preserved berries, have a similar good effect. I had only opportunity in a single case to try whortleberries (*Vaccinium Vitis Idæa*), and their action was good. Both the pickles and the horse-radish also acted well, and the preserved milk was not without value. According to the view that this disease is caused by a diminution of the potash-salts in the blood, the extract of meat ought to have been specially effective. It was consumed in larger quantities, but I could never perceive any good effect it had. It may be urged, on the other hand, that if we had not had it, the disease would have raged to a greater extent.

Only of the greatest necessity did I permit a scurvy patient to lie still and keep within doors; if they could not walk crutches were made for them, and they had to go out into the fresh air a couple of hours daily. As a local application I employed principally camphorated spirits, which were highly valued by the patients as relieving the pain in the infiltrations already mentioned. The shortest period any scurvy patient was under treatment was

14 days, and the longest 132 days. The total number of days during which the scurvy patients were under treatment amounted to the considerable sum of 1,900, or on an average 67 days for each patient.

Of eye diseases there were some cases of simple conjunctivitis, and seven attacks of snow-blindness, not including the cases, also seven in number, which occurred during the ice journeys, some of which are said to have been very intense. They always occurred in the case of those who did not use glasses, some from obstinacy, others because they thought them inconvenient to walk with. None who properly used glasses were attacked, though on the other hand many who went without them also escaped.

This disease, so common in the Arctic regions, arises in working or marching out upon the snow-fields, where the eye has not a single dark spot to rest upon. The attack was very sudden; to the patient all appeared as if wrapped in mist, and he was unable to go forward alone. Soon after pain commenced, in most cases very suddenly, and after some hours, five to ten, there was the most intense conjunctivitis, the conjunctiva, and even the eyelid, being much swelled. Tears streamed in floods over the cheeks, and the patient complained like a child of the pains, which he described as feeling deep in the eye, and in the forehead over the eyebrow, and in the head. In most cases there was tenderness over the ciliary tract, and sooner or later there was developed a superficial keratitis with a clouding, commonly diffuse, of the whole cornea. In these cases the intolerance of light was raised to the uttermost, and the eyelids were kept spasmodically closed. Some cases which I examined with the ophthalmoscope only showed hyperæmia in the fundus of the eye.

By using cold compresses, and prescribing calabar, and, in the cases in which there was pain in the forehead, atropine, the treatment was over in a couple of days, and no sign remained of what the patient had suffered.

I cannot give any distinct indication for calabar, but it is certain that, in the cases where I employed it early, the disease was sooner overcome than in those in which I delayed or altogether omitted its use. Lieutenant Palander also valued the use of calabar in the attacks of snow-blindness which occurred during the ice-journeys. I had always considered snow-blindness as a hyperæsthesia of the nerves of the eye, and a blinding whereby the patient lost the power of vision, and from this point of view I looked upon calabar as useful, and this turned out to be the case. Except in the accounts of the Englishmen's and Americans' journeys in the Arctic regions, I had nowhere seen snow-blindness described in detail. They, however, appear to have registered under this name various diseases of the eye. Their treatment was very simple, consisting in dropping in "wine of opium." This I have also tried in two cases, and cannot deny that it was attended with very good results—calabar, however, shortened the treatment. In two cases the pains were so intense that it was only by the use of atropine and injections of morphia, and an artificial leech, that I could arrest them. In the general sick list I have placed them under the head of kerato-conjunctivitis, though that perhaps is not quite exact.

Of external injuries there have only occurred some trifling incised wounds and contusions. During the summer, and so long as we were on board, every injury, even the most inconsiderable, the least scratch in the skin, showed a disposition to go on to suppuration, which, however, I do not ascribe as any peculiarity to Spitzbergen; but it occurs, in my experience, also in common sea-voyages in cold weather, and perhaps is caused by contact with salt water.

Of injuries by frost there were some quite mild cases on the ears and nose, and above all around the palms of the hands. I cannot omit to state here the composition of the salve I used in such cases with great success, and the value of which I learned many years ago, how I do not remember. I consider it deserving of recommendation.

Rc. Chloret. hydrargyric. corrosiv. . . grm. 1.
    Ol. Ricini . . . . gtt. 40.
    Aetherol. terebinth. depur. . . . gtt. 60.
    Collodii . . . . grm. 50.

A man was lost during the ice-journeys by going astray on the ice among the drifting snow. He was probably frozen to death when overcome by fatigue.

Besides the care of the sick belonging to the expedition, I had several opportunities of giving medical advice to the Norwegian walrus-hunters, who during the summer visit Spitzbergen in great numbers. The diseases which principally occurred among them were catarrhs in the alimentary tract. An attack of gonorrhœa, one of spermatorrhœa, and some external ailments—among these a case of inflammation in a finger from a neglected panaritium—also occurred. The finger was amputated, and this was the only operation during the whole period.

Two persons with gunshot wounds, one on an English vessel, the other on a Norwegian, sought my assistance. In the former case a rifle-ball had passed through the muscular part of the forearm without damage either to the bone or to any large blood vessel; in the latter the gun had exploded, and the pieces had badly wounded the man's left hand, from the muscles of the thumb of which a small splinter of iron was extracted. Both these wounds were dressed with carbolic acid without permanent injury. That none of the Norwegians who wintered in Ice Fiord survived may appear wonderful, as they were as well provided with food as the Swedes, in other respects even better, and in no respect worse. But when one is informed how they passed the time in the most complete inactivity, lived like brutes in the most abominable filth and disorder, and that there was none to exercise authority over them or warn them of the danger of such inactivity and such a way of living, there is no ground for surprise that the scurvy took the upper hand, and that all succumbed to it. The advice and information they obtained from me during my visit to them, partly for some occasional ailments that then occurred among them, partly for possibly impending attacks of scurvy, they appear completely to have forgotten.

The corpses of two men who wintered at Grey Hook were examined by me, and showed evident and strong signs of scurvy.

Those at Ice Fiord were already buried at the time of our visit, but that they too fell a sacrifice to scurvy I believe cannot be doubted.

For further particulars I refer to the sick list.

NOTE.—In a communication addressed to the writer, Professor Nordenskiöld draws special attention to the fact that during the journey over the inland ice (see pages 220—263) no lime juice was used, the whole stock having been thrown away when it was found necessary to reduce the equipment of the exploring party.

APPENDIX I.

Dietary adopted till the 1st October, 1872.

Morning.	Noon.	Evening.
No. 1. 　　　　　　Grm. Butter . . . 25·5 Coffee . . . 31·875 Sugar . . . 31·875	Grm. Smoked bacon or dried 　fish . . . . . 321·0 Sourkrout . . . . 321·0 Preserved potatoes . 51·0 Preserved vegetables 26·4 Extract of meat . . 6·35 Brandy or rum 60 cub. cm. 　or beer . 350 ,, ,,	Grm. Butter 25·5 Sugar. 32·0 Tea . 6·35
No. 2. Same as No. 1.	Grm. Preserved meat . . 491·0 Preserved potatoes . 51·0 Preserved vegetables 26·4 Extract of meat . . 6·35 Brandy or rum 60 c.c.m. 　or beer . 350 ,,	Same as No. 1
No. 3. 　　　　　Grm. Butter . . . . 25·5 Chocolate . . 32·0 Sugar . . . . 32·0	Grm. Salt pork . . . . 425·0 Peas . . . . . 197·0 Barley . . . . . 40·6 Brandy or rum 60 c.c.m. 　or beer . 350 ,,	Same as No. 1
No. 4. Same as No. 1.	Grm. Salt meat . . . . 425·0 Peas . . . . . 197·0 Extract of meat . . 6·35 Barley . . . . . 40·6 Brandy or rum 60 c.c.m. 　or beer . 350 ,,	Same as No. 1
No. 5. 　　　　　Grm. Butter . . . . 25·5 Cheese . . . . 51·0 Bread . . . . 212·5 Brandy or rum 60 c.c.m. 　or beer . 350 ,,	Same as No. 2.	Grm. Butter 25·5 Cheese 51·0

Per day: Bread 531·0, tobacco 10·6 grm.
Per week: Salt 90·0, mustard 30·0, pepper 12·5 grm., vinegar 60 c.c.m.
Of the different dietaries, No. 1 was in force 1 day; No. 2, 3 days; No. 3, 2 days; No. 4, 1 day; No. 5, on extraordinary occasions.

APPENDIX I.

Dietary intended to be adopted from 1st October, 1872.

Morning.	Noon.	Evening.
No. 1. Grm. Butter . . . 25·5 Coffee . . . 32·0 Sugar . . . 32·0	Grm. Smoked bacon or dried fish . . . . . 324·0 Sourkrout . . . . 321·0 Preserved potatoes . 51·0 Preserved vegetables 26·4 Extract of meat . . 6·35 Rice . . . . . . 210·0 Raisins or currants . 21·0 Brandy or rum 60 c.c.m. or beer . 350 ,,	Grm. Butter . . 25·5 Sugar . . 32·1 Tea . . . 6·35
No. 2. Same as No. 1.	Grm. Preserved meat . . 292·0 Preserved potatoes . 51·0 Preserved vegetables 26·4 Extract of meat . . 6·35 Brandy or rum 60 c.c.m. or beer . 350 ,,	Same as No. 1.
No. 3. Grm. Butter . . . 25·5 Chocolate . . 32·0 Sugar . . . 32·0	Grm. Salt pork . . . . 425·0 Peas . . . . . 196·6 Extract of meat . . 6·35 Brandy or rum 60 c.c.m. or beer . 350 ,,	Same as No. 1.
No. 4. Same as No. 3.	Grm. Salt pork . . . . 425·0 Fruit soup . . . 1 portion Brandy or rum 60 c.c.m. or beer . 350 ,,	Same as No. 1.

Per day : Bread 531·0, tobacco 10·6 grm., lime-juice 15 c.c.m.
Per week : Flour 425·0, butter 125·0, salt 90·0, mustard 30, pepper 12·5 grm., vinegar 60 c.c.m.
Of the different rations No. 1 is in force 1 day ; No. 2, 4 days ; No. 3, 1 day ; and No. 4, 1 day a week.

APPENDIX I.

Dietary adopted during the Winter 1872-73.

Morning.	Noon.	Evening.
No. 1. Butter . . . 21·0 Grm. Sugar . . . 25·5 Coffee . . . 21·0	Grm. Smoked bacon or dried fish . . . . 300 Sourkrout . . . . 210 Preserved potatoes . 42·5 Extract of meat . . 6·35 Rice . . . . . 142·0 Currants . . . . 4·25 Brandy or rum 60 c.c.m. or beer . 350 „	Grm. Butter . . 21·0 Sugar . . 27·6 Tea . . . 4·25
No. 2. Same as No. 1.	Grm. Preserved meat . . 194·6 Preserved vegetables 26·4 Extract of meat . . 6·35 Brandy or rum 30 c.c.m. or beer . 350 „	Same as No. 1.
No. 3. Same as No. 1.	Grm. Salt meat . . . . 265·6 Preserved potatoes . 42·5 Sago . . . . . . 8·5 Barley . . . . . 20·3 Raisins . . . . . 17·0 Prunes . . . . . 4·25 Dried fruit . . . 12·5 Brandy or rum 30 c.c.m. or beer . 350 „	Same as No. 1.
No. 4. Butter . . . 21·0 Grm. Chocolate . . 21·0 Sugar . . . 25·5	Grm. Salt pork . . . . 265·6 Preserved potatoes . 42·5 Peas . . . . . . 145·2 Brandy or rum 30 c.c.m. or beer . 350 „	Same as No. 1.

Per day: Bread 425 grm. (two-thirds wheat, one third rye), Tobacco 5·95 grm.

Per week: mustard 19·4 grm., vinegar 60 c.c.m., pepper 8·5 grm., salt 38·0 grm.

No. 1 Sundays, No. 2 Mondays, Wednesdays, and Fridays, No. 3 Saturdays, No. 4 Tuesdays and Thursdays.

From 1st January to 1st May 15 c.c.m. lime juice.

From 1st February 85 grm. cheese per week, and 51 grm. flour per day.

APPENDIX I.

Dietary on board the SOFIA, 1868.

Morning.	Noon.	Evening.
No. 1. 　　　　　lb.[1] Butter . . 0·05 Coffee . . 0·07 Sugar . . 0·075	lb. Smoked bacon . . 0·75 Extract of meat . 0·0013 Preserved potatoes 0·12 Preserved vegetables 0·055 Rice . . . . . 0·5 Raisins or currants. 0·05 Brandy or rum 2 cub. in.	lb. Butter . 0·05 Tea . . 0·014 Sugar . . 0·075
No. 2. Same as No. 1.	lb. Preserved meat . . 0·596 Preserved potatoes. 0·12 Extract of meat . . 0·0013 Preserved vegetables 0·055 Brandy or rum 2 cub. in.	Same as No. 1.
No. 3. 　　　　　lb. Butter . . 0·05 Chocolate . 0·064 Sugar . . 0·075	Salt pork . . 0·75 lb. Peas . . . 7·5 cub. in. Extract of meat 0·0013 lb. Brandy or rum 2 cub. in.	Same as No. 1.
No. 4. Same as No. 3.	Salt meat . . 1·0 lb. Preserved potatoes ·12 lb. Groats . . . . 2 cub. in. Preserved vegetables 0·055 lb. Brandy or rum . 2 cub. in.	Same as No. 1.

Per day: Bread 1·25 (half rye, half wheat), 0·45 cub. in. lime-juice.
Per week: Butter 0·3, mustard 0·03, pepper 0·01, salt 0·12, vinegar 1 cub. in., wheat-flour 1·0, tobacco 0·135.
Sourkrout when it is given out, 0·5.
No. 1 Sundays, No. 2 Mondays, Wednesdays, and Fridays, No. 3 Tuesdays and Thursdays, No. 4 Saturdays.

[1] 1 Swedish lb. = 0·937133 lb. avoirdupois.

APPENDIX I.

Table showing the Mean Height of the Barometer, and the Mean, Maximum and Minimum Temperatures during the Swedish Polar Expedition 1872–1873.

Months.	Mean Height of the Barometer.	Mean Temperature.	Maximum Temperature.	Minimum Temperature.
August, 1872	760·40	+ 2·1	+ 7·5	- 3·0
September ,,	755·44	- 6·7	+ 8·7	- 29·6
October ,,	756·70	12·6	- 0·6	- 27·2
November ,,	756·60	8·2	+ 2·6	19·5
December ,,	757·28	14·5	- 3·4	26·6
January, 1873	750·63	- 9·9	+ 3·6	- 32·4
February ,,	753·08	- 22·7	- 0·0	- 38·2
March ,,	756·72	- 17·63	- 0·4	- 38·0
April ,,	762·42	18·12	+ 0·2	- 32·6
May ,,	770·77	-- 8·2	+ 3·6	- 19·4
June ,,	755·01	+ 1·11	+ 9·4	3·9

Table of the Nutritive Value of various Rations during various Expeditions.[1]

	Albumen	Gelatine.	Fat.	Carbo-hydrates.	Extractive Matter.
	Gram.	Gram.	Gram.	Gram	Gram
Swedish Man-of-war	162·43	—	87·1	431·57	4·57
Swedish Merchant-ship	196·81	—	52·42	604·63	10·1
English Arctic Expeditions	144·63	—	27·43	422·72	5·57
McClure's reduced rations (⅔)	96·42	—	18·28	281·81	3·7
Sofia, 1868	137·23	5·35	70·35	444·7	5·1
Polhem, 1872 till 1 Oct.	139·26	5·87	65·65	380·99	5·29
,, the intended winter ration	134·49	7·21	77·38	414·02	5·83
,, from 1 Oct., 1872, till 1 May, 1873	89·79	2·37	49·25	305·13	2·8
,, 1873, from 1 May to 1 July	91·54	4·19	50·13	358·83	4·02
Onkel Adam, from Oct., 1872	117·38	0·59	36·63	265·9	6·98

[1] All per man per day.

APPENDIX I.

Sick List of the Swedish Polar Expedition, 1872–1873.

	Under 20 years	21–30 years	31–40 years	Above 40 years	Total	January—March	April—June	July—September 1872	July—September 1873	October—December	Total	In good health and recovered	Dead	Total (Brought forwd.)
Officers and Staff of the Expedition		1			1	—	1				1	1	—	1
Inferior Officers, &c.	—	1	11	4	16	3	4	1		1	7	16	16	—	16
Carpenters			2	2	4	1	2			1	4	4	—	4
Sailors and Apprentices	—	12	2	—	14	—	4	4	1	5	14	14	—	14
Boatmen	—	12	17	1	30	1	13	4	—	12	30	28	2	30
Cooks (one female)	—	2		—	2	1	—			1	2	2	—	2
Private and Hired		2	11	—	2	15	5	6	—	1	3	15	15	—	15
Total	2	38	33	9	82	11	30	9	3	29	82	80	2	82

There were on board the *Polhem:* officers and staff of the expedition, 4; inferior officers, &c., 4; carpenter, 1; sailors and boatmen, 12; hired men, 6: total, 29. *Gladan:* officers, 2; inferior officers, 2; carpenter, 1; sailors and boatmen, 20; total, 25. *Onkel Adam:* master and inferior officers, 4; cook, 1; crew, 8: total, 13. Total of the whole, 67.

Number of days of treatment.—For the *Polhem*, 513; *Gladan*, 969; *Onkel Adam*, 1,051.

Average of sick per day.—On board the *Polhem*, 1·13; *Gladan*, 2·23; *Onkel Adam*, 3·1.

Cost of medicines.—For the *Polhem* and *Gladan*, 443·85 rixdollars rixmynt (about £24 12s.).

List of the Diseases.

Disease	Under 20 years	21-40 years	Above 40 years	Total	January-March	April-June	July-September, 1872	July-September, 1873	October-December	Total	In good health and recovered	Dead	Total
Scorbutus	2	14	8	128	9	13	—	—	6	28	28	—	28
Chloro-anæmia	—	1	—	1	—	—	—	—	1	1	1	—	1
Melancholia	—	1	—	1	—	—	1	—	—	1	1	—	1
Neuralgia supraorbitalis	1	1	—	2	—	—	—	—	2	2	2	—	2
Conjunctivitis simplex	1	3	1	5	1	2	—	1	1	5	5	—	5
Kerato-conjunctivitis [1]	3	4	—	7	—	7	—	—	—	7	7	—	7
Otitis externa	1	—	—	1	—	1	—	—	—	1	1	—	1
Angina tonsillaris	2	1	1	4	—	1	—	2	4	4	4	—	4
Pericarditis	—	1	—	1	—	—	1	—	—	1	1	—	1
Bronchitis acuta	1	1	—	2	1	—	—	1	2	2	2	—	2
Pneumonia	1	1	—	2	—	—	—	2	2	2	2	—	2
Pleuritis exsudativa	—	2	—	2	—	—	1	—	2	1	1	1	2
Catarrh, ventric. acutus	4	2	—	6	1	1	—	2	2	6	6	—	6
,, ventric. chron.	2	3	—	5	—	2	—	—	3	5	5	—	5
,, gastro-intestinal	2	1	—	3	—	2	—	—	1	3	3	—	3
Typhlitis stercoralis	1	—	—	1	—	—	—	—	1	1	1	—	1
Rheum. muscularis	1	2	2	5	1	—	1	—	3	5	5	—	5
Rheum. articularis acutus	1	2	—	3	1	—	1	—	1	3	3	—	3
Synovitis genu	1	1	1	3	—	1	—	—	2	3	3	—	3
Distorsio	—	1	—	1	—	1	—	—	—	1	1	—	1
Contusio	—	1	—	1	—	—	—	—	1	1	1	—	1
Vulnus contusum	2	1	—	3	—	—	3	—	—	3	3	—	3
Congelatio et perniones	1	2	1	4	1	3	—	—	—	4	4	—	4
Ulcus	—	—	1	1	—	—	—	1	—	1	1	—	1
Panaritium	—	2	—	2	—	—	—	2	—	2	2	—	2
Carbunculus	—	1	—	1	—	—	—	1	—	1	1	—	1
Furunculus	1	—	—	1	—	—	—	—	1	1	1	—	1
Accident [2]	—	1	—	1	—	1	—	—	—	1	—	1	1
TOTALS	24	47	38	109	97	16	34	13	3	31	97	95	2	97

[1] Snow blindness. [2] Lost in a snow storm during the ice-journey

APPENDIX II.

LIST OF BOOKS AND MEMOIRS RELATING TO THE SWEDISH ARCTIC EXPEDITIONS.

GEOGRAPHY.

1. Torell, O.—Bref om Island. (Letter on Iceland.)
K.V.A. Ofvers, 1857, pp. 325-332.

2. Chydenius, K. Svenska expedition en till Spetsbergen år 1861, under ledning af Otto Torell. (The Swedish Expedition to Spitzbergen in the year 1861, under the direction of Otto Torell.)
Stockholm, 1865. 8vo, pp. 489, 1 map, 16 pl.
Translated, see No. 4.

3. Svenska expeditionen till Spetsbergen och Jan Mayen, utförda under åren 1863 och 1864, af N. Dunér, A. J. Malmgren, A. E. Nordenskiöld, och A. Quennerstedt. (The Swedish Expedition to Spitzbergen and Jan Mayen, carried out during the years 1863 and 1864 by N. Dunér, A. J. Malmgren, A. E. Nordenskiöld, and A. Quennerstedt.)
Stockholm, 1867. 8vo, pp. 268, 1 map, 7 pl.
Translated, see No. 4.

4. Die schwedischen Expeditionen nach Spitzbergen und Beren-Eiland, ausgeführt in den Jahren 1861, 1864 und 1868, unter Leitung von O. Torell und A. E. Nordenskiöld. Aus dem Schwedischen übersetzt von L. Passarge. Jena, 1869.

5. Grad, Ch. A.—Esquisse physique des îles Spitzbergen et du Pôle Arctique.
Paris, 1866. 8vo, pp. 164, 1 map.

6. Fries, Th. M.—Resultaterna af de Svenska expeditionerna till Spetsbergen, af —— o——. (Results of the Swedish Expeditions to Spitzbergen.)
Svensk litteratur tidskrift, edited by C. R. Nyblom. 1868, pp. 216-240.

7. Nordenskiöld, A. E.—1868 års Svenska Polarexpeditionen under ledning af A. E. Nordenskiöld och Fr. v. Otter. (The Swedish Polar Expedition of 1868 under the leadership of A. E. Nordenskiöld and Fr. von Otter.)
Framtiden, edited by C. v. Bergen. 1869, pp. 642–657.
Translated, see No. 4.
,, Petermann, Mittheil., 1868, pp. 298–304.
,, London, R. Geogr. Soc. Proc., Vol. 13, pp. 151–165.
,, London, R. Geogr. Soc. Journal, Vol. 39, pp. 131–146.
,, Paris, Soc. de la Géogr. Bulletin, 1869, pp. 357–378.

8. Fries, Th. M. and Nyström, C.—Svenska Polarexpeditionen år 1868 med Kronoångfartyget *Sofia*. Reseskizzer. (The Swedish Polar Expedition of 1868 with the Royal steamer *Sofia*. Sketches of the Voyage.)
Stockholm, 1869. 8vo, pp. 237, 1 map, 4 pl.

9. Heer, Osw.—Ueber die neuesten Entdeckungen in hohen Norden. Vortrag gehalten den 28 Januar, 1869, auf dem Rathhaus in Zürich.
Zürich, 1869. 8vo, pp. 28. A Swedish translation was published at Stockholm in 1869.

10. Nordenskiöld, A. E.—Redogörelse för en expedition till Grönland år 1870. (Narrative of an Expedition to Greenland in the year 1870.)
K.V.A. Öfvers, 1870, pp. 973–1082, 4 pl.
Translated, see No. 34, 51.
,, Geol Mag., Vol. IX. 1872.
,, Paris, Soc. de la Géogr. Bulletin, 1873, pp. 318–325.

11. Fries, Th. M.—Grönland, dess natur och innevånare ; efter äldre och nyare författares skildringar samt egen erfarenhet tecknade. (Greenland, its nature and inhabitants ; delineated after the sketches of old and recent writers and the author's own experience.)
Upsala, 1872. 8vo, pp. 180, 11 pl.

12. Heer, Oswald.—Die schwedischen Expeditionen zu Erforschung des hohen Nordens vom Jahr 1870 und 1872 auf 1873.
Zürich, 1874. 8vo, pp. 14.

13. Nordenskiöld, A. E.—Redogörelse för den Svenska Polarexpeditionen år 1872–1873. (Narrative of the Swedish Polar Expedition, 1872–1873.)
K.V.A. Trans. App., Part 2, No. 18, pp. 118, 1 map, 1 pl.

Translated, Petermann, Mittheil., 1873, pp. 444-453.

14. Kjellman, Fr. — Svenska Polarexpeditionen, 1872-1873. (The Swedish Polar Expedition, 1872-1873.)
Stockholm, 1875. 8vo, pp. 355, 1 map, 1 pl.

15. Lindhagen, D. G.—Geografiska ortbestämmelser på Spetsbergen af Prof. A. E. Nordenskiöld ; beraknade och sammanställda. (Geographical determinations of places on Spitzbergen, by Prof. A. E. Nordenskiöld : calculated and collected.)
K.V.A. Handlingar, Part 4 (1861-1862), No. 5, pp. 47.
Transl., Petermann, Mittheil., 1864, pp. 127-135.

16. Nordenskiöld, A. E.—Geografisk och geognostisk beskrifning öfver nordöstra delarne af Spetsbergen och Hinloopen-Strait. (Geographical and geognostic description of the north-eastern parts of Spitzbergen and Hinloopen Strait.)
K.V.A. Handlingar, Part 4 (1861-1862), No. 7, pp. 25, 1 map.
Transl., Petermann, Mittheil., 1864, pp. 127-135, 208-215.

17. Dunér, N., and Nordenskiöld, A. E.—Anteckningar till Spetsbergens geografi. (Notes on the Geography of Spitzbergen.)
K.V.A. Handlingar, Part 6 (1865-1866), No. 5, pp. 15, 1 map.
Transl., Explanatory Remarks in illustration of a map of Spitzbergen. Translated from the Transactions of the Royal Swedish Academy of Sciences.
Stockholm, 1865.

18. Nordenskiöld, A. E., and v. Otter, F. W.—Karta öfver hafvet emellan Spetsbergen och Grönland utvisande ångfartyget *Sofias* kurser under den Svenska Polarexpedition, 1868, äfvensom drifisens läge under olika tider af aret, lodningar m.m. (Map of the sea between Spitzbergen and Greenland, showing the courses of the steamer *Sofia* during the Swedish Polar Expedition of 1868, also the position of the drift ice at different seasons of the year, soundings, &c.) Stockholm, 1869. Fol.

19. Petermann, A.—Das Relief des Eismeer. Bodens bei Spitzbergen. Nach den Tiefsee-Messungen der Schwedischen Expedition unter Nordenskiöld und v. Otter, 1868.
Petermann, Mittheil., 1870, pp. 142-144, 1 map.

20. Nordenskiöld, A. E.—Astronomiska ortbestämningar under Svenska Polarexpeditionen, 1868. (Astronomical determinations of places during the Swedish Polar Expedition of 1868.)
K.V.A. Ofvers, 1870, pp. 569-580.

21. Daa. L. K.—Om Spitsbergens Russiske navn Grumant. (On Grumant, the Russian name of Spitzbergen.)

K.V.A. Öfvers, 1870, pp. 899–907.

22. Jäderin, E.—Geografiska ortbestamningar under Svenska expeditionen till Grönland, 1870. (Geographical determinations of places during the Swedish Expedition to Greenland in 1870.)

K.V.A. Öfvers, 1871, pp. 925–940.

23. Wijkander, A.—Astronomiska observationer under den Svenska arctiska expeditionen, 1872–1873. 1. Tidsoch ortbestämningar.

K.V.A. Handlingar, Vol. 13 (1874), No. 9.

24. Chydenius, K.—Om den Svenska expeditionen till Spetsbergen ar 1861 företagna undersökning af en gradmätnings utförbarhet derstades. (On the explorations undertaken during the Swedish Expedition to Spitzbergen in the year 1861, with the view of ascertaining the practicability of measuring an arc of meridian there.)

K.V.A. Öfvers, 1862, pp. 89–111, 1 map.

Transl., Petermann, Mittheil., 1863, pp. 24–27.

25. Torell, O.—Explorations in Spitzbergen, undertaken by the Swedish Expedition in 1861, with the view of ascertaining the practicability of the measurement of an arc of meridian.

London, Royal Society's Proceedings, Vol. 12 (1862–1863), pp. 658–662.

26. Torell, O.—Extract of a Letter to General Sabine, dated from Copenhagen, Dec. 12, 1863.

London, Royal Society's Proceedings, Vol. 13 (1863–1864), pp. 83–84.

27. Skogman, C.—Completion of the preliminary survey of Spitzbergen, undertaken by the Swedish Government with the view of ascertaining the practicability of the measurement of an arc of the meridian. In a letter addressed to Major-General Sabine, dated Stockholm, Nov. 21, 1864.

London, Royal Society's Proceedings, Vol. 13 (1863–1864), pp. 551–553.

28. Dunér, N., and Nordenskiöld, A. E.—Förberedande undersökningar rörande utförbarheten af en gradmätning på Spetsbergen. (Preliminary surveys with a view to ascertain the practicability of measuring an arc of meridian on Spitzbergen.)

K.V.A. Handl., Vol. 6 (1865–1866), No. 8, pp. 19, 1 map.

151.[1] Arnell, W.— Journey to Siberia.
Revue bryologique, 1877, pp. 32–41.

152. Berggren. Sv.—Ett isbetäckt land i höga norden. (An ico-covered land in the high north.)
Läsning för folket, 1872, Nos. 50, 52.

153. Fries, Th. M.— De senaste polar-färderna. (The latest Polar Expeditions.)
Svensk Tidskr. f. literatur, politik och ekonomi, 1876, pp. 60–104, 132–162.

154. Jaderin, E.—Geografiska ortbestämningar under Svenska expeditionen till Novaja Semlja och Kariska hafvet år 1875. (Geographical determinations of places during the Swedish Expedition to Novaya Zemlya and the Kara Sea in the year 1875.)
Öfvers, af K.V.A. Handlingar, 1876, No. 2, pp. 39–56.

155. Kjellman, F. R.—Redogörelse för *Pröven's* färd från Dicksons hamn till Norge samt för Kariska hafvets växt och djurverld. (Narrative of the voyage of the *Pröven* from Dickson's Harbour to Norway, with an account of the vegetable and animal world of the Kara Sea.)
Reprinted from No. 158.

156. Lundström, A. N.—Expedition Polaire Suédoise, sous la direction de M. le Prof. A. E. Nordenskiöld, 1875.
De Dickson's Hamn à Stockholm a travers la Sibérie.
Le Tour du Monde, No. 848, pp. 209–224. Paris, 1877.

157. Nordenskiöld, A. E. —On the former Climate of the Polar Regions.
The Geological Mag., Nov., 1875, pp. 525–532.

158. Nordenskiöld, A. E.--Svenska färden till Novaja Semlja och mynningen af Jenissej, sommaren 1875. (The Swedish Expedition to Novaya Zemlya and the mouth of the Yenissej in the summer of 1875.)
Gothenburg, 1875 (error of the press for 1876). 8vo, pp. 58.

159. Nordenskiöld, A. E.- Resplan för en expedition till Jenissej år 1876 utrustad af Hernr O. Dickson och Alex. Sibiriakoff. (Plan of an Expedition to the Yenissej in the year 1876, fitted out by Messrs. O. Dickson and Alex. Sibiriakoff.)
Gothenburg, 1876. 8vo, pp. 3.

[1] This and the following numbers are taken from a later list.

160. Nordenskiöld, A. E.— Berättelse om Jenissej Expeditionen år 1876. (Report of the Yenissej Expedition in the year 1876.)
Gothenburg. 1876. 8vo, pp. 6.

161. Nordenskiöld, A. E.— Redogörelse för en expedition till mynningen af Jenissej och Sibirien 1875. (Narrative of an expedition to the mouth of the Yenissej and Siberia, 1875.)
Appendix to K.V A. Transactions. Stockholm, 1877. 8vo, pp. 114.

162. Nordenskiöld, A. E. Programme de l'expédition de l'année prochaine (Juillet, 1878) à la mer glaciale de Sibérie.
Comptes Rendus, 1877, pp. 658–662.

163. Nordenskiöld, A. E.— Framställning rörande 1878 års Ishafsfärd. Inlagd till H. M. Konungen.
Gothenburg, 1877. 8vo, pp. 23.
(Memorial concerning the Arctic Expedition of 1878.)
Gothenburg, 1878.
Translated into *Danish* in Geogr. Tidskrift, 1878, into *German* in Petermann's Geogr. Mittheil., 1878, and into *French* in Bull. Soc. Geogr. 1878.

164. Nordenskiöld, A. E., and Theel, Hj.—Expéditions Suédoises de 1876 au Yenissei.
Upsala, 1877. 8vo, pp. 106.

165. Nordenskiöld, A. E., and Theel, Hj.—Redogörelser för de Svenska expeditionerna till mynningen af Jenissej ar 1876. (Narratives of the Swedish Expeditions to the mouth of the Yenissej in the year 1876.)
Appendix to K.V.A. Handlingar. Stockholm, 1878. 8vo, pp. 81, 1 map.

166. Parent, Eugenio.—Breve Rapporto sui procedimenti della Spedizione polaire artica svedese dall' agosto 1872.]
Estratto dalla Rivista Marittima del mese di Agosto. Anno VI. Fasc. VIII., 1873. 8vo, pp. 48.

167. Stuxberg, A.— Erinringar från Svenska expeditionerna till Novaja Semlja och Jenissej 1875 och 1876. (Reminiscences from the Swedish Expeditions to Novaya Zemlya and the Yenissej in 1875 and 1876.)
Stockholm, 1877. 8vo, pp. 112.

168. Theel, Hj. - Expédition Polaire Suédoise, sous la direction de M. le Prof. A. E. Nordenskiöld, 1875.

De la Norwège au Yenissei. Le Tour du Monde. No. 816 and 817. Paris, 1877.

169. Berättelse om Landt—Expeditionen till Jenissej år 1876. (Report of the Land Expedition to the Yenissej in the year 1876.)
Gothenburg, 1877. 8vo, pp. 36.

PHYSICS AND METEOROLOGY.

29. Agardh, J. G.— Om den Spetsbergska drif-vedens ursprung. (On the origin of the Spitzbergen drift-wood.)
K.V.A. Öfvers, 1869, pp. 97–119.

30. v. Otter, F. W.—Finnes det öppet vatten vid Nordpolen ? af. F. v. O. (Is open water to be found at the North Pole?)
Carlskrona, K. Örlogsmanna-Sällsk. Tidskrift, 1870, pp. 47–58, 121–137.

31. Johannesen, E. H.—Observationer, Isforholde og Dybde under Fangstreisen på Novasemlia i sommeren, 1869. Uddragen af Journalen ombord i Skonnerten *Nordland*. (Observations, state of the ice and soundings during a walrus-hunting excursion on Novaya Zemlya in the summer of 1869. Extracted from the Log of the schooner *Nordland*.)
K.V.A. Öfvers, 1870, pp. 111–115.
Transl. Petermann, Mittheil., pp. 870, 194–199, map.

32. Johannesen, E. H.—Hydrografiske iakttagelser under en Fangsttour, 1870, rundt om Novaja-Semlia. (Hydrographical observations during a walrus-hunting tour round Novaya Zemlya in 1870.)
K.V.A, Öfvers, 1871, pp. 157–168, map.
Transl Petermann, Mittheil., 1871, pp. 35–36, 230–232.

33. Meteorologiska iaktagelser anställda på Beeren-Eiland vintern 1865-6, af skepparen Sievert Tobiesen, och in om Norra Polarhafvet sommaren 1868 af Kaptenen Friherre Fr. von Otter och Löjtnant L. Palander. Meddelade af A. E. Nordenskiöld. (Meteorological observations made on Bear Island in the winter of 1865–1866, by skipper Sievert Tobiesen, and in the North Polar Sea in the summer of 1868 by Captain Baron Fr. von Otter and Lieut. L. Palander. Communicated by A. E. Nordenskiöld.)

K.V.A. Trans., Vol. 8 (1869), No. 11, pp. 28. Transl. Petermann, Mittheil., 1870, pp. 249-254.

34. Nordenskiöld, A. E.—Temperatur von Omenak, Westgrönland. Wien, Österreich. Ges. f. Meteorol. Zeitschr., red. v. Jelinek u. J. Hann. 1872, pp. 114-142.

35. Wijkander, A.—Observations météorologiques de l'expédition arctique Suédoise, 1872-73.
K.V.A. Handl., 1873, No. 3.

36. Nordenskiöld, A. E.—Foredrag vid K. Vet. Akad.'s årshögtid 31 Mars, 1875 (Om det forna polarklimatet). (Address at the Anniversary meeting of the Royal [Swedish] Academy of Sciences, 31st March 1875.) (On the former climate of the Polar lands.)
Aftonbladet, 1875. No. 82.

37. Chydenius, K.— Bidrag till kännedomen om de jordmagnetiska for hållandena vid Spetsbergen, samlade under den Svenska expeditionen är 1861. (Contributions to a knowledge of the relations of terrestrial magnetism on Spitzbergen, collected during the Swedish expedition in the year 1861.)
K.V.A. Öfvers, 1862, pp. 271-300.

38. Lemström, K. S.—Magnetiska observationer, under Svenska Polarexpeditionen år 1868. (Magnetical observations during the Swedish Polar expedition of 1868.)
K.V.A. Trans., Vol. 8, 1869, No. 8, pp. 47.

39. Observationer på luftelektriciteten och polarljuset under 1868 års Svenska Polarexpedition. (Observations on atmospheric electricity and the aurora during the Swedish Polar Expedition of 1868.)
K.V.A. Öfvers, 1869, pp. 663-688.

40. Dunér, N. C.—Magnetisk inclinations-bestämningar på Spetsbergen. (Determinations of magnetic inclination on Spitzbergen.)
K.V.A. Öfvers, 1870, pp. 584-596.
Transl. Archiv. des Sc. phys. et nat. Nouv. pér. 1871, pp. 147-165. De la Rive, A., Quelques remarques à l'occasion du mémoire de M. Lemström. Ib, pp. 165-168.

41. Wijkander, A.—Iaktagelser öfver luftelektriciteten under den Svenska Polarexpeditionen, 1872-73.
K.V.A. Öfvers, 1874, pp. 31-40.
Transl. Archiv des Sc. phys. et natur. Nouv. per. Vol. 51, pp. 31-42.

42. Wijkander, A.— Om Norrskenets, spektrum. (On the spectrum of the aurora.)
K.V.A. Öfvers, 1874, pp. 41-45.
Transl. Archiv des Sc. phys. et nat. Nouv. pér. Vol. 51, pp. 25-30.

43. Wijkander, A.— Observations magnétiques pendant l'expédition arctique suédoise en 1872-1873.
K.V.A.—Vol. 13 (1874), No. 16.

170. Wijkander, A.—Ueber die magnetischen Störungen und ihre Zusammenhang mit dem Nordlichte.
Zeitschr. der oesterr. meteorol. Gesellschaft. Bd. XII. No. 11.

171. Wijkander, A.—Sur la périodicité des perturbations de la declinaison magnétique dans la Scandinavie septentrionale. Lunds Univ. Årsskrift, Tom. xii. pp. 1-9.

172. Wijkander, A.—Observations magnétiques, faites pendant l'expédition arctique suédoise en 1872-1873, II.
K.V.A. Trans., Vol. 14 (1874), No. 15.

173. Wijkander, A.—Bidrag till kännedom om vindforhållendena i de Spetsbergen omgifvande delarne af Norra Ishafvet. (Contributions to a knowledge of the relations of the winds in the parts of the North Polar sea surrounding Spitzbergen.)
K.V.A. Öfvers, 1875, No. 8.

GEOLOGY AND PALÆONTOLOGY.

44. Torell, O.—Bidrag till Spitsbergens mulluskfauna. Jemte en allmän öfversigt af arktiska regionens naturfö hållendena och forntida utbredning. (Contributions to the mollusc-fauna of Spitzbergen. Together with a general view of the natural relations and former extent of the Arctic Regions.)
Stockholm, 1859. 8vo, 154 pp. 2 pl.
Transl. Petermann, Mittheil., 1861, pp. 49-67.

45. Nordenskiöld, A. E.—Geografisk och geognostisk beskrifning öfver nordöstra delarne af Spetsbergen och Hinloopen-Strait. (Geographical and geognostic description of the north-eastern parts of Spitzbergen and Hinloopen Strait.) See No. 16.

46. Blomstrand, C. W.—Geognostika iakttagelser under en resa till Spetsbergen år 1861. (Geognostic observations during a journey to Spitzbergen in the year 1861.)

K.V.A. Trans., Vol. 4 (1861-62), No. 6, pp. 46, 2 pl.
Transl. Petermann, Mittheil., 1865, p. 191-195.

47. Nordenskiöld, A. E.—Utkast till Spetsbergens geologi. (Sketch of the Geology of Spitzbergen.)
K.V.A. Vol. 6 (1865-66), No. 7. pp. 35, 2 maps.
English Translation. Stockholm, 1867.

48. Lindström, G.—Analyser på bergarter från Spetsbergen. (Analyses of rocks from Spitzbergen.)
K.V.A. Öfvers, 1867, pp. 671-674.

49. Nordenskiöld, A. E.—Föredrag, på K. Vet. Akad. årshägtid 31 Mars 1871 (Om Grönlands inlandsis). (Address at the Anniversary meeting of the Royal [Swedish] Academy of Sciences). (On the inland ice of Greenland.)
Stockholms Dagblad, 1871, No. 104.

50. Nordenskiöld, A. E.—Utkast till Isfjordens och Belsounds geologi.
Stockholm, Geol. Fören, Förhandl., 1875, pp. 243-260, 301-322, 356-372, map.
Transl. Geol. Mag., 1876.

51. Nordenskiöld, A. E.—Der Eisenfund bei Ovifak in Grönland.
Tschermak, Mineral. Mittheil., Bd. 1 (1871), pp. 109-112 (Extracted from No. 10).

52. Nordström, Th.—Kemisk undersökning af meteorjern från Ovifak på Grönland. (Chemical examination of meteoric iron from Ovifak in Greenland.)
K.V.A. Öfvers, 1871, pp. 453-462.

53. Meteoric iron from Greenland.
Geol. Mag., 1871, pp. 570-571.

54. Nauckhoff, G.—Om forekomsten af meteorjern i en basaltgång vid Ovifak i Grönland. Geognostisk och kemisk undersökning. (On the occurrence of meteoric iron in a basalt vein at Ovifak in Greenland. A geognostic and chemical examination.)
K.V.A. Transl. Appendix. Vol. 1, No. 5. pp. 38. Transl. Tschermak, Mineral. Mittheil., 1874, pp. 109-126.

55. Nordenskiöld, A. E.—Remarks on the Greenland meteorites.
London, Geolog. Soc. Quarterly Journ., Vol. 28 (1872), pp. 44-46.

56. Daubrée, G. A.—Examen des roches avec fer natif, decouvertes en 1870, par M. Nordenskiöld, au Groenland.
Paris, Acad. des Sc., Comptes Rendus, T. 74 (1872), pp. 1541-1549.

57. Daubrée, G. A. Examen des météorites d'Ovifak (Groenland), au point de vue du carbone et des sels solubles qu'ils renferment.
Paris, Acad. des Sc., Compt. Rend., T. 75 (1872), pp. 240–246.

58. Wöhler, F.—Analyse des Meteoreisens von Ovifak in Grönland. Nachträgliche Bemerkungen.
Göttingen, K. Ges. d. Wiss., Nachrichten, 1872, pp. 197–204, 499–501.

59. Nordenskiöld, A. E.—Föredrag på K. Vet. Akad. högtidsdag, 5 April, 1872 (Om meteorjernet från Ovifak). (Address at the Anniversary Meeting of the Royal [Swedish] Academy of Sciences, 5th April, 1872.) (On the meteoric iron from Ovifak.) Stockholms Dagblad, 1872, No. 107.
Transl. Revue scientifique de la France et de l'étranger, 1872, pp. 128–131.

60. Steenstrup, J.—Oplysninger om de Grönlandske Jernmasser. (Information about the Greenland iron masses.)
Copenhagen, Naturhist. Foren. Videnskab. Meddelelser, 1872, p. 11.

61. Das gediegene Eisen von Ovifak in Grönland. (The native Iron at Ovifak in Greenland.)
Der Naturforscher. Hrsg. v. W. Sklarek, 1874, pp. 473–475.

62. Flight, W.—A chapter in the history of meteorites.—Meteoric irons found August, 1870.—Ovifak (or Uigfak) near Godhavn, Kekertarssuak or island of Disko, Greenland.
Geol. Mag., 1865, pp. 115–123.

63. Tschermak, G.—Der Meteoritenfund bei Ovifak in Grönland.
Tschermak, Mineralog. Mittheil., 1874, pp. 165–174.

64. Nordenskiöld, A. E.—(Lettre contenant des observations sur les poussières charbonneuses, avec fer métallique, qu'il a observé dans la neige; communiquée par M. Daubrée.)
Paris, Acad. des Sc., Compt. Rend., T. 77 (1873), pp. 463–465.

65. Nordenskiold, A. E.—Om kosmiskt stoft, som vid nederbörden faller till jordytan. (On cosmic dust which falls with rain [or snow] to the surface of the earth.)
K.V.A. Öfvers, 1874, No. 1, pp. 3–12.
Transl. Poggendorf, Annalen, 1874, pp. 154–165.
„ Archiv. des. Sc. phys. et nat. Nouv., 1874, pp. 282–284.
„ Philos. Mag., Ser. 4, Vol. 48 (1875), pp. 456–457.

66. Lindström, G.—Om Trias och Juraförstenningar från Spetsbergen. (On Triassic and Jurassic fossils from Spitzbergen.)

K.V.A. Trans., Vol. 6 (1865-66), No. 6, pp. 20, 3 pl.
Transl. Geol. Mag., 1868, p. 29-30.

67. Hulke, J. W.—Memorandum on some fossil vertebrate remains collected by the Swedish expeditions to Spitzbergen in 1864 and 1868.
K.V.A. Handl. Appendix, Vol. 1 (1873), No. 9, pp. 11.

Heer, Osw.—Flora fossilis arctica.
Die fossile Flora der Polarländer. Bd. 1-3, Zurich, 1868-75.

68. Bd. 1.—Die in Nordgrönland, auf der Melville Insel, im Banksland, am Mackenzie, in Island und in Spitzbergen entdeckten fossilen Pflanzen. Mit einem Anhang über versteinerte Hölzer der arctischen Zone. Von Carl Cramer. pp. 199, 1 map, 50 pl.

69. Bd. 2 : 1.—Fossile Flora der Bären Insel. Enthaltend die Beschreibung der von den Herrn A. E. Nordenskiöld und A. J. Malmgren im Sommer 1868 dort gefundenen Pflanzen.
K.V.A. Handl., Bd. 9 (1870), No. 5, pp. 51, 15 pl.

70. Bd. 2 : 2.—Flora fossilis Alaskana. Fossile Flora von Alaska.
K.V.A. Handl., Bd. 8 (1869), No. 4, pp. 41, 10 pl.

71. Bd. 2 : 3.—Die miocene Flora und Fauna Spitzbergens. Mit einem Anhang über die diluvialen Ablagerungen Spitzbergens.
K.V.A. Handl., Vol. 8 (1869), No. 7, pp. 98, 16 pl.

72. Bd. 2 : 4.—Contributions to the Fossil Flora of North Greenland.

73. Bd. 3 : 1.—Beiträge zur Steinkohlen Flora der arctischen Zone.
K.V.A. Handl., Vol. 12 (1873), No. 3, pp. 11, 6 pl.

74. Bd. 3 : 2.—Die Kreide-Flora der arctischen Zone, gegründet auf die von den Schwedischen Expeditionen von 1870 and 1872 in Grönland und Spitzbergen gesammelten Pflanzen.
K.V.A. Handl., Vol. 13 (1874), No. 2, pp. 138, 38 pl.

75. Bd. 3 : 3.—Nachträge zur miocenen Flora Grönlands, enthaltend die von der Schwedischen Expedition im Sommer 1870 gesammelten miocenen Pflanzen.
K.V.A. Handl., Bd. 13 (1874), pp. 29, 5 pl.

76. Bd. 3 : 4.—Uebersicht der miocenen Flora der arctischen Zone.
Zürich, 1874, pp. 24.

77. Heer, Osw.— Om de af A. E. Nordenskiold och C. W. Blomstrand på Spetsbergen upptäckta fossila växter. (On the Fossil Plants discovered by A. E. Nordenskiöld and C. W. Blomstrand, on Spitzbergen.)
K.V.A. Öfvers, 1866, pp. 149-153.

78. Heer, Osw.—Utdrag ur ett bref af Prof. Oswald Heer rörande fossila växter från nordvestra Amerika, insamlade af Bergmästare Hj. Furuhjelm. Meddeladt af A. E. Nordenskiold. (Extract from a letter from Prof. Oswald Heer, concerning fossil plants from north-western America, collected by Mining Inspector Hj. Furuhjelm. Communicated by A. E. Nordenskiöld.)
K.V.A. Öfvers, 1868, pp. 63-68.

79. Heer, Osw.—On the miocene flora of the Polar Regions. Two lectures given at the annual meeting of the Natural History Society of Switzerland, on the 9th and 11th September, 1867, at Rheinfelden. (Transl. by Edward John Lee.)
Geol. Mag., 1868, pp. 273-280.

80. Heer, Osw.—Ueber die meiocäne Flora der Polarregionen.
Das Ausland, 1868, pp. 277-280.

81. Stur, O. Heer.—Flora fossilis arctica.
Wien. k.k. geol. Reichsanstalt, Verhandl., 1868, pp. 179-181.

82. Heer, Osw.—Die miocene Flora von Spitzbergen. Vorgetragen den 23 August, 1869, bei der Versammlung der schweiz. naturf. Gesellschaft in Solothurn.
Schweiz. Naturf. Ges. Verhandl., 1869, pp. 156-168.

83. Heer, Osw.—La flore miocène du Spitzberg.
Arch. des Sc. phys. et nat. Nouv. pér., 1869, pp. 289-300.

84. Heer, Osw.—Förutskickade anmärkningar öfver Nordgrönlands kritflora, grundade på den Svenska expeditionens upptäckter, 1870. (Preliminary remarks on the Cretaceous Flora of North Greenland, founded on the discoveries of the Swedish Expedition of 1870.)
K.V.A. Öfvers, 1871, pp. 1173-1184.

85. Heer, Osw.—On the Carboniferous Flora of Bear Island.
London, Geol. Soc. Quart. Journ., 1872, pp. 161-169.

86. Dawson, J. W.—Note on the relations of the supposed Carboniferous plants of Bear Island, with the Palæozoic Flora of North America.
Geol. Mag., 1873, p. 43.

87. Heer, Osw.—Om de miocena växter, som den Svenska expeditionen 1870, hemfort från Grönland. (On the Miocene plants which the Swedish Expedition of 1870 brought home from Greenland.)
K.V.A. Öfvers, 1873, No. 10, pp. 5–12.

88. Heer, Osw.—Anmärkningar öfver de af Svenska Polarexpeditionen 1872-73 upptäckte fossila växter. (Remarks on the fossil plants discovered by the Swedish Polar Expedition of 1872-73.)
K.V.A. Öfvers, 1874, No. 1, pp. 25–32.

174. Chydenius, J. L.—Undersokning af fossilt hartz från Grönland. (Examination of fossil resin from Greenland.)
Geologiska Foreningens Stockholm Forhandl., 1875, pp. 549–551.

175. Daubrée, G. A.—Observations sur la structure intérieure d'une des masses de fer natif d'Ovifak.
Comptes Rendus, T. 74 (1877), pp. 66–70.

176. Heer, Osw.—Flora fossilis arctica. Die fossile Flora der Polarländer.
Bd. IV., Zürich, 1877.

1. Beiträge zur fossilen Flora Spetsbergens. Gegründet auf die Sammlungen der Schwedischen Expeditionen vom Jahre 1872 auf 1873. Mit einem Anhang: Uebersicht der Geologie des Eisfjordes und des Bellsundes von Prof. A. E. Nordenskiold.
K.V.A. Handl., Bd. 14, No. 5 (1876), pp. 141, 32 pl.

177. Oberg, P.—Om Trias försteningar från Spetsbergen. (On Triassic fossils from Spitzbergen.)
K.V.A. Handl., Bd. 14, No. 14 (1877), pp. 19, 5 pl.

ZOOLOGY.

89. Quennerstedt, A.—Några anteckningar om Spetsbergens däggdjur och foglar (Akad. afhandl.). Some notices of the Mammalia and Birds of Spitzbergen (Academic treatise).
Lund, 1862. pp. 33.

90. Andersén, C. H.—Om Spetsbergsrenen, *Cervus tarandus*, forma Spetsbergensis. (On the Spitzbergen reindeer, *Cervus tarandus*, forma Spetsbergensis.)
K.V.A. Öfvers, 1863, pp. 457–461.

91. Malmgren, A. J.—Jakttagelser och antechningar till

Finmarkens och Spetsbergens däggdjursfauna. (Observations and notes regarding the Mammalia Fauna of Finmark and Spitzbergen.)
K.V.A. Öfvers, 1863, pp. 127-155.
Transl. Zeitschr. f. d. gesammt. Nat. wiss. von Giebel u. Siewart. Bd. 24 (1864), pp. 454-458.
Petermann, Mittheil., 1865, pp. 112-114.

92. Malmgren, A. J.—Om tandbyggnaden hos Hvalrossen (*Odobænus rosmarus*, L.) och tandombytet hos hans of ödda unge. (On the formation of the tooth of the Walrus [*Odobænus rosmarus*, L.], and on the change in the teeth in its unborn young.)
K.V.A. Öfvers, 1863, pp. 505-522.

93. Malmgren, A. J.—Anteckningar till Spetsbergens fogel fauna. (Notes on the Bird Fauna of Spitzbergen.)
K.V.A. Öfvers, 1863, pp. 87-126.

94. Malmgren, A. J.—Nya anteckningar till Spetsbergens fogel fauna. (New notes on the Bird Fauna of Spitzbergen.)
K.V.A. Öfvers, 1864, pp. 377-412.

95. Newton, A.—Notes on the Birds of Spitzbergen.
The Ibis, 1865, pp. 199-219, 496-525.

96. Malmgren, A. J.—Zur Vogelfauna Spitzbergens. Auf Anlass von Mr. Alfred Newton's "Notes on the Birds of Spitzbergens" in "The Ibis," 1865.
Journal für Ornithologie, 1865, pp. 385-400.

97. Newton, A.—Zur Vogelfauna Spitzbergens. Auf Anlass von Dr. A. J. Malmgren's Aufsatz im Journal für Ornithologie, 1865.
Journal für Ornithologie, 1867, pp. 207-211.

98. Sundevall, C. J.—Spetsbergens foglar med hufvudsakligt avseende på dem som blifvit funna under Prof. Nordenskiölds resor dit åren 1868 och 1872-73. (The Birds of Spitzbergen with special reference to those found during Prof. Nordenskiöld's journeys thither in the years 1868 and 1872-3.)
K.V.A. Öfvers, 1874, No. 3, pp. 11-25.

99. Malmgren, A. J.—Om Spetsbergens fisk-fauna. (On the Fish Fauna of Spitzbergen.)
K.V.A. Öfvers, 1864, pp. 489-539.
Transl. Petermann., Mittheil., Ergänz., 1865, pp. 34-39.

100. Boheman, C. H.—Bidrag till kännedomen om Spetsbergens insekt-fauna. (Contributions to the knowledge of the Insect Fauna of Spitzbergen.)

Förhandl. vid de Skand. Naturforsk. nionde möte i Stockholm, 1863, pp. 393-399.
Transl. Petermann, Mittheil., 1866, pp. 181-183.

101. Boheman, C. H. — Spetsbergens insekt-fauna. (The Insect Fauna of Spitzbergen.)
K.V.A. Öfvers, 1865, pp. 563-577.

102. Holmgren, A. E.—Bidrag till kännedomen om Björen Eilands insekt-fauna. (Contributions to the knowledge of the Insect Fauna of Bear Island.)
K.V.A. Handl., Bd. 8 (1869), No. 5, pp. 56.

103. Holmgren, A. E. — Insekter från Nordgrönland samlade af Prof. A. E. Nordenskiöld ar 1870. Granskade och beskrifna. (Insects from North Greenland collected by Prof. A. E. Nordenskiöld in the year 1870. Examined and described.)
K.V.A. Öfvers, 1872, No. 6, pp. 97-105.

104. Thorell, T.— On Arachnider från Spetsbergen och Björen Eiland. (On Arachnids from Spitzbergen and Bear Island.)
K.V.A. Öfvers, 1871, pp. 683-701.

105. Thorell, T.— Om några Arachnider från Grönland. (On some Arachnids from Greenland.)
K.V.A. Öfvers, 1872, No. 2, pp. 147-166.

106. Göes, A.—Crustacea decapoda podophthalma marina Sueciæ, interpositis speciebus norvegicis aliisque vicinis, enumerat A. Göes.
K.V.A. Öfvers, 1863, pp. 161-180.

107. Göes, A. — Crustacea amphipoda maris Spetsbergiam alluentis, cum speciebus aliis arcticis, enumerat A. Göes.
K.V.A. Öfvers, 1865, pp. 517-536.

108. Sars, G. O.—Cumaceer fra de store Dybder i Nordishavet, insamlede ved den Svenske Arktiske Expeditioner Aarene 1861 og 1868. (Cumacea from great depths in the North Polar Sea, collected by the Swedish Arctic Expeditions in the years 1861 and 1868.)
K.V.A. Öfvers, 1871, pp. 797-802.

109. Lilljeborg, W.—De under Svenska vetenskapliga expeditionen till Spetsbergen 1872-1873 derstädes samlade Hafs-Entomostraceer. (The Marine Entomostraca collected during the Swedish Scientific Expedition to Spitzbergen in 1872-73.)
K.V.A. Öfvers, 1875, No. 4.

F F

110. Lovén, S.—Om Molluskslägtet Pilidium Midd. (On the Mollusc Tribe, Pilidium Midd.)

K.V.A. Öfvers, 1859, pp. 119–120.

Torell, O.—Bidrag till Spetsbergens mollusk fauna. (Contributions to the Mollusc Fauna of Spitzbergen.) See No. 44.

111. Mörch, O. A. L.—Catalogue des mollusques du Spitzberg recueillis par le Dr. H. Kroyer, pendant le voyage de la corvette *La Recherche* en juin 1838. (Contains matter relating to the mollusca collected by the Swedish Expedition.)

Bruxelles Soc. Malacol. de Belgique, Annales, T. 4 (1869).

112. Lindahl, J.—Om Pennatulid-slagtet Umbellula, Cuv. (On the Pennatulid tribe, Umbellula, Cuv.)

K.V.A. Handl., Bd. 13 (1874), No. 3, pp. 22, 3 pl.

113. Smith, F. A.—Kritisk förteckning öfver Skandinaviens Hafs-Bryozoer 1–5. (Critical List of the Marine Bryozoa of Scandinavia.)

K.V.A. Öfvers, 1865, pp. 116–142, 1 pl.; 1866, pp. 395–533, 11 pl.; 1867, pp. 279–429, 5 pl.; 1867, appendix, pp. 230, 5 pl.; 1871, pp. 1115–1134, 2 pl.

114. Smith, F. A.—Bryozoa marina in regionibus arcticis et borealibus viventia recensuit F. A. S.

K.V.A. 1867, pp. 443–487.

115. Malmgren, A. J.—Nordiska Hafs Annulater. (Marine Annulata of the North.)

K.V.A. Öfvers, 1865, pp. 51–110, 181–192, 355–410, 20 pl.

116. Malmgren, A. J.—Annulata polychæta Spetsbergiæ, Grönlandiæ, Islandiæ et Scandinaviæ hactenus cognita.

K.V.A. Öfvers, 1867, pp. 127–235, 14 pl. Also published in Swedish at Helsingfors, 1867.

117. Théel, H.—Borst- och Stjernmaskar, tagna i grannskapet af 80 degraden under Svenska expeditionen 1872–73. (Annelids taken in the neighbourhood of 80° N.L., during the Swedish expedition in 1872–73.)

118. Ljungman, A.—Ophiuroidea viventia huc usque cognita enumerat A—L.—.

K.V.A. Öfvers, 1866, pp. 303–336.

119. Lovén, S.—Till frågan om Ishafsfaunans fordna utsträckning afver en del af Norden fast land. (On the question of the

former extension of the fauna of the Polar Sea over a part of the mainland of the North.)
K.V.A. Öfvers, pp. 463-468.

120. Lovén S.—Om resultaten af de af den Svenska Spetsbergs-expeditionen 1861 utförda djupdraggningar. (On the results of the deep dredgings carried out by the Swedish expedition to Spitzbergen in 1861.)
Förh. vid de Skand. Naturf. nionde möte, Stockholm, 1863, pp. 384-386.

121. Malmgren, A. J.—Om förekomsten af djurlif på stora hafsdjup. (On the occurrence of animal life at great depths in the sea.)
Helsingfors, Finska Vet. Soc. Öfvers, 12 (1869-70), pp. 40-49.

122. Quennerstedt, A.—Anteckningar om djurlifvet i Ishafvet mellan Spetsbergen och Grönland. (Notes on animal life in the Polar Sea between Spitzbergen and Greenland.)
K.V.A. Handl., Bd. (1867) No. 3, pp. 35, 3 pl.

123. v. Gëes.—Om Tardigrader, Anguillulæ m.m. från Spetsbergen. (On Tardigrada, Anguillulæ, &c. from Spitzbergen.)
K.V.A. Öfvers, 1862, pp. 18.

178. Eisen, G.—On the Oligochotæ collected by the Swedish expeditions to the Arctic Regions, under the direction of Prof. A. E. Nordenskiöld.
K.V.A. Handl., 1877, Bd. 15.

179. Eisen, G.—Redogörelse för Obligochæter samlade under de Svenka expeditionem till arktiska trakter. (See No. 178.)
K.V.A. Öfvers, 1878, No. 3.

180. Holmgren, A. E.—Novaja Semljas insekt fauna.
(In preparation.)

181. Koch, L.—Arachnider från Novaja Semlja och Sibericn. (Arachnida from Novaya Zemlya and Siberia.)
(In preparation.)

182. Leche, V.—Ofversigt öfver de af de Svenska expeditionerna till Novaja Zemlja och Jenissej 1875 och 1876 insamlade Hafs-Mollusker. (Review of the Marine Mollusca collected by the Swedish expeditions to Novaya Zemlya and Yenissej in 1875 and 1876.)
K.V.A. Handl., 1877, Bd. 16.

183. Lilljeborg, W.—Synopsis crustaceorum succicorum Ordinis Branchiopodorum et Subordinis Phyllopodorum.

Nova Acta Reg. Soc. Sc. Ups. Ser. III. vol. extra ordinem editum.
Upsala, 1877, pp. 20, 4to.

184. Mäklin, Fr. W.—Diagnoser öfver några nya siberiska insekt-arter. (Descriptions of several new Siberian species of insects.)

185. Sars, G. O.—Om Cumaceer fra de store Dybder i Nordishavet. (On Cumacea from great depths in the North Polar Sea.)
K.V.A. Handl., Bd. II., No. 6, pp. 12, 4 pl.

186. Smitt, F. A.—Recensio systematica animalium Bryozoorum, quæ in itineribus ad insulas Novaja Semlja et ad ostium fluminis Jenissej, duce Professore A. E. Nordenskiöld, invenerunt Doctores A. Stuxberg et H. Théel.
K.V.A. Öfvers, 1878, No. 3.

187. Stuxberg, A.—Myriopoder från Sibirien och Waigatsch ön samlade under Nordenskiöldska expeditionen, 1875.
K.V.A. Öfvers, 1876, No. 2, pp. 11–38, 2 pl.
On the Myriopoda, from Siberia and Waigatsch Island, collected during the expedition of Prof. Nordenskiöld, 1875.
Ann. and Magazine of Natural History, 4th series, Vol. 17, pp. 306–318, London, 1876.

188. Stuxberg, A.—Crustacea malacostraca från Murmanska och Kariska Hafven. (Crustacea malacostraca from the Murman and Kara Seas.)
K.V.A. Handl., Appendix, Bd. 5.

189. Stuxberg, A.—Echinodermer från Novaja Semljas haf samlade under Nordenskiöldska expedionerna 1875 och 1876. (Echinodermata from the sea of Novaya Zemlya collected during Prof. Nordenskiöld's expeditions in 1875 and 1876.)
K.V.A. Öfvers, 1878, No. 3.

190. Théel, Hj.—Etudes sur les Gephyriens inermes des Mers de la Scandinavie, du Spitzberg et du Grœnland.
K.V.A. Handl., Bd. 3, No. 6, pp. 30, 4 pl.
Compare Journal de Zoologie, 1875, pp. 366–390, 475–488.

191. Théel, Hj.—Några bidrag till Novaja Semljas fogel-fauna. (Some contributions to the Bird Fauna of Novaya Zemlya.)
K.V.A. Öfvers, 1876, No. 5, pp. 43–53.
Note sur les oiseaux de la Nouvelle Zemble.

Ann. Sci. naturelles, 6me Sér. (zoologie). Tome IV., Art. No. 6, pp. 1-7.

192. Théel, Hj.—Note sur l'Elpidia, genre nouveau du groupe des Holothuries.
K.V.A. Handl., App., Bd. 4, No. 1, pp. 7.

193. Théel, Hj.—Mémoire sur l'Elpidia, nouveau genre d'Holothuries.
K.V.A. Handl., Bd. 14, No. 8.
Stockholm, 1877. pp. 30, 5 pl., 4to.

194. Théel, Hj.—Note sur quelques Holothuries des Mers de la Nouvelle Zemble.
Nova Acta Reg. Soc. Sc. Ups., Ser. III. Vol. extra ordinem editum.
Upsala, 1877, pp. 18, 2 pl., 4to.

195. Théel, Hj.—Les Annélides Polychètes des Mers de la Nouvelle Zemble.
(In preparation.)

196. Trybom, F.—Dagfjärilar insamlade af Svenska expeditionen till Jenissej 1876. (Diurnal Lepidoptera collected by the Swedish Expedition to the Yenissej in 1876.)
K.V.A. Öfvers, 1876, No. 6, pp. 35-51.

197. Tullberg, T.—Collembola borealia. Nordiska Collembola.
K.V.A. Öfvers, 1876, No. 5, pp. 23-47, pl. 8 to 11.

198. Westerlund, C. A.—Sibiriens Land- och Sötvatten-Mollusker. (The Land and Fresh-water Molluscs of Siberia.)
K.V.A. Handl., Bd. 14, No. 12.
Stockholm, 1877, pp. 111, 1 pl., 4to.

BOTANY.

124. Malmgren, A. J.—Öfversigt af Spetsbergens fanerogamflora. (Review of the Phanerogamous Flora of Spitzbergen.)
K.V.A. Öfvers, 1862, pp. 229-268.
Translated, Petermann. Mittheil., pp. 47-53.

125. Anderson, N. J.—Bidrag till den nordiska floran. 1. Ett hittils obeskrifvet gräs från Spetsbergen. (Contributions to the Flora of the North. 1. A hitherto undescribed grass from Spitzbergen.)
K.V.A. Öfvers, 1866, pp. 121-124, 1 pl.

126. Fries, Th. M.—Tillägg till Spetsbergens fanerogam-flora. (Additions to the Phanerogamous Flora of Spitzbergen.)
K.V.A. Öfvers, 1869, pp. 121–144, 1 pl.

127. Fries, Th. M.—Om Beeren-Islands fanerogam-vegetation. (On the Phanerogamous Vegetation of Bear Island.)
K.V.A. 1869, pp. 145–156.

128. Fries, Th. M.—Plantæ vasculares insularum Spetsbergensium hactenus lectæ. Plantæ vasculares in insula "Beeren-Eiland" repertæ. Upsaliæ, 1871, fol., pp. 2.

129. Berggren, S.—Bidrag till kännedom om fanerogmafloran vid Diskobugten och Auleitsivik-fjorden på Grönlands vestkust. (Contributions to a knowledge of the Phanerogamous Flora at Disko Bay and Auleitsivik Fjord on the West Coast of Greenland.)
K.V.A. Öfvers, 1871, pp. 853–897.

130. Kjellman, F. R.—Några tillägg till kännedomen om Spetsbergens Plantæ vasculares. (Some contributions to the knowledge of the Plantæ vasculares of Spitzbergen.)
K.V.A. Öfvers, 1874, No. 3, pp. 31–42.

131. Lindberg, S. O.—Mossor år 1858 på Spetsbergen insamlade af Professor A. E. Nordenskiöld. (Mosses collected on Spitzbergen in 1858, by Professor A. E. Nordenskiöld.)
K.V.A. Öfvers, 1861, pp. 189–190.

132. Lindberg, S. O.—Förteckning öfver mossor, insamlade under de Svenska expeditionerna till Spetsbergen 1858 och 1861.
K.V.A. Öfvers, 1866, pp. 533–561.

133. Berggren, S.—Musci et Hepaticæ Spetsbergenses.
K.V.A. Handl., Bd. 13 (1874), No. 7.

134. Berggren, S.—Undersökning af mossfloran vid Diskobugten och Auleitsivikfjorden. (Examination of the Moss Flora at Disko Bay and Auleitsivik Fjord.)
K.V.A. Handl., Bd. 13 (1874), No. 8.

135. Agardh, J. G.—Om Spetsbergens alger. (On the Algæ of Spitzbergen.)
Univ. Progr. Lund, 1862, fol., pp. 4.

136. Agardh, J. G.—Bidrag till kännedomen af Spetsbergens alger, jemte Tillägg. (Contributions to the knowledge of the Algæ of Spitzbergen, with an addition.)

K.V.A. Handl., Bd. 7 (1867–1868), No. 8, pp. 49, 3 pl.

137. Cleve, P. T.—Diatomaceer från Spetsbergen. (Diatoms from Spitzbergen.)
K.V.A. Öfvers, 1867, pp. 661–669, 1 pl.

138. Berggren, S.—Alger from Grönlands inlandsis. (Algæ from the Inland Ice of Greenland.)
K.V.A. Öfvers, 1871, pp. 293–296, 1 pl.

139. Agardh, J. G.—Bidrag till kännedomen af Grönlands Laminareer och Fucaceer. (Contributions to the knowledge of the Laminaria and Fucacea of Greenland.)
K.V.A. Handl., Bd. 10 (1871), No. 8, pp. 31.

140. Nordstedt, O. Desmidiaceæ ex insulis Spetsbergensibus et Beeren Eiland in expeditionibus 1868 et 1870 succanis collectæ.
K.V.A. Öfvers, 1872, No. 6, pp. 23–24, 2 pl.

141. Lagerstedt, N. G. W.—Sötvattens-diatomaceer från Spetsbergen och Beeren Eiland. (Freshwater Diatoms from Spitzbergen and Bear Island.)
K.V.A. Handl., Bih., Bd. 1 (1873), No. 14, pp. 52, 2 pl.

142. Cleve, P. T.—On Diatoms from the Arctic Sea.
K.V.A. Handl., Bih., Bd. 1 (1873), No. 13, pp. 28, 4 pl.

143. Kjellman, F. R.—Om Spetsbergens marina klorofyllförande Thallophyter. (On the Marine Chlorophyll-bearing Thallophytes of Spitzbergen.) I. Florideæ.
K.V.A. Handl., Bih., Bd. 3.

144. Fries, Th. M.—Lichenes Arctoi Europæ Groenlandiæque hactenus cogniti. Collegit, examinavit, disposuit Th. M. F.
Upsala, R. Soc. Sc. Ups., Nova Acta Ser. III., Vol. III. (1861), pp. 103–398.

145. Fries, Th. M.—Lichenes Spetsbergenses determinavit Th. M. F.
K.V.A. Handl., Bd. 7 (1867), No. 2, pp. 53.
Translated, Petermann, Mittheil., 1868, pp. 62–64.

146. Karsten, P. A.—Fungi in insulis Spetsbergen et Beeren Eiland collecti. Examinavit, enumerat P. A. K.
K.V.A. Öfvers, 1872, No. 2, pp. 91–108.

199. Kjellman, F. R.—Om Spetsbergens marina klorophyllförande Thallophyter. II. (On the Marine Chlorophyll-bearing Thallophytes of Spitzbergen.)

K.V.A. Handl. Bih., Bd. 4, No. 6.
Stockholm, 1877, pp. 64, 5 pl.

200. Kjellman, F. R.—Bidrag till kännedomen af Kariska hafvets algvegetation. (Contributions to the knowlelge of the Algæ of the Kara Sea.)
K.V.A. Öfvers, 1877, No. 2, pp. 3–30, 1 pl.

201. Kjellman, F. R.—Ueber die Algenvegetation des Murmanschen Meeres an der West Küste von Novaja Semlja und Wajgatsch.
Nova Acta Reg. Soc. Sc. Ups., Ser. III., Vol. extra ordinem editum.
Upsala, 1877, pp. 86, 1 pl., 4to.

202. Lundström, A. N.—Kritische Bemerkungen über die Weiden Nowaja Semljas und ihren genetischen Zusammenhang.
Nova Acta Reg. Soc. Sc. Ups., Ser. III., Vol. extra ordinem editum.
Upsala, 1877, pp. 44, 1 pl., 4to.

HYGIENE.

147. Nyström, C.—Om den sista Svenska Spetsbergs-expeditionens utrustning och hygien. (On the equipment and hygiene of the last Swedish expedition to Spitzbergen.)
Upsala, Läk.-Fören. Forhandl., Bd. 4 (1868–69), pp. 419–439.

148. Nyström, C.—Om jäsnings- och forruttnelseprocesserna på Spetsbergen. (On the processes of fermentation and putrefaction on Spitzbergen.)
Upsala, Läk.-Foren. Forhandl., Bd. 4 (1868–69), pp. 551–571.

149. Från Spetsbergs-expeditionen.—Bref från Axel Envall. (Vinterquarteret Polhem i Mossel Bay d. 16 Juni 1873.) (From the Spitzbergen expedition.—A letter from Axell Envall.) (The winter-quarters Polhem in Mussel Bay, 16th June, 1873.)
Hygeia, Bd. 35 (1873), pp. 408–412.

150. Envall, A.—Rapport till kongl. Sundhetskollegium öfver hygienen och sjukvården under den Svenska Polarexpeditionen 1872–73. (Report to the Royal [Swedish] Board of Health on the hygiene and care of the sick during the Swedish Polar Expedition of 1872–73.)
Stockholm, Sv. Läkare Sällsk., Nya Handl., Ser. II., D. 5, 3, pp. 87–122.

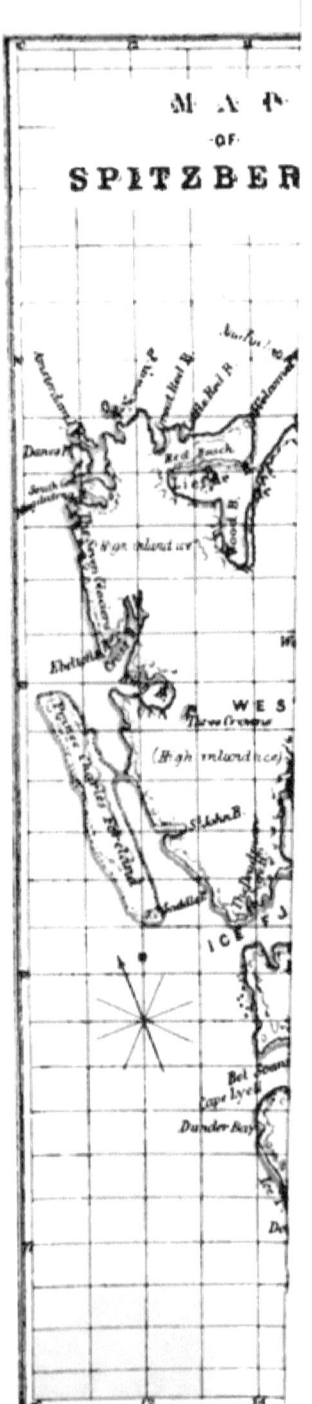

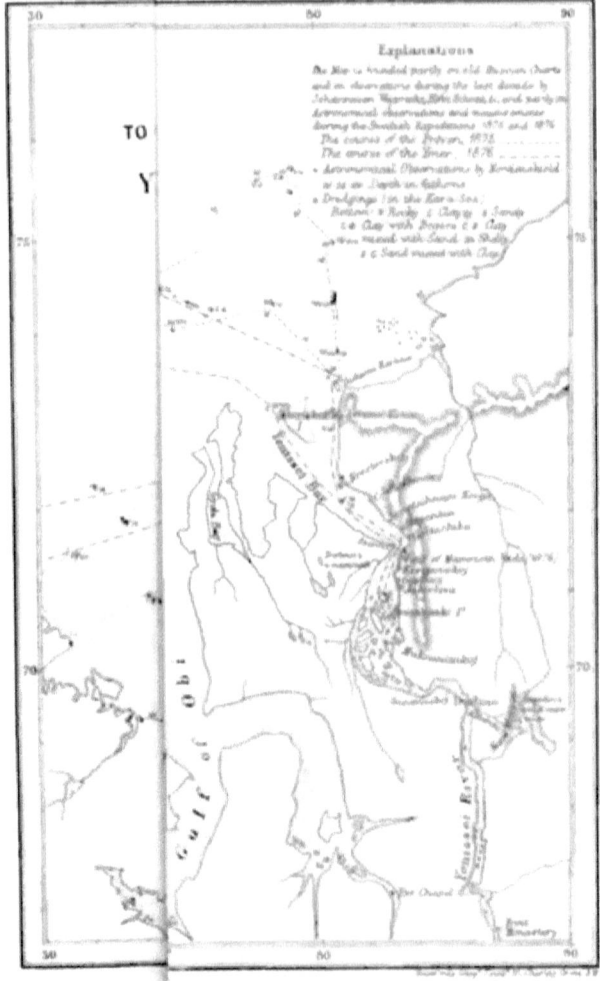

INDEX.

INDEX.

A.

ACARIDÆ, 287
Actinia Haven, 358
Advent Bay, 46, 98, 99
Æolus, 48, 92, 93, 102
Aira, 93
Aldert Dircks's Bay, 93
Alecto, 283
Alecto exchrichtii, 336, 357, 369
Alectoria, 95
Alga on inland ice, 163
Alnus fructicosa, 293
Alopecurus, 76, 93
Alsine, 94
Amphipoda, 283
Amsterdam Island, 46, 53
Andromeda, 99
Andromeda tetragona, 291
Angelica, 295
Angelin's Mount, 69
Annelids, 51, 102
Anser bernicla, 53
Anser brachyrhynchus, 109
Appendicularia, 287
Apseudes, 102
Arabis, 94
Arctic current, 118
Arctic fox, 68
Arctic willow, 94
Arnell, Docent H. W., 320
Astarte, 109
Asterida, 336, 357
Auks, 51, 53, 109
Aulacomnium, 79
Aurora, 225

B

BEAR pasturing, 285
Bear Island, 61, 104, 128, 133
Bear Islands, 370
Bears, 235

Beaver skins, 375
Bell sound, 45, 48, 52, 100, 114
Beluga catodon, 57
Berg, Governor-general Count von, 9, 13, 14, 15, 16, 17, 18
Berggren, Dr. Sven, 31, 131, 155
Beros, 109
Beroidæ, 287
Biloculina, 102
Birch, dwarf discovered on Spitzbergen, 136
Bird Bay, 74
Birkbeck, Mr E., 113
Blomstrand, 49, 97
Bove, Lieut. G., 352
Brachiopoda, 299
Brandywine Bay, 58, 84, 88, 141, 233
Brenner, Rector M., 320
Brookes' apparatus, 51
Brown, Dr. R., 157
Bruzewitz, E. C., 352
Bryas, 95
Bryopogon, 95
Bryozoa, 336
Buccinum glaciale, 94
Buchan, Captain, 44
"Bulldog" machine, 51, 101, 146

C.

CALAMAGROSTIS, 93
Calamites, 136
Canals in the Inland Ice of Spitzbergen, 253
Cape Boheman, 109
Cape Chelyuskin passed, 359
Cape Crozier, 59
Cape Fanshawe, 70
Cape Mitre, 95
Cape Platen, 241
Cape Schelagskoj, 371
Cape Severo, 359
Cape Thordsen, 33, 274

INDEX.

Cape Wrede, 52
Cardamine, 63, 65, 77, 89, 186
Cardium, 100
Carex chordorrhiza, 291
Castrén's Islands, 77, 79, 83
Catabrosa, 77
Catharine, Czarina, 43
Cerastium, 58, 63, 65, 76, 94
Cetraria, 58, 95
Chabarova, 354
Charadrius hiaticula, 78
Charles XII.'s Island, 52
Chydenius, K., 49, 74, 84, 92, 104
Chrysosplenium, 92
Cirratulus, 102
Cladonia, 95
Clavering, 44
Clio, 287
Cloudberries, 259
Cloven Cliff, 46, 53
Coal, 96, 302
Cochlearia, 58, 63, 76, 94, 98
Copepoda, 119, 253
Cortusa, 292
Cosmic dust, 36, 127
Cottus, 100
Crenella, 100
Crevasses, 251
Cribella, 336
Cross Bay, 52, 95
Crozier, Lieut., 52
Crustacea,102, 337
Ctenodiscus, 336
Cuma, 102, 149
Cumacea, 283
Cydippe, 100
Cylichna, 102
Cyprina Islandica, 150
Cystopteris, 95

D.

DANES' Island, 52, 92
Deevie Bay, 110
Deep dredging, 118
Delphinium, 292
Dentalina, 102
Desmidieæ, 52
Dianthus, 291
Diatomaceæ, 52, 102
Dickson, Mr. Oscar, 29, 30, 36, 37, 177, 278, 345
Dickson Bay, 140
Dickson Harbour, 286, 326, 355
Dicranum, 58, 95
Diptera, 63
Down Islands, 115
Draba, 63, 65, 77, 94, 99, 131
Drepanopsetta, 100
Dryas, 77, 99
Dunder Bay, 114

Danér, 49, 104, 112, 114, 121
Dupontia, 76
Dym Point, 79

E.

ECHINI, 336
Echinodermata, 336, 337
Ehrensvärd, Count A., 123
Eider, 94, 109, 115, 201
Emberiza nivalis, 51
Empetrum nigrum, 291
Encalypta, 95
English Bay, 46
Entada gigalobium, bean of, 72
Envall, Dr A., 183; report on hygiene of expedition of 1872-3, 321
Erigeron, 94
Eriophorum, 99
Erratic blocks, absence of, on Siberian coast, 373
Extreme Hook, 50, 233

F.

FEODOR, 292, 329
"Finners," 51, 52
Forests, Siberian, 308
Foster's Islands, 68
Franklin, Sir John, 44, 146
Fries, Th. M., 131
Frugord, 2, 5, 7, 16, 23

G.

GADUS, 100
Galium, 291
Gasterosteus aculeatus, 290
Gephyrea, 102
Giles, Commander, 123
Giles' Land, 150, 215
Gladan, 175
Glaucous gulls, 216
Globigerina, 102
Goes, 49
Gold diggings on the Yenissej, 318
Green Harbour, 97, 137
Greenland, Nordenskiöld's journey to, 30, 153
Grey Hook, 93
Guillemots, 202
Gulf stream, 51, 118, 132
Gymnomitrium, 58, 85

H.

HALOS, 224
Harpalus, 287
Hecla Cove, 59
Hecla Mount, 60, 65
Hedysarum, 292
Heer, Prof. Oswald, 153

INDEX.

Helis Sound, 122, 124
Hinloopen Strait, 68, 83, 84
Hippuris vulgaris, 291
Holmgren, A. E., 131
Holothuria, 51, 102
Hope Island, 119
Horn Sound, 109
Horn Sounds Tinder, 111
Hoogaard, Lieut. A., 322
Hydromedusæ, 339
Hypnum, 58, 78

L.

ICEBERGS, formation of, 122
Ice-crystals, large, 249
Ice, the crystalline form of, 225;
 showers of, 255
Idothea Sabinei and *entomon*, 336, 362
Inland Ice of Greenland, 159, 171
Irkiapi, 373
Isopoda, 283
Ivory gull, 202

J.

JOHANNESEN, CAPTAIN, 358, 365
Juncus, 99 ; *J. castaneus*, 291

K.

KARA GATE, 281
Kara Sea, 37, 38, 323
Keilhau, Prof., 44, 125
King Carl's Land, 246
King of Sweden, 47, 345
King's Bay, 52, 96, 140
Kjellman, Dr., 36, 37, 183, 186, 279, 321, 352, 357
Kobbe Bay, 58, 94
Kryokonite, 153
Kuylenstjerna, Captain, 19

L.

LAMINARIA, 69
Laminaria Agardhi, 362
Lamont, Mr., 124
Lapps, games of the, 204
Laptjeff, 369
Larus eburneus, 56
Larus glaucus, 56, 56
Larus tridactylus, 54, 65
Lee's Foreland, 129
Leigh Smith, Mr., 189, 269, 271
Lemstrom, S., 131
Lena, voyage of the, 365
Lepidodendra, 136
Lestris parasitica, 56

Liachoff's Island, 368
Lickle Bay, 142
Lilliehook, 49
Limacina, 65
Lovén, Professor, 44
Lumbricus, 287
Lumpenus, 102
Lundstrom, Docent, 37, 279, 303
Luzula, 77, 91, 99

M.

MACK FRITZ, 272
McClintock, Sir Leopold, 47
Magdalena Bay, 45, 46
Magdalena Hook, 52
Magdalena, the, 48, 92, 43, 97, 100, 102
Malmgren, A. J., 49, 75, 104, 110, 114, 121, 131
Mammoth tusks, 306
" Marked " reindeer, 84
Marten's Island, 79
Matotschkin Schar, 279, 280, 281, 322
Mattilas, 53, 73, 97, 126, 195; death of, 268, 272
Medusæ, 287
Mergulus albo, 52
Meteoric iron, discovery of, 174
Middle Hook, 46, 114
Mollusca, 102
Molpadia borealis, 363
Mormon arcticus, 147, 148
Mosander, Professor, 19, 20
Mount Misery, 106, 139
Muffin Island, 28
Murchison Bay, 67, 72
Murchison, Sir Roderick, 47
Murder discovered and punished, 117
Mussel Bay, 35, 36, 191
Myriotrochus Rinki, STEENSTRUP, 102
Mytilus edulis, 189

N.

NATHORST, DOCENT H., visits Spitzbergen, 32
Natica, 100
Nauckhoff, G., 131
Neratrum, 293
New Siberian Islands sighted, 365
New Vriesland, 69
Nuniomina, 102
Nord Fjord, 102
Nordenskiold, Adolf Erik, his birth
 and parentage, 1 ; education, 5 ;
 university studies, 7 ; first published
 works, 8 ; dismissal from his offices,
 12 ; visit to Berlin, 12 ; leaves

Finland, 16; refused permission to revisit Finland, 18; applies for the professorship of mineralogy and geology in the University of Helsingfors, 18; takes part in Torell's first Expedition to Spitzbergen, 20; appointed successor to Mosander, 20; makes a tour through Jemtland and Dalecarlia, 22; takes part in Torell's second expedition, 22; visits Finland, 23; proposes a new Arctic Expedition, 27; reaches the highest latitude attained by a vessel in the old hemisphere, 28; visits Greenland, 30; sits in the House of Nobles, 34; is elected a representative of Stockholm in the Diet, 34; starts on a new Polar Expedition, 35; sails to the mouth of the Yenissej and ascends the river, 37; returns to the Yenissej, 38; accompanies Torell in his first expedition to Spitzbergen, 45; shares with Torell the command of the second Expedition to Spitzbergen, 42; makes a boat voyage through Hinloopen Strait, 67; has an adventure with a Polar bear, 81; leader of the Expedition of 1864, 104; of 1868, 123; goes to Greenland, 153; starts on the Expedition of 1872, 183; holds a Council, 197; starts on a journey over the inland ice of Spitzbergen, 220; starts on a voyage to the Yenissej in 1875, 278; receives the thanks of the Russian government, 319; starts on a second voyage to the Yenissej, 320; his programme of the North-East Passage Expedition, 346; joins the Expedition; passes Behrings Straits, 356; arrives at Yokohama, 357

Nordenskiold family, the, 1
Nordquist, Lieut. O., 352, 357
Nordstrom, Dr. Theodor, 31, 155
North Cape, 378
North-East Cape, 359
North-East Land, 58, 74, 75, 243, 248
Norways, the, 46, 54, 92
Nostoc commune, 65

O.

Öberg, Docent P., 30, 155
Obuk, Mr., 157
Onkilon race, the, 379
Ophiurida, 283, 336
Osborne, Captain Sherard, 47
Otter, Baron Fr. von, 37, 155
Oxyria, 76
Oxytropis, 223

P.

Palander, Lieut., 36, 138, 183, 352, 382, 384
Palliser, the brothers, 133
Papaver, 77
Parent, Lieut., 36, 183
Parry, 44, 58, 64, 65
Parry Island, 78, 150, 235
Peat moss, 139
Pedicularis, 94
Pennatulidæ, 357
Permian fossils, 93
Petermann, 245
Petersen, Carl, 47, 49, 68, 69, 71, 79, 82, 83, 94
Phalaropus, 65, 94
Phipps, Constantine John, 44
Phipps' Island, 78
Phoca groenlandica, 84
Phosphorescent crustacea, 209
Physa, 232
Poa, 76, 97, 98
Podura, 63, 144
Poduridæ, 287
Polar bear, 80, 144; its flesh, 124
Polar Expedition of 1868, 123; of 1872-3, 175
Polar night, 207
Polar willow, 63, 133
Pole, routes to the, 153
Polygonum, 99
Polythalamia, 51, 102
Polytricha, 58, 95, 99
Potentilla, 76, 99
Pottia, 77
Prince Charles' Foreland, 52
Productus, 46
Procren, the, 272
Pteropoda, 142
Ptilidium, 55
Pycnogonids, 357, 363

R.

Radiolaria, 102
Raised beaches, 324
Ranunculus, 76, 94, 99, 133
Red Bay, 64
Reindeer as a draught animal, 176; quantity of flesh yielded by, 182; killed, 222
Reindeer moss as food, 203
Reindeer Valley, 139
Rhacomitrium, 58, 95
Rink, Mr., 157
Rockfolds, 247
Rotge, 116
Rubus arcticus, 295
Runeberg, J. L., 6

S.

Sabine, Sir Edward, 44, 187
Safe Haven, 108, 114
Sagani, 134
Sahlberg, Dr. J., 320
Salix, 58, 99
Samoyedes, 281, 313, 354
Sassen Bay, 110
Saurian Mountains, 139
Sauric Hook, 109
Saxifraga oppositifolia, 270
Saxifraga rivularis, 266
Saxifrages, 63, 94, 99, 134
Schalavroff, 369
Schvanenberg, 340
Scoresby, 145
Scoresby's Island, 80, 82
Scurvy, an attack of, 211
Sea, temperature of, 364
Seals floating, 125
Seebohm, Mr., 340
Seven Icebergs, 52
Seven Islands, 74, 77, 141, 143, 150
Shark fishing, 132
Siberia, its fertility, 299
Sibiriakoff, Herr Alex., 38, 39, 321, 345, 353, 367
Sibiriakoff's Island, 327
Sidoroff, Herr M., 340
Sigillaria, 139
Silene, 94
Sipunculus, 102
Skoptzi, 310
Smeerenberg, 91
Smitt, F. A., 49, 131
Snow Bunting, 218
Sofia, 130; springs a leak, 151
Solorina, 95
Sotnikoff, 304
South Cape, 118, 119, 136
South Gat, 94, 149
Sphærophoron, 95
Spiders, 63
Spiriter, 46, 109
Spitzbergen, 41; land north of, 53; change of its climate, 139
Stans Foreland, 48
Staphylinidæ, 287
Staratschin, 112, 137
Stellaria, 77, 98
Stichaster, 336
Stor Fjord, 74, 84, 105, 108, 119
Stuxberg, Dr., 37, 279, 321, 352
Summer, approach of, 265
Sutton, Mr. Graham Manners, 113
Svjatoi, Nos, 369

T.

Tchuktches, 372; barter with, 375; dress and manners of, 377, 385

Tellina, 100
Temple Mount, 111
Terns, 94, 114
Théel, Dr. Hj., 279, 285, 320, 337
Thousand Islands, the, 47, 113
Thumb Point, 123
Thymus, 293
Tofieldia borealis, 277
Torell, Otto, 40, 45, 47, 48, 49, 100
Treurenberg Bay, 58, 60
Triassic strata, 110, 139
Tringa maritima, 65, 94
Tritorium, 100
Trybom, F., 320
Tundra, the, 294, 320

U.

Umbellula, 337
Umbilicaria, 58, 95
Uria grylle, 52, 53
Usnea, 77
Uusimaa, 55

V.

Van Keulen Bay, 114
Van Mejen Bay, 114
Vega, the, 345; frozen in, 383; released, 386; passes Behrings Straits, 383; arrives at Yokohama, 384
Von Yhlen, 49, 97

W.

Wachtmeister, Count, 33
Wagstaffe, Dr. W. W., 113
Waldenberg Bay, 68, 261, 262
Walden Island, 74
Wabrushunt, 54; hunting, 89
Walter, Thymen's Strait, 120
Waygatz Islands, 84
Whales Bay, 118
Whales Head, 120
Whales Point, 118, 119, 120
White Island visited, 355
White Mount, 122
White whale, 87, 137
Whortleberry, 289
Whymper, Mr., 157, 379
Wiggins, Captain Joseph, 339
Wijde Bay, 93
Wijkander, Dr., 30, 183, 186
Wilander, Hj., visits Spitzbergen, 32
Worm, 63

Y.

Yalmal, 283, 293
Yenisej, the 37, 38; reached by sea, 285; ascent of, 286; the fish of, 297, 312; a steamer on, 301; coal seams near, 302
Yuser, the, 320

www.ingramcontent.com/pod-product-compliance
Lightning Source LLC
Chambersburg PA
CBHW022112300426
44117CB00007B/678